GROWTH AND DECLINE IN
COLCHESTER, 1300–1525

This is a study of economic and institutional change in one of England's principal cloth towns during the late Middle Ages, drawing extensively upon unpublished records in Colchester borough archives and elsewhere. The approach to urban history is an exceptionally broad one; this is the first history of a medieval English town to analyse in conjunction changes in the pattern of overseas trade, in industrial organisation and output, in urban government, and in the economy and society of the countryside. First it describes Colchester in the earlier fourteenth century, its trade, its agricultural setting and its form of government. At this time the town was a small one even by English standards, with fewer than 4,000 inhabitants. The book then shows how clothmaking grew in Colchester after the Black Death and how the population increased until about 1414 it was perhaps twice what it had been before the plague years. The implications of this for the wealth of Colchester's merchant class, the government of the borough and for the town's rôle in the local economy are discussed. It is suggested that urban growth on this scale was not great enough to make much impact upon the course of rural development. The last section of the book shows that Colchester's growth was not sustained through the fifteenth century and that the trade and population of the town contracted, particularly after 1450. Some of the causal links between economic contraction and institutional change in the borough are examined, and it is suggested that for the most part increasing economic regulation and the growth of oligarchic principles of government are not to be explained by reference to economic misfortune. The study closes with an examination of Colchester's contribution to agrarian depression in the Essex countryside.

GROWTH AND DECLINE IN COLCHESTER, 1300–1525

R. H. BRITNELL
Lecturer in History, University of Durham

The right of the
University of Cambridge
to print and sell
all manner of books
was granted by
Henry VIII in 1534.
The University has printed
and published continuously
since 1584.

CAMBRIDGE UNIVERSITY PRESS

Cambridge
London   New York   New Rochelle
Melbourne   Sydney

CAMBRIDGE UNIVERSITY PRESS
Cambridge, New York, Melbourne, Madrid, Cape Town, Singapore, São Paulo

Cambridge University Press
The Edinburgh Building, Cambridge CB2 8RU, UK

Published in the United States of America by Cambridge University Press, New York

www.cambridge.org
Information on this title: www.cambridge.org/9780521305723

First published 1986
This digitally printed version 2008

A catalogue record for this publication is available from the British Library

Library of Congress Cataloguing in Publication data
Britnell, R. H.
Growth and decline in Colchester, 1300–1525.
Includes index.
1. Colchester (Essex)—Economic conditions.
2. Colchester (Essex)—Politics and government.
I. Title.
HC258.C65B75 1986   330.9426'723   85-9644

ISBN 978-0-521-30572-3 hardback
ISBN 978-0-521-07315-8 paperback

CONTENTS

MAPS

For Jennifer

ACKNOWLEDGEMENTS

My thanks are due to the late Sir Michael Postan and to Dr Marjorie Chibnall. They launched me into the economic history of the Middle Ages and supervised the earlier stages of my research. I am also obliged to Dr Wendy Childs, Mrs Linda Drury and to the late Miss Susan Flower for information brought to light in the course of their work. I have profited from discussing Colchester with Dr Maryanne Kowaleski, who showed me some points of comparison with medieval Exeter, and with Dr Larry Poos, who gave me advance notice of his important findings in the demography of medieval Essex.

Access to Colchester borough records has become easier over the years, and it is a pleasure to acknowledge the help of those who, at different stages of play, have allowed me to use them, often at some inconvenience to themselves: to the last town clerk of Colchester, Mr N. Catchpole, to Mr T.-D. Clarke and his staff at the Colchester and Essex Museum, and more recently to Mr Paul Coverley, Colchester's first archivist. For money my obligations are wholly to the University of Durham.

In preparing my manuscript for publication I have benefited at each stage from the secretarial expertise of Mrs Margaret Hall. My colleague Dr Duncan Bythell kindly looked out passages likely to cause difficulty to readers, and persuaded me to write an Introduction.

Finally I must record this book's debt to my wife, who has helped it forward with encouragement and advice.

R. H. B.

ABBREVIATIONS

Texts and calendars published by the Record Commissioners

Rot. Hund.	*Rotuli Hundredorum* (2 vols., 1812–18)
Rot. Parl.	*Rotuli Parliamentorum* (6 vols., 1783)
Statutes	*The Statutes of the Realm* (11 vols., 1810–28)

Public Record Office texts and calendars

Cal. Chart. R.	*Calendar of Charter Rolls*
Cal. Close R.	*Calendar of Close Rolls*
Cal. Fine R.	*Calendar of Fine Rolls*
Cal. Inq. P.M.	*Calendar of Inquisitions Post Mortem*
Cal. Pat. R.	*Calendar of Patent Rolls*
Feudal Aids	*Inquisitions and Assessments relating to Feudal Aids*
L. and P.	*Letters and Papers, Foreign and Domestic, of the Reign of Henry VIII*

Journals and Reports

Annales E.S.C.	*Annales, économies, sociétés, civilisations*
B.A.R.	*British Archaeological Reports*
E.H.R.	*English Historical Review*
Ec.H.R.	*Economic History Review*
T.E.A.S.	*Transactions of Essex Archaeological Society*

Other printed works

Colch. Cart.	*Cartularium Monasterii Sancti Johannis Baptiste de Colecestria*, ed. S. A. Moore, Roxburghe Club (2 vols., London, 1897)
Essex Fines	*Feet of Fines for Essex*, ed. R. E. G. Kirk and others, Essex Archaeological Society (4 vols., Colchester, 1899–1964)
Morant, *Colchester*	P. Morant, *The History and Antiquities of the most Ancient Town and Borough of Colchester* (London, 1748)
Morant, *Essex*	P. Morant, *The History and Antiquities of the County of Essex* (2 vols., London, 1768)
O.E.D.	*The Oxford English Dictionary*, ed. J. A. H. Murray and others, 2nd edn (12 vols., Oxford, 1933)
Return of Names	House of Commons, *Every Member of the Lower House of the Parliaments of England, Scotland and Ireland, i: England, 1213–1702* (London, 1878)

MANUSCRIPTS

A. Record repositories other than Colchester borough records

B.L.	British Library
E.R.O.	Essex Record Office
P.C.C.	Prerogative Court of Canterbury
P.R.O.	Public Record Office
W.A.M.	Westminster Abbey Muniments

B. Colchester borough muniments

CR	Court roll
LB	The Ledger Book of St John's Abbey, Colchester (Davis no. 269)
OB	The Oath Book
RPB	The Red Paper Book

DATES

Dates given in the form 1310/11 signify the office year from Michaelmas to Michaelmas. The convention is useful for Colchester's own records, since borough officers began their term of office on the Monday after Michaelmas. It may also be employed in references to manorial records, since manorial officers normally took up their duties on Michaelmas day or the day after. Accounts or other records which do not correspond to these terms (e.g. many royal receivers' accounts) are dated in the form 1310–11 where no more exact information is necessary; this date implies a period from some time in 1310 to some time in 1311.

REFERENCES TO COLCHESTER
BOROUGH RECORDS

Except in the case of the Cartulary of St John's Abbey, which is adequately edited (*Colch. Cart.* above), references to Colchester borough records are to the original manuscripts. A number of Colchester records were edited in translation earlier in the century by I. H. Jeayes and W. G. Benham, and these editions are invaluable as calendars and indexes to the original records. They are not complete or reliable enough, however, to be used as substitutes for the manuscripts in a study of this kind.

THE REGISTERS

In the case of the Red Paper Book and the Oath Book the folio numbers used in citing references are the modern pencilled ones, since there is no coherent original numbering of the leaves. The Ledger Book of St John's Abbey has fourteenth-century foliation in Arabic numerals, and this has been used in references to the texts it contains.

THE COURT ROLLS

References to the court rolls are given in the form CR 1/1, where the first number is the modern number given to the roll (in this case the earliest one, that for 1310/11), and the second number is that of the membrane. Each roll comprises a number of membranes sewn Exchequer fashion, and for some rolls there are several alternative numberings of the membranes. References here are always to the earliest numbering, which is usually a medieval one, added at a time when each roll was complete. These were the membrane numbers used by the compilers of the Oath Book index to the rolls. This oldest system of numeration, though it presents some awkwardnesses, has the advantage that there is no ambiguity about which sequence of numbers is in question, and also has the merit of drawing attention to gaps in the record which are obscured by more recent numberings of the membranes. However, not all membranes have clearly visible numbers, and in some instances the original ones must be deduced from the sequence of the membranes or from the Oath Book. The following list is designed as a check list to facilitate the finding of references. From this list may be found (a) the year of each surviving roll, (b) the modern numbering of the rolls and (c) the original numbering of those membranes which survive, together with the sequence in which they are now sewn. The oldest roll, for example, dates from 1310/11, is numbered CR 1 and has 12 surviving membranes, those originally numbered 10 and 13 having been lost.

The medieval numbering of the rolls is not usually hard to find. Before 1352 (CR 1–9) it is mostly in the bottom left-hand corner; between 1353 and 1400 (CR 10–31) at the top, in or towards the right-hand corner; from 1400 to 1449 (CR 32–64) at the foot; from 1451 to 1485 (CR 65–82) in the bottom right-hand corner; and in the early sixteenth century (CR 83–102) at the foot or in one of the lower corners. Where there is no surviving trace of a number this has been indicated below by the use of brackets.

Some rolls are sewn up with the membranes in reverse sequence (*i.e.* with the first membrane at the bottom and the last at the top). These are indicated in the list with an asterisk following the membrane numbers.

1310/11	CR 1/1–9, 11, 12, 14
1311/12	CR 2/1–4, (5), 6, 7, (8), 9, 10, (11), 12, 13*
1329/30	CR 3/(1), 2–5, (8)*
1333/4	CR 4/1, (2, 3), 4, 7, 9, 8, 10–14
1336/7	CR 5/1–6, (7), 8–10
1340/1	CR 6/1–6, 8–11
1345/6	CR 7/1–4, (5), 6–10, 12, 14
1349/50	CR 8/10
1351/2	CR 9/(1), 2–8*
1353/4	CR 10/1–14*
1356/7	CR 11/1–14*
1359/60	CR 12/1–19
1360/1	CR 13/7–9, 14, 15
1364/5	CR 14/(1), 2–8, 10–15
1366/7	CR 15/1–18
1372/3	CR 16/1–17
1374/5	CR 17/1–12, 14–18, 20
1376/7	CR 18/2, 4–14, 16–23
1378/9	CR 19/1–8, 10, 11, 9, 12–25, (26), 27, 28
1379/80	CR 20/2, 5, 6, 8, (9), 10, 11, 13–34, 36, 37
1381/2	CR 21/(1), 2–32, (32a), 33–56

1382/3	CR 22/2–57, (58), 1
1383/4	CR 23/22, 23, 25, 26, 29–34, 36–8, 46, 48, 49, 52, 55–7, 59, 63, 20[a]
1384/5	CR 24/1–26, (26a), 27–59[b]
1385/6	CR 25/1–36, (37), 38–47, 49–59, 61[c]
1387/8	CR 26/(1), 2–48, (49), 50–71
1391/2	CR 27/3–42, 44, 45
1392/3	CR 28/1–29, 35–42[d]
1395/6	CR 29/1–26, 29
1398/9	CR 30/1–25[e]
1399/1400	CR 31/1–29
1400/1	CR 32/(1), 2–24
1403/4	CR 33/4–20, (21), 22, (22a), 23–8, (29), 30
1404/5	CR 34/(1), 2–7, 9–26
1405/6	CR 35/1–36
1406/7	CR 36/1–32
1409/10	CR 37/3, 14–20, 29–37
1411/12	CR 38/1–21, (22, 23), 24–36, (37)
1413/14	CR 39/1–6, 6(a), 7–30, 32, (33), 34, (35), 36–8, (38a), 39–46, (47)
1416/17	CR 40/45(a), 3–11, (46), 44, 12–15, 18–28, 31–43, 45[f]
1418/19	CR 41/1–13, (14), 15–28, (29), 30–4, (35)
1419/20	CR 42/(1), 2–32
1422/3	CR 43/1–7, (8), 9–28
1423/4	CR 44/3–33
1424/5	CR 45/3–39
1425/6	CR 46/1–28
1426/7	CR 47/4–12, 15–31
1427/8	CR 48/3–12, 14–32
1428/9	CR 49/1, 3–35
1429/30	CR 50/1–27, (28), 29–36, (37)
1432/3	CR 51/1–9, (11), 12, 10, 13–20, (21–3), 24–33, (34, 35)
1434/5	CR 52/1–29
1435/6	CR 53/1–30
1436/7	CR 54/1, 2, 4–32
1437/8	CR 55/1–15, (16), 18–50
1438/9	CR 56/1–20, 20(a), 21–39, (40)

[a] Membrane 56 reversed.
[b] Membranes 43, 48, 50, 51, 53–9 reversed. Appended to this roll is a single membrane (m. 6) of a roll of business devolved from the royal assizes, mostly instructions to seize Colchester men or to form juries.
[c] Membrane 2 reversed.   [d] Membrane 1 reversed.
[e] Membrane 1 reversed.   [f] Membranes 45(a), 8, 46, 44, 45 reversed.

1439/40	CR 57/1–4, 6–29
1442/3	CR 58/1–18, (18a), 19, 20, (21)
1443/4	CR 59/17–24, 1–16
1444/5	CR 60/2, 4–11, 13–25, (27), 28, (29), 30[g]
1446/7	CR 61/4–14, (15), 16, (17), 18–21, (23)
1447/8	CR 62/1–3, 7, 4–6, 8–23, (24–6)
1448/9	CR 63/1–3, 14, 15, 4–8, 10–13, 16–23
1451/2	CR 64/1–28, (29)
1452/3	CR 65/1–4, 6–25
1455/6	CR 66/1–28
1456/7	CR 67/1–7, (8), 9–13, (14), 15–17, (18), 19–24, (25), 26, 27
1457/8	CR 68/3–12, (13), 14–20, (21), 22–30
1458/9	CR 69/1–19, (20), 21–4
1459/60	CR 70/1–22, (23), 24, (25), 26
1460/1	CR 71/1–19, (20), 21–5
1463/4	CR 72/1–32
1466/7	CR 73/1–4, (5), 6, (7), 8–10, (11), 12–26, (27), 28–37, (38), 39–41
1470/1	CR 74/1–8, (9), 10–15, (16), 17, (18–23), 24, 25, 27, 28, (29–31)
1473/4	CR 75/1–11, (12, 13), 14–25, (26)
1476/7	CR 76/1–10, (11–13), 14, (15, 16), 17, (18–21), 22, (23–7), 28, (29, 30), 31
1477/8	CR 77/1–3, (4), 5–18, (19), 20–6, (27), 28, (29)
1480/1	CR 78/1–6, (7), 8, 9, (10), 11–13, (14), 15, (16–18), 19, (20), 21, (22, 23)
1481/2	CR 79/(1, 2), 3–7, (8), 9–17, (18), 19–25, (26, 27), 28–37, (38), 39
1483/4	CR 80/(4), 5, 6, (7, 8), 9–12, (13–18), 19, 20, (21), 22, 23, (24–8)[h]
1484/5	CR 81/1, 3–17, (18), 19–22, (23), 24–9, (30), 31
1509/10	CR 82/3–12, (13), 14–18, 20–30
1510/11	CR 83/(1–10), 11, (12–17)
1511/12[i]	CR 84/(1–5), 6, (7, 8), 9, (10–15), 19, 17, (18, 21), 20
1512/13	CR 85/(1, 2), 4, 4(a), (5), 6, 7, (8–10), 11, (12–15)
1514/15	CR 86/1–29, 31
1515/16	CR 87/1, 2, 6–21, (22, 23)
1516/17	CR 88/(1–3), 5–24
1517/18	CR 89/1–7, (8), 9–27

[g] Membrane 9 reversed.
[h] Membrane 22 reversed.   [i] Membranes 14–21 belong to 1510/11.

[j] Membranes 16 and 18 reversed.   [k] Membrane 18 is numbered xvij.

INTRODUCTION

The number of England's inhabitants recovered only slowly from the demographic disasters of the fourteenth century. The best current estimates suggest that, having stood at between 4.5 and 6.0 million in 1348, the population of the kingdom was only somewhere between 2.25 and 2.75 million in the 1520s.[1] If output per head had remained unchanged throughout the period from 1348 to 1525 this would mean that national income in the latter year was approximately one half what it had been in the former. But during the later fourteenth and fifteenth centuries a larger part of the population than before was able to find regular employment, and more resources were available per head of the population. Wage levels rose, and families were able to buy more food and manufactured goods as a reward for their labours. The later fifteenth century was a golden age in the history of standards of living. Even in the 1520s, though real wages had fallen a long way from their fifteenth-century peak, skilled craftsmen could earn 25 per cent more than equivalent wage earners at the opening of the fourteenth century.[2] The implications of these changes for the level and composition of national income are imperfectly understood. There are as yet no aggregate estimates either of incomes or of output sufficiently dependable to assess the combined effect of lower population and higher output per man. Interpretations of the economic history of these centuries vary considerably according to the emphasis which different historians place upon the main economic variables.

The want of national statistics has encouraged local and sectoral researches into a wide range of topics relating to England's economic performance, and the accumulation of such studies has led to general agreement on some issues which were once controversial. It is now

---

[1] J. Hatcher, *Plague, Population and the English Economy, 1348–1530* (London, 1977), pp. 68–9.

[2] E. H. Phelps Brown and S. V. Hopkins, *A Perspective of Wages and Prices* (London, 1981), pp. 28–9.

commonly accepted that agricultural output was slow to recover from the crises of the fourteenth century, and that land was cultivated both less extensively and less intensively in the earlier sixteenth century than in the early fourteenth. But there is less agreement concerning urban experience, despite the well documented arguments of Mr Phythian-Adams and Professor Dobson to the effect that contraction was more common than growth.[3] Dr Bridbury, in particular, has argued that evidence of increased urban wealth between 1334 and 1524 jeopardises any pessimistic interpretation of England's economic performance between these dates.[4] The difficulty of establishing what happened in towns results chiefly from the poor quality of available statistical data. It is harder to establish how urban economies were faring than to trace developments in those smaller, rural communities for which good estate documents survive. Arguments about variations in urban prosperity are liable to flounder into quantitative statements which cannot be tested or even closely defined.

Besides the obvious uncertainties concerning urban populations, economic activity and wealth, there are other research problems currently linked to the question of urban prosperity. In recent years the *Economic History Review* has accepted articles relating to town government, borough office-holders and the recruitment of burgesses.[5] The nature of urban oligarchies in the late Middle Ages, pioneered as a topic in constitutional history, is now examined as much for its relevance to the characteristics of urban wealth.[6] A related issue which has received less attention is the development of restrictive by-laws; Dr Hibbert has argued that the level of regulation in industry and trade was in part determined by expectations of growth, stagnation or contraction, and that townsmen in the late Middle Ages were more constrained by public controls than their forebears because of the typically poorer commercial environment in which they lived.[7] The documentation needed to study these institutional changes is

---

[3] C. Phythian-Adams, 'Urban Decay in Late Medieval England', in P. Abrams and E. A. Wrigley, eds., *Towns in Societies: Essays in Economic History and Historical Sociology*, Past and Present Publications (Cambridge, 1978), pp. 159–85; R. B. Dobson, 'Urban Decline in Late Medieval England', *Transactions of the Royal Historical Society*, 5th ser., xxvii (1977), pp. 1–22.

[4] A. R. Bridbury, *Economic Growth: England in the Later Middle Ages* (London, 1962), pp. 74–82; idem, 'English Provincial Towns in the Later Middle Ages', *Ec.H.R.*, 2nd ser., xxxiv (1981), pp. 17–22.

[5] R. B. Dobson, 'Admissions to the Freedom of the City of York in the Later Middle Ages', *Ec.H.R.*, 2nd ser., xxvi (1973), pp. 1–21; Bridbury, 'English Provincial Towns', pp. 1–24; J. I. Kermode, 'Urban Decline? The Flight from Office in Late Medieval York', *Ec.H.R.*, 2nd ser., xxxv (1982), pp. 179–98.

[6] *E.g.* R. S. Gottfried, *Bury St. Edmunds and the Urban Crisis, 1290–1539* (Princeton, 1982), pp. 131–66.

[7] A. B. Hibbert, 'The Economic Policies of Towns', in M. M. Postan, E. E. Rich and E. Miller, eds., *The Cambridge Economic History of Europe, iii: Economic Organization and Policies in the Middle Ages* (Cambridge, 1963), pp. 179–229.

more often extant than good economic statistics. The questions are of interest in their own right, and a great deal of work remains to be done. Yet without direct information relating to economic performance the economic interpretation of social change is a hazardous pursuit. The study of institutional change in towns of the fourteenth and fifteenth centuries provides no substitute for economic evidence and in fact runs into difficulties when that evidence is not forthcoming.

There is, however, no corpus of statistical evidence adequate to chart the economic development of most English towns. General surveys have to depend upon an eclectic range of material, and their conclusions must accordingly be confined to broad generalisations about the outcome of changes over long periods. Causal relationships between economic, social and constitutional changes cannot be investigated closely in this type of study because in so many towns the evidence is confined to one or two strands of relevant information. Only in the case of a few well documented towns is it feasible to examine in close conjunction all the various types of evidence relating to economic change which occupy historians working on a larger scale. The present study of Colchester takes up this challenge. It aims to establish with greater precision the chronology of change than a general survey could do. It sets out, too, to examine a variety of themes in close juxtaposition, and to sound out some causal explanations more thoroughly than it would be possible to do with many towns together. The results, though in no way a substitute for general surveys, can serve as a reference point for scrutinising their conclusions. A study of Colchester has the particular advantage that the town is recognised as a principal witness in the case for urban growth, which means that it is legitimate to form some general observations on the strength of its evidence alone.

Though Colchester is a well documented town by the standards of medieval England, the economic evidence is nevertheless of a low quality. The assessment presented here of Colchester's economic performance through the years between 1300 and 1525 depends heavily upon the statistical series printed in the Appendix, all of which are tantalising in that, though related to economic quantities, they do not directly measure outputs or inputs. Most of the series are discussed in the course of the book with a view to assessing their value; each on its own would be open to multiple objections as an economic indicator. However, the agreement between the different sets of figures concerning Colchester's economic growth in the later fourteenth century and contraction during the fifteenth century means that some generalisations may be made which do not depend only upon the independent reliability of the separate series. There is here a point of inductive method which has been widely employed in agrarian studies[8] but which has found less application in the investigation of urban economies. If it is more probable than not that a measured series implies an associated economic change, then that probability is increased if other evidence of similar quality points in the same direction. An increase in the number of mills at work would carry little conviction on its own as evidence of increasing consumption of foodstuffs. It would be *prima facie* more likely to mean this than anything else, however, and the probability that it does so is enhanced by evidence of an increase in the brewing of ale. The combined testimony of these series could be overturned only by showing (1) that there is some non-economic reason why all the series should move in the same direction, or (2) that one or more of the series is more likely than not to imply something other than it seems to do, or (3) that there is new evidence to indicate a different set of conclusions.

The relationship in this study between the different aspects of Colchester's history to be discussed is as follows:

	1300– 49 Chapter	1350– 1414 Chapter	1415– 1525 Chapter
A Colchester cloth and its markets	1	4	11
B Industrial organisation	1	5	12
C Urban population and consumption	1	6	13
D Credit and wealth	1	7	14
E The borough constitution	2	8	15
F Regulation of industry and trade	3	9	16
G The urban impact upon agriculture	3	10	17

Movements of population are of prime importance for the interpretation of urban development, and the sections dealing with this topic are the core around which other matters are organised. Some explanation of Colchester's changing size is offered (chiefly in the sections designated A and B) and some of its consequences are illustrated (chiefly in those designated D, E, F and G). The intricacy of these themes in conjunction, and the scarcity of comparable integrated studies, precludes extensive comparison with other towns, though many points of similarity and dissimilarity are noted in passing. But the fact that the town was exceptionally fortunate during the period under review, when it emerged

[8] This principle is fundamental to the methods of enquiry pioneered by Professor Postan.

from the backwaters of English commerce to become one of the dozen wealthiest towns in the kingdom, implies a convenient standard of comparison with other towns. Particular attention is drawn to this point in the further conclusions at the end of the book, but it is implicit in much of the earlier discussion.

PART I

Rusticity, 1300–49

1

Urban economy

I

At the opening of the fourteenth century Colchester preserved the four-square features of its Roman origins. The walls of the ancient *colonia* enclosed a rectangular area of 109 acres, and inside the gates the main thoroughfares formed a T-shape more or less aligned with the principal Roman streets.[1] The trunk of the T, the modern High Street, was unambiguously the town centre. From its highest point at Cornhill down to the church of St Nicholas it was wide enough to contain the markets for grain, dairy produce, poultry, fish and meat.[2] Despite the inevitable noise and dirt this was a residential street, and some of the best stone-built accommodation in the town was to be found there.[3] On its northern side stood the Norman moothall where sessions of the borough courts were held and where town revenues were collected.[4] The walled area was also the ecclesiastical heart of Colchester; eight of the twelve urban parish churches were built there, two of them beside the high street, and one of them in the middle of it surrounded by stalls.[5] It was supposed that Colchester had been King Coel's capital city, and that the defences had been first built either by him or by his daughter St Helen.[6] For all that, the convenience of the walls as a source of building stone had not been overlooked, and they were consequently in too poor a state of repair to

[1] Morant, *Colchester*, i, p. 6; P. Crummy, *Aspects of Anglo-Saxon and Norman Colchester*, Colchester Archaeological Report, i; Council for British Archaeology Report, xxxix (London, 1981), pp. 48–9.
[2] CR 34/11d (corn); CR 32/1r (dairy produce); OB, fos. 31v, 33r (fish); OB, fos. 31v, 32r, 33v, 34r (meat).
[3] P. Crummy, *Colchester: Recent Excavations and Research* (Colchester, 1974), p. 32.
[4] Crummy, *Aspects of Anglo-Saxon and Norman Colchester*, pp. 60–3.
[5] Morant, *Colchester*, ii, p. 1; OB, fo. 168v.
[6] OB, fo. 20r; Henry of Huntingdon, *Historia Anglorum, 55 B.C.–A.D. 1154*, ed. T. Arnold, Rolls ser. (London, 1879), p. 30.

be considered any longer as effective fortifications.[7] Houses were built up against them, and one family had assumed the surname Upthewall.[8]

The residential part of Colchester was not restricted to streets within the walls. As in other walled towns at this time the occupied area extended into suburbs outside the gates.[9] This was not because the centre was packed with people. The north-eastern quarter was almost devoid of townsmen's houses; a royal castle stood there, reputedly on the site of King Coel's palace,[10] and in the angle of the walls there was a Franciscan friary with its grounds.[11] Near the castle lay the fields and meadows attached to it; here, and in the south-western angle of the walls, there were crops growing in the spring and summer months.[12] Even the more populated parts of the town contained many intramural gardens and orchards, and each of the parish churches had its own churchyard.[13] But beyond the walls there was no physical constraint on development other than the River Colne to the north and east, and on all sides suburban locations had some positive attractions. The river drew artisans who needed water for industrial purposes, and there were further supplies of water from springs and wells.[14] The most important developments were by Colchester's larger monastic foundations, the Benedictine abbey of St John the Baptist and the Augustinian priory of St Botolph, both of which stood to the south of the town centre with populous streets at their gates.

Besides the town walls, castle and monastic buildings, none of which had been built by burgesses, there was no grand architecture in Colchester. The parish churches were small and mostly rubble-built, with a conspicuous ingredient of re-used Roman tile and brick in their construction.[15] Domestic architecture was even less imposing. Stone buildings, where they occurred, were also built of rubble, and were often a patchwork of alterations.[16] Houses were small, since even the wealthier townsmen lived in only a handful of rooms; in 1301 John Menny the tanner had a hall, chamber, kitchen, granary, bakehouse and tannery; Roger Dyer's house

---

[7] CR 7/10d; CR 9/6r; CR 9/6r; CR 10/10d.

[8] OB, fo. 56v; CR 2/6r, 12r; *Rot. Parl.*, i, p. 258.

[9] R. H. Hilton, *A Medieval Society: The West Midlands at the End of the Thirteenth Century* (London, 1966), pp. 185–7.

[10] OB, fo. 20v.

[11] Morant, *Colchester*, ii, pp. 43–4.

[12] *Ibid.*, i, p. 10; P.R.O., S.C.6/839/18, mm. 1r, 2d; S.C.6/839/19, mm. 1d, 2d; J. H. Round, 'Berryfield, Colchester', *T.E.A.S.*, new ser., xvii (1926), p. 37.

[13] St Runwald's churchyard was beside West Stockwell Street, separate from the church: Morant, *Colchester*, ii, p. 10.

[14] RPB, fo. 65v; Morant, *Colchester*, i, pp. 1–2.

[15] Morant, *Colchester*, ii, p. 1; Crummy, *Aspects of Anglo-Saxon and Norman Colchester*, pp. 47–8.

[16] Crummy, *Colchester: Recent Excavations*, pp. 29–31.

comprised a living room, a chamber, a kitchen, a brewhouse and probably a separate dyehouse; Peter le Wylde had a hall, a chamber, a kitchen and a barn in which to store his grain.[17] Most townsmen occupied or shared premises smaller than these. The contrast between Colchester housing and that in nearby village streets would not have been very marked, and the town churches were no finer than those of rural parishes. There was accordingly a sharp contrast in size and quality between the properties to be seen in the streets of Colchester and those of neighbouring monastic and manorial lords.

The inhabitants of Colchester were seemingly well placed to trade with the outside world. The Colne flowed by the northern wall and then meandered southwards, rapidly broadening into an estuary approachable from the sea. On the river bank to the east of the town, half an hour's walk from the centre, a detached settlement of seafarers and fishermen had grown up at Hythe.[18] Within the past hundred years wharves here had superseded those at Old Heath further to the south, and warehouses had been constructed to accommodate merchandise awaiting shipment. Though subordinate to Ipswich for customs administration, Colchester was a port of call for merchant ships and a point of embarkation for local agricultural produce and manufactures.[19] Large vessels could ride in the mouth of the Colne estuary in a reach known as the Wodesende between Brightlingsea and Wivenhoe, and from there smaller craft made their way to and from Hythe, sometimes over a distance of as much as five miles.[20] Besides fishing boats, some merchant shipping belonged to men of the town.[21] But the rate of growth of Colchester's sea-borne trade had been surpassed by that of other east-coast ports. Because of the restricted mooring facilities at Hythe, Colchester probably had fewer ships than Brightlingsea at the mouth of the estuary or Salcott along the coast to the south-west.[22] And though the community at Hythe owed its existence to developments in Colchester's fishing and maritime trade, neither its size nor its dynamism bore comparison with that of Harwich or Manningtree,

---

[17] *Rot. Parl.*, i, pp. 243, 244, 248.
[18] An agreement concerning the tithes of St Leonard at Hythe dates from 1227, and the earliest references to 'old hythe' occurs soon after this: *Colch. Cart.*, i, p. 178, and ii, pp. 307–8, 545–6.
[19] For warehouses, see P.R.O., E.101/556/14r, 19Ar. In 1296–7 wheat from north-eastern Essex was collected in Colchester for shipment to Gascony: E.101/556/1, m. 2r.
[20] P.R.O., E.101/556/14r.
[21] *Documents illustrating the Crisis of 1297–98 in England*, ed. M. C. Prestwich, Camden 4th ser., xxiv (London, 1980), no. 199, p. 187.
[22] The provisioning of Edward II's muster at Newcastle upon Tyne in 1319 and of his Scottish campaign of 1322 employed ships from Brightlingsea and Salcott but none from Colchester: P.R.O., E.101/556/7r, 10r.

two nearby coastal towns of thirteenth-century foundation, whose growth of population and wealth had been more rapid than that of their neighbours.[23]

Colchester had direct communications with London which, though not drawn on the fourteenth-century Gough Map, are indicated by the inclusion there of Brentwood, Chelmsford and Witham.[24] A growing trade on this route in the thirteenth century induced the founding of seven markets along it between 1199 and 1312.[25] To the north Colchester had highway communications with Ipswich, and to the west two separate routes led, through numerous small market towns, to Cambridge and Bishop's Stortford. Even eastwards, in the Tendring peninsula, though there were no major thoroughfares, there was some traffic to Manningtree and Harwich, as well as to a number of large villages with little industry of their own which were dependent upon urban manufactures. For all this, the principal urban development of the region in the thirteenth century had been in communities which started off much smaller than Colchester. Brentwood, Chelmsford and the nucleus of modern Witham were new towns of the thirteenth century, and Chelmsford was already of sufficient administrative importance to be functioning as county town for Essex. To the west of Colchester, Braintree, Coggeshall and Halstead all had free messuages appropriate to occupation by artisans and tradesmen.[26] The growth of population in the market towns of Essex during the thirteenth century had greatly exceeded that within Colchester, and in this sense Colchester had benefited less than smaller and newer communities from the expansion of inland trade.

In spite of sea communications and road connections, Colchester in 1300 was a town whose products and services were primarily sold to men of the surrounding countryside. Its interests in this respect were sufficiently pronounced to affect the development of rural marketing in north-eastern Essex. Within a radius of eight miles only one new market was founded during the thirteenth century, by a road junction four miles to the east of

---

[23] Mistley and Harwich accounted respectively for 3.1 and 1.0 per cent of the thirtieth collected in Tendring Hundred in 1237, before Manningtree was founded in the parish of Mistley. In 1334, however, Mistley and Manningtree together contributed 4.6 per cent of the fifteenth collected in Tendring Hundred; Harwich contributed 5.4 per cent: P.R.O., E.179/107/1; *The Lay Subsidy of 1334*, ed. R. E. Glasscock, The British Academy: Records of Social and Economic History, new ser., ii (London, 1975), pp. 88–9.

[24] *The Map of Great Britain* c. *A.D. 1360*, issued by the Bodleian Library (Oxford, 1958); F. M. Stenton, *Preparatory to Anglo-Saxon England*, ed. D. M. Stenton (Oxford, 1970), p. 240.

[25] R. H. Britnell, 'Essex Markets before 1350', *Essex Archaeology and History*, xiii (1981), p. 18.

[26] R. H. Britnell, 'Burghal Characteristics of Market Towns in Medieval England', *Durham University Journal*, new ser., xlii (1981), pp. 147–9.

the town at Elmstead Market.[27] Other large villages nearby, which in other locations might have supported a market, went without one. At an inquest held in Colchester in 1317 in response to a writ from the king, the jury could complain only of markets held at St Osyth, Manningtree, Earls Colne, Coggeshall and Salcott,[28] all of which were beyond what was normally considered neighbouring in this context. There were few markets in adjacent villages partly because the borough markets were too well established for rivalry to succeed. But Colchester did not command a large enough hinterland to be able to support an extensive overseas trade. In this respect the borough was outstripped by Ipswich, whose local mercantile ascendancy was of long standing. The Colchester region even depended to some extent on supply through Harwich and other minor ports.[29] Some wine, coal, iron, salt and other staple commodities were shipped through Hythe for the town and its environs, but the range of imports was narrower than that through Ipswich; local landlords sent to Ipswich rather than to Colchester for their millstones.[30] And such direct maritime trade as Colchester had was heavily dependent upon merchants and shipping from other ports.[31] From the taxation lists of 1295 and 1301,[32] in conjunction with the later court rolls, a handful of resident merchants likely to have engaged in long-distance trade can be identified, but neither their numbers nor their wealth were sufficient to give them much weight in Colchester society. The borough was closer in character to a rural market town than to a centre of mercantile activity.

Colchester industry, as this implies, attracted little investment. From at least the middle decades of the thirteenth century the town had had a reputation for russets, which were taken to many parts of England to be made up as outer garments.[33] The early Colchester court rolls contain several examples of townsmen who were distrained to appear in court by the seizure of russet cloth or clothing made of russet,[34] and in the borough's assessment for the fifteenth of 1301 russet was the only woollen cloth to be repeatedly mentioned as a distinct type.[35] Colchester at this time still

[27] *Cal. Chart. R.*, i, p. 429.   [28] RPB, fo. 56r.

[29] In 1301 Colchester taverners were buying wine through a Harwich merchant: *Rot. Parl.*, i, p. 265. The supply of coal at the hands of Mersea shippers is recorded in 1311: CR 1/11d–12d.

[30] P.R.O., S.C.6/839/19, m. 1r (king's manor, Colchester); S.C.6/841/9r (Feering).

[31] CR 4/8r (London), 9v (Sandwich). Flemish ships, too, called at Colchester: *Cal. Pat. R., 1340–3*, p. 286; *Cal. Close R., 1346–7*, pp. 203–4, 234.

[32] *Rot. Parl.*, i, pp. 228–38, 243–65.

[33] *English Historical Documents, 1189–1327*, ed. H. Rothwell (London, 1975), p. 881; E. M. Carus-Wilson, *Medieval Merchant Venturers: Collected Studies*, 2nd edn (London, 1967), pp. 213–14.   [34] CR 1/1d, 2d, 8r, 14r; CR 2/8r.

[35] *Rot. Parl.*, i, pp. 246 bis, 247, 251, 259 bis, 262, 263.

sent cloth to distant parts, and these cloths are mentioned alongside those of Coggeshall, Maldon and Sudbury in a list of customs payable in Ipswich at the end of the thirteenth century.[36] In 1301, however, only six men were taxed on fullers' utensils and only three on dyestuffs and dying vats. This small number of fullers and dyers, who might reasonably be expected to figure in such a tax assessment, is more significant than the fact that there were only eight recorded weavers. Colchester was plainly not primarily a cloth town. Industry here had probably suffered from the development of clothmaking in the countryside. Fulling mills occur in early fourteenth-century sources in the villages of Finchingfield, Bocking, Lawford, Boreham and perhaps Wethersfield, as well as in the market towns of Coggeshall, Witham, and Manningtree.[37] Occupational names derived from the finishing trades occurred in many north-eastern Essex communities, particularly in the market towns. In the tax roll of 1327 the surname Dyer and its equivalents occurs three times in Colchester, and once in Mistley or Manningtree, Witham, Little Coggeshall, Great Bardfield, Bocking and Halstead. The surnames Fuller and Webb are absent from the Colchester list, but both occur in Dedham, and there were two Fullers in West Bergholt, one in Witham and one in Fairstead.[38] While none of this evidence proves that Colchester clothmaking had contracted from some earlier level, the burgesses cannot have been successful in capturing the growing market for cloth.

Of greater prominence in the 1301 tax assessment than textiles was the preparation of skins by tanning and tawing, and this has more claim to be considered the town's main industrial specialisation. Thirteen taxpayers were described as tanners or occupied tanneries, of whom Henry Pakeman was the most heavily taxed man in Colchester with movables valued at nearly £10.[39] A further 17 inhabitants who were taxed upon leather and shoes, or described as cobblers, indicate the main use to which leather was put in meeting demand in the local market. There were at least two parchment makers, who also used to make gloves. The number of men in

---

[36] *The Black Book of the Admiralty*, ed. T. Twiss, Rolls ser., (4 vols., London, 1871–6), ii, p. 186. A Coggeshall cloak occurs in Leicester in 1320: *Records of the Borough of Leicester, 1103–1327*, ed. M. Bateson (London, 1899), p. 376.

[37] P.R.O., C.133/93/9 (Finchingfield, 1300); C.133/117/15 (Coggeshall, 1305); C.134/34/4 (Boreham, 1315); C.134/63/27 (Wethersfield, 1319); E.142/1/10 (Witham, 1307); B.L., Galba E.IV, fo. 108r (Bocking, 1303); *Cal. Inq. P.M.*, ii, no. 628, p. 380 (Lawford, 1287); *A Descriptive Catalogue of Ancient Deeds in the Public Record Office*, H.M.S.O. (6 vols., London, 1890–1915), i, no. C.906, p. 476 (Manningtree, 1309).

[38] *The Medieval Essex Community: The Lay Subsidy of 1327*, ed. J. C. Ward, Essex Record Office Publications, lxxxviii (Chelmsford, 1983), pp. 13, 17, 18, 23, 27, 28, 31, 54, 63, 66; E. Miller, 'The Fortunes of the English Textile Industry during the Thirteenth Century', *Ec.H.R.*, 2nd ser., xviii (1965), p. 78.

[39] *Rot. Parl.*, i, p. 252.

these industries suggests that their sales were not restricted to Colchester itself. But the presence in the subsidy roll of 1327 of two men with the surname Tanner in Witham, one in Halstead and one in Fairstead, implies that this industry too met with some competition in rural markets.[40] It is unlikely that the Colchester leather industry produced much that was surplus to local requirements, and there is no evidence of regular leather exports to London or abroad. The earliest detailed evidence of Colchester's exports, almost a century later, shows some export of skins but not of leather. The textile and leather industries between them exhaust the manufacturing industries worthy of comment in Colchester in 1301.

The sea may have offered more employment than either the textile or the leather industries at this time. Seventeen taxpayers in 1301 had at least part ownership in boats, and four of these were also taxed on fishing tackle. There were two other fishermen without boats of their own.[41] The amount of employment on merchants' ships was no doubt greater than this, though no estimate is possible before the early 1340s. When the sheriff of Essex and Hertfordshire was commissioned in about 1340 to hold all ships of 120 tons or more in preparation for war he took four at Colchester, the *James*, the *Katerine*, the *Mariotte* and the *Nicholas*.[42] A Colchester vessel of about 100 tons, the *Eline*, occurs in 1338 and another, the *Seintemaricog*, in 1342 and 1347. The *Margarete*, which the king used in 1338, was perhaps of about 60 tons. Other ships occurring in the performance of wartime naval duties were the *Margerie* in 1338 and the *Petit James* in 1342, both little more than fishing boats to judge from the size of their crews.[43] Since a ship of 120 tons would employ a crew of about 28,[44] it may be supposed that Colchester's merchant shipping then employed fewer than 200. Not all the crews needed to be of Colchester men, so that an estimate of 200 would overstate the importance of this employment for the town. Moreover, there had probably been some increase in Colchester's merchant shipping during the 1330s. It nevertheless looks probable that fishing, coastal trade and overseas trade together figured prominently in Colchester's employment structure in the early fourteenth century.

Population estimates for medieval towns are always problematic, but in Colchester's case there is little doubt about the order of magnitude. Even by English standards it was not very big. London, with perhaps 40,000 people, was in the same class as Bruges, Ghent, Ypres and Rouen on the

---

[40] *The Medieval Essex Community*, ed. Ward, pp. 27, 28, 66.
[41] *Rot. Parl.*, i, pp. 247–54. Geoffrey 'his brother' (p. 251) is Geoffrey Dounyng, sailor (p. 252).   [42] P.R.O., E.101/556/37r.
[43] P.R.O., E.36/203, fo. 151v; E.36/204, fo. 116v; E.372/193, m. 31r. I owe these references to Mrs Linda Drury.
[44] C. Platt, *Medieval Southampton: The Port and Trading Community, A.D. 1000–1600* (London, 1973), p. 71.

other side of the Channel. Bristol, Norwich and York may each have had about 10,000 inhabitants, and so, according to one definition, would count by medieval standards as large towns.[45] Colchester never would. From the records of a tax levied on the borough and liberty in 1301 it has been estimated that the number of inhabitants was then about 3,000.[46] In 1312–13, according to a document in existence in the eighteenth century, 'a tallage was assessed upon every particular person (or master of a family) in this town and the liberties, according to the value of his chattels or rents. The number of persons taxed was 518.'[47] This again, allowing for clergy, castle garrison, vagabonds and paupers, suggests a population of 3,000–4,000. This estimate accords well with Colchester's low status as a commercial and manufacturing town.

All the indicators of Colchester's size and economic characteristics imply that the town was not a wealthy one. This is fully confirmed by taxation records. Since the town was assessed for tax along with four dependent villages, Lexden, Mile End, Greenstead and West Donyland, the total figures of each assessment exaggerate the amount of urban taxable wealth. But it is unnecessary to make any allowance for this to demonstrate Colchester's poor standing; even with rural appendages it would still have to be omitted from a list of England's wealthiest 50 towns in 1334.[48] It does not compare with the main east-coast ports, its taxable wealth being less than half that of Ipswich and only a quarter or less that of Newcastle upon Tyne, Boston and Great Yarmouth. Colchester also compares badly with some nearby towns; Bury St Edmunds, Sudbury and Writtle all had more taxable wealth.[49]

Even large towns retained pronounced rural features at the end of the thirteenth century,[50] so it is not surprising to find that agrarian pursuits were important in Colchester's economy. The tax assessments of 1295 and 1301 show that the chief single kind of movable wealth in Colchester was

---

[45] L. Genicot, 'Les Grandes Villes de l'Occident en 1300', in *Économies et sociétés au Moyen Âge: mélanges offerts à Edouard Perroy* (Paris, 1973), pp. 200, 206–19; G. A. Williams, *Medieval London: From Commune to Capital*, 2nd edn (London, 1970), pp. 315–17; J. C. Russell, *British Medieval Population* (Albuquerque, 1948), p. 285; E. Miller, 'Medieval York', in P. M. Tillott, ed., *A History of Yorkshire: The City of York*, The Victoria History of the Counties of England (Oxford, 1961), p. 40.

[46] G. Rickword, 'Taxations of Colchester, A.D. 1296 and 1301', *T.E.A.S.*, new ser., ix (1906), pp. 145–6. Professor Russell, projecting backwards on false assumptions from the evidence of Colchester's poll tax assessment of 1377, estimates the town's population at 7,400 before the Black Death: J. C. Russell, *Medieval Regions and their Cities* (Newton Abbot, 1972), p. 124.   [47] Morant, *Colchester*, i, p. 47.

[48] R. E. Glasscock, 'England circa 1334', in H. C. Darby, ed., *A New Historical Geography of England* (Cambridge, 1973), pp. 179–85. For further discussion, see J. F. Hadwin, 'Evidence on the Possession of "Treasure" from the Lay Subsidy Rolls', in N. J. Mayhew, ed., *Edwardian Monetary Affairs (1279–1344)*, *B.A.R.*, 36 (Oxford, 1977), p. 161.

[49] *The Lay Subsidy of 1334*, ed. Glasscock, pp. 85, 169, 198, 226, 291, 294.

[50] Hilton, *A Medieval Society*, p. 185.

agricultural. This is implied by the number of taxpayers assessed on grain and livestock.[51] By this criterion the proportion of taxpayers involved in agriculture (other than those from the villages of the liberty) was 81 per cent in 1295 and about 69 per cent in 1301.[52] It is true that in many instances wealth in these forms was combined with possessions indicating employment in industry or trade, whether raw materials, craftsmen's utensils or finished goods. The number of urban taxpayers taxed only on household goods (including brewing utensils) and agricultural produce was 51 per cent of the total in 1295 and about 40 per cent in 1301. The list of 1301 shows a lower proportion of such people because it included many more of the town's poorer households, who were less likely than wealthier households to have land. This figure for 1301 overstates the proportion of urban taxpayers concerned exclusively in agriculture and brewing, since a number of those taxed only on household goods and agricultural produce had occupational names suggesting employment off the land. But even with these allowances it is likely that two-thirds of the taxpayers of 1301 had some wealth in land and that one third had no significant wealth other than land or other property. This implies that the fluctuations of yields and prices which affected incomes in the countryside around Colchester were a principal determinant of incomes in the borough itself.

II

During the 1330s and 1340s the history of Colchester's long-distance trade shows developments which make an interesting prelude to events after the Black Death. Successful applications for burgess status by sailors and shipmen in the early thirties suggest a burst of interest in trade through Hythe; three mariners became burgesses in 1330 together with William Buk of Mersea, who rapidly became a leading Colchester shipowner and merchant, and at least two more mariners were admitted to the burgage during 1331/2.[53] Perhaps this was the result of increasing denizen trade in wool during the later 1320s and the temporary abolition of staple ports for the wool trade in April 1328.[54] Some royal experiments in regulating the wool trade served the turn of Colchester seamen, who are to be found in 1339 exporting wool through Maldon on behalf of big Italian firms, the Bardi and Peruzzi.[55] These developments might be supposed transient, and

[51] Taxpayers with horses but no other grain or livestock are excluded.
[52] The figure for 1301 is more approximate than that for 1295 because not all taxpayers from the villages of the liberty can be separately identified.
[53] OB, fos. 30r, 31r; CR 3/3r, 8d. For Alexander Archer, see n. 55.
[54] T. H. Lloyd, *The English Wool Trade in the Middle Ages* (Cambridge, 1977), p. 120.
[55] *Cal. Pat. R., 1338–40*, p. 206, Alexander Archer and John Belch were burgesses of Colchester: OB, fos. 30r, 36v.

even illusory, were they not followed by more evidence for a growth of
interest in Hythe as a port. In 1339/40 a plot at Hythe was leased by the
community of Colchester to John Aleyn, a Colchester shipowner. It lay
in the meadow called Saltmed and occupied 2,000 square feet. He was also
granted a strip of land between this plot and the river bank on condition
that he made no charge for wares placed there by other burgesses or for
moorings there. Then in 1342 three similar plots, each of 5,400 square feet,
were granted by the community to John Peldon, Nicholas le Chapman and
John Lucas. The plots were expressly for building on, and in each case there
was an extension to the river bank for quayage, as in the case of John
Aleyn's plot. A similar plot of 1,120 square feet, granted to John Tenham
at the same time, was described as vacant, implying that it was already
recognised as a unit of tenure. The others, however, are neither described
as vacant nor as having been surrendered by previous tenants, and they
appear to constitute a new scheme accepted by the bailiffs and community
of the borough for extending warehousing and wharfage at Hythe.[56] The
community's concern with shipping is further in evidence in 1341/2, a year
when two merchants, William Buk and John Fordham, were bailiffs.
At the beginning of their term of office at Michaelmas 1341 they
successfully negotiated with Sir John de Sutton, lord of Wivenhoe,
concerning rights at the Wodesende in Old Heath. By this agreement the
bailiffs, community and all merchants plying to Colchester were allowed
to anchor and wharf at the Wodesende and to cart their tackle and wares
to and from the banks of the Colne. The bailiffs and community were
authorised to make docks for shipbuilding and maintenance work at a plot
there called the Sole, measuring six perches by five. This site was valuable
because it could be used by sea-going vessels which could not navigate
higher up the river, and its development may indicate an increase in volume
of trade through Colchester.[57]

One component of the export trade through Hythe in the early
fourteenth century was local agricultural produce. Though less noteworthy
than Ipswich as a port for wool shipments, Colchester had a small stake
in the trade, both legal and illegal.[58] Rabbit skins and cheeses also figure
amongst exports here.[59] Local agricultural producers were amongst those
who showed an interest in the port. William Buk, who had three
warehouses at Hythe in 1337, was probably drawn to trade in Colchester
through his interests as a wool producer, since he owned 100 acres of
marshland in West Mersea.[60] Elias le Herde of Wivenhoe, who in 1335/6

[56] OB, fos. 35v, 37r.
[57] RPB, fo. 139r.
[58] *Cal. Close R., 1341–3*, pp. 204, 292, 327; *Cal. Pat. R., 1340–3*, p. 286.
[59] *Cal. Pat. R., 1340–3*, p. 286; *Cal. Close R., 1343–6*, pp. 478–9.
[60] P.R.O., E.101/556/19Ar, 37r; *Essex Fines*, iii, p. 39.

took up a messuage at Hythe from a Colchester fisherman, was earlier a servant at Wivenhoe manor, where he was still a tenant in the 1330s. He had taken advantage of his manorial responsibilities to develop as a middleman, like James le Herde, his contemporary at Langenhoe on the other side of Colne Water.[61] Small operators from coastal villages were in a good position to seize opportunities in local trade. Colchester's exports in the 1330s and 1340s also included some cloth.[62]

Of imported goods, wine is the most prominent in the very fragmentary extant evidence. Some came by way of other English ports; John Fynch the London vintner sued a couple of burgesses for debt in 1334, and Walter Daulard, a wine importer of Sandwich, was trading in Colchester about the same time.[63] From the 1330s, however, a group of wine importers among Colchester's own merchants becomes prominent in the records. This may be a trick of documentary survival or it may be related to the contemporary development of properties at Hythe. John Fynch of Colchester, joint owner of the *Nicholas* in the early 1340s, was a seller of wine in the borough,[64] and so was Roger Belch who, in addition to owing the *James*, bought a crayer called the *Skynkewyn of Breel* in 1343.[65] John Tenham, who acquired one of the new building plots at Hythe in 1342, was another vintner, who had only recently become a burgess.[66] William Buk and John Aleyn both handled wine in the 1350s and are likely to have done so already in the 1340s.[67] Colchester's wine trade implies the existence of outward cargoes appropriate to the Gascon market. In the later fourteenth century the only such export was woollen cloth.

The immediate effect of these commercial developments on enterprise and employment in Colchester was nevertheless slight. There is nothing in the records of this period to suggest any change in the fortunes of the textile industry. If clothmaking in the town had increased other things might be expected to follow. Labour relations in the cloth industry were subject to hazards rare in agriculture because of the greater irregularity of employment in the former and the greater possibilities for employees to deceive their employers. Even if additional industrial employment was achieved by a transfer of men out of agriculture, some increase in the number of pleas of broken contract might be expected. In the second place, if Colchester merchants were expanding their credit to finance industrial

[61] OB, fo. 33v; E.R.O., T/B 122; R. H. Britnell, 'Production for the Market on a Small Fourteenth-Century Estate', *Ec.H.R.*, 2nd ser., xix (1966), pp. 381–2.
[62] *Cal. Pat. R., 1340–3*, p. 286; *Cal. Close R., 1343–6*, pp. 478–9.
[63] CR 4/8r, 9r, 10r,d, 11r,d, 12r (John Fynch of London); CR 4/9d, 10r (Walter Daulard of Sandwich). [64] P.R.O., E.101/556/37r; CR 3/1d, 3d; CR 6/1d, 5r; CR 7/2r.
[65] P.R.O., E.101/556/37r; *Cal. Pat. R., 1343–5*, p. 27; CR 3/3d; CR 6/1d.
[66] OB, fos. 34v, 37r; CR 7/2r.
[67] CR 9/5d; CR 10/1r, 5d; CR 11/1d, 5d, 9d; CR 12/1r, 11d.

Table 1.1 *Pleas of broken contract and debt brought to Colchester courts,
1310/11–1345/6*

	29 September–24 December		25 December–24 March		25 March–24 June		25 June–28 September	
	Broken contract	Debt	Broken contract	Debt	Broken contract	Debt	Broken contract	Debt
1310/11	2	7	0	9	?	?	?	?
1311/12	1	8	0	4	3	9	1	1
1329/30	1	3	1	5	?	?	?	?
1333/4	?	?	?	?	?	?	?	?
1336/7	0	10	0	4	0	8	0	4
1340/1	3	16	2	8	?	?	1	13
1345/6	1	9	1	8	?	?	?	?

Source: CR 1–7.

expansion, the number of pleas of debt in the borough might be expected
to increase. The evidence does not favour either of these possibilities. Table
1.1 shows the number of pleas of broken contract and debt in each quarter
of the years for which there is some record. It may be observed, in passing,
how small the number of such pleas was at this period. There were only
22 pleas of debt in 1311/12 and 26 in 1336/7, these being two years for
which the record is complete enough for a count to be made. There was
no increase in this litigation during the 1330s and 1340s sufficiently great
to indicate a surge of growth or structural change in the economy of the
town. An increase in Colchester's industry might also be expected to have
encouraged some immigration from Flanders,[68] particularly in view of the
town's location on the east coast, but no Flemings occur in the court rolls
before the Black Death. The absence of these various features of industrial
development makes it improbable that there was much expansion of the
cloth industry in Colchester at this time.

It is improbable, moreover, that after 1311/12 there was any increase
in employment or population in Colchester above earlier levels. On the
contrary, population may have contracted after the famines of 1316–18.
At Michaelmas 1311 there were eight water mills at work in the liberty of
Colchester. On the stretch of the Colne to the north of the town were North
Mill by North Bridge, Stokes Mill at the end of Land Lane[69] and between

[68] E. Lipson, *The Economic History of England*, i, 12th edn (London, 1959), pp. 452–3.
[69] Stokes Mill was near the lands of Colchester castle, which included arable in Stocmel-
nelond and meadow in Stocmelnemede: P.R.O., S.C.6/839/18, m. 2r,d. A will proved
in 1330 bequeaths meadowland lying in Estmadwe lying south of Stockesmelne: CR 3/5r.

them, Middle Mill lying to the north of the castle. East Mill stood by East Bridge. To the south were Bourne Mill, where Bourne Pond now lies, the Eld Mill of St Botoloph's priory,[70] probably at the north end of Old Heath where Distillery Pond is now, and the New Mill of St Botolph's, whose site is uncertain.[71] There was also a mill belonging to Lexden manor on the bank of the Colne a mile or so to the west of Colchester.[72] But Stokes Mill seems to have been abandoned by the 1330s, which meant that Colchester had only seven water mills in operation in the 1340s. Simultaneously there was apparently a reduction in ale consumption.[73] The evidence from 1310/11 and 1311/12 is difficult to interpret because irregular brewing is very imperfectly recorded, but the 112 alewives reported at the Michaelmas lawhundred in 1311 exceeded the number at any subsequent assizes before the Black Death. The total was particularly low in 1329/30 and thereafter picked up to range between 92 and 109 in the years 1336–46.[74] Since food prices were lower in the 1330s and 1340s than they had been earlier in the century,[75] a lower level of milling and brewing would strongly imply a contraction rather than an expansion of population since the opening decades of the century. This again argues against there having been any appreciable increase in employment in Colchester during the decades preceding the Black Death.

On this showing, Colchester was not one of the towns to benefit from the growth of English clothmaking during the 1330s and 1340s.[76] Any increase in cloth shipments through Hythe was the consequence of mercantile developments in some of the smaller market towns of northern Essex and southern Suffolk, such as the borough of Clare, which clearly enjoyed opportunities for economic expansion during the 1330s. No count of pleas of debt in Clare can be readily made, but the number terminating in licences to agree or failure to prosecute increased during these years and this was the prelude to a permanently higher level of litigation for debt in the later fourteenth century. The level of brewing activity simultaneously increased to a peak level in the years 1339–49, about half as high again as in the second decade of the century.[77] Clare borough court rolls also

---

[70] This is the *molendinum iuxta Wykam* of CR 2/2r. It was later called Canwick (*i.e.* Canons' Wick) Mill, and it occurs in 1777 as Kennic Mill: J. Chapman and P. André, *A Map of the County of Essex* (London, 1777, reprinted Chelmsford, 1950), plate ix.

[71] All seven mills are listed in the jury reports at the Michaelmas lawhundred of 1311: CR 2/2r. Stokes Mill last occurs as a grain mill at the following lawhundred: CR 2/5r.

[72] *Colch. Cart.*, i, pp. 53, 97, 160; P.R.O., C.134/31/3; *Essex Sessions of the Peace, 1351, 1377–1379*, ed. E. C. Furber, Essex Archaeological Society Occasional Publications, iii (Colchester, 1953), p. 63.   [73] Appendix, Table 1.

[74] For comparison, the number of brewers amerced in Sudbury in the years 1336–46 ranged between 58 and 98 (average 73): P.R.O., S.C.2/203/114, 115; S.C.2/204/3.

[75] J. Z. Titow, *English Rural Society, 1200–1350* (London, 1969), pp. 98–9, 102.

[76] Carus-Wilson, *Medieval Merchant Venturers*, pp. 242–3.

[77] P.R.O., S.C.2/203/38, 43–7.

record numerous new rents in Clare in the 1340s.[78] These signs of vigour are likely to be related to industrial growth, though of modest dimensions. Such development was unlikely to be widespread in the textile centres of the region. Sudbury, which like Colchester was an old-established centre of clothmaking, showed no signs of economic expansion in these years.[79]

Colchester's economic fortunes were thrown into yet more uncertainty in 1348 by the arrival of the Black Death. Between 1327/8 and 1347/8 an annual average of 2.35 wills had been proved in the borough court, but in 1348/9 there were 111.[80] These figures cannot be converted into any remotely plausible indicator of what happened to the death rate; either more burgesses than usual made their wills in the plague year or a higher proportion than usual of wills was proved in the borough court. It is likely, however, that at least a quarter of the population died in the epidemic. Brewing activity fell so that at Michaelmas 1351 there were only 70 brewers amerced, where at Michaelmas 1345 there had been 94.[81] Two mills out of the seven which operated during the 1340s were abandoned as grain mills,[82] so that only five grain mills were at work for about 20 years afterwards. This mortality caused a great upheaval in the economy of the town. To a survivor of the epidemic it would have seemed that the blow must have affected the prosperity of the borough for the worse.

[78] G. A. Holmes, *The Estates of the Higher Nobility in Fourteenth-Century England* (Cambridge, 1957), p. 157.
[79] P.R.O., S.C.2/203/112–15; S.C.2/204/3; S.C.6/1006/9–16.
[80] OB, fos. 29v–40r.
[81] CR 7/2r; CR 9/1d.
[82] The last occurrence of North Mill and Middle Mill as grain mills is at the Hocktide lawhundred of 1346: CR 7/9d.

Parish churches
1. St Mary at the Wall
2. St Peter
3. St Martin
4. St Runwald
5. Holy Trinity
6. St Nicholas
7. All Saints
8. St James
9. St Giles
10. St Botolph
11. St Mary Magdalen
12. St Leonard
—— The town walls

Colchester in 1300

23

2

Urban liberty

I

Despite its small size, Colchester was a privileged town in the fourteenth century. It had no overlord but the king, whose predecessors had long since granted it a measure of self-government under the law. The burgesses elected annually two bailiffs to preside over the judicial and police work of the borough, to supervise the collection of borough revenues, to assess and collect royal taxes and to represent the burgesses in cases of conflict with the Crown, local landlords or other towns. Officers of the borough had some authority over four dependent hamlets which with the town itself made up the liberty of Colchester; this division of Essex was in fact the Hundred of Colchester, since Colchester was one of numerous English boroughs which constituted hundreds in themselves and whose courts of law developed as hundred courts.[1] Because of its privileges, Colchester was more independent of seigneurial authority than many small boroughs of comparable size and wealth, and this autonomy was conducive to a certain civic dignity. If the borough was nevertheless not particularly attractive to newcomers, an explanation is not hard to find. Ordinary tradesmen benefited little from royal favours which left them, in most respects, no better off than the inhabitants of market towns elsewhere. The financial charges upon them were no lighter for having been imposed by wealthy townsmen rather than royal officers. They were subject to tallages for the necessary expenses of the community; they were amerced for infringing petty rules of trade; they paid more tax than would have been required of them in a less privileged environment. The chief advantages of being a burgess were the right to put animals on the borough common[2] and to engage in middleman activities in the town.[3] A man with these

---

[1] *Cal. Chart. R.*, i, p. 411; Morant, *Colchester*, i, pp. 78–9; J. Tait, *The Medieval English Borough* (Manchester, 1936), pp. 32–3, 45–6.
[2] Morant, *Colchester*, i, p. 88; CR 3/1d, 3d; CR 4/1d. [3] See Chapter 3, pp. 35–8.

interests might feel strongly enough to defend them if they were assailed from without, but such rights were no more than those similarly guarded by the men of many a smaller settlement. The liberties most distinctive of the borough community were of greatest advantage to the richer men of the town to whom they gave scope for the exercise of public authority.

As yet the government of Colchester was conducted with little pomp, the constitution being informal and the number of borough officers small. The bailiffs handled judicial matters with the assistance of a town clerk and three sergeants, who were officers of the court. The burgesses also appointed their own coroners.[4] How these eight positions were filled is unknown, but it was achieved without elaborate elective apparatus. There were no appointed treasurers and no audited accounts. Nor was there a town council.[5] The bailiffs sought the burgesses' assent to any ordinances they might make,[6] probably at an annual meeting when new borough officers were elected. Such a constitution depended on frequent co-operation amongst the wealthier burgesses from whom bailiffs might be chosen and from whom advice was best had. If the bailiffs needed formal consultation with their peers they summoned an *ad hoc* assembly at which opinions might be aired. In May 1311 a meeting was held to discuss whether the bishop of London's tenants at Chelmsford and Braintree should pay tolls in Colchester, and the ensuing deliberations were briefly noted in the current court roll, together with a list of the 30 men, not including the bailiffs, who had been present.[7] Joseph Elianor's indentures of 1341 for the founding of his chantry imply that the community could act even in the absence of bailiffs. His provision that the patronage of the chantry should be exercised by the bailiffs and community, or if there were no bailiffs by the community *per se*, shows a high degree of confidence in the ability of his fellow burgesses to organise themselves.[8] In part this informality arose from the small size of the community. In part, too, it corresponded to the nature of the bailiffs' obligations as they were then understood. The tradition of self-government was tightly circumscribed by law and custom. There had been too little growth of wealth in the borough to generate pressures for change in the system, and the ruling group itself was too diffuse in its interests, and perhaps too hidebound in legalistic thinking, to generate any desire for innovation. The everyday administration of the borough had all the appearance of routine, the occasional breaks coming in response to shocks from outside the community rather than from initiatives within it.

---

[4] For the number of sergeants, see CR 9/1r; CR 10/1d. For the borough coroners, see RPB, fo. 47v.

[5] See Chapter 8, pp. 118–19.

[6] RPB, fo. 124r.

[7] CR 1/11r.

[8] B.L., Stowe 841, fo. 35v.

The heaviest demand on the bailiffs' time was the work of the courts, which involved a more constant attention to duty than it would have done in a rural hundred. Colchester was sufficiently urban to have moulded its legal system away from the normal pattern. The hundred court met fortnightly, rather than every three weeks,[9] and even this did not solve the problems of commercial life, since procedure there was too slow for the effective prosecution of outsiders who might be here one day and gone the next. The burgesses therefore operated a second court, the court of pleas, inspired by the more rapid forms of procedure developed for merchant law.[10] As against the eight weeks' delay which a defendant in the hundred court could expect as a matter of right,[11] the court of pleas could bring a man to court within a few days. When Adam le Orloger of Mersea was sued in June 1311 for detaining a boat and its cargo of coal, his right to three essoins gave him only two days' respite, since the bailiffs were willing to hold sessions two days running to speed the matter along.[12] Courts of pleas made the bailiffs' timetable more unpredictable than it would otherwise have been. In 1311/12 there were at least 23 sessions of the hundred court and 36 sessions of the court of pleas, but in 1336/7 there were 26 sessions of the former and only 8 sessions of the latter.[13] Despite this element of discretion in their work, the bailiffs had little independence in judicial matters. They were more concerned with the correct handling of procedure than with the interpretation of laws. Few pleas had to do with property, since burgesses preferred to defend their freeholds in the king's courts.[14] Pleas before the bailiffs mostly involved allegations of minor assault or indebtedness, where there was little occasion for independent judicial opinion.

Maintenance of law and order was another element of the bailiffs' duties, and many breaches of the peace came before the courts not as private pleas but through the working of normal policing. Constables and a night watch were appointed to each of the four main gates of the town, in accordance with the Statute of Winchester,[15] and on their report the courts investigated people said to wander round the town at night.[16] Whenever a disturbance occurred or was threatened it was up to bystanders to raise the hue to apprehend the aggressor; an inquest was then held in the hundred court

[9] For the normal pattern, see H. M. Cam, *The Hundred and the Hundred Rolls* (London, 1930), p. 168.

[10] *Select Cases concerning the Law Merchant*, ed. C. Gross and H. Hall, Selden Society, xxiii, xlvi, xlix (3 vols., London, 1908–32), i, pp. xvi–xxii; L. F. Salzman, *English Trade in the Middle Ages* (Oxford, 1931), pp. 161–2.

[11] R. H. Britnell, 'Colchester Courts and Court Records, 1310–1525', *Essex Archaeology and History*, xvii (forthcoming, 1986).

[12] CR 1/11d–12d. [13] CR 2 and 5. [14] *Essex Fines*, ii, pp. 101, 105, 121, etc.

[15] CR 1/11r, 12r, 14r; CR 2/7d; *cf.* 13 Edward I, 2, c. 4 (*Statutes*, i, p. 97).

[16] *E.g.* CR 2/7r, CR 3/5r.

to determine whether the hue had been raised justly. But the court's competence in these instance was limited to minor offences, and the bailiffs had no power to try cases of felony (murders, rapes, maimings, robberies, thefts) for which death or mutilation were prescribed penalties. Such matters had to be handed over to the king's justices. In practice Colchester courts distinguished thefts to the value of less than 1*s* 0*d* from more serious ones. A thief who in 1310 entered a smithy by night and stole some iron was brought before the bailiffs and coroner, but because the iron was worth only 5*d* he was merely put in the pillory.[17] In the summer of 1311, however, some men caught by the night guard and suspected of having been stealing were ordered to be detained until the next gaol delivery early in the new year. One of the offenders, Richard Musse the miller, was then convicted and hanged for the theft of four geese worth 1*s* 0*d*.[18] The policing of the borough can be seen as a matter for routine co-operation between the bailiffs, the coroners and the king's justices, the bailiffs attending to minor breaches of the peace but passing on the more serious cases.

The policing function of the borough courts achieved its most formal expression at the thrice-yearly lawhundreds, which were enlarged sessions of the hundred court.[19] On these occasions the principal landowners in the liberty were required to put in an appearance or to make a formal excuse for their absence. An agreement of 1338 between the burgesses and the abbot of Colchester specified his obligation for suit of court at three lawhundreds held the Monday after Michaelmas (29 September), the Monday after the feast of St Hilary (13 January) and the Monday after Hockday (the second Tuesday after Easter).[20] The court rolls show that this timing was retained throughout the later Middle Ages. Lawhundred juries did not have to concern themselves with frankpledge, the system which required men to associate in groups of 10 or 12 to be responsible for each other's good conduct; Colchester was one of the boroughs free of this institution. Lawhundred business was nevertheless extensive. A jury of burgesses came before the bailiffs to answer questions designed to elicit the names of offenders against certain statutes, ordinances and by-laws. The regulations in question were very varied, for besides matters relating to the king's peace and to public morals they covered agrarian and commercial offences.[21] Lawhundred proceedings are accordingly a rich source of information about economic organisation in the liberty.

In addition to the regular meetings of the lawhundred, the bailiffs were empowered to hold inquests to investigate flagrant abuses or matters which

[17] CR 1/4d.
[18] CR 1/14r; CR 2/5d.
[19] For this institution in rural areas, see Cam, *The Hundred and the Hundred Rolls*, p. 176.
[20] *Colch. Cart.*, ii, p. 507; OB, fo. 148r.
[21] *Cf.* W. A. Morris, *The Frankpledge System* (Cambridge, Mass., 1910), pp. 147–50.

could not suitably be accommodated to the lawhundred timetable. In the latter category came inquests into the keeping of the assize of bread, which were conducted, whenever the bailiffs saw fit, by a specially empanelled jury including four bakers.[22] But any other item of law enforcement might be handled similarly. The bailiffs held occasional inquests, described as inquests *ex officio*, to establish points needing to be cleared up quickly. On 23 August 1334, William le Salter and Ida Hotfot were found buying up eight mullets before the fish market had opened, so they were guilty of forestalling. The bailiffs had them arrested and called an inquest, probably the same day. The pair confessed, and were ordered to forfeit the price of the mullets. On this occasion, however, at the request of two royal officials who happened to be in the moothall at the time, the penalty was reduced from 1*s* 9*d* to 10*d* with the proviso that if caught forestalling again the couple should be put in the pillory.[23]

In addition to judicial and policing obligations, the bailiffs at this period had responsibility for handling the borough finances. In most cases they had little real freedom to spend money as they pleased since they had difficulty enough in funding what had to be done. Judicial administration brought in a steady income from fines, and bailiffs were always more eager to impose money penalties than to inflict less remunerative forms of punishment.[24] There was some revenue, probably very small, from properties owing rent to the community.[25] But these receipts together were insufficient to maintain the fixed structures around the town for which the bailiffs were responsible, and to meet these costs it was necessary to raise subsidies or tallages from time to time. A few are known from the earliest surviving court rolls; a subsidy for East Bridge was being collected in the autumn of 1310 and during the following winter; in the summer of 1312 a burgess was in arrears in his payment of a tallage assessed 'throughout the whole community' for the repair of the walls and gates of the town.[26] Starting at Easter 1339 the abbot of Colchester paid the community 13*s* 4*d* a year to be free of such tallages.[27] The administrative duties of the bailiffs as collectors of revenue for the community's use must have been the chief reason for the existence of a common chest, which was also used for the custody of important documents.[28]

Other sums collected by the bailiffs passed through their hands in their capacity as collectors of revenue for the Crown. The burgesses' regular liability was limited to £35 a year for the fee farm of the borough,[29] a sum

---

[22] *E.g.* CR 2/4r.

[23] CR 4/12d.

[24] There is no reference to the pillory's being used.

[25] CR 1/6r; CR 2/6d; B.L., Campb. Ch. ii, 5.

[26] CR 1/2r, 7d; CR 2/11d, 12d.

[27] *Colch. Cart.*, ii, pp. 506–8; OB, fo. 148r.

[28] B.L., Campb. Ch. xxiii, 14.

[29] Tait, *The Medieval English Borough*, pp. 171, 178, 188–9; OB, fos. 11r–18r.

secured annually by a lease of the local duties payable on goods unloaded at Hythe, together with the market tolls. The dues were collected on behalf of the lessee by the borough sergeants.[30] Though leases ran from Michaelmas to Michaelmas, payment from the lessee was due in coin a fortnight earlier in order to allow time for the money to reach Westminster.[31] But not all the king's normal revenues arising within the liberty passed through the bailiffs' hands. They had nothing to do with the sums separately collected at Colchester castle from the king's fields, pastures and woods on the northern side of the town.[32]

II

In fact the bailiffs of Colchester could regard the liberty of the borough as an administrative unit for very few purposes. The Colchester coroners had authority both in the town and in the hamlets;[33] the bailiffs were entitled to issue summonses, levy debts and issue writs throughout the liberty on the king's behalf;[34] the liberty was also a unit for the assessment and collection of taxes.[35] But in other respects the bailiffs' authority and that of the borough courts was curtailed by manorial rights. Although the burgesses had no feudal overlord but the king, they lived in close proximity to landlords who penned them in with restrictions. Moreover, conflict of interest between the burgesses and neighbouring lords bred disputes and sometimes open conflict, both within the liberty and beyond. The wealthiest lordship in the liberty was that of the abbot of Colchester, whose demesnes in West Donyland and Greenstead were said in the early fourteenth century to include about 480 acres of arable, 100 acres of wood, 100 acres of pasture and 40 acres of meadow.[36] The abbot's assized rents in the liberty were reported to amount to £33.[37] Lexden manor, the second largest estate, had at least 323½ acres of arable in 1313 with 160 acres of pasture and 24½ acres of meadow. Rents there were said to be £4 5s 4d a year.[38] These two manors were the main source of trouble to the burgesses both because of their size and because their lords exercised jurisdiction over tenants. Leet courts were held both in Greenstead and Lexden to exercise

---

[30] CR 7/1r. In 1312 a sergeant was appointed 'to collect tolls, make attachments and perform other duties of his office': CR 2/10r.
[31] CR 1/1d; CR 2/5d.
[32] P.R.O., S.C.6/839/18, 19.
[33] RPB, fos. 46v–47v, 52v, 53r, 67r and detached folio (formerly fo. lv); OB, fo. 175r; *Essex Sessions*, ed. Furber, p. 88.
[34] *British Borough Charters, 1216–1307*, ed. A. Ballard and J. Tait (Cambridge, 1923), pp. lxi, 171.
[35] *Rot. Parl.*, i, pp. 228–38.　　[36] RPB, fo. 54v.
[37] *Ibid.* A lower figure from 1312–13 is cited in Morant, *Colchester*, i, p. 48, note E.
[38] P.R.O., C.134/31/3.

basic policing responsibilities.[39] The smaller lordships in the liberty – Colchester Priory's properties in Canwick and Greenstead,[40] St Osyth Abbey's manor of Mile End[41] and the lands attached to the king's castle[42] – had no jurisdiction sufficient to affect the burgesses. The king's manor was potentially able to cause trouble, since its properties included Kingswood over which the burgesses had pasture rights, but no disagreement seems to have arisen concerning them.[43]

It was in disputes between the burgesses and their neighbours that independence of judgement and action by the bailiffs had most potential for good or ill. There were a number of recurrent problems. Manorial leet jurisdiction was one of them because it inevitably reduced the authority of Colchester courts. During the early fourteenth century, for example, the Fitz Walters at Lexden successfully prevented their water mill from coming within the purview of Colchester lawhundreds.[44] It was a matter of course for Colchester juries to call in question the legitimacy of such independent jurisdiction, as in 1317 and 1321/2, even though they had little hope of overturning long established rights.[45] To this extent some of the contentions between the town and its neighbours were a formality. But the burgesses were seriously afraid that the lord of Lexden might achieve complete independence; between 1313 and 1327 they went so far as to compile an abstract of evidence for Lexden's belonging to the liberty, designed as a brief for legal counsel.[46] This issue could not be evaded, since it was clearly the duty of the bailiffs to resist the dismemberment of the liberty. Other conflicts between burgesses and landlords were less clear cut. In a period of land hunger and assertive demesne husbandry new problems of land use were bound to arise around the town. The enclosure of land by burgesses themselves caused some trouble,[47] but the activities of landlords were more difficult for the burgesses to monitor, and the rights of the burgesses were often uncertain. The abbots of Colchester pursued a vigorous policy of estate improvement during the first quarter of the fourteenth century, expanding the area of their demesnes and encouraging enclosures,[48] and this gave rise to problems about access to pastures.[49]

[39] LB, fo. 305r; *Rot. Hund.*, i, p. 163; RPB, fo. 56v.

[40] Morant, *Colchester*, ii, pp. 28(2), 39; *Rot. Parl.*, i, p. 253. In 1312–13 the prior's rents in the liberty were reputedly £10 2s 0d: Morant, *Colchester*, i, p. 48, note E.

[41] Morant, *Colchester*, ii, p. 27(2); *Rot. Parl.*, i, p. 263.

[42] Morant, *Colchester*, i, p. 8.

[43] The king's manor received a sum called *communis preda* each year for animals commoning on Kingswood Heath: P.R.O., S.C.6/839/18, mm. 2r, 3r; S.C.6/839/19, mm. 1r, 2r.

[44] The miller of Lexden Mill was not reported by lawhundred juries in any documented court before 1352: CR 9/3d, 6r. Cf. *Essex Sessions*, ed. Furber, p. 63.

[45] RPB, fos. 48r, 56r.

[46] *Ibid.*, fos. 67r–68r.   [47] *E.g.* CR 2/2r.

[48] LB, fos. 60v–62r, 97r,v, 100r,v, 181v–182r, 199v–201v.

[49] CR 6/1d, 5d.

Another running dispute concerned the burgesses' pasture rights in Lexden.[50] On this issue feelings ran sufficiently high for large numbers of burgesses to take the law into their own hands; pasture riots are more in evidence than any other form of civil disturbance in Colchester's history during the first half of the fourteenth century.[51] To judge from the abbots' successes in establishing their case, the burgesses were inclined to rush into bad causes, making life difficult for any bailiff who did not want unnecessary disturbances. In a dispute involving pasture rights in the Sawenwode in 1328/9 the bailiffs were explicitly exonerated from complicity, implying that the invasion of the wood had not been plotted inside the moothall.[52]

In some kinds of dispute the bailiffs assumed a diplomatic rôle. The texts of several agreements between the community and neighbouring landlords have survived from the thirteenth and early fourteenth centuries, all of which are described as having been ratified with the borough's common seal.[53] Much depended upon both the bailiffs' room for manoeuvre and upon the quality of personal contacts. In 1338 the burgesses came as near as they ever did to a diplomatic victory in relations with the abbey, in an agreement achieved, it is said, by the mediation of all their friends.[54] The points at issue concerned the abbot's financial obligations towards the borough and his suit of court there. The bailiffs could negotiate such matters without constraint from the pressure of popular feeling. There was another agreement in 1343 whereby the burgesses abandoned their claim to certain rights of common.[55] But while enjoying these better relations with the abbey the bailiffs had completely lost control over the town's relations with Lexden. Large number of burgesses invaded Lexden Park in 1343, apparently to assert rights of pasturing, hunting and fishing there. John Fitz Walter and his retinue laid siege to the town, ambushing merchants until some townsmen bought him off, violating the rules of trade in the market place and refusing to pay his share of a subsidy. Where feelings ran so high the bailiffs had the authority neither to lead the community effectively nor to negotiate with its enemies.[56]

On many issues there were bound to be differences of judgement and interest between the leading burgesses and the rest of the community. The character of Colchester's ruling group before the Black Death may be

---

[50] *Cal. Pat. R., 1307–13*, pp. 530–1; *Cal. Pat. R., 1343–5*, pp. 98–9.

[51] But see *Cal. Pat. R., 1317–21*, pp. 366–7, 474–5, 479–80.

[52] LB, fo. 40r,v.

[53] There are agreements with Colchester Abbey from 1254, 1338 and 1343: *Colch. Cart.*, ii, pp. 505–9; OB, fo. 148r,v; RPB, detached folio (formerly fo. xlvij). An agreement with the lord of Wivenhoe manor dates from 1341: RPB, fo. 139r.

[54] *Colch. Cart.*, ii, pp. 506–8; OB, fo. 148r,v.

[55] *Colch. Cart.*, ii, pp. 508–9.

[56] *Cal. Pat. R., 1343–5*, pp. 98–9; *Essex Sessions*, ed. Furber, pp. 62–3.

deduced from the kind of men who were chosen to be bailiffs. That they were drawn from the wealthiest of Colchester's townsmen goes without saying, so that most of them, even those from a mercantile background, owned property around the town. But the available biographical information about them strongly suggests that these men were not usually merchants. Only one third of them had any interest in trade or industry.[57] At the apex of Colchester's social pyramid the community of the borough merged into the lower ranks of the community of the shire. Burgesses owned properties all over northern Essex. William le Clerk had 95 acres in West Donyland in 1308.[58] In 1303 Ellis son of John and his wife held in dower a manor in Latton and a third of the manor of Marks Tey, but in 1317 they exchanged the Latton manor for a life interest in 265 acres in Ovington and Belchamp St Paul.[59] Arnold de Mounteny, at the time when he was elected bailiff in 1319, was heir to a lordship in Mountnessing.[60] William Buk had 120 acres in West Mersea in 1336.[61] Joseph Elianor in 1338 had a hereditary title to 102 acres in Colchester together with another estate of much the same size in Great Wigborough and Salcott.[62] Thomas de Dedham in the early 1340s had 75 acres in Dedham and a share in 103 acres in Great Oakley.[63] Warin son of William occurs in an undated tithe list as owner of 39½ acres of arable together with some fields of unknown acreage in Lexden.[64] Inevitably Colchester's leading burgesses were drawn into interest groupings and matrimonial alliances with other landed families of comparable status.[65]

Additional contacts with county society were created by the day-to-day business of Colchester's professional lawyers. John Parles, the most prominent of these, followed the king's courts and was consequently away from Colchester most of the time, though he represented the borough in at least 11 parliaments.[66] Ralph Ode was similarly reported to be away in

---

[57] Peter de Aston, alias le Salter (CR 3/3r, 8v; OB, fo. 161v); Richard le Barbour (CR 6/8r; OB, fos. 35v, 36v, 160r); Roger Belch (P.R.O., E.101/556/37r); William Buk (*ibid.*); Adam de Castro (*Rot. Parl.*, i, pp. 235, 262); Edmund le Chaloner (evidence of the name alone); Richard de Colne (*Rot. Parl.*, i, p. 259); John le Dyer (*ibid.*, p. 229); John Fordham (CR 5/7d; CR 7/8r); John Fynch (P.R.O., E.101/556/37r); John de Ratlesden (*ibid.*); Matthew son of Robert, alias le Verrer (CR 1/2d; CR 2/2d, 10r); William de Sartria (*Rot. Parl.*, i, pp. 234, 243); John de Tendring (*ibid.*, p. 229; and H. M. Cam, *Liberties and Communities in Medieval England* (Cambridge, 1933), p. 170).

[58] *Essex Fines*, ii, p. 121 (*cf.* p. 239).

[59] *Feudal Aids*, ii, pp. 139, 172; *Essex Fines*, ii, pp. 173, 219, 237, 242; *Cal. Close R.*, *1302–7*, p. 358; *Cal. Close R.*, *1313–18*, p. 458.

[60] RPB, fo. 2r; *Essex Fines*, ii, p. 196.   [61] *Essex Fines*, iii, p. 39.

[62] P.R.O., C.143/245(9); *Essex Fines*, iii, p. 6. Two acquisitions in Colchester are recorded in B.L., Add. Ch. 41,691 and 41,692.

[63] *Essex Fines*, iii, pp. 54, 63; *Cal. Close R.*, *1341–3*, p. 538.

[64] LB, fo. 210r,v. One of these fields was the 'large field' called Chesterweldefeld.

[65] *E.g.* Britnell, 'Production for the Market', pp. 381–2.

[66] *Essex Fines*, ii, pp. 151, 175, 185, etc.; *Return of Names*, pp. 55–143.

1314; he had to be replaced as a coroner for Essex because his time was taken up with the affairs of certain great men.[67] Others remained in Colchester, acting as attorneys in the borough courts offering clerical and legal services to local landlords. In the early 1330s Warin atte Welle, one of Colchester's leading clerks, collaborated with the abbey's lay steward in acquiring lands in Benningham, Pitsea, North Benfleet and Colchester; these were held on the abbey's behalf until Edward III's licence for the abbey to acquire them was obtained in 1336.[68] At the same period Colchester Priory was using the services of other clerks, Joseph Elianor and Robert le Clerk, to acquire property in Greenstead.[69] By these transactions members of Colchester's ruling group became intimately involved in the concerns of local landlords, both secular and religious. Hubert Bosse is known to have become a sworn member of the abbot of Colchester's council only two months before his election as a bailiff of Colchester in 1315.[70]

There are many reasons why, through the centuries, men of independent means have been willing to give up time for work in local government. Political principles had no bearing on the decisions of fourteenth-century townsmen, and the advantages of office were more a private matter, but there was nevertheless a range of considerations which drew men to accept election. There may sometimes have been direct financial rewards, but these can only have been slight; even in the fourteenth century the distinction between the community's income and that of individual bailiffs was clear in principle, and the community's income in any case left little to spare after its commitments had been met. Economic inducements were, at the most, very indirect ones. High standing in the community enabled a man to cultivate goodwill among his neighbours, and may have significantly enhanced the reputation of those burgesses who offered clerical services to others, but financial considerations of this kind were probably not the main inducement to men who accepted office. Had it been so in a small town like Colchester it would have been worthwhile for a few established families to have closed the door to newcomers. This did not happen, probably because the work was not duly rewarded in material terms. That is to say that, in addition to any financial benefits, there were others relating to personal satisfaction, self-esteem and social standing. Office in the borough allowed individuals scope to exercise organisational skills valued by their fellow burgesses. It also offered a dignified authority in the king's service to men of modest means who could not have aspired to rise so high in the county hierarchy. Even though in this instance royal

---

[67] *Cal. Close R., 1313–18*, p. 114.
[68] LB, fos. 199r–201r.   [69] *Colch. Cart.*, ii, pp. 502–3.
[70] LB, fo. 239r,v. For Bosse as bailiff, see *ibid.*, fos. 97v, 98v, 179v, 182v.

service was not a highway to riches, it held some appeal for men of substance in the liberty, and was occasionally an accolade to men who had already enjoyed exceptional success in enriching themselves and establishing a family name. Even in the early fourteenth century, when successful mercantile careers in Colchester were so few, the high posts in the community were open to men with relevant talents who were willing to do the work involved.

3

Food supplies

I

The officers of medieval Colchester were obliged to control trade to a variety of different ends. One set of rules, some of them established by statute law, was designed to protect urban consumers from monopolistic practices and to ensure that victuallers earned only conventional rates of profit. But the attitude of the authorities to middlemen and processors of food and drink could not be antagonistic. These groups made up a large sector of urban society, and their reasonable interests had to be safeguarded; brewing alone involved perhaps one sixth of all borough households, including some of the most influential. Rules to limit the profits of middlemen did not derive from hostility to hucksters as such. Other regulations, in fact, were intended to give privileges to burgesses as traders and to protect their livelihood against competition from non-burgesses. In this context the borough community acted like a gild to look after the interests of its members. Only burgesses could set up as craftsmen in the borough, for example, so that their employment was to some extent protected against external competition.[1] The burgesses' jealousy was directed chiefly against outsiders, whose interests were systematically disregarded by urban regulations, sometimes with the connivance of statute law.

Because the rules concerning burgesses' activities were of diverse inspiration and date, urban constitutions varied in the degree to which they restricted freedom to trade.[2] Some limited the free retailing of goods outside the market place to a small group of families and exacted licence fees from others. Other towns, of which Colchester was one, were more

---

[1] CR 1/6r.
[2] Dobson, 'Admissions to the Freedom of the City of York', p. 16; M. Kowaleski, 'The Commercial Dominance of a Medieval Provincial Oligarchy: Exeter in the Late Fourteenth Century', *Medieval Studies*, xlvi (1984), pp. 356–7.

generous in their policy. Colchester had never had a gild merchant, and to trade freely here one had simply to be a burgess or a burgess's wife. The community had only loose control over its membership, since any man born in the liberty of the borough could claim burgess status as of right.[3] Outsiders who wished to trade regularly might become burgesses on payment of a modest entry fine, provided that they found two burgesses to sponsor them. The highest entry fines on record from the early fourteenth century were 13s 4d, and some paid as little as 2s 0d.[4] This relatively open policy meant that the courts were not accustomed to exact fines from non-burgesses for licences to trade. When lawhundred juries reported non-burgesses for usurping commercial privileges the charge involved a real offence against the community, not merely a pretext for taxing traders.[5]

Both middlemen and consumers were expected to benefit from the control of public markets where the prices of grain, livestock, fish and other basic commodities were determined. These controls were the foundation of urban economic regulation. The rules are not all known, but their characteristics are evident from the prosecution of burgesses who defied them. The burgesses operated an offer-price system for those bringing goods into Hythe, and the same will have been true of the corn and beast markets; outsiders responsible for marketing consignments of grain were expected to offer a price in ignorance of the state of the market. It was an offence for an urban middleman to give information about current expectations in order to raise prices or keep them higher than they would otherwise be.[6] The price offered might be well below the market-clearing price on a particular day, in which case rationing schemes were adopted. Burgesses had a right to a share in cargoes at Hythe at the offer price,[7] and there was probably, as in other ports,[8] some provision for ordinary householders to buy what they required before bulk buyers moved in. The same ethos prevailed in the beast market. A lawsuit in 1312 concerns two calves which two butchers had been interested in purchasing. One had bought them, whereupon the other had demanded his share, but to no avail, and this was considered a fit matter for a plea of trespass.[9] To the extent that urban policy was successful in holding prices for lengthy periods below the market-clearing price, benefits of trade which should have gone to producers were diverted to consumers. This was potentially

---

[3] CR 11/4d; Morant, *Colchester*, i, p. 98, note L.
[4] CR 2/13r (13s 4d); CR 1/1r and CR 2/4r, 7d (2s 0d).
[5] Non-burgesses might be fined for evading tolls: CR 9/3d; CR 10/1r, 6r.
[6] CR 2/12d.   [7] CR 1/7r.
[8] C. Gross, *The Gild Merchant* (2 vols., Oxford, 1890), ii, pp. 184–5 (Newcastle upon Tyne), 228 (Southampton), 291 (Andover); Miller, 'Medieval York', p. 99.
[9] CR 2/9r.

more damaging for urban supply than the activities of forestallers which incurred repressive public disapproval. The system of trade worked strongly in favour of burgesses who knew the state of the market and against the interests of external suppliers who did not, and to that extent they protected the interests of Colchester's own middlemen at the expense of those from farther afield.

A burgess trading in Colchester had two advantages over outsiders quite apart from his superior knowledge of market conditions there. The first concerned acquisition of supplies. The rules of trade in the main commodity markets, especially at Hythe, allowed burgesses, under regulated conditions, to buy foodstuffs or raw materials wholesale in the borough. Retailers of foodstuffs might buy large quantitites at Hythe in order subsequently to retail them in smaller lots for the convenience of consumers; five fishwives who did this in the summer of 1311 ran into trouble because the fish stank by the time they could get it to market.[10] Other middlemen bought up quantities of produce to be processed before selling it; bakers and brewers required grain in bulk, butchers required livestock. The second advantage was the right of burgesses to buy and sell without paying tolls. Non-burgesses owed toll on both their purchases and their sales, unless they were buying for their own households. These sums were collected at the gates of the town on goods entering and leaving,[11] so that any outsider coming to sell something and buy in exchange was obliged to pay to come in and to go out again. The system depended upon burgesses being known to the men on the gates. Burgesses were occasionally tempted to collaborate with outsiders by selling products on their behalf; in 1312 Richard Smart was charged by the bailiffs with receiving grain brought to market by an outside seller and selling it as his own 'under cover'.[12] Sometimes, too, burgesses made secret deals in such a manner as to allow outside buyers to evade their obligations.[13] But it was absolutely forbidden to give outsiders such encouragement, and the spirit of the by-laws was hostile to any sort of partnership between burgess and non-burgess. The rules were no doubt often evaded, but it was more difficult to do so on large deals than on small ones, and it was this that really mattered. Tolls were much more frequently due on wholesale transactions than on retail ones because of the exemption of all urban households from liability for toll on the purchase of their domestic requirements. In view of the ways in which the rules of trade were stacked against outsiders, it is hardly

---

[10] CR 1/8d.

[11] This all rests on late evidence. The freedom of all townsmen from toll on purchases for their households was an old custom in the early fifteenth century: OB, fo. 8r. The collection of tolls at the borough gates is recorded in the early sixteenth-century will of Thomas Christmas: P.C.C., Ayloffe, 28.

[12] CR 1/1r; CR 2/6d.   [13] CR 7/5v.

surprising that the provisioning of Colchester was a major activity of burgesses themselves.

Some of the town's supply came from within the liberty itself. Besides the demesne lands of the abbey, Lexden manor, Mile End manor, the priory and the castle, there were many burgesses who had sufficient land to produce a marketable surplus. If Willard was right to suppose that grain assessed for taxation was superfluous to household needs and destined to be sold, then in 1301 there were at least 191 households within the liberty which had grain for sale.[14] Many of these probably marketed their grain directly to consumers. Townsmen might still buy bread grain to be ground on handstones, or, more probably, to be ground on contract at one of the local mills. They bought oats, too, for domestic brewing and for porridge. Direct contact between such consumers and the original growers was commoner here than in London because grain producers made up a larger proportion of the urban population. But local suppliers also sold grain to brewers, bakers and other intermediaries, some of whom bought large quantities. On the king's manor between 1278 and 1281 crops not needed for wage payments or seedcorn were sold in bulk, and at Lexden manor in 1287/8 the manorial officers accounted for a rye stack and an oats stack sold to a single buyer.[15]

Even some grain purchased to supply individual households was diverted into the hands of tradesmen. In order to secure supplies as they required them, as well as to obtain the miller's profit on the grinding of corn, Colchester bakers leased water mills in the liberty, paying money rents to the landlords. In 1345/6, for example, John son of Robert leased the East Mill, John Pottere and Richard Dollard leased the New Priory Mill, and John Wyger and Thomas Deynes leased the North Mill; all these men were bakers.[16] The connection with milling gave them a source of meal for which they did not have to engage in active trade, since they received payment in kind for milling grain, and indeed frequently took more payment in this form than they were legally entitled to. They were allowed by statute to take at least one twenty-fourth of the grain,[17] so presumably the proportion which actually found its way into the town bakeries was higher. Because of the additional elements of profit involved, it was more advantageous for a baker to secure cheap supplies by infringing the assize of millers than by breaking the Statute of Forestallers.

Some middlemen, meanwhile, expended more energy in their search for

[14] J. F. Willard, *Parliamentary Taxes on Personal Property, 1290 to 1334: A Study in Mediaeval English Financial Administration* (Cambridge, Mass., 1934), pp. 84–5; Rickword, 'Taxations of Colchester', p. 148.

[15] P.R.O., S.C.6/839/18, m. 2r; S.C.6/839/19, m. 1r; S.C.6/845/13r.

[16] CR 7/2r, 5d (millers); CR 6/11r; CR 7/2d, 4d (bakers).

[17] Statutum de Pistoribus, etc.: *Statutes*, i, p. 203.

supplies. Langenhoe was a regular source of grain to the south, and when the lord of the manor there had exceptionally large surpluses of oats in the late 1330s and early 1340s townsmen were there to buy them.[18] In 1337 Thomas de Balton is on record buying five quarters of oats in Ardleigh from the vicar there.[19] Although some landlords had their own produce marketed in the borough, the outward movement of middlemen seeking grain was a normal feature of urban supply and the acceptable alternative to forestalling. Middlemen might still fall foul of the law in other ways. A jury report of January 1334 lists 11 burgesses who had between them conspired to defraud the community of toll on 530 quarters of grain since the previous Michaelmas. The volume of grain in question demonstrates that the burgesses were not intending to use it solely for their own household requirements.[20] It is likely, from these various indications of the presence of Colchester middlemen in the grain trade, that the town was not primarily dependent upon fortuitous arrivals at Hythe, and that most suppliers were well aware of the current state of the market. Urban policy would not, in these circumstances, have held the market price of grain below the equilibrium level in times of normal trade.

Middlemen in the grain trade were not, however, specialised merchants. It was uncommon to find merchant capitals tied up in grain outside London and the large east-coast ports. The nine offenders of 1334 included three women and four husband-and-wife partnerships, and none of Colchester's leading merchants was involved. The grain was probably destined for brewing. In Colchester most middlemen in the grain trade were probably bakers and brewers themselves rather than additional links in the chain of urban supply. In London it was not uncommon for bakers and brewers to derive supplies from cornmongers,[21] so that there were two intermediaries between the grower and the consumer. In Colchester it was unusual for there to be more than one. This lack of specialism meant that knowledge of supplies amongst the townsmen was geographically restricted, and that in times of scarcity search costs rose steeply and dependence upon external enterprise increased. It was at such times that the cost of grain was most likely to be affected by the offer-price system at Hythe.

The regulation of middlemen's profits in the interests of consumers was an ancient obligation for all urban authorities. By statute the price of bread and ale was fixed with reference to the price of grain. The price of wine was also subject to regulation; in Colchester vintners had to fix retail prices in line with those in London.[22] These assizes did nothing, however, to

[18] Britnell, 'Production for the Market', pp. 382–3. [19] CR 7/1d, 4r.
[20] CR 4/4d. The nature of the toll in question is uncertain.
[21] Williams, *Medieval London*, pp. 161–3. [22] RPB, fo. 124r.

regulate the prices of basic supplies, and it was to this purpose that the law against forestalling was implemented. The operation of this law in Colchester, although perhaps of little significance for price levels in the borough, nevertheless constitutes a further source of information about the food trades.

A forestaller, by definition, undermined the system of price setting in urban markets by intercepting goods on their way to market. Either in collusion with the seller, or by buying up produce with the intent to sell it on his own account, he raised the price at which it was publicly put on offer to townsmen. He might also raise prices by restricting supply. It was further possible that the interception of normal supplies would induce panic buying by consumers, and so raise prices from the demand side. Forestalling had first been proscribed by statute in 1285 (or thereabouts)[23] and had since attracted more attention from the government early in Edward II's reign. Commissions had been detailed to look into the enforcement of this law in each county, and it so happens that the commissioners' findings at Colchester in 1308 are extant.[24] Not surprisingly the borough's lawhundreds from the years 1310–12 show the campaign against forestalling in full swing, with larger numbers of forestallers being reported than at any time in the following 200 years.[25] In fact, however, the effect of forestallers on the borough food supply can have been only a slight one at this period. John Profete the fishmonger had sufficient capital to intercept large incoming cargoes at Hythe, and was therefore the sort of middleman against whom the Statute of Forestallers was aimed, but his control of the market, and the capacity of his operations to provoke stockpiling by consumers, must have been severely curtailed by the perishable nature of his merchandise.[26] Other forestallers, even if they forestalled as habitually as the lawhundred reports imply, appear to have done so on very small capitals. Most were women, the wives of stallholders, who hung around lane ends in the hope of turning a quick penny, or who bought up items before the market was officially open.[27] These were disreputable ways of going on, but their impact upon the urban price level was surely negligible. It was a curious comment on the capacity of these common forestallers to oppress the poor that, in 1311, of the thirteen presented by the Epiphany lawhundred jury two were pardoned on account of their poverty.[28] Many families in the food trades made a meagre

---

[23] Statutum de Forstallariis: *Statutes*, i, pp. 203–4.
[24] *Cal. Pat. R., 1307–13*, pp. 29–31 (*cf. ibid.*, pp. 42, 53–5); Cam, *Liberties and Communities*, pp. 168–72.
[25] CR 1/1d, 6r; CR 2/1d, 2r, 9d. See Appendix, Table 4.
[26] CR 1/2r, 7r.
[27] See R. H. Hilton, 'Women Traders in Medieval England', *Women's Studies*, ii, (1984), pp. 149–52.   [28] CR 1/6r.

living, and their misdemeanours were more a strategy for survival than a monopolistic conspiracy.

Forestalling in early fourteenth-century Colchester was primarily a problem in the supply of fish, secondly in the supply of poultry and fruit, hardly at all in the grain trade. This was chiefly the consequence of differing costs. A fishmonger wanting to buy up cheap supplies had little alternative to acquiring fish on its way to market since the costs of seeking supplies at another fishing port would have been likely to outweigh the advantages of their cheapness. Seeking supplies of poultry or fruit did not involve such long journeys, but search costs were again high because of the characteristically small size of units of production, which meant that supplies became available haphazardly and in small lots. This contrast between fish, poultry and fruit trades explains why a burgess with sufficient capital could forestall fish in large quantities, even a boatload at a time,[29] whereas forestalling in the grand manner is unknown amongst poulterers or fruiterers. In the grain trade search costs were significantly lower because there were so many large producers in the near vicinity of the town. It was easier for a middleman to obtain supplies from the producer without resorting to forestalling in order to do so.

II

From what is known of normal levels of productivity in medieval agriculture it may be calculated that a town of 3,000 inhabitants required arable resources of at least 11½ square miles.[30] Conceivably, if the whole surface of the land was under the plough, such a town might be supplied with grain within a radius of two miles, implying in Colchester's case that the population could have lived comfortably off lands within the liberty and still have had a surplus for pasturing sheep and cattle. In reality this minimal estimate of agricultural requirements rests on such stringent assumptions that it cannot have applied to many actual towns, and Colchester was not one of them. Neither the pattern of land utilisation nor the productivity of the soil were compatible with so restricted an area of supply. As the evidence from Langenhoe implies, even in years of normal harvest the town had to derive much of its grain from villages beyond the liberty.

In the first place, allowance has to be made for the proportion of the land in the vicinity of Colchester which was not used for the cultivation of cereals. The evidence of the Feet of Fines between 1290 and 1330

[29] CR 4/7d; CR 6/8r.
[30] G. Duby, *L'Economie rurale et la vie des campagnes dans l'Occident médiéval* (2 vols., Paris, 1962), pp. 223–4.

concerning those estates in the liberty whose arable lands contained at least 30 acres suggests that about 15 per cent of such properties were made up of pasture, meadow and wood.[31] The proportion of uncultivated land in the region must have been higher than this, however, because of extensive common lands within the liberty which were not represented in these examples. The map of Essex by Chapman and André published in 1777 shows a belt of heath and woodland stretching from the head of the Blackwater estuary as far as the River Stour and passing directly across the liberty of Colchester. From the extensive Tiptree Heath, where Tiptree Priory held a cattle fair in the early fourteenth century,[32] and the smaller Paternoster Heath to the east of it, the heathlands stretched north-eastwards towards Dedham. Chapman and André also show a belt of woodland across the northern part of the liberty, occupying the spaces between the heaths in what is still the most wooded part of the borough. For the most part these heaths and woodlands stood on glacial sands and gravels whose infertility predisposed them to be unsuited to the growing of crops. They impinged heavily upon the agricultural potential of the region. In 1777 nearly one fifth of the land within $3\frac{1}{2}$ miles of Colchester was under heath or wood – 5.3 per cent under wood, 13.4 per cent under heath. The proportion of woodland in the early fourteenth century was still larger than it was in 1777. 'Even within the two hundred years last past,' Morant observed in 1748, 'King's Wood made a considerable appearance on the north-side of this town but is entirely gone: and smaller parcels are cleared round it almost every year.'[33] Woodlands had been cleared for timber and for extending the cultivated area in the thirteenth century,[34] but this process had stopped well short of denuding the liberty. Welshwood was reckoned to contain 40 acres in 1330 and in the same year the Sawenwode still contained 220 acres. In this part of the liberty the woods were dense enough to conceal poachers and other criminals; at least 24 men took deer in Kingswood without detection for six months in 1291; an inquest of 1308 speaks of Crockleford Wood and Ralph Pycot's wood which enabled robbers to prey on travellers between Colchester and Ardleigh, so that men hardly dared to use the roads there.[35]

The quality of arable land in Colchester introduced a further constraint upon the cultivation of bread grains. The sandy nature of the soil, which

---

[31] *Essex Fines*, ii, pp. 73, 74, 105, 121, 130, 157, 218.

[32] A stot was bought there for Feering manor in 1332/3: P.R.O., S.C.6/841/6r. *Cf.* Morant, *Essex*, ii, p. 141.

[33] Chapman and André, *A Map of Essex*, plate ix; Morant, *Colchester*, i, p. 12.

[34] *Building Accounts of King Henry III*, ed. H. M. Colvin (Oxford, 1971), p. 22 *ter*; *Rot. Hund.*, i, p. 163. The name Sawenwode ('sown wood') occurs in 1311: CR 1/12d.

[35] LB, fos. 40r, 197r; C. R. Young, *The Royal Forests of Medieval England* (Leicester, 1979), p. 105; Cam, *Liberties and Communities*, p. 169.

Table 3.1 *Grain assessed for the fifteenth of 1301 on various demesnes in the liberty of Colchester*

	Wheat q.	Rye q.	Barley q.	Small oats q.
Abbot of St John in Greenstead	–	8	–	15
Abbot of St John in Monkswick	–	20	–	30
Prior of St Botolph in Canons' Wick	–	6	3	10
Lord of Lexden manor	–	10	–	20
Abbot of St Osyth in Mile End	–	–	–	–

Source: Rot. Parl., i, pp. 249, 253, 256, 259, 263.

made it vulnerable to drought[36], implied the inadvisability of extensive wheat cultivation and induced a preference for rye as a winter-sown crop. Accounts of the king's manor of Colchester between 1278 and 1281 indicate that in the course of a three-year crop cycle three times as much rye was sown as wheat. The grain given to farm servants on the manor for their subsistence contained no wheat at all. The Fitz Walter manor of Lexden was also in the rye country; an account of 1288 shows that only rye and oats were sold from the harvest of the year before.[37] There is, too, a preponderance of rye over wheat in the grain upon which the people of Colchester were taxed in 1301; Rickword counted 133 quarters of rye to 26 quarters of wheat.[38] The tax assessments of known demesne farms are shown in Table 3.1. If rye was the predominant bread grain in the liberty it must be supposed that it was a staple bread grain in the borough. This is implied in a contract of 1316; when Petronilla le Walsches surrendered her rights to Walscheslond, in exchange for a pension from the abbot of Colchester, it was stipulated that she should receive every year two quarters of rye and one of oats.[39]

The management of these rye-growing lands around Colchester and to the east followed a more flexible system than that of the wheat lands to the west, where a three-course rotation of wheat, oats and fallow was the normal pattern. In the wheatlands the sown acreage under winter-sown crops, mostly wheat, was usually about the same as the area under

[36] Morant, *Colchester*, i, p. 1; A. Young, *General View of the Agriculture of the County of Essex* (2 vols., London, 1807), i, p. 25 and map opposite p. 1.
[37] P.R.O., S.C.6/839/18, mm. 1r, 2d; S.C.6/839/19, mm. 1d, 2d; S.C.6/845/13r.
[38] Rickword, 'Taxations of Colchester', p. 146.   [39] LB, fos. 182v–183r.

spring-sown crops, mostly oats.[40] But such details as survive of arable husbandry around Colchester show great variation. On the king's demesne lands between 1278 and 1281 the winter-sown and spring-sown acreages were about the same in three out of the four years.[41] This is not so either at Wivenhoe or on an appendage of Wivenhoe manor at East Donyland on the opposite side of the Colne estuary, where the winter-sown acreage was usually appreciably smaller than the spring-sown. The Wivenhoe accounts show that the rotation scheme employed was a flexible one which may be expressed as (i) rye, or sometimes wheat, (ii) oats, or sometimes legumes or barley, (iii) rest for one or more years. Side by side with parcels of land under this pattern of rotation there were some lands which were put under oats for several years in succession before reverting to pasture.[42] Altogether the pattern of husbandry in Wivenhoe demonstrates the unsuitability of the land there for the intensive cultivation of bread grains. It is improbable, on this showing, that anything like one third of the arable land in the liberty of Colchester was sown with bread crops each year.

For all these reasons, harvests within the liberty were inadequate to cope with total market demand there. Even in rural areas the proportion of families who needed to buy or earn some of their bread or bread-stuffs was commonly as high as 45 per cent,[43] and it was certain to be above this in an urban society – three-quarters would be a reasonable guess. In view of the characteristics of arable farming in the liberty it was inevitable that some bread grain must come from outside even in normal years, and villages up to about eight miles away by road were regular sources of supply. In 1333, not a year of any peculiar harvest conditions, the reeve of Westminster Abbey's manor of Feering had 40 quarters of wheat carted to Colchester over this distance, which represents the limits of a comfortable day's journey; a longer haul would involve an overnight stop.[44] The constraints of agrarian geography created a marketing area of asymmetric shape. The Colne valley west of Fordham and the loams around the River Pant were lands where wheat was the main winter-sown crop, and the chief source of cash for both landlords and tenants. The coastal villages to the south-west also grew some wheat, and had the advantage of communication with Colchester by sea.[45] To the east of the borough, however, the soils

[40] R. H. Britnell, 'Utilization of the Land in Eastern England, 1350–1500', in E. Miller, ed., *The Agrarian History of England and Wales*, iii (Cambridge, forthcoming).

[41] P.R.O., S.C.6/839/18, mm. 1r, 2d; S.C.6/839/19, mm. 1d, 2d.

[42] E.R.O., T/B 122.

[43] M. M. Postan, 'Medieval Agrarian Society in its Prime: England', in *idem*, ed., *The Cambridge Economic History of Europe*, i: *The Agrarian Life of the Middle Ages*, 2nd edn (Cambridge, 1966), p. 619.

[44] P.R.O., S.C.6/841/6r,d.

[45] Britnell, 'Production for the Market', p. 381; *idem*, 'Agricultural Technology and the Margin of Cultivation in the Fourteenth Century', *Ec.H.R.*, 2nd ser., xxx (1977), pp.

were more akin to those of Colchester itself and rye was the main winter-sown crop.[46] The sheriffs' accounts of grain purveyed in Essex for the king's armies confirm that wheat was derived more from the parts to the west of Colchester than from Tendring Hundred to the east, despite the greater proximity of the latter to the sea.[47] The trade in bread grains was accordingly more active on the western and southern sides of the borough than on the eastern side.

Despite its prominent pastoral component, the agriculture of the liberty of Colchester was similarly unable to meet all the town's requirements of wool, dairy produce or meat. The most organised of these trades was that in wool. The marshlands south and south-west of the town depended upon wool as their chief source of cash, and there were wool fairs at Coggeshall[48] and St Osyth. Philip de la Rokele of Colchester, who traded in both wool and cloth, was at St Osyth fair in 1310, and while there balanced his account with a merchant who was his partner.[49] On occasion the wool trade involved journeys further into Essex and Suffolk,[50] but since Colchester was not a significant wool-exporting port its wool trade was not normally a far-ranging activity. In the case of cheese and dairy produce the main source of supply outside the liberty was the region between Colchester and Tiptree Heath. The sheriff's account of cheeses purchased in Essex in 1337 reveals a major dairying centre on the Layer plateau around the Layers and Tolleshunts.[51] On Palm Sunday 1339 William de Brome contracted in Colchester with John le Herde of 'Layer' that the latter should supply 12 cheeses to Brome's house in Colchester on Midsummer Day.[52] Livestock to replenish Colchester's pastures as well as for the shambles came from beyond the liberty, probably from all sides. In 1312 Henry atte Felde alleged he had negotiated to buy 42 sheep in Ardleigh.[53]

59–65; *idem*, 'Agriculture in a Region of Ancient Enclosure, 1185–1500', *Nottingham Medieval Studies*, xxvii (1983), pp. 46–50; manorial accounts from Lexden (P.R.O., S.C.6/845/15d), Great Tey (S.C.6/847/16d), Layer Marney, Great and Little Totham, Faulkbourn, Hatfield Peverel (S.C.6/1120/5d), Messing and Birch (E.R.O., D/DH X17d).

[46] Manorial accounts from Wix (E.R.O., D/DU/40/75–7), Wivenhoe (E.R.O., T/B 122), Dovercourt (P.R.O., S.C.6/840/1–13); lease of lands in Lawford (LB, fo. 47r,v); custumal of Dedham (P.R.O., D.L.43/2/19); W. J. Ashley, *The Bread of our Forefathers: An Inquiry in Economic History* (Oxford, 1928), pp. 40, 123–5.

[47] P.R.O., E.101/556/1, mm. 2r, 3r, 14r, 19Ar.

[48] A fair was granted in 1250 and became known as a source of wool: *Cal. Chart. R.*, iii, p. 480; W. Cunningham, *The Growth of Industry and Commerce during the Early and Middle Ages*, 5th edn (3 vols., Cambridge, 1910), i, pp. 551, 553; Britnell, 'Agricultural Technology', p. 57.   [49] CR 1/9d.

[50] *Cal. Close R., 1341–3*, p. 205; *Cal. Pat. R., 1340–3*, pp. 296, 317–18. Thomas de Canterbury bought wool in Bardfield in 1343: P.R.O., S.C.6/836/10r,d. For his Colchester connection, see OB, fo. 32r; CR 6/6d; CR 7/1d, 2d, 3r,d, 4r; *Cal. Pat. R., 1343–5*, p. 98.   [51] P.R.O., E.101/556/19Ar.

[52] CR 6/9d.   [53] CR 2/9d, 12r.

By the early fourteenth century, growth of population had stimulated
the production of food in western Europe to the point where, in many
regions, further increases could not be obtained without an agricultural
revolution.[54] There were no signs of new technology in the scourging
rotations of the Essex wheatlands or in the rye husbandry of Colchester
and the Tendring peninsula. Though the area of woodland was larger than
it is today, it was valued as a source of pasture, fuel and construction
materials, and its reduction to modern levels would not have led to any
corresponding increase in total agricultural output. As elsewhere in
England the main phase of land clearance was over by 1300, and landlords
and tenants cultivated the available arable and pasture as intensively as
they could without much chance of increasing their output. Some evidence
for the intensity of cultivation in the Colchester region comes from the
marshlands south of the town. Here soils were of heavy but fertile clay,
capable of supporting the triennial rotations of the wheatlands to the west.
At Langenhoe Hall, five miles from Colchester's grain market, Lionel de
Bradenham ploughed up his cow pasture as a means of raising cash during
the price depression of the late 1330s and early 1340s, but he cultivated
oats on the newly ploughed soils. This was presumably because the land
capable of growing wheat, with the supplies of manure available, was
already drawn into the regularly cultivated demesne lands.[55] The case was
similar at Bourchier Hall in Tollesbury, 12 miles from Colchester but with
easy access along the coast out of the Blackwater estuary into the Colne.
Not only was the wheat-growing area here maintained by a three-course
rotation of crops, as at Langenhoe, but cereals cultivation had been
pursued to the detriment of crop yields. Of four wheat harvests recorded
between 1338 and 1351 the best produced a return of 2.4 times the seed
sown.[56] If the land in these marshland villages was being used as intensively
as contemporary arable techniques permitted it is reasonable to suppose
that the same was true of the lands around Colchester, within the same
marketing region as Langenhoe and Tollesbury and nearer the marketing
centre.

Colchester market place was the main single centre of agricultural trade
within an eight-mile radius, and it was this local prominence which had
hampered the development of marketing in nearby villages. But even
within this region the town did not dominate supplies in such a way as
to capture all the available marketable surplus. Colchester and its liberty
contained only about one tenth of the taxpayers within this radius in 1327,

[54] Duby, *L'Économie rurale*, i, pp. 183–4, 216–19.
[55] Britnell, 'Production for the Market', pp. 384–5; *idem*, 'Minor Landlords in England
and Medieval Agrarian Capitalism', *Past and Present*, lxxxix (1980), p. 15.
[56] Britnell, 'Agricultural Technology', pp. 58–61.

and perhaps about this proportion of the population of the region.[57] And though no doubt the urban population was more dependent upon marketed foodstuffs than those of rural communities, there were a number of villages within eight miles of Colchester, or on the perimeter, which had sufficient numbers employed in seafaring or manufacturing to create a regular market demand. Manningtree, West Mersea, Brightlingsea, Coggeshall, Earls Colne, Bures, East Bergholt and Dedham were all independent *foci* of consumption. From the coastal villages, too, some produce left the region altogether for the supply of London or other east-coast markets.[58] It would therefore be inappropriate to ascribe intensive land use, even within Colchester's own marketing area, exclusively to demand in the borough. The burgesses faced more competition for supplies during the early fourteenth century than they had done a century earlier.

[57] *The Medieval Essex Community*, ed. Ward; *Suffolk in 1327, being a Subsidy Return (a Twentieth)*, ed. S. H. A. Hervey, Suffolk Green Books, ix, vol. ii (Woodbridge, 1906).
[58] As from Westminster Abbey's manor of Feering: P.R.O., S.C.6/841/6d, 7d, 8d, 9d.

SURVEY, 1300–49

Colchester in the early fourteenth century had antiquity and chartered privilege strongly in its favour. Legend, unaware of any breach of continuity there since the time of the Romans, hallowed streets, churches, walls and wells with ancient associations. In recent centuries the borough had kept pace with major constitutional developments elsewhere; the burgesses elected their own officers, held their own courts of law, paid taxes on movables at the borough rate and sent members to parliaments. The court of pleas had come into existence to meet distinctive urban needs. The law administered in the borough courts had changed over the years in response to successive royal ordinances and statutes, so that business in 1310, the year of the first surviving court roll, was very different from what it would have been in 1178 when elected bailiffs first took over the hundred court.[1] Moreover the urban economy had shown some response to the general commercial expansion of the thirteenth century, chiefly at Hythe. The number of inhabitants had increased, woods had been cleared and there were more enclosures than there had been. Colchester had moved with the times in predictable fashion.

But in some respects the borough's circumstances had become less favourable during this period. Administrative autonomy carried little power to mould the commercial and industrial environment to the burgesses' advantage. Ipswich, rather than Colchester, was the chief beneficiary of growing international trade, and new ports had been created at Harwich and Manningtree. Industrial activity had spread to surrounding villages, leaving Colchester as one amongst many rather small centres of production. In its relation with the surrounding agrarian society, Colchester's stature had diminished. For all their traditional dignity, burgesses were troubled and, on occasion, plainly threatened by local magnates, and in an age of aggressive landlords and self-confident estate administration it was doubtful how far all their ancient liberties would survive intact.

[1] Tait, *The Medieval English Borough*, pp. 171, 188.

Colchester's share in local agricultural trade was smaller than in the twelfth century. Though local agricultural output had doubtless increased, the demand for food and raw materials had grown more rapidly in ordinary villages and market towns than in Colchester itself, and London's growing requirements had put additional pressure on supplies. Colchester in the early fourteenth century was hemmed in by regional developments beyond its control, and its inhabitants were more characteristically reacting to external threats than engaged in novel economic or constitutional initiatives of their own.

During the first half of the fourteenth century there were no unambiguous signs that Colchester's fortunes might improve. Overseas trade through Hythe seems likely to have grown a little during the 1330s and 1340s, and the number of shipmen may consequently have increased. The wine trade with France interested the borough's small merchant class during these decades. But there can have been little or no development of clothmaking in Colchester, and any increase in cloth exports benefited textile villages further inland. If there were increasing exports of agricultural produce, this brought benefits chiefly to local landlords and tenants by offsetting the adverse effects of low prices. The overseas trade of Colchester merchants had only meagre implications for urban employment at this stage. The population of the borough was probably lower in the fourth and fifth decades of the century than it had been during the first, and in 1348 the Black Death caused a further decrease. If there were 3,000–4,000 inhabitants in 1300, as seems likely, then by 1350 the number was below 3,000.

PART II

Growth, 1350–1414

4

Colchester cloth and its markets

I

During the later thirteenth and the fourteenth centuries commercial clothmaking in north-western Europe became more widespread than it had been before. The overland routes which had linked the Flemish cloth towns by way of Champagne to markets in France, central Europe and the Mediterranean gave way to a variety of new ones pioneered first by Italian and German, later by English and Dutch merchants. Opportunities for making cloth broadened as the pattern of trade became more extended.[1] Meanwhile the larger cloth towns, Ypres, Ghent and Bruges, paid a heavy penalty for their greatness. Divided by social conflict, and challenged from without by the expansive ambitions and fiscal rapaciousness of Philip IV of France, they suffered a period of crisis between 1285 and 1314 from which their fortunes never recovered.[2] Their difficulties confirmed the advantages of mercantile activity in smaller towns. The most remarkable achievements were in the Leie valley in southern Flanders; cloths of Kortrijk and Wervik were already well known to French drapers in the late thirteenth century, and their fame spread more widely during the fourteenth.[3] Brabant also gained from these circumstances; cloths of Louvain, Malines and Brussels sold in Paris from the 1290s.[4] After 1320 cloths of the Leie valley and Brabant transformed the textile trade of the Mediterranean world, and as they did so new centres of production like Comines and Menen began to supply the new arteries of trade.[5] In England

[1] H. Laurent, *Un Grand Commerce d'exportation au Moyen Âge: La draperie des Pays-Bas en France et dans les pays méditerranéens (xiie–xve siècles)* (Paris, 1935), pp. 138–44.
[2] *Ibid.*, pp. 117–18, 126–8.
[3] *Ibid.*, pp. 132–3.   [4] *Ibid.*, pp. 129–38.
[5] J. Heers, 'La Mode et les marchés des draps de laine: Gênes et la montagne à la fin du Moyen Âge', *Annales E.S.C.*, xxvi (1971), pp. 1110–11; L. Liagre-de Sturler, *Les Relations commerciales entre Gênes, la Belgique et l'Outremont d'après les archives notariales génoises (1320–1400)* (2 vols., Brussels and Rome, 1969), i, p. cxxxiv; *Recueil*

too, the manufacture of cloth for new markets engaged a number of regions, though industrial progress here came later than in southern Flanders or Brabant. In the 1330s and 1340s increasing clothmaking in England reduced the need for imports from Flanders, though as yet it had little impact on foreign markets.[6] Subsequently, however, the annual export of English cloths increased from fewer than 4,000 in 1353/4, a year of rapid improvement, to 10 times that number by the end of the century.[7]

The more successful cloth industries in this period were often in old centres, and Colchester is not the only instance of a new cloth town whose reputation can be taken back to the early thirteenth century.[8] Nor did the success of fourteenth-century cloth towns depend upon their introduction of any particular fashions. The range of textiles from north-western Europe entering into long-distance trade was a wide one, embracing both the fine fabrics of Kortrijk and Menen, at one extreme, and at the other the says of Hondschoote and the even cheaper *matten* of Poperinge.[9] There were no common styles or techniques, and some centres were conspicuously conservative. The towns of the Leie valley continued to use English wool and to eschew mechanical fulling despite the duties charged on the former and despite higher labour costs.[10] In Colchester the finishing trades remained in the hands of Englishmen and maintained a long tradition. Admittedly cloths made there were of different qualities and colours, some of which had no particular association with the town. In 1376 a fuller was charged with having neglected to full two *decene* of blanket, a cheap white cloth.[11] Some cloths of brighter colour emerged from a few workshops, and from the late fourteenth century there are recorded disputes with fullers concerning cloths of blue, tawny, ruby and musterdevillers.[12] Such cloths were not intended solely for local consumption; in 1406, at the time of his death, a London draper stocked 18 cloths of blue medley from Colchester, each valued at £3 6s 8d.[13] But far more common in references

de documents relatifs à l'histoire de l'industrie drapière en Flandre, ed. H.-E. Sagher and others, part ii (3 vols., Brussels, 1951–66), ii, p. 2, and iii, p. 2.

[6] Carus-Wilson, *Medieval Merchant Venturers*, pp. 241–3.

[7] E. M. Carus-Wilson and O. Coleman, *England's Export Trade, 1275–1547* (Oxford, 1963), p. 138.

[8] D. M. Nicholas, *Town and Countryside: Social, Economic and Political Tensions in Fourteenth-Century Flanders* (Bruges, 1971), pp. 81–93.

[9] E. Coornaert, 'Draperies rurales, draperies urbaines. L'évolution de l'industrie flamande au Moyen Âge et au xvie siècle', *Revue belge de philologie et d'histoire*, xxviii (1950), pp. 72–4; *Recueil de documents*, ed. Sagher and others, iii, p. 256.

[10] Coornaert, 'Draperies rurales, draperies urbaines', p. 73; J. A. van Houtte, *An Economic History of the Low Countries, 800–1800* (London, 1977), p. 82.

[11] CR 18/4r.

[12] CR 24/56r; CR 33/5d, 26r.

[13] *Calendar of Plea and Memoranda Rolls of the City of London, A.D. 1413–1437*, ed. A. H. Thomas (Cambridge, 1943), pp. 2–3.

to Colchester cloth are the russets for which the town had long been known, and in this respect the history of industrial growth here illustrates well the conservative character of up-and-coming textile towns in the later Middle Ages.

During the fourteenth century the word russet embraced shades of grey and brown not now normally grouped together. Such ambiguity is to be explained by the technicalities of the dyeing operation by which russets were made. There was no suitable grey or brown dyestuff – though at the cheapest end of the market a sheep-coloured cloth was obtained by leaving wool undyed[14] – and in consequence these colours were produced industrially through a combination of other dyes. Like sanguines, murreys and violets they were obtained by colouring wool with a weak solution of woad and subsequently dipping it into a weak bath of madder. The shade of colour was determined by the qualities of the dyestuff used and the strength of the dyeing solution, the browner shades requiring slightly greater intensities of colour than the grey.[15] One advantage of greys was that they required little dye, and could consequently be made more cheaply than richly coloured cloths. Not surprisingly, many different results were obtainable by these means, and although grey russets and brown russets were capable of being distinguished they were linked by so many inter-mediate variations that the term russet was appropriately employed for the whole range. As late as 1611 Cotgrave's dictionary gave 'light-russet' as a translation of the French *gris*, implying that intermediate colours between grey and brown might be envisaged as shades of lighter or darker russet.[16] In the fourteenth century russet cloth was most characteristically near the grey end of the range. Both poets and prose writers take this for granted. In *The Parlement of the Thre Ages*, written perhaps in 1352, Medill-Elde is described with alliterative variation both as 'a renke alle in rosette' and 'this gome alle in graye'.[17] The author of *Piers the Plowman* makes the same assumption when he describes how Charity is to be found

---

[14] W. L. J. de Nie, *De Ontwikkeling der Noord-Nederlandsche Textielververij van de Veer-tiende tot de Achttiende Eeuw* (Leiden, 1937), p. 228. Such cheap cloths had only a local market: Heers, 'La Mode et les marchés', pp. 1111–12, 1115; C. Carrère, *Barcelone, centre économique à l'époque des difficultés, 1380–1462* (2 vols., Paris, 1967), i, p. 445.

[15] G. Espinas, *La Draperie dans la Flandre française au Moyen Âge* (2 vols., Paris, 1923), ii, pp. 148–9; G. de Poerck, *La Draperie médiévale en Flandre et en Artois: Technique et terminologie*, Rijksuniversiteit te Gent, Werken uitgeven door de Faculteit van de Wijsbegeerte en Letteren, cx, cxi, cxii (3 vols., Bruges, 1951), i, pp. 193–5; de Nie, *De Ontwikkeling der Nord-Nederlandsche Textielververij*, p. 229. Woad and madder are the only dyestuffs recorded as imported into Colchester in 1397–8: P.R.O., E.122/193/33, fos. 12r, 13v.

[16] R. Cotgrave, *A Dictionarie of the French and English Tongues* (London, 1611). In J. Florio, *A Worlde of Wordes* (London, 1598) *bigio* is translated 'gray or russet colour'.

[17] The Parlement of the Thre Ages, lines 137–8, 182: *The Parlement of the Thre Ages*, ed. I. Gollancz (London, 1915).

in all ranks of society, russet and grey standing together to represents the dress of the lower orders:

> For I haue seyn hym in sylke. and somme tyme in russet,
> Bothe in grey and in grys. and in gulte herneys.[18]

Another indication of the prevalence of grey among russets is found in the history of Lollard priests, whom Thomas of Walsingham describes as dressed in russet.[19] This meant they wore grey, as Friar Daw observed in debate with Jack Upland:

> But Jacke, amonge oure chateryng yit wolde I wite
> Whi that the lollardis weren moost greye clothis.[20]

In the colour of their dress Lollard priests followed the Franciscans, who wore russet and were known, in England, as the grey friars.[21]

The manufacture of grey cloths in fourteenth-century Europe had distinctive features. Grey was universal among the poorer classes both in town and country.[22] The author of *Piers the Plowman* uses russet to typify poverty both in the passage already quoted and when he describes how Charity craves nothing,

> And is as gladde of a goune. of a graye russet
> As of a tunicle of Tarse. or of trye scarlet.[23]

From 1363 English statute law required farm workers, and all whose chattels were worth less than £2 to clothe themselves in russet or blanket costing below 1*s* 0*d* an ell.[24] Most grey fabrics were accordingly of the very lowest quality of materials and manufacture, including amongst them undyed woollens. Being dressed as a shepherd or dressed as a sheep was all one.[25] Manufacturers of fine cloths, by contrast, were rarely interested in making greys because the market for them was so limited. Contemporary fashion in secular society required cloths of vivid colours to combine with

[18] Piers the Plowman, B, xv, lines 214–15 (*cf.* C, xvii, lines 342–3); *The Vision of William concerning Piers the Plowman*, ed. W. W. Skeat (2 vols., Oxford, 1886), i, pp. 450–1.

[19] Thomas of Walsingham, *Historia Anglicana*, ed. H. T. Riley, Rolls ser. (2 vols., London, 1863–4), i, p. 324.

[20] Friar Daw's Reply, lines 382–3: *Jack Upland, Friar Daw's Reply and Upland's Rejoinder*, ed. P. L. Heyworth (Oxford, 1968), p. 85.

[21] J. Moorman, *A History of the Franciscan Order from its Origins to the Year 1517* (Oxford, 1968), p. 359; H. Kurath and S. M. Kuhn, eds., *Middle English Dictionary* (Michigan, 1956 – in progress), iv, p. 326.

[22] G. F. Jones, 'Sartorial Symbols in Medieval Literature', *Medium Aevum*, xxv (1956), pp. 66, 68–9.

[23] Piers the Plowman, B, xv, lines 160–3 (*cf.* C, xvii, lines 296–9): *The Vision of William concerning Piers the Plowman*, ed. Skeat, i, pp. 446–7.

[24] 37 Edward III, c. 14: *Statutes*, i, pp. 381–2.

[25] The author of Piers the Plowman, robed in russet (A, ix, line 1; B, viii, line 1; C, xi, line 1) was clothed as a sheep (A, i, line 2; B, i, line 2) or as a shepherd (C, i, line 2): *The Vision of William concerning Piers the Plowman*, ed. Skeat, i, pp. 2–3, 252–3.

silks, furs and jewellery.[26] Hardly any fine greys were made in the main Flemish or Brabantine cloth towns;[27] they were left to the outlying textile regions of northern Normandy (centring on Montivilliers) where they were a local specialism. Here dyeing was controlled, and older techniques of fulling were preferred to the use of fulling mills. Such greys were worthy of the households of royalty and princes of the Church, where they were used for a variety of sombre purposes.[28]

Colchester russets did not belong to either extreme of the market. They were not fine cloths, being usually fulled mechanically,[29] but they were dyed and manufactured to recognised standards and were better made than the fabrics of the poor. Greys of this quality were used to make cloaks for men outside the ranks of the poor, partly for everyday convenience,[30] partly for symbolism's sake. Walsingham acidly observed that Lollard preachers wore russet 'in token of fuller perfection', and Friar Daw knew that grey was 'the colour that signefieth symplenesse'.[31] There was accordingly a reliable market for greys amongst religious men. Russets also had their place in lay piety. They could be used for mourning, as an alternative to black,[32] and had other funerary uses. When Sir John Cheyne, the Lollard knight, made his will in 1413 he asked for his body to be laid out upon russet at 1s 3d a yard, this being an appropriate material with which to express contempt for the flesh.[33] Colchester russets combined a humility of status and soundness of quality which suited them for symbolic uses of this kind. One elaborate form of knighthood ceremony required squires to spend the hours of darkness before the great day in chapel, at prayer, clothed 'in hermytis aray of Colchestir russet'.[34] The very fact that Colchester russet was recognised by name distinguishes it from the cheapest quality of russets, most of which were not known by their place of manufacture.

---

[26] S. Thrupp, *The Merchant Class of Medieval London* (Chicago, 1948), p. 149.

[27] De Poerck, *La Draperie médiévale en Flandre*, i, pp. 195–6; R. H. Bautier, 'La Place de la draperie brabançonne et plus particulièrement bruxelloise dans l'industrie textile du Moyen Âge', *Annales de la Société Royale d'Archéologie de Bruxelles*, li (1966), p. 55.

[28] Laurent, *Un Grand Commerce*, pp. 217–18; M. Mollat, *Études sur l'économie et la société de l'Occident médiéval, xiie–xve siècles* (London, 1977), item 5, p. 409. For the high reputation of Norman greys, see R. van Uytven, 'Cloth in Medieval Literature of Western Europe', in N. B. Harte and K. Ponting, eds., *Cloth and Clothing in Medieval Europe: Essays in Memory of Professor E. M. Carus-Wilson* (London, 1983), pp. 167, 173.

[29] See Chapter 5, pp. 76–7.

[30] Thrupp, *The Merchant Class*, pp. 149–50.

[31] Thomas of Walsingham, *Historia Anglicana*, i, p. 324; Friar Daw's Reply, line 384: *Jack Upland*, ed. Heyworth, p. 85.

[32] *A Book of London English, 1384–1425*, ed. R. W. Chambers and M. Daunt (Oxford, 1931), p. 143.

[33] K. B. McFarlane, *Lancastrian Kings and Lollard Knights* (Oxford, 1972), p. 211.

[34] A. Way, 'Illustrations of Medieval Manners, Chivalry and Costume, from Original Documents', *The Archaeological Journal*, v (1848), pp. 260, 265.

Colchester cloths were also of a distinctive size. The standard measure was the *decena*, a local peculiarity which appears to mean a length of 10 ells (equal to 12½ yards). The ulnage accounts use the word as if it were synonymous with the more familiar *duodena*, or dozen,[35] a cloth about 13 yards long which was a characteristic product of the Suffolk textile industry,[36] and though Colchester sources do not use the term *duodena*, this equivalence was about right. In 1375 a clothmaker was reported by a lawhundred jury for fraud because he used to have *decene* of cloth imperfectly shorn and then sold them as cloths of 14 ells. This implies that the *decena* was shorter than 14 ells, but that a rolled up *decena* which was rougher than usual might look like a properly made cloth of 14 ells.[37] Two 'whole cloths' of grey russet were valued in 1407 at £2 6s 0d each, which was twice the normal price of a *decena*. They were equivalent to the piece of grey russet 24 yards long and 2 yards wide worth £2 5s 0d which was purloined by a Colchester fuller about the year 1411.[38]

Colchester *decene* came in two widths, some called broad cloths or large cloths and others called narrow cloths or straits. Table 4.1 shows prices of russets in these two categories taken from pleadings in Colchester courts. Some disputes concern cloths which had been taken to fullers for fulling, but the prices cited in these instances are no lower than in other cases; the plaintiffs in question claimed the full price of the finished cloth on the understanding that they would pay the fuller a standard charge for his labour once the cloth was returned. Broad cloths in the period 1385–1413 were priced between £1 0s 0d and £1 8s 0d a *decena*, which would mean between 1s 7d and 2s 3d a yard. Both limits of the range are independently attested, for 14 ells sold in 1405 for £1 6s 8d, implying a price of about 1s 6d a yard, and in 1398 a piece of grey russet 4½ yards long was valued at 10s 0d, which is about 2s 3d a yard.[39] Straits from Colchester sold at prices from 9s 8d to 12s 0d a *decena*, which implies between 9d and 1s 0d a yard. Since straits were about half the price of broad cloths they were probably half the width. Straits in this region were traditionally a yard wide,[40] which implies that broad cloths were two yards wide. This was no longer the normal width for English broad cloths, but it had been so in the early thirteenth century when Colchester's reputation for russets was first established.[41] At times even broader cloths were woven, as in an

---

[35] In the account of 1399–1400 cloths are listed as *decene* but totalled as dozens: P.R.O., E.101/342/14.

[36] In a Suffolk ulnage account of 1394–5 each dozen of strait cloth was taxed at a quarter the rate paid for a standard broadcloth of 26 yards: P.R.O., E.101/342/8r,d.

[37] CR 17/7r.

[38] CR 36/20d; *Cal. Pat. R., 1408–13*, p. 352.

[39] CR 35/7r; CR 36/13d.   [40] *Rot. Parl.*, iii, p. 320.

[41] A. R. Bridbury, *Medieval English Clothmaking: An Economic Survey* (London, 1982), pp. 106–7.

Table 4.1 *Prices of Colchester russets in Colchester, 1383–1413*

	Valuation		Implied price of a *decena*		Year	Reference
	s	d	s	d		
BROAD CLOTHS						
vna decena et tres vlne panni lanei de russet	38	0	–		1383	CR 24/51r
duo decene panni lanei de colore de russet et mede viridi	56	0	28	0	1385	CR 25/30d
vna decena panni de russet largi	24	4	24	4	1387	CR 28/21r
duo panni de russet	60	0	–		1388	CR 26/51r
vna decena panni de russet largi	28	0	28	0	1389	CR 28/24r
vna decena de russet	20	0	20	0	1390	CR 28/6d
tres decene panni de russet grey	71	0	23	8	1390	CR 27/11r
duo decene panni de russet	46	0	23	0	1390	CR 27/18r
duo decene de grey russet largi	48	0	24	0	1391	CR 28/37d
vna decena et tres vlne panni de russet largi	36	0	–		1394	CR 29/5d
ij decene de grey russet panni lati	48	0	24	0	1394	CR 30/9d
duo decene et dimidia panni largi de tane russet	60	0	24	0	1395	CR 29/8d
vna decena panni et dimidia de grey russet	33	0	22	0	1395	CR 29/9d
quatuor virge et dimidia de grey russett	10	0	–		1398	CR 36/13d
x decene panni de grey russet	220	0	22	0	1401	CR 32/17d
vna decena de grey russet	24	0	24	0	1401	CR 32/24r
vnus pannus latus de russet	26	8	–		1405	CR 35/16r
vnus pannus de russet	26	8	–		1405	CR 35/6d
xiiij vlne panni lati de grey russet mixti	26	8	–		1405	CR 35/7r
vj decene panni lanei lati de greye russet	150	0	25	0	1405	CR 36/25d
vna decena panni lanei de tany russet	26	0	26	0	1410	CR 38/17d
tres decene de russet	72	0	24	0	1413	CR 39/38d
NARROW CLOTHS						
vna decena panni lanei stricti de russet	10	0	10	0	1392	CR 28/8r
vij decene panni stricti de russet	84	0	12	0	1393–4	CR 29/22r
v decene de russett stricti	50	0	10	0	1397	CR 30/15d
ij decene stricte panni russeti de grey[a]	19	4	9	8	1398	CR 30/5d
ij decene panni stricti de russet	20	0	10	0	1400	CR 32/23d
vna decena de grey russet stricti	12	0	12	0	1403	CR 33/18d

[a] Sold in Dedham.

instance from 1376, when a weaver was allegedly given 17 *lb* of warp thread and 17 *lb* of weft to make a *decena* 2¾ yards wide.[42] Broad cloths were more characteristic of Colchester's own industry than straits were. The ulnage accounts of 1395–7 record sales of only 238 *decene* of narrow cloth in Colchester, the equivalent of 2.6 per cent of the broad cloth sold,[43] and few straits were exported through Colchester in 1397–8, though they were more prominent in trade through Ipswich.[44] Broad cloths were also more commonly the subject of disputes in the borough courts, as Table 4.1 shows. In the 1390s straits were more associated with Essex village industries; they were the chief object of trade in Dedham, and they were numerous in the markets of Coggeshall and Braintree.[45] In Suffolk they accounted for 65 per cent of the cloth trade between 1 February 1396 and Easter 1397.[46] In its concentration on broad cloths Colchester differed from its neighbours. This means that Colchester's speciality may be approximately described as a medium-grade, mechanically fulled, russet cloth, usually grey, measuring about 12 yards long by 2 yards wide, and costing in the region of £1 4s 0d at the end of the fourteenth century.

On Tuesday, 10 March 1388, William Okle, weaver, pleaded in a Colchester court of pleas that Matilda Westoneys owed him 10s 6d for a broad *decena* of tawny whose manufacture he had organised on her behalf about Christmas time in 1386. In order to justify his claim he itemised his costs in having the wool spun and dyed, in weaving the cloth and in having it fulled. In addition he claimed he had lent Matilda part of the wool, and that he had paid for the 'lyste' required to hold the cloth on tenter hooks after washing and fulling.[47] These claims supply a coherent analysis of the manufacturing costs of this particular cloth, the details of which are shown in Table 4.2. But the total implied cost was only 16s 6d, and even allowing some margin for Okle's enterprise, the selling price of such a cloth must have been below £1. These expenses cannot be assumed to be directly relevant to the normal quality of Colchester russet, which sold for prices higher than this, and indeed there is sufficient evidence in the Colchester records to show what adjustments need to be made to explain the higher price of russets.

The dyed yarn from which Okle made his cloth was worth about 5¼d a pound, but this was cheaper than the yarn usually used for Colchester cloths. In 1386, 3½ *lb* of 'white russet' yarn were sold for 1s 11d, which implies a price of about 6½d a pound, and in 1387 31½ *lb* of 'white russet' yarn were valued at £1 6s 8d, implying a price of about 10d.[48] On this

[42] CR 18/13r.
[44] P.R.O., E.122/193/33.
[46] P.R.O., E.101/342/10r.
[48] CR 25/58r; CR 26/2d.

[43] P.R.O., E.101/342/9, mm. 1r–3d, 8r–10r, 11r.
[45] P.R.O., E.101/342/9, mm. 5r–7d, 10d, 13r, 14r.
[47] CR 26/41r,d.

Table 4.2 *Manufacturing costs of a large* decena *of tawny, 1386*

	s	d
26 *lb* of wool @ 3*d* each	6	6
spinning	1	7
dyeing	3	3
weaving	2	6
fulling	2	6
'lyste'		2
	16	6

Source: CR 26/41r.

showing the yarn used for russets varied considerably in price, so that 26 *lb* of russet yarn might vary in cost between 14*s* 1*d* and £1 1*s* 8*d*. There were two elements in these variations in the price of yarn, one the price of the raw wool, the other the quality of dyeing. Dyeing costs were likely to have constituted about half the price of the most expensive russet yarn on record, but far less than this in most cases. These variations are important because they must account for most of the differences in price between one Colchester russet and another.

The price of 2*s* 6*d* claimed by Okle for weaving a *decena* of broad cloth was also exceptionally low, and a more usual charge was 4*s* 0*d*. In the summer of 1377 William Pykhood allegedly received a horse worth 16*s* 0*d* for weaving four *decene* on the understanding that he should complete them before taking on other work.[49] This implies that at that time 4*s* 0*d* was a good rate, but subsequently Thomas atte Welle claimed £1 2*s* 0*d* for weaving 5½ *decene* of cloth in the year following 24 February 1379,[50] and William Grenewey claimed 4*s* 0*d* for weaving a *decena* early in 1381.[51]

In a further respect, too, Okle's costs were low, since the charge made by fullers for handling a *decena* was commonly 3*s* 0*d* in the later fourteenth century. There are two instances of this higher rate from 1370, one from 1383 and one from 1388;[52] the last was expressly the charge for two large *decene* of russet. In 1372, too, Richard Lyard claimed 3*s* 3*d* for fulling a *decena* and one yard more of so-called bastard cloth.[53]

These qualifications all imply that the normal costs of a *decena* of russet ought to be increased above those of Okle's tawny. Table 4.3 illustrates a likely structure of costs for a *decena* of russet about 1391, when local

[49] CR 19/14d.   [50] CR 26/48d.   [51] CR 22/49r.
[52] CR 18/10d, 21r; CR 24/51r; CR 29/16r.   [53] CR 18/12r.

Table 4.3 *Estimated manufacturing costs of a broad* decena *of russet,*
c. *1391*

	s	d
26 *lb* of wool @ 4*d* each	8	8
spinning	1	7
dyeing	3	10
weaving	4	0
fulling	3	0
'lyste'		2
sealing		2¼
	21	5¼
entrepreneur's costs and margin	2	6¾
	24	0

Source: Table 4.2 and subsequent discussion.

fleeces were priced at 6*d*.[54] The estimate assumes that the normal cost of russet yarn was 6½*d* a pound rather than any higher recorded value, and it adds a further 2¼*d* to the costs of production to cover the cost of having each cloth sealed by the king's ulnager.[55] Allowing some margin for entrepreneur's profit (about 10 per cent) this estimate accords well with the price of Colchester russets recorded in Table 4.1.

These calculations suggest some points of comparison with the contemporary manufactures of the Datini enterprise at Prato, whose organisation was more highly capitalist than anything in eastern England and whose structure is better recorded. The share of raw wool in the cost of producing a Colchester cloth, about 36.0 per cent, was similar to that in Prato, which averaged 37.8 per cent in the years 1392–3. In some cloths made by Datini the proportion of total costs taken by wool was slightly larger, and in some slightly lower, but not by much.[56] Cloths made from Provençal wool, whose market value in northern Italy was close to that of Essex cloths, had only 35.5 per cent of their manufacturing costs in raw wool.[57] The similarity between these proportions shows that that the ability of cloths

[54] See Table 10.5. Local fleeces weighed about 1½ *lb*: R. H. Britnell, 'Agricultural Techniques in Eastern England', in E. Miller, ed., *The Agrarian History of England and Wales*, iii (Cambridge, forthcoming).

[55] Each *decena* owed 2*d* for subsidy and ¼*d* for ulnage: P.R.O., E.101/342/9, 10, mm. 10r, 11r.

[56] F. Melis, *Aspetti della vita economica medievale*, i (Siena, 1962), p. 561 and Table 27 opposite p. 554.

[57] Between 1385 and 1402 *panni di Sex* were valued at 1.1 *fl* per *canna* on average. Cloths of Provençal wool were valued at 1.3 *fl* per *canna*: F. Melis, 'Uno sguardo al mercato dei panni di lana a Pisa nella seconda metà del trecento', *Economia e storia*, vi (1959), pp. 329n, 347; *idem*, *Aspetti della vita economica medievale*, i, p. 550.

of the Colchester type to compete in European markets was not due simply to the cheapness of the wool from which they were made. The level of manufacturing costs was equally important to their success.

II

Between 25 February 1397 and 24 February 1398 Hythe was visited by 32 ships engaged in overseas trade. Of these, 19 were foreign, mostly from the Low Countries. These foreign ships were engaged chiefly in short hauls across the North Sea, bringing beer, fish and a few manufactures, and either leaving empty or taking hides, butter and cheese.[58] They had little relevance for the cloth industry. Cloth exports direct from Hythe were mostly shipped by Colchester men in English ships, and they travelled beyond the shores of the North Sea. Only a few Colchester cloths passed through Bruges on their way to other destinations.[59] The main export markets were farther afield, where there was less local industrial competition and where diplomatic relations were easier than those between England and Flanders. The pattern of trade created by Colchester merchants before the Black Death assumed a greater significance for the economy of the borough during the period of recovery.

The wine trade remained attractive to Colchester merchants throughout the later fourteenth and early fifteenth centuries. John de Scotland and William Buk of Colchester traded with Gascony in the 1350s,[60] and Geoffrey Dawe and William Hunt did so in the 1360s. Dawe and Hunt also imported salt from the Bay of Bourgneuf.[61] Later customs records from 1397–8, 1410–11 and 1413–14 show that these were simple bilateral trades in exchange for cloth.[62] Through their direct contact with the source of these fabrics, drapers in Bordeaux recognised Colchester cloth by name. The archbishop of Bordeaux on one occasion bought Colchester cloth to clothe members of his household.[63] Gascony, which depended heavily on England for its supply of cloth,[64] was the main destination for Colchester's overseas enterprise throughout the later fourteenth century. During the 12 months following 25 February 1397 wine imports into Colchester amounted to 369 tuns, whose commercial value was in the region of £1,800.[65] Imports from the rest of the continent cannot have equalled this sum.

[58] P.R.O., E.122/193/33, fos. 11v–17r, 24r–25r.
[59] *Die Handelsbücher des hansischen Kaufmannes Veckinchusen*, ed. M. P. Lesnikov, Forschungen zur mittelalterlichen Geschichte, xix (Berlin, 1973), p. 45.
[60] *Cal. Pat. R., 1350–4*, p. 130; CR 12/2d.
[61] *Cal. Pat. R., 1361–4*, pp. 497, 511, 515.
[62] P.R.O., E.122/193/33; E.122/51/29, 40.
[63] Carus-Wilson, *Medieval Merchant Venturers*, p. 270n.   [64] *Ibid.*, pp. 38–9, 270.
[65] P.R.O., E.122/193/33, fos. 11v–13v, 24r–25r. The price of Gascon wine was around £5 a tun: M. K. James, *Studies in the Medieval Wine Trade*, ed. E. M. Veale (Oxford, 1971), pp. 30, 37, 51.

Meanwhile Colchester men had opened up a new commerce with the Baltic, where their principal destination was Prussia. This region had in abundance silvan products which were in short supply in the west, and its inhabitants' lack of established textile industries made them dependent upon imported cloth.[66] Direct contact with the Baltic did not depend wholly upon the efforts of Colchester merchants; some German shippers crossed the North Sea to call at Hythe. In 1371 a cog on its way from Elbing to Colchester was among 39 vessels boarded and searched by Flemish officials seeking to arrest the property of English merchants.[67] But Englishmen were made welcome in Prussia in the third quarter of the fourteenth century; their commercial privileges even allowed them to retail cloth there. Such were the opportunities that merchants from a number of towns took advantage of them: Bristol, London, Colchester, Norwich, King's Lynn, Boston, Beverley, Hull and York.[68] In this list Colchester is one of the least predictable members. It would not have seemed likely 50 years earlier that the town should become associated with such an adventurous field of merchant activity.

Colchester enterprise in the Baltic was established by the early 1360s, when a number of leading merchants, including William Buk and William Hunt were involved.[69] In the more troubled days of the trade under Richard II, a handful of Colchester merchants was amongst those seeking redress for losses incurred in Prussia.[70] Later fourteenth-century customs accounts show that imports from the Baltic were more varied than those from Gascony; in addition to fish and wheat, the main items in 1397, there were small consignments of wax, bitumen and timber from the eastern Baltic, salt and iron from Scandinavia, linen cloth, thread and beer from northern Germany.[71] This implies that Colchester merchants did not confine their contacts to Prussian ports. Indeed, when trade with Prussia was interrupted in the spring of 1388 attempts were still made to trade with

---

[66] M. M. Postan, *Medieval Trade and Finance* (Cambridge, 1973), pp. 314–19; F. Renken, *Der Handel der Königsberger Grossschäfferei des Deutschen Ordens mit Flandern um 1400*, Abhandlungen zur Handels- und Seegeschichte, v (Weimar, 1937), pp. 18–19, 95–103.

[67] D. M. Nicholas, 'The English Trade at Bruges in the Last Years of Edward III', *Journal of Medieval History*, v (1979), pp. 37, 41.

[68] F. Schulz, *Die Hanse und England von Eduards III bis auf Heinrichs VIII Zeit*, Abhandlungen zur Verkehrs- und Seegeschichte im Auftrag des Hansischen Geschichtsvereins, v (Berlin, 1911), p. 15.

[69] *Cal. Close R., 1360–4*, p. 248; *Cal. Pat. R., 1361–4*, pp. 291, 511.

[70] *Hanseakten aus England, 1275 bis 1412*, ed. K. Kunze (Halle, 1891) no. 229, pp. 159–60; *Cal. Close R., 1385–9*, pp. 67–8, 163, 194–5; *Die Rezesse und andere Akten der Hansetage von 1256–1430*, ed. K. Koppman (8 vols., Leipzig, 1870–97), iii, nos. 404A, 404B, pp. 406, 413.

[71] See, for example, the cargoes of the *Cristofre* of Danzig and of the *Seintemarishyp* of 'Danburgh': P.R.O., E.122/193/33, fos. 13r, 16r,v.

Skåne, presumably for fish.[72] In exchange the Baltic took Colchester cloth, which eventually established itself as one of the few English fabrics to be known by its place of origin.[73] Some of the earliest references to Colchester cloth as a recognised type are from the records of the Teutonic Knights who, besides the possibility of contact with English exporters to Danzig, had opportunities to obtain English fabrics through their own trading activities in England.[74] Accounts of the Seneschalcy of Königsberg at the start of the fifteenth century show the bishop of Samland indebted to the Order for ten Colchester half cloths, five grey and five brown. Accounts of the Seneschalcy of Marienburg from 1404 list stores of cloth in various places, including four Colchester halves in the cloth cellar at Elbing. The accounts also record debts claimed from resident Prussians for cloth dispatched far into the interior of the country. Money for Colchester cloth was owed in Elbing, Heilsberg, Schippenbeil, Rössel, Löbau, Danzig and Lontschitcz.[75] However, within Colchester's own sphere of operations the Baltic trades were subordinate to Gascony. Imports from the region were considerably less valuable than the wine trade, and recorded cloth exports were smaller.

Gascony and Prussia together accounted for most of Colchester's enterprise abroad. The third main overseas outlet for local cloth, which opened up in the 1380s, was one in which Colchester men were never directly involved. This was the Mediterranean trade. Because Italian merchants bought their cloth in London and had no direct contact with Colchester, and because they saw Colchester *decene* as one type amongst many similar products from the eastern counties, they spoke only of Essex cloth. This term included the russets for which Colchester had a reputation; an account of cloths sent from London by way of Southampton on behalf of the Datini companies in 1389 is concerned with Guildford blanket and Essex dark grey.[76] The first contacts with the Mediterranean world were about the early 1380s, when the London agents of Florentine trading companies were buying Essex cloth to be sold in eastern Spain and

---

[72] *The Diplomatic Correspondence of Richard II*, ed. E. Perroy, Camden 3rd ser., xlviii (London, 1933), no. 83, pp. 54–5; *Bronnen tot de Geschiedenis van den Handel met Engeland, Schotland en Ierland, 1150–1485*, ed. H. J. Smit, Rijks Geschiedkundige Publikatiën, lxv, lxvi, (2 vols., The Hague, 1928), i, no. 680, p. 397.

[73] H. Ammann, 'Deutschland und die Tuchindustrie Nordwesteuropas im Mittelalter', *Hansische Geschichtsblätter*, lxxii (1954), pp. 50–1; P. Dollinger, *The German Hansa*, trans. D. S. Ault and S. H. Steinberg (London, 1970), p. 245.

[74] Renken, *Der Handel der Königsberger Grossschäfferei*, p. 125, n. 87.

[75] *Handelsrechnungen des Deutschen Ordens*, ed. C. Sattler, Verein für die Geschichte von Ost- und Westpreussen, v (Leipzig, 1887), pp. 16–17, 37, 40–2, 55, 123–4, 254.

[76] *Documenti per la storia economica dei secoli xiii–xvi*, ed. F. Melis, Istituto Internazionale di Storia Economica 'F. Datini' (Florence, 1972), no. 62, p. 254.

northern Italy. The Datini companies provide the best documented instance of this, and they may have performed a pioneering rôle in establishing the reputation of these cloths in southern Europe. By the time Colchester cloths had become familiar to the Teutonic Knights' Grossschäfferei in Prussia, Essex cloths had become a regular item of commerce for Datini partnerships in Tuscany, Catalonia and elsewhere. The recorded distribution of these cloths in southern Europe follows the route of shipments to the Mediterranean from the North Sea through the Straits of Gibraltar.[77] Small numbers of them reached Málaga, where in 1402 a correspondent writing to Barcelona distinguished between larger and smaller varieties.[78] They reached the Datini *fondaco* at Barcelona in the 1390s, and rather more were sent on to that on Majorca: 12 in 1395, 50 in 1397 and 44 in 1400.[79] Documentation from Pisa shows Essex cloths, with those from elsewhere in England, becoming prominent at the end of the fourteenth century; they are of much greater account in the records of cloth sold annually by Datini between 1383 and 1402 and by the Bracci company between 1391 and 1397 than they are in those of the Pisan company of Baldo da Sancasciano in the years 1354–71. Datini records suggest that English cloth was in particularly heavy demand from the late 1380s, and that between 1387 and 1402 Essex cloths accounted for 24.0 per cent, by value, of all cloths sold by Datini in Pisa.[80] Throughout the west-central Mediterranean at this period Essex cloths were able to survive the stiff competition of those from Tuscany because of their relatively low prices.[81] The channels by which Essex cloths reached this region in the late fourteenth and early fifteenth centuries were nevertheless few. The Genoese, whose dealings in English cloth date from the 1380s, did not at this early stage recognise Essex cloths as a type,[82] and the port of Marseilles handled little English cloth of any sort.[83] The share of Essex cloths in the total trade of the western Mediterranean was not as great as it was in the trade of the Datini companies. But once known in the Mediterranean world, Essex cloths gained some hold. They perhaps never established themselves in

---

[77] I. Origo, *The Merchant of Prato*, 2nd edn (Harmondsworth, 1963), p. 73.

[78] F. Melis, *Mercaderes italianos en España (Siglos xiv–xvi)* (Seville, 1976), p. 6.

[79] C. Verlinden, 'Draps des Pays-Bas et du Nord-Ouest de l'Europe au Portugal du xve siècle', *Anuario de estudios medievales*, iii (1966), p. 259; F. Melis, 'La diffusione nel Mediterraneo occidentale dei panni di Wervicq e delle altre città della Lys attorno al 1400', in *Studi in onore di Amintore Fanfani* (6 vols., Milan, 1962), iii, pp. 223, 225.

[80] Melis, 'Uno sguardo al mercato', pp. 326–7, 347.

[81] Melis, *Mercaderes italianos en España*, p. 51.

[82] Liagre-de Sturler, *Les Relations commerciales*, i, pp. cxxviii, cxxxiv–cxxxvii, and ii, p. 929.

[83] E. Baratier, 'De 1291 à 1423', in G. Rambert, ed., *Histoire du commerce de Marseille* (7 vols., Paris, 1949–66), ii, p. 301.

Genoese trade,[84] but they were taken up by the Venetians, who introduced them to Damascus by 1416.[85]

In its ability to export cloth to continental markets during the later fourteenth century, Colchester shared the fortunes of the English cloth industry as a whole, which was increasingly able to benefit from overseas markets because of the competitive prices of its characteristic products. The argument which relates this competitiveness to the higher taxes on exports of wool imposed by Edward III in 1336 is of doubtful relevance in Colchester's case.[86] The tax did not discriminate between different qualities of wool, and so impeded the export of cheaper wools even more than that of finer ones. The cloths of Essex and Suffolk were mostly made of cheap wools which it was no longer profitable to export.[87] But the poorer quality of these wools meant that continental producers had less difficulty in finding substitutes for them. English customs duties were unlikely to raise the costs of manufacturing inferior woollens abroad to the extent that they raised those of the luxury cloth industry. The success of Colchester russets in the later fourteenth century therefore implies that the relatively favourable terms on which the English could make cloth were not only the consequence of tariff policy.[88] In this instance the ability of entrepreneurs to benefit from cheap water power for mechanical fulling was probably of great importance to them.[89] The directness of Colchester's communications with the continent by water was also a greater advantage after the Black Death than before, since high transport costs were a severe deterrent to trade in cheap fabrics. These advantages allowed more effective price competition between Colchester cloths and those from other sources of supply, and particularly, perhaps, against those from Brabant.[90]

The importance of change on the demand side is difficult to assess. A town making cheap cloth might benefit after the Black Death from increases in real income amongst the lower ranks of society, especially in the immediate wake of the disaster, when wages rose rapidly and inheritance

---

[84] J. Heers, *Gênes au xve siècle: Activité économique et problèmes sociaux* (Paris, 1961), pp. 457–8; *idem*, 'La Mode et les marchés', pp. 1112–13. In these discussions of the Genoese cloth trade Essex cloths attract no attention; nor is there any reference to grey or brown cloths from England.

[85] E. Ashtor, 'L'Exportation de textiles occidentaux dans le Proche-Orient musulman au bas Moyen Âge (1370–1517)', in *Studi in memoria di Federigo Melis* (5 vols., Naples, 1978), ii, p. 343.

[86] The real effect of these taxes on the export of finer wools has recently been reasserted in J. H. Munro, 'Monetary Contraction and Industrial Change in the Late-Medieval Low Countries, 1335–1500', in N. J. Mayhew, ed., *Coinage in the Low Countries (880–1500)*, *B.A.R.* International Ser., 54 (Oxford, 1979), p. 110.

[87] *Rot. Parl.*, iii, p. 320.

[88] Bridbury, *Medieval English Clothmaking*, pp. 89–97.

[89] See Chapter 5, pp. 76–7.   [90] *Cf.* Mollat, *Études*, item 5, pp. 408–9.

effects contributed to the consequent spending spree. But since Colchester's cloth was not produced for the lower ranks of society this explanation for increasing sales is not readily available. Perhaps Colchester russets were substituted for local fabrics among some groups whose income was rising. It is also possible that Colchester russets were substituted for finer fabrics by groups whose income was falling. There is no sure way of deciding whether either or both of these hypotheses is relevant.

Observation so far has been confined to sales abroad, simply for lack of evidence about the home market. There were local sales of Colchester russet in the eastern counties, and some travelled farther, but references to this trade are rare. Probably, in fact, domestic sales were smaller than those overseas, at least after the 1350s. The size of consignments exported implies that there was little surplus for home demand. If, for example, the import of wine from Gascony during 52 weeks in 1397–8 was financed by exports of Colchester cloth the total required would have been 1,500 *decene*. This figure may be compared with the 4,330 *decene* sealed in Colchester by the ulnager during 95 weeks in the period 1395–7.[91] The relative slightness of home sales is also suggested by the narrowness of the trading pattern of Colchester merchants in England. An analysis of trade in the home market between 1390 and 1410 may be derived from the record of litigants from outside the liberty of the borough who were named in the borough courts either as plaintiffs or defendants in pleas of debt.[92] This evidence shows that outside the clothmaking region of Suffolk the only town to trade regularly with Colchester was London. Londoners came to Colchester for the fairs[93] and, in the opposite direction, Colchester men went to London to sell their cloth in the markets there.[94] But the London connection was not wholly, or even primarily, an orientation to the home market. It was in London that Essex cloths were acquired by Italian exporters, and some Hanseatic exports were also marketed by this route.[95] The predominance of export markets for Colchester's cloth, at a time when the growth of demand in England can hardly have lagged much behind that of her neighbours, implies that the reason for industrial development in the town was a greater ability to compete in new markets as a result of cost advantages over foreign manufacturers, rather than any increase in the demand for this sort of cloth.

[91] P.R.O., E.101/342/9, mm. 8r, 10r, 11r.
[92] CR 27–37.
[93] *Calendar of Letters from the Mayor and Corporation of the City of London, circa 1350–1370*, ed. R. R. Sharpe (London, 1885), p. 105.
[94] Guildhall Library Muniments, Recognisance Roll 12, m. 12r.
[95] Melis, *Aspetti della vita economica medievale*, i, pp. 278–9; *Cal. Close, R., 1402–5*, p. 439.

III

As Colchester's trading connections increased, so did activity on the waterfront at Hythe, particularly during the last quarter of the fourteenth century. The rising value of shipments contributed not only to the incomes of individual families who profited from the growth of trade but also to that of the community as a body. Between 1372 and 1400 there was an increase of perhaps 18 per cent in the annual income from the lease of tolls there,[96] but variations in the terms of this lease were trammelled by customary expectations and do not indicate at all well changes in the real level of receipts.[97] Of greater value was a group of separately leased sources of income at Hythe, of which measurage was the first to appear. If there was such a charge on traders before 1373 its yield was included with the lease of tolls. At Michaelmas 1373, however, a measurer was publicly elected, and he was prevailed upon to pay £2 10s 0d for the year.[98] The value of the lease subsequently rose to £3 6s 8d in 1374/5 and £4 in 1385/6.[99] Then, either in 1386 or 1387, Hythe rents were increased by the leasing of a new crane, the first on record here, and one of the earliest known in England. Its introduction coincided with the earliest reference to poundage as a separate element of income from Hythe; measurage, poundage and the new crane were leased together for £14.[100] The next step was the community's acquisition of a second crane, called Robert Sewale's crane or Philip Neggemere's crane, together with some new buildings. These assets, which were added between Michaelmas 1396 and Michaelmas 1398, raised the combined value of the Hythe leases, other than tolls, to £36 at the latter date and to £39 at Michaelmas 1400. These late fourteenth-century contracts also included quayage and wharfage as items of the lease.[101] Yet another source of income from Hythe, introduced between Michaelmas 1400 and Michaelmas 1404, was a charge for manhandling bulky goods which was leased for £1.[102] The increase in the community's income from assets at Hythe was greater than that from any other source during the years 1350–1410, and it made Hythe of prime importance in borough finances. The estimates in Table 4.4 suggest that in 1372/3 the lease of tolls at Hythe accounted for about 36 per cent of the community's income from rents, but that in 1406/7 this lease and the new Hythe leases together made up about 57 per cent of the total.

[96] Appendix, Table 5.
[97] See Chapter 8, p. 122.   [98] RPB, fo. 6v.
[99] CR 17/1d; CR 25/2r.
[100] The first recorded lease including the crane is for two years from Michaelmas 1387: CR 26/16r.
[101] CR 29/7d; CR 30/3r; CR 31/2d; CR 32/1r. For a parallel development of port facilities, see Platt, *Medieval Southampton*, p. 143.   [102] CR 34/1d.

Table 4.4 *The community's income from rents in 1372/3 and in 1406/7*
(estimates)

	Hythe leases			Other rents		
	Measurage, cranage, etc. £	Water tolls £	Land tolls £	Moothall cellar £	Fixed rents £	Total £
1372/3	–	17ᵃ	18ᵃ	–	12.6ᵇ	47.6
1406/7	35ᶜ	20ᵈ	20ᵈ	7.3ᵉ	13.4ᵇ	95.7

ᵃ The water and land tolls were leased together for £35. Here they are separated as in the lease of 1392/3: CR 28/2r.

ᵇ From the community rental of 1387/8: OB, fos. 158r–170r. The estimate for 1372/3 excludes some rents contracted in 1373/4 recorded in the Red Paper Book: RPB, fos. 7v, 8r. The figure for 1406/7 includes additions made to the rental up to and including those in the handwriting of Thomas Stampe.

ᶜ CR 36/1r, adding £1 for porterage.

ᵈ Water and land tolls were leased together for £40. But water tolls were leased for £20 in 1395/6, 1413/14 and 1418/19: CR 29/7d; CR 39/1r; CR 41/1d.

ᵉ CR 36/2d.

Many of the boats calling at Hythe were engaged in coastal trade. Morant possessed 'an account taken in the 17th of Richard II of all the vessels that arrived at Hyth'.[103] The nature of this document may be guessed from the circumstance that in 1392/3 and 1395/6, and presumably in the intervening years for which no court rolls survive, measurage and poundage at Hythe were not leased out but committed to William Wytham with instructions to render account to the borough receivers.[104] Morant's document was probably such an account, recording sums received for measuring and weighing of cargoes to establish what dues they should pay. These local charges were paid on most, if not all, cargoes coming into port, and relate to coastal trade as well as to imports from overseas. All that is known about the documents concerns the number of ships, and may be told in Morant's words: 'it appears that from the 9th of July to the 29th of December, anno 1393, there came into that port no less than seventy-two'. The royal customs accounts show only 14 ships through Hythe between 9 July and 29 December 1397.[105] This contrast suggests that most ships calling there in the 1390s were trading along the coast, though the numerical contrast is more accentuated than the economic reality, since vessels on coastal routes were likely to be smaller than those trading

[103] Morant, *Colchester*, ii, p. 23, note U.
[104] CR 28/2r; CR 29/7d.
[105] P.R.O., E.122/193/33, fos. 14r–17r, 24r–25r.

abroad. It is unlikely, therefore, that the level of trade at Hythe was primarily determined by the size of cloth exports.

Cloth exports were likely, however, to have been an important determinant of income and employment in Colchester, and so to have governed other facets of trade there. It is interesting, in this context, that the high level of income at Hythe at the end of the 1390s was soon followed by a decline, to the point that by 1420 receipts had fallen by almost a half. This turning point corresponds to a change in the fortunes of Colchester merchants. A severe depression afflicted the trade of western Europe in the last years of the fourteenth century and the early years of the fifteenth, a period of acute monetary crisis.[106] General problems were compounded by particular difficulties in Colchester's main markets. Conditions in the Baltic deteriorated from 1402, when the Anglo-Hanseatic treaty of ten years earlier was revoked, and trade was interrupted between 1403 and 1407.[107] On the southern route the period 1403–6 was one of mounting uncertainty. The people of Bordeaux were threatened with invasion, and though they defeated the French just before Christmas 1406, their future remained in doubt. The year 1406/7 was a dismal one for the Gascon trade.[108] Though the enterprise of Colchester merchants in these regions partially recovered during the second decade of the fifteenth century, it was incapable of further growth. The peak level of income from Hythe therefore corresponds to the zenith of the fortunes of Colchester's merchants overseas.

By the 1390s, however, Colchester cloth had come to interest groups of merchants other than Colchester's own, so that the fortunes of the industry were less dependent than in the past on the level of exports through Hythe. A larger proportion of exports than in the past was going through London in the hands of Italians and Germans. This means that the level of activity at Hythe is not a dependable guide to the fortunes of clothmaking in the fifteenth century, and the industrial history of the borough between 1400 and 1420 was not as unfortunate as the evidence from Hythe might suggest. An examination of how manufactures in Colchester responded to opportunities overseas will show how by the first decade of the fifteenth century the cloth industry was less dependent than in the past on native enterprise and traditional markets.

[106] J. H. Munro, *Wool, Cloth, and Gold: The Struggle for Bullion in Anglo-Burgundian Trade, 1340–1478* (Toronto, 1972), pp. 58–63; H. van der Wee, *The Growth of the Antwerp Market and the European Economy (Fourteenth–Sixteenth Centuries)* (3 vols., The Hague, 1963), ii, pp. 15–17; J. Day, 'The Great Bullion Famine of the Fifteenth Century', *Past and Present*, lxxix (1978), pp. 12–35.

[107] Schulz, *Die Hanse und England*, pp. 55–65.

[108] R. Boutruche, *La Crise d'une société: Seigneurs et paysans du Bordelais pendant la Guerre de Cent Ans* (Paris, 1963), pp. 219–21; Y. Renouard, ed., *Bordeaux sous les rois d'Angleterre*, Histoire de Bordeaux, iii (Bordeaux, 1965), pp. 414–16. Wine imports from Gascony were very low in 1406/7: James, *Studies in the Medieval Wine Trade*, p. 108.

5

Industry

I

Perhaps not all the so-called Colchester cloth exported in the late fourteenth century was made in Colchester itself. But there can be little doubt, given the town's specialisation in russets within its own region, that this was the major source. Predictably, then, the evidence of increasing sales abroad is paralleled by indications of industrial development. Signs of rapid recovery, or even new growth, were evident soon after the Black Death, when Colchester received its first influx of immigrants from abroad. The sudden burst of Flemish names into the records between 1352 and 1354 implies that a number of families came more or less together in the early 1350s, the burgesses being willing to accept them the more readily because of the recent loss of manpower.[1] From this time onwards the number of textile workers in the borough increased, so that by the mid 1370s there were already appreciably more than there had been in the earlier fourteenth century. The taxation of Colchester in 1301 had recognised only six fullers and three dyers, but the court roll of 1376/7 alone permits the identification of thirteen fullers and two dyers.[2]

The best evidence for continuing industrial growth in Colchester is the record of the changing annual rent of the wool market after its reorganisation in 1373. The wool trade before that time had no established location in the public market place; it was held under cover to keep the wool dry, in the hall and gateway of a privately owned tenement near the moothall, and this without any formal authorisation from the bailiffs and community. The council decided in 1373 to transfer the market to the empty cellar of the moothall, which was accordingly provided with better windows and whitewashed at the community's expense. From then on the cellar was

---

[1] CR 9/7r; CR 10/2r,d, 3r, 5r, 8r, 10r, 11r,d.
[2] *Rot. Parl.*, i, pp. 243, 246, 247, 255, 261, 262; CR 18/4r, 6r, 7r,d, 8d, 10d, 12r,d, 13r, 14r, 16d, 19r, 20r, 21r,d.

annually leased to woolmongers who would take charge of the market's organisation and pay a rent to the community.[3] This rent was paid out of the tolls levied on sales of wool, which means that it should have fluctuated with the total volume of sales. The duties paid on goods sold in the borough were fixed ones; a later list of tolls in the hand of John Hayward, town clerk between 1428 and *c.* 1434, notes that wool paid toll at the rate of one farthing for each pound by weight, and that these tolls had been levied time out of mind.[4] It is noteworthy, therefore, that having originally been set at £4 in 1373/4 and £3 10*s* 0*d* the following year, the rent of the cellar rose to £5 6*s* 8*d* by the end of the century.[5]

This was not, however, the limit of its growth. One of the most problematic features of Colchester's statistical history in the early fifteenth century is a marked rise in the rent of the moothall cellar despite the adverse circumstances of the town's overseas trading ventures from 1402 and the contraction of waterborne trade. In 1404/5 the rent reached £7 6*s* 8*d* for the first time on record, and it stood at this level again in 1406/7, a year which must have been poor for exports to Gascony and Prussia.[6] After that the rent rose still higher, to reach a peak of £9 6*s* 8*d* in 1411/12 and 1413/14. These figures imply a growth of wool sales and some concomitant increase in the volume of cloth produced. If Colchester's wool trade was so little affected by crises in the cloth trade built up by its merchants, then either there must have been powerful forces for expansion in the home market during the early fifteenth century or exports of Colchester cloth to new markets must have increased rapidly. Both options sound far-fetched. Though there was some slight increase in real wages during the early fifteenth century,[7] it was hardly enough to cause an expenditure boom. And in view of the falling level of cloth exports through the port of Ipswich (of which Colchester was part) and the falling level of the Colchester community's receipts from Hythe,[8] it cannot be supposed that Colchester merchants were responsible for any new overseas initiatives during these years. Probably the problems facing Colchester merchants were offset by new export opportunities opening up through the London market. Italian trade would be the most likely to have filled this rôle in view of the rapid increase in the importance of Essex cloth in the Datini enterprise at the end of the fourteenth century. If this is so it means a new phase in the history of Colchester's cloth industry opened at the end of the fourteenth century when, as a result of Italian demand, the growth of

[3] RPB, fos. 6v, 7r.   [4] OB, fos. 5r, 7r.
[5] Appendix, Table 5.   [6] See Chapter 4, p. 71.
[7] M. M. Postan, *Essays on Medieval Agriculture and General Problems of the Medieval Economy* (Cambridge, 1973), pp. 199, 201; Brown and Hopkins, *A Perspective of Wages and Prices*, p. 28.   [8] Appendix, Table 5.

exports was no longer related to mercantile enterprise in the town. It also means that Colchester was exceptionally fortunate during the early years of the fifteenth century, since cloth exports for England as a whole reached a peak in 1401/2 and then sank to a lower level for 20 years; total exports during the years 1405–9 were only three-quarters of their volume in the years 1395–9.[9]

II

From the late fourteenth century some account can be given of the technology and organisation of clothmaking in Colchester. Raw wool came in over distances of many miles,[10] some of it purchased in bulk by Colchester contractors. The wool clip from Langenhoe was often bought by Colchester men – Henry Bosse in 1370, John Middelion in 1384, John Prentis in 1388.[11] Other raw materials were acquired from wholesalers; a consignment of fullers' earth sold at Hythe by a merchant of Hadleigh about 1374 suggests that Colchester industry drew partly on trade networks created by Suffolk clothiers;[12] John Tollere of Ipswich sold woad to William Boot the dyer in 1383.[13] Some imported materials came by merchants from more distant ports; Nicholas Brembre, the prominent London grocer, had woad in Colchester in 1388 shortly after his arrest;[14] Thomas Fulmard of Newcastle upon Tyne had eight tons of woad at Hythe, and a similar amount in Hadleigh, in 1391.[15] Some of Colchester's dyestuffs and other necessities were imported by foreign merchants; a ship from the lost port of Remereswale in Holland was at Hythe in 1379 after unloading woad at Great Yarmouth.[16] Colchester's own merchants also had a hand in importing dyestuffs and woodashes and retailing them to craftsmen in the town.[17]

In the process of clothmaking, the raw materials, and then the woven fabric, passed many times from hand to hand and from place to place. Wool bought in the moothall cellar[18] was washed, broken up[19] and combed

---

[9] Carus-Wilson and Coleman: *England's Export Trade*, pp. 88–92, 138; Munro, 'Monetary Contraction', pp. 138, 151.

[10] There are recorded wool sales by men from Layer Marney, Birch, Stoke by Nayland and Bungay: CR 12/7r; CR 15/14d; CR 18/10d; CR 19/26d.

[11] E.R.O., D/DC 2/13r; D/DE1 M225r; D/DE1 M226r.

[12] CR 17/6r.   [13] CR 22/46r.

[14] *Cal. Close R., 1385–9*, p. 362.

[15] *Cal. Close R., 1389–92*, p. 374. Fulmard's origin is established from *Cal. Pat. R., 1388–92*, p. 204.

[16] *Cal. Close R., 1377–81*, p. 258.

[17] CR 20/17r, 25d; CR 21/23d, 51r; CR 24/56r.

[18] Many buyers of wool were small producers of whom little is known: *e.g.* William Crabbe (CR 18/7r), John Bures (CR 18/18r), Robert Barbour (CR 18/21r), John Kentyssh (CR 19/9r), Richard Ram (CR 19/18r), William Strattone (CR 19/24r).

[19] For breaking of wool by a hired woman, see CR 16/8r.

or carded[20] before being dyed[21] and spun with spinning wheels.[22] These preparatory operations were often co-ordinated by minor entrepreneurs, whose stake in the industry was protected by regulations to prevent the engrossment of wool entering the town.[23] Many cloths were brought so far by weavers themselves, who enjoyed considerable freedom of man- oeuvre in this period; John Tynnot the weaver was alleged in 1375 to have contracted with a dyer for the dyeing of wool,[24] and in 1377 William Pykhood the weaver was charged with debt for wool he had purchased.[25] The terms on which cloth was made varied greatly. Some weavers accepted yarn to be woven at piece rates, and some contracted to work for a stated length of time for wages or other acceptable remuneration.[26] Weavers were rarely dependent upon a single employer, and they were usually able to combine contract work with trading on their own account, so that the distinction between independent weavers and wage earners was blurred by the many weavers who were both.[27]

A few weavers attempted to be wholly independent of wage earning; a plea before the bailiffs in 1382 involved two men who had gone into partnership for the weaving of cloth,[28] and another a few years later concerns a weaver who was contracted to weave cloths in return for one third of the price his partner could obtain for them.[29] The implication of such freedom is that weavers commonly owned their looms or hired them independently of an employer. John Grom had a loom constructed in his home in 1375 for which he was alleged still to owe money many years later.[30] The price of looms varied with size, but twice in the course of litigation looms in Colchester were valued at 18s 0d,[31] and in addition a weaver needed shuttles which were variously valued at 1s 0d or 1s 10d a

---

[20] A number of women were designated 'kempster', which was an occupational description and not a family name: *e.g.* Christine, Mabel and Agnes in 1384/5. The last of these was distrained by a pair of combs: CR 24/13r,d, 16d. Carding as a normal technique is implied by the presence of cardmakers – *e.g.* Edmund Porter and Robert Nevill: CR 21/10d, 18d.

[21] Contracts for dyeing in the wool are mentioned, for example, in CR 17/14r; CR 18/6r, 10d, 16d. The dyeing of russets in this way is indicated by a recorded theft of grey wool: CR 24/55r.

[22] Spinning wheels occurs as objects stolen (CR 16/11r, attached schedule) and as objects distrained (CR 18/9r).

[23] CR 15/12r.

[24] John Tynnot the weaver (CR 14/4r) contracted to have dyeing done in 1375 (CR 17/14r).

[25] Pykhood occurs in 1377 as a buyer of wool, presumably for clothmaking on his own account (CR 18/10d) but he also wove on contract (CR 19/14d).

[26] For examples of long contracts, see CR 17/14d, CR 19/21r.

[27] Richard Silvester several times claimed debts for cloths sold (CR 14/5d; CR 17/10r; CR 18/22r) but in 1373 he was alleged to have woven on contract (CR 16/10r). John Shipman similarly both sold cloth (CR 17/12r) and wove on a wage contract (CR 19/21r, 24r).

[28] CR 21/32r.

[29] CR 24/37r.

[30] CR 23/30r.

[31] CR 26/57d; CR 31/10r.

pair in 1382.[32] These sums were well within a weaver's reach, particularly when credit was available.

Completed cloths were first washed and then fulled by machinery. The growth of clothmaking in Colchester was accompanied by the redeployment of milling facilities from grain milling to fulling, and the conversion of redundant water mills to the purpose of clothmaking occurred in the countryside as well.[33] Within the liberty of Colchester the course of change is imperfectly recorded, but it is more in evidence after 1349 than before. Stokes Mill stopped milling grain sometime after 1312,[34] but in 1356 it was leased as a fulling mill.[35] North Mill and Middle Mill, both abandoned as grain mills about the time of the Black Death, were converted for fulling soon afterwards; Middle Mill was in the hands of a fuller by 1360,[36] and North Mill was probably similarly converted by 1359, though there is no unambiguous reference to fulling there before 1380.[37] New Mill, too, was converted for fulling by 1405, and probably soon after the summer of 1383.[38] These modifications to water mills were not irreversible, for later in the century Stokes Mill temporarily served again as a grain mill, and Middle Mill ground grain again in the early fifteenth century.[39] From the 1350s, however, there was always some mechanical fulling in Colchester.

The fulling mills of the fourteenth and early fifteenth centuries stood on the banks of the Colne to the north of the town centre; North Mill, Middle Mill, Stokes Mill and probably New Mill all stood within three-quarters of a mile downstream of North Bridge, and the river banks and mill races of this stretch of river could be seen hanging day and night with new cloths put out to wash and dry.[40] Supervision was haphazard, and from time to time cloths were stolen or damaged.[41] Fullers who did not themselves lease mills paid a charge called millhire in order to have access to milling facilities; in 1385 a fuller was sued for 3s 4d which he was alleged to owe 'for melleher' due from fulling 100 ells and two *decene* of cloth'.[42] Between Michaelmas 1385 and Michaelmas 1386 Henry Snow took 502 *decene* of cloth to John Sebern the elder at North Mill on the understanding that

---

[32] CR 22/5d, 7r.

[33] W.A.M., 25677r, 25682r.   [34] See Chapter 1, pp. 20–1.

[35] In 1356 Stokes Mill was leased by John Trige (CR 11/2d, 3r) who was connected with the cloth industry rather than with grain milling (*e.g.* CR 11/6r).

[36] See Chapter 1, p. 22n. Middle Mill in 1360 was in the hands of Thomas Clerk the fuller (CR 12/12d) and John Byrch: CR 12/7r.

[37] In 1359 the servant of Hugh Love the fuller (CR 18/21r) claimed to have been assaulted at North Mill: CR 12/4r. Use of North Mill for fulling in 1380 is shown in CR 20/21r and implied in CR 20/11r.

[38] CR 35/6d, 16r. No miller of New Mill was reported for taking excessive toll after Hocktide 1383: CR 22/35d.

[39] See Chapters 6 and 8, pp. 88, 198.

[40] CR 26/51r; CR 35/6d, 16r.

[41] *E.g.* CR 35/7r.   [42] CR 25/7d.

he would settle up at the latter date.[43] Types of cloth handled at the mills may be known only from disputes in which the details were recorded, but such instances often have to do with russet. Richard Hykeman, for example, alleged that his former servant, John de Eyk, had damaged a *decena* of grey russet in 1401 when he was supposed to have taken it to be fulled at North Mill.[44] Presumably the development of mechanical fulling in the liberty helped to keep down costs of production after the Black Death and thereby improved the competitive edge of Colchester manufactures. At the very least the distances travelled by fullers were appreciably reduced, and it is possible that the availability of local mills hastened the transition away from more laborious methods of fulling.

Sources of entrepreneurship in the 1370s and 1380s cannot be narrowly defined. Many urban families were dabbling in the cloth trade, employing craftsmen to work up materials in the hope of a profit on the final product.[45] However, fullers were more likely than any other group to be earning large trading profits. Some put out wool to be dyed and yarn to be woven, and so co-ordinated the whole process of manufacture from the start.[46] More characteristically, however, they would accept unfinished cloth to full and sell, later paying the weaver his due.[47] Their hand was strengthened by a by-law prohibiting the sale of unfulled cloth to buyers who were not burgesses of Colchester.[48] Leading Colchester fullers also bought and sold cloth which had been fulled already.[49] These features of the fullers' stake in the cloth trade, which became more pronounced towards the end of the century, did not amount to a very advanced degree of capitalist organisation. Fullers were craftsmen as well as traders, and though some of the time they finished cloth on their own account, they also worked on contract, often for minor producers.[50]

In view of the loose pattern of industrial organisation, it is implausible to ascribe the growth of Colchester's cloth industry in the later fourteenth century to the entrepreneurial abilities of a new class of merchant clothmakers. The typically small units of mercantile organisation in the borough would in any case present some awkward obstacles to such an argument. To judge from the independence of action enjoyed by individual craftsmen, the increased manufacture of textiles should be regarded as a response to new opportunities by small producers who made their

---

[43] CR 26/26d, 40d.   [44] CR 32/24r.

[45] *E.g.* John Barbour, skinner, was prosecuted for a debt incurred in having cloth fulled: CR 18/10d.

[46] *E.g.* John Lyard, fuller (CR 19/10r), occurs doing both in 1377: CR 18/8r, 10d.

[47] *E.g.* CR 29/9d; CR 31/4d, 8d, 27d; CR 32/6d.

[48] CR 9/6r; CR 15/6d; CR 19/19r.

[49] *E.g.* John Lyard (CR 18/13d, 22d; CR 19/18r) and Hugh Love (CR 18/11d).

[50] As in the case of Hugh Love: CR 18/21r; CR 24/51r.

Table 5.1 *Distribution of cloth sales between men paying subsidy and ulnage in Colchester, 30.xi.1395–29.ix.1397*

Number of *decene* sold	Number of sellers	Share of total sales %
10 or fewer	83	9.2
10½ to 20	39	13.2
20½ to 30	23	12.9
30½ to 40	14	11.0
40½ to 50	9	9.4
50½ to 60	5	6.1
60½ to 70	6	9.1
70½ to 80	2	3.6
80½ to 90	4	8.0
90½ to 100	0	0.0
100½ or more	4	17.6
	189	(100.0)

Source: P.R.O., E.101/342/9, mm. 8r–10r, 11r.

decisions within a spectrum of choice determined by the commercial enterprise of similarly small merchant enterprises. By the standards of contemporary Flanders such industrial relations were primeval.[51] Though this is well demonstrated by the details of organisation which have already been given, it may be substantiated even better from evidence of the 1390s. The customs accounts of the port of Ipswich between 25 February 1397 and 25 April 1398, which distinguished exports through Colchester from those through Ipswich, may be compared with the ulnage accounts for Colchester from 30 November 1395 to Michaelmas 1397.[52] Ulnage had to be paid on cloths which were to be exported whether they changed hands in England or not.[53] From the customs accounts it is evident who were cloth exporters, and from the ulnage accounts may be learned the names of cloth sellers. During the 95 weeks of the ulnage accounts, only 380 of the 4,330 *decene* sealed in Colchester (that is 8.8 per cent of the total) were sold by merchants who exported cloth through Colchester.[54] Most of those

[51] Coornaert, 'Draperies rurales, draperies urbaines', p. 68.
[52] P.R.O., E.101/342/9; E.122/193/33. [53] *Cal. Fine R.*, xi, p. 122.
[54] Total sales were 6 *panni integri* (counted as two each), 4,199 *decene panni de assiso* (counted as one each) and 238 *decene panni stricti* (counted as ½ each): P.R.O., E.101/342/9, mm. 8r–10r, 11r. The first 56 entries on m. 11r are repeated from m. 10r. Such repetition is uncharacteristic of these accounts, so I have interpreted it as a copyist's error and have excluded these entries from the total. They amount to 280 *decene panni de assiso*.

listed in the ulnage accounts had no recorded share in the export trade; of the 189 men who paid subsidy and ulnage on cloth in this period only 10 were exporters of cloth through the port. Many of those listed in the ulnage accounts sold little; six of them sold only one cloth each. The distribution of sales between sellers is shown in Table 5.1, which demonstrates the extent to which clothmaking remained in the hands of small entrepreneurs during the years of Colchester's most rapid growth.

III

Colchester stood on the edge of a larger clothmaking region lying partly in Essex and partly in Suffolk, with Colchester, Braintree, Bury St Edmunds, Hadleigh and Ipswich on its perimeter.[55] Something of the development of the region as a whole, and of Colchester's relative importance within it, is to be discovered in records relating to the collection of the king's subsidy on cloths sold. The earliest accounts, those for 1353–61,[56] may be compared with those between July 1394 and October 1397.[57] During both these periods the subsidy was collected by royal servants who accounted at the Exchequer, rather than leased for fixed payments.[58] The briefest analysis of these records establishes that at neither period was there any standardised system of collecting the subsidy or accounting for it, and that the figures recorded must understate the total number of cloth sales. There was no fixed list of places where the subsidy was collected even at the end of the 1390s.[59] The quality of this source is accordingly low. But where single markets can be identified for both periods some credence may be given to the evidence for increased marketing of cloths between the 1350s and the 1390s. The 85 cloths sold in Coggeshall during a twelve-month period in 1355–6, and the 75 cloths sold in Bradwell and Braintree during an eleven-month period in 1360–1,[60] may be compared with the proportionally higher figures recorded in Table 5.2 for a sixteen-month period in 1394–5. Colchester has no separate figure from the 1350s, when it paid subsidy together with the other ports of

[55] H. L. Gray, 'The Production and Exportation of English Woollens in the Fourteenth Century', *E.H.R.*, xxxix (1924), p. 31; E. M. Carus-Wilson, 'The Woollen Industry', in M. M. Postan and E. E. Rich, eds., *The Cambridge Economic History of Europe, ii: Trade and Industry in the Middle Ages* (Cambridge, 1952), pp. 418–19.

[56] P.R.O., E.356/7, mm. 1r–5d.

[57] P.R.O., E.101/342/9.

[58] For leases between 1382 and 1394, see *Cal. Close R., 1381–5*, pp. 225–6; *Cal. Close R., 1385–9*, pp. 252, 426; *Cal. Close R., 1389–92*, p. 292. For a clear statement of the abandonment of leases in 1394, see *Cal. Pat. R., 1391–6*, p. 514. Details of collectors appointed in the July of that year are in *Cal. Fine R.*, xi, pp. 122–4, and later appointments are on pp. 166, 193, 231. The subsequent return to a system of leases is indicated on pp. 255, 301.

[59] P.R.O., E.101/342/9, 13.   [60] P.R.O., E.356/7, mm. 4r, 5d.

Table 5.2 *Cloths paying subsidy and ulnage in Essex markets, 20 July 1394–30 November 1395*

	Cloths of assize without grain
Colchester	849¾
Braintree	631
Coggeshall	361½
Dedham	190¾
Maldon	185¾
Chelmsford	181¾

Source: P.R.O., E.101/342/9, mm. 1r–5d.

Norfolk, Suffolk and Essex, but between Michaelmas 1354 and Michaelmas 1358 all these ports together averaged only 587 cloths a year.[61]

The growth of Colchester's trade encouraged the development of the cloth fairs there. In the 1350s and 1360s, when they were only informally organised, they were held on 20 and 21 June and again on 18 and 19 July in the market place to the west of St Runwald's church. No market rents accrued to the community on these occasions because trading took place in cellars, in the nooks between houses, in gateways, in private houses and from private stalls. In 1374 the fairs were reformed at the instance of William Reyne, one of the bailiffs. Trading was reorganised to take place in the moothall and its entrance and on booths erected opposite the moothall and southwards from it, stretching from the west end of St Runwald's church as far as the corn market at the top of the high street. These booths, to be maintained at the community's expense, were to yield rents to the common chest. The fairs were retimed to be held on 22, 23 and 24 June and again on 20, 21 and 22 July, the object of this second change being apparently to bring the fairs closer to the feasts of St John the Baptist (24 June) and St Mary Magdalen (22 July) with which they were associated. That the duration of the fair was in each case extended indicates that these reforms were partly inspired by the growth of trading at fair time. The new regulations of 1374 demonstrate that merchants from outside Colchester were bringing cloth to sell there; burgesses were sternly prohibited from allowing outsiders to make use of private houses as outlets through which to sell their cloth, and none might allow an outsider to share the use of his booth or to sublet it. Measures were also taken to regulate trade in cloth on market days throughout the year by confining transactions

[61] P.R.O., E.356/7, mm. 1r,d, 2r,d.

to the moothall, and the terms of these provisions imply that clothiers from the county came into Colchester to sell cloth outside fair times.[62]

The figures in Table 5.2 suggest that in 1394–5 Colchester had established itself as the leading cloth market in Essex. This was not a freak year; the account of subsidy and ulnage collected on cloth sales in 1398–9, though it does not cover the period of Colchester's cloth fairs, shows a level of sales higher than that in the borough's closest rivals, Braintree and Dedham, put together.[63] There is unfortunately no corresponding evidence from Suffolk of the numbers of cloths paying subsidy in individual towns. The total annual number of cloths sold in Suffolk was slightly larger than that from Essex,[64] but the trade was more scattered between the various centres of manufacture. Colchester may already have been in the 1390s, as it was in the 1460s, the largest single cloth market in the Essex and Suffolk textile region.[65] If it had a rival, that must have been Hadleigh, whose dynamic importance in the development of Suffolk industry during the later fourteenth century is evident from Colchester's own records.

An analysis of litigation for debt in Colchester courts between 1390 and 1410 suggests that the borough did not trade regularly with many places outside its immediate vicinity. But Hadleigh and London, each with 31 recorded litigants, were outstanding in this respect. These two towns, for different reasons, were the principal partners in Colchester's internal trade. Hadleigh's lead amongst the Suffolk towns was followed at some distance by Sudbury, with twelve litigants, Boxford with seven, Clare and Long Melford with five each. Lavenham, with only one litigant, had yet to make its mark.[66] The development of these contacts between Colchester and the Suffolk cloth towns, Hadleigh in particular, did not follow a simple pattern of complementarities. To some extent the links were those between a port and its hinterland, but this pattern was greatly weakened by the Suffolk clothmakers' trade through Ipswich and by their direct contacts with London. Trade was encouraged by differences between the cloths of the different towns; those from Suffolk were characteristically more colourful than Colchester's own, with blues and reds in the forefront. Mercantile enterprise, in response to local, sometimes temporary, needs, also maintained a frequent interchange of grain, wool and dyestuffs between the various centres of manufacture. Some examples of contacts between Hadleigh and Colchester illustrate these complexities. In 1374 Thomas Lane bought barley in Kersey from a Hadleigh merchant.[67] Stephen Smyth

[62] RPB, fo. 8r,v.
[63] P.R.O., E.101/342/13.
[64] P.R.O., E.101/342/8, 10.
[65] See Chapter 12, pp. 188–9.
[66] CR 27–37.
[67] CR 18/14d.

of Hadleigh bought wool in Colchester from a servant of John Beneyt of
Ramsey in 1398.[68] John Coleman of Hadleigh was in Colchester in 1401
to sell coverlets, linen sheets and sailcloth.[69] In 1403 Thomas Hosyere of
Colchester was in Hadleigh buying red, green and black straits.[70] Too few
transactions are recorded in detail for any closer analysis of the composition of trade on this route, but these instances suggest that it was very
miscellaneous.

Details from the records of these different cloth towns make it possible
to assess some of the variations in their fortunes during the later fourteenth
century, and so to gauge the relative strength of Colchester's performance.
Hadleigh is the only major Suffolk textile centre for which a poll tax
assessment has survived. In 1377 it was a town about a quarter of the size
of Colchester, to judge from the 705 names listed, and at least one tenth
of the population was directly dependent upon the cloth industry. In recent
decades the number of small plots let to tenants had increased and the
manorial rent roll had greatly expanded with the growth of employment
there.[71] Hadleigh merchants were outstanding for the range of their
commerce, and probably handled fabrics from other clothmaking villages.
They dealt directly with Londoners, occasionally using Colchester as a
meeting point for the fulfilling of contracts or the settlement of debts;[72]
some of the cloths which reached London through their agency may have
been included amongst the so-called Essex cloths sent to Italy.[73] The
growth of trade around Hadleigh during the later fourteenth century may
also be illustrated by a manorial account of Kersey in 1398/9 which shows
how valuable the market place there had become. The rental refers to a
drapers' market and a cloth hall as well as markets for spicers, linendrapers,
shoemakers and tanners, and besides £7 10s 7d of old stallage rents there
was 13s 6d from newly leased plots.[74] Kersey had few direct trading links
with Colchester, probably because its manufactures were handled by
Hadleigh clothiers.

Hadleigh's reputation for prosperity as early as 1372 is suggested by an
anecdote from the Red Paper Book.[75] In that year, following the naval
disaster at La Rochelle inflicted by the Castilians on 23 June, Edward III

---

[68] CR 31/5d.   [69] CR 32/21d.   [70] CR 33/10d.
[71] E. Powell, *The Rising in East Anglia in 1381* (Cambridge, 1896), pp. 111–14; G. Unwin,
    Studies in Economic History, ed. R. H. Tawney (London, 1927), p. 264; M. Mate,
    'Agrarian Economy after the Black Death: The Manors of Canterbury Cathedral Priory,
    1348–91', *Ec.H.R.*, 2nd ser., xxxvii (1984), p. 351.
[72] James, *Studies in the Medieval Wine Trade*, pp. 202, 204–6; Guildhall Library Muniments,
    Recognisance Roll 12, mm. 2r, 11r, 12r; CR 32/23r, 24r.
[73] Coloured straits were traded by the Datini companies as *panni di Sex: Documenti per
    la storia economica*, ed. Melis, no. 88, p. 308.
[74] P.R.O., S.C.6/1001/3r.   [75] RPB, fo. 5r,v.

ordered several cities and boroughs to supply barges for the defence of the coast,[76] and made Colchester and Ipswich jointly responsible for making one barge at their own expense. The two town councils, considering the expense of fulfilling this obligation, and the undeserved good fortune of their neighbours who had escaped it, conferred together and decided to approach the king's council for an amendment of the order. Richard Haverland[77] was to report to the council on their behalf how they had been impoverished since the beginning of the king's war, so that they had not the resources to build a barge without help, and he was to raise the question whether Hadleigh ought not be be made jointly liable with Colchester and Ipswich. Haverland's diplomacy was successful; in order to hasten the building of the barge the king issued instructions to the bailiffs and community of Hadleigh that they should assess the town to make a contribution.[78]

By contrast with Hadleigh and Kersey the Stour valley clothmaking towns, Clare and Sudbury, had known little economic development since the Black Death, and this may in part account for the prominence of Sudbury as a source of discontent in 1381.[79] Here, as a previous chapter has shown, the cloth industry was already well established before the middle of the fourteenth century. Thereafter a seigneurial tax on looms in Sudbury continued to be levied until 1405, and the figures are shown in Table 5.3. There are obvious weaknesses in the figures as a reliable guide to the fortunes of the cloth industry. The sharp drop between 1371 and 1372 in the number of looms taxed suggests an institutional change of some sort rather than an economic one. Furthermore, the unconvincing fluctuations of the years 1396–1405, and more particularly the auditor's correction of the figure for 1398, imply that the level of taxation was a matter in dispute between lord and tenants. Nonetheless, the figures for 1398 and 1401 are founded on real counts; in the latter year the names of those paying tax are listed for the first time on record, and some of these occur as sellers of cloth in the Suffolk ulnage account of 1396–7.[80] This implies that the cloth industry here was at its peak in the later 1350s and was slightly smaller at the end of the century. That this is not implausible is shown by other economic indices in the court rolls. The number of bakers amerced in Sudbury for breaking the assize of bread never exceeded those in October 1347 or May 1348, and declined further in the last quarter of

---

[76] J. W. Sherborne, 'The Battle of La Rochelle and the War at Sea, 1372–5', *Bulletin of the Institute of Historical Research*, xlii (1969), p. 25.

[77] Haverland was a member for Ipswich in the parliament of October 1372: *Return of Names*, p. 189.

[78] *Cal. Pat. R., 1370–4*, p. 219.

[79] *The Peasants' Revolt of 1381*, ed. R. B. Dobson (London, 1970), no. 39, pp. 248–54.

[80] P.R.O., S.C.2/204/13, m. 2d; E.101/342/10r.

Table 5.3 *Number of looms taxed in Sudbury, 1340–1405*

Date	Magne lame	Parue lame	Source
(Nov.) 1340	23	6	S.C.6/1006/12r
(Nov.) 1342	23	9	S.C.6/1006/13r
(Nov.) 1345	20	12	S.C.6/1006/14r
(Nov.) 1346	20	12	S.C.6/1006/15r
30.xi.1348	20	12	S.C.6/1006/16r
30.xi.1350	20	12	S.C.6/1006/17r
30.xi.1352	22	9	S.C.6/1006/18r
30.xi.1355	21[a]	7[b]	S.C.6/1006/19r
17.x.1356	25	11	S.C.2/204/4, m. 5r
20.xi.1357	24	12	S.C.2/204/4, m. 8d
23.xii.1358	30	5	S.C.2/204/4, m. 10r
18.i.1361	25	5	S.C.2/204/5, m. 1d
30.xi.1361	25	4	S.C.6/1006/21r
17.iv.1363	30	3	S.C.2/204/5, m. 10r
8.iv.1364	31	2	S.C.2/204/5, m. 14r
24.xii.1366	27	3	S.C.2/204/6, m. 1r
17.xii.1369	20	2	S.C.2/204/6, m. 3d
1.xii.1371	30	1	S.C.2/204/6, m. 5r
13.xii.1372	12	1	S.C.2/204/6, m. 8r
18.xii.1374	18	2	S.C.2/204/7, m. 1r
11.xii.1375	12	2	S.C.2/204/7, m. 4d
4.i.1378	12	2	S.C.2/204/10, m. 1d
25.xii.1378	13	2	S.C.6/1006/24r
28.xi.1379	14	2	S.C.2/204/10, m. 5r
15.xii.1382	10	3	S.C.2/204/10, m. 12r
7.xii.1383	10	3	S.C.2/204/10, m. 13d
(Dec.) 1385	12	2	S.C.6/1006/10r
7.xii.1388	12	2	S.C.2/204/11, m. 1d
3.xii.1391	12	2	S.C.2/204/11, m. 4r
2.xii.1396	12	2	S.C.2/204/12, m. 1d
25.xii.1398	27[c]	6[d]	S.C.6/1006/26r
25.xii.1400	22	4	S.C.6/1006/27r
12.ix.1401	22	4	S.C.2/204/13, m. 2d
c. 15.vi.1405	12	2	S.C.2/204/13, m. 4d

[a] Changed from 10.　　　　　　　　[b] Changed from 5.
[c] Changed from 12.　　　　　　　　[d] Changed from 2.

the century to a level below that of the third quarter. The number of brewers who broke the assize of ale never exceeded those of the years 1346–8, and shows a marked contraction from about the time of the Peasants' Revolt. The numbers of butchers amerced for failure to keep their assize remained fairly stable through the fourteenth century; the largest count on record is from 1359. In this instance the figures for 1347 and 1348 were occasionally exceeded in the later fourteenth century, but never by more than one fifth. The court roll evidence of Sudbury suggests that the town never regained the population it had had in the 1340s and that the textile industry barely maintained the level it had enjoyed then.[81]

Clare borough records contain no details of clothmaking to compare with the tax on looms at Sudbury, but the industry there was small and failed to expand during the later fourteenth century above the level it had attained before the Black Death. Between 1358 and 1377 dyers were annually amerced at the court leet in April for throwing waste into the streets. Three dyers were so amerced in 1358, and thereafter the number was invariably two or three but never more.[82] This amercement was not made in the court of 3 April 1380 or subsequently. Other evidence from Clare suggests that the borough economy developed little if at all in the later fourteenth century. All through the third quarter of the century the number of brewers amerced in the leet court remained below the level of the 1340s. After that some rather higher figures are recorded, which suggest that the brewing of ale may have been at a peak in the period *c.* 1378–90, but the differences do not amount to any conclusive evidence for a higher output than that of the 1340s. The number of bakers amerced shows no sustained increase during these 50 years. By the standards of the age this was a good record, and suggests that the economy of Clare was resilient in the face of the disasters of 1349 and 1362. On the other hand, there is nothing here to suggest much in the way of industrial growth.[83]

The combined evidence of continuing industrial growth in Colchester into the second decade of the fifteenth century, the local prominence of the cloth trade there in the 1390s and the poorer performance of some other textile towns in the area suggests that between the early 1350s and about 1414 the town was a major centre of development in the local economy, and not simply a participant on the margin of more rapid developments. Evidently the concept of industrial development as a regional phenomenon needs to be handled with some care. Most villages within the clothmaking region of Essex and Suffolk had no cloth industry worth mentioning. Amongst those that did, not all were enjoying industrial growth. And the cloth industries of Colchester and Hadleigh on the periphery were performing better than that of Sudbury and Clare at the centre.

[81] P.R.O., S.C.2/204/3–7, 10–13.
[82] P.R.O., S.C.2/203/52, m. 4r; S.C.2/203/55–61.
[83] P.R.O., S.C.2/203/43–65.

6

Population

Industrial development implied improving prospects for industrial employment. The effect upon total urban employment depended upon what was happening elsewhere in the economy, and it would be rash to make assumptions about the outcome. But amongst the regular reports of lawhundred juries which at first sight repeat themselves monotonously from term to term there is information of considerable interest for this aspect of Colchester's economic development in the late Middle Ages, implying that the consumption of foodstuffs in the town increased for over 50 years after the Black Death and that the number of inhabitants was growing. This is not the sort of evidence that can be used to calculate levels of income or production; the figures relate to burgesses reported for trading offences rather than to the measured output of goods and services. However, with a certain amount of interpretation the evidence is both free from serious ambiguity and consistent with other facets of the borough's economic history. The most valuable part of this material relates to the food and drink trades, which were subject to exceptionally close supervision at the lawhundreds.

The first set of details to be examined concerns millers, whose profession was well known for its proclivity towards sharp practice. Mill toll ought to have been taken at the rate of one grain in 24,[1] but millers notoriously took more than they were entitled to.[2] At every lawhundred a list of the mills where the miller had broken the rules was presented by the jury, and few mills in operation could be expected to run for more than a year or two without appearing in these lists. Lawhundred reports accordingly indicate the changing number of corn mills in the period of economic recovery. During the 1350s and 1360s, when only five mills were in

---

[1] OB, fo. 176r; CR 22/4d. *Cf.* Statutum de Pistoribus, etc.: *Statutes*, i, p. 203.

[2] H. S. Bennett, *Life on the English Manor: A Study of Peasant Conditions, 1150–1400* (Cambridge, 1937), p. 135.

operation,[3] restrictive trade practices were a mounting problem as the demand for milling services increased. The community was drawn into new areas of economic regulation to prevent this from happening. In November 1359 six bakers and four millers were fined for conspiring that all the bakers' wheat should be ground before that of anyone else, which had meant that for some time townsmen had been unable to get their grain milled.[4] This method of checking millers was undermined, however, by the community's continuing tolerance of bakers who themselves leased mills. At the Hilary lawhundred of 1360, for example, Thomas Deynes the baker was amerced for taking excessive toll at Bourne Mill.[5] Sometime during the years that followed the community closed this loophole by ordaining that in future no Colchester baker might lease a mill or any part of a mill, and in 1374 a baker was accordingly amerced for having taken part share in the lease of Bourne Mill.[6] This, then, was a feature of the smaller ring of millers and bakers supplying Colchester in the decades after the Black Death.

Then, in the late 1360s, there began a recovery of investment in corn mills. The Hocktide lawhundred of 1367 amerced the millers of the five mills which had been employed over the previous 20 years. At the Michaelmas lawhundred of 1372 these mills were listed again, now joined by three new mills belonging to William Reyne, John atte Ford and Henry Bosse.[7] Whereas the older mills were all owned by manorial lords, even if these lords had not set them up in the first place,[8] the three new mills had all been constructed by leading merchants of the borough. There was excessive optimism here, since one of the new mills does not occur again after the Hocktide lawhundred of 1373, and was presumably not a success.[9] But with seven mills in operation the town was back at least to the number it had had before the Black Death. Because water power in the borough was now being used for the cloth industry as well, expansion of corn milling could no longer be accommodated on the banks of the Colne. Both the new mills successfully established were windmills, probably situated to the south of the town near the abbey, which is where Colchester's windmills

---

[3] East Mill, New Mill, Bourne Mill, Eld Mill, Lexden Mill: CR 10/1d, 5d; CR 11/1d, 5d, 9d; CR 12/1r, 7r, 11d; CR 13/8d; CR 14/1r, 8d; CR 15/1r, 6d, 12r.

[4] CR 12/3d.

[5] CR 12/7r.

[6] CR 17/1d.

[7] CR 15/12r; CR 16/1d.

[8] East Mill, New Mill and Eld Mill belonged to St Botolph's Priory; Stokes Mill and Bourne Mill belonged to the abbey: CR 2/2r. Lexden Mill belonged to the lord of Lexden manor: P.R.O., C.134/31/3.

[9] William Reyne acquired John atte Ford's mill in 1372 and so possessed two mills (CR 16/6d, 11d) but one of these does not occur again.

were to be found in the eighteenth century.[10] New Mill went over to the cloth trade after 1383, but for a few years its place was taken by Stokes Mill, which had not been grinding corn since the early years of the century.[11] Another mill, known as the Mill in the Wood, began to operate about 1386, so that there were still seven corn mills normally at work during the late 1380s.[12]

An episode in 1392 shows how much the power resources of the town were under pressure in the late fourteenth century. At the Hilary lawhundred of that year the jury reports listed two horse mills grinding corn in the liberty, and three such horse mills were reported at the Hocktide lawhundred.[13] Another mill called John Bird's mill occurs in 1392 for the first and last time.[14] Probably as many as 11 corn mills were functioning that year. The implied increase in milling capacity suggests that demand for foodstuffs in the town was growing. The occurrence of horse mills is further evidence of constraints on development along traditional lines. After 1392, all three horse mills disappear from the record, along with John Bird's mill, never to return. They were probably all small and temporary affairs whose profitability was never established, or whose usefulness was diminished by some expansion of capacity at one of the larger mills. During the later 1390s there were seven mills in active employment.[15] After Michaelmas 1399 one of these, Eld Mill, disappeared from the lawhundred lists, but its place was taken by Canwick Mill, which re-entered the picture in about 1404[16] and remained a corn mill for many years. A new Middle Mill was built for the purpose of corn milling about 1406,[17] so that there were eight active mills towards the end of this decade.[18]

Even in isolation the history of milling in Colchester suggests that demand for foodstuffs there had grown, at least from the late 1360s. This evidence is reinforced by that of the brewing industry, again derived from

10 Morant, *Colchester*, i, map opposite p. 4. These were not Colchester's earliest windmills; there was a disused mill mount in Munkesdoune in 1325: LB, fos. 60v–62r.

11 CR 22/4d, 22d, 35d; CR 23/37r. Stokes Mill no longer occurs after the Hilary lawhundred of 1388: CR 26/28r. It was rebuilt by Thomas Godeston for fulling about 1402: *Cal. Pat. R., 1429–36*, pp. 205, 333.

12 East Mill, Bourne Mill, Eld Mill, Lexden Mill, the mills of Henry Bosse and William Reyne, the Mill in the Wood: CR 23/37r; CR 24/2r, 19d, 35d; CR 25/1d, 23d, 42d; CR 26/1d, 28r, 46d. The Mill in the Wood, called 'new' in 1386, stood south of Hythe Hill at the end of Cattelane: RPB, fo. 58r.

13 CR 27/14d, 28d.

14 CR 27/14d, 28d; CR 28/1r.

15 East Mill, Bourne Mill, Lexden Mill, Eld Mill, the Mill in the Wood, William Reyne's mill (from 1395 called Simon Fordham's), Henry Bosse's mill: CR 28/17r, 28r; CR 29/1d, 12r, 20r; CR 30/1r, 10r, 16r; CR 31/2r, 11r, 18r. The first four were water mills, the last three windmills.

16 CR 33/13r.   17 CR 35/26d; CR 37/14r.

18 East Mill, Bourne Mill, Lexden Mill, the Mill in the Wood, Marjory Fordham's windmill, Henry Bosse's windmill, Canwick Mill, Middle Mill: CR 36/3r, 11d, 21d; CR 37/3r.

the reports of lawhundred juries. At every lawhundred the jury presented a list of names of all who had brewed and sold ale against the assize. This had nothing to do with the measures by which ale was sold; the use of irregular measures was a separate matter, more severely dealt with by the court.[19] The assize of ale had two components. First, as in the case of the assize of bread, the price of ale was statutorily tied to the price of grain (in this case malt), so that when a quarter of malt sold for 2s 0d a gallon of ale sold for two farthings, and the price of ale could rise by a farthing a gallon for each subsequent rise of 1s 0d a quarter in the price of malt.[20] Secondly, there was supposed to be a public check on the quality of ale. The brewer was required to call a public aletaster to sample each brew before putting it up for sale.[21] In practice no attempt was made in Colchester to enforce the law. The records contain no references to public aletasters and there were no borough officers to enforce this part of the assize. Even the monitoring of ale prices was apparently treated as a matter not to be interfered with; lawhundred jury reports never comment on what prices should have been or on what prices had been actually charged. It was deemed simpler to fine all ale brewers a small and unpunitive sum which could formally be regarded as a punishment for breaking the assize though in effect it was a tax on brewing. The preparation of a list of brewers was delegated to a small number of assessors, whose own fine for breach of the assize was condoned. The lists were compiled ward by ward, and the level of amercement was noted by each name. As a rule the charge was 3d at each lawhundred, but some brewers were amerced 6d or even 1s 0d, presumably because they sold more than the rest. The amercement of brewers was demonstrably treated as a source of income for the community and implied no criticism of those amerced.[22] Besides the absence of aletasters and the repeated amercement of the same women at a low standard rate, it may also be observed that the wives of the town's most respected men were regularly included in the lists. Brewing for sale was an activity which engaged the wealthiest burgesses' households. In 1377 it was observed that, in spite of statutory provisions to prevent it, Colchester bailiffs were retailing wine and ale during their term of office, and measures were taken to ensure that the law was respected.[23] The brewers amerced at the Hilary lawhundred of that year[24] include the wives

[19] *E.g.* CR 10/1r; CR 12/11d.

[20] RPB, fo. 16v; Assisa Panis et Cervisie, and Statutum de Pistoribus, etc.: *Statutes*, i, pp. 200, 203.

[21] R. H. Hilton, 'Lords, Burgesses and Hucksters', *Past and Present*, xcvii (1982), p. 14; RPB, fo. 16v.

[22] R. H. Hilton, *The English Peasantry in the Later Middle Ages* (Oxford, 1975), pp. 45, 104.

[23] RPB, fo. 11r. For the statutory provisions in question, see 25 Edward III, 3, c. 2: *Statutes*, i, p. 315.   [24] CR 18/9d.

of George Fordham (bailiff in 1362/3), John Lucas (bailiff in 1370/1 and 1371/2), John Keek (M.P. for Colchester in 1369, bailiff in 1368/9 and 1377/8), Simon Fordham (M.P. for Colchester at least six times between 1373 and 1388; bailiff in 1382/3 and later), Thomas Fraunceys (M.P. for Colchester at least 11 times between 1372 and 1399; bailiff in 1381/2 and later) and Thomas Clerk (bailiff in 1381/2 and later).[25] An offence of which so many estimable women were guilty cannot have carried any social stigma.

The community could afford to neglect the monitoring of ale prices and quality because of the size of the industry and its particular organisation. So many households brewed for sale that there was no possibility of brewers colluding to fix prices or quality. The market mechanism in practice provided some guarantee that prices would be only so high as to recompense brewers for their material costs and their time and trouble. Brewing was the responsibility of women and required only the resources of a household kitchen, except in a few rare instances. Seldom can brewing have been the mainstay of a family's income,[26] though it might have had more importance for some single women. In all these respects the statistics for brewing make a better economic indicator than the figures of millers amerced. The proportion of the market which any one brewer could command was always small. A variation in the number of alewives suggests more about changes in output than a change in the number of millers amerced, both because of the tax-like character of the amercement and because the average brewer's output was unlikely to vary very much.[27]

To gauge the number of brewers it is necessary simply to count the number presented at each lawhundred whose records are in a fit state. Figure 6.1 shows how markedly the number grew during the later fourteenth century. After the Black Death there was recovery during the 1350s to a level of activity which surpassed that of the 1340s, and thereafter the number rose to even higher levels. There was average annual growth of 1.8 per cent a year between 1358 and 1406, but this growth was not even. There were setbacks in the late 1350s (*c.* 1357–61) and in the 1390s (*c.* 1392–8). The main periods of expansion were the earlier 1350s (*c.* 1351–6), the later 1370s (*c.* 1375–80) and about the turn of the century (*c.* 1398–1405). By 1405 the number of alewives brewing for sale was well over twice the number brewing in the decades before the Black Death.

The only other drink subject to assizes in the fourteenth century was wine. This was a very different trade from that in ale since the quantity

[25] OB, fos. 46v–57r; *Return of Names*, pp. 182–258.
[26] There were a few exceptions; see Chapter 13, p. 196.
[27] For a comparable use and discussion of brewing statistics, see E. B. Dewindt, *Land and People in Holywell-cum-Needingworth* (Toronto, 1971), pp. 235–6.

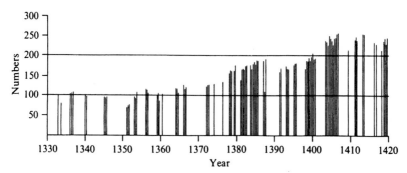

Figure 6.1 Numbers amerced in Colchester for brewing against the assize, 1330–1420

available depended upon overseas trade rather than local production, and the relatively small number of importers meant that there was more danger of collusion between sellers. Outlets for wine by retail were more restricted than those for ale, and were often controlled by the importers, who acquired taverns and put servants in charge of them. Like ale the price of wine was subject to direct regulation, but the community had no locally verifiable standard by which to regulate it. An ordinance of 1316/17 had stipulated that the price of wine in Colchester should be the same as that in the city of London,[28] where the retail price of wine was fixed twice a year by a committee of vintners and other merchants whose combined expertise and impartiality was likely to produce a sounder result than anything Colchester could muster.[29] London prices remained the determinant of Colchester's assized prices throughout the fourteenth century; in 1381 Thomas Clerk broke the assize of wine because he sold it at 2*d* a gallon more than the current London price.[30] A further requirement of vintners was that their measures should be open to scrutiny by their customers, and they were penalised if such scrutiny was made impossible; the usual charge against vintners was that they had sold wine against the assize and retracted their measures. For these offences they were subject to fines larger than those paid by alewives, usually 1*s* 0*d* in the late fourteenth century. However, this higher fine corresponded to the vintners' greater specialisation, and it was perhaps no more punitive than the fines imposed upon brewers.

The number of vintners in Colchester does not give an accurate account of quantities of wine sold because vintners could vary greatly in the extent of their trade. But the increase is so marked during the course of the

[28] RPB, fo. 124r.
[29] Salzman, *English Trade in the Middle Ages*, pp. 386–7.   [30] CR 21/1d.

Table 6.1 *The greatest and smallest number of vintners presented for breach of the assize of wine in a single lawhundred (by decades), 1310–1409*

Decade	Number of documented lawhundreds	Greatest number of vintners	Smallest number of vintners
1310–19	3	6	3
1320–9	1	5	5
1330–9	5	1	0
1340–9	5	3	0
1350–9	9	12	4
1360–9	8	15	4
1370–9	8	13	3
1380–9	18	21	6
1390–9	12	22	8
1400–9	16	20	1

Source: Appendix, Table 2.

fourteenth century that it adds substantially to the case for increasing expenditure upon drink in the town. Table 6.1 shows decade by decade the greatest number of vintners reported to have broken the assize of wine at a single lawhundred, together with the smallest number. The early figures are of dubious relevance because they are based on so small a number of lawhundreds, though it is probably no coincidence that the number drops at the start of the Hundred Years' War.[31] After 1350, however, while the evidence is still very imperfect, the fact that both the greatest number and the smallest number show a tendency to rise means that the evidence for an increasing number of taverns is trustworthy. It is plausible, on this showing, that there were twice as many taverns at the end of the fourteenth century as there had been before the Black Death.

The evidence of the baking trade, like that of the wine trade, defies close interpretation because of the wide variation from year to year in the number of bakers amerced.[32] The number of recorded bakers does, however, drop to a low level in the 1350s and then show evidence of recovery, and the number in 1405/6 was larger than in any earlier year. There is, therefore, even in these figures some support for the interpretation of the late fourteenth century as a period of increasing consumption in Colchester. However, this series of figures differs from the others which have been examined in that even the largest number of bakers recorded after the Black Death showed little advance on that in the earlier

[31] James, *Studies in the Medieval Wine Trade*, p. 15.
[32] Appendix, Table 3.

fourteenth century. It is not likely that there should have been any real difference of experience between the brewing of ale and the baking of bread. Perhaps there was a contraction in the number of occasional bakers or a change in the attitude of the authorities towards them.

These sets of figures from lawhundred presentments, though each of them has its shortcomings as an economic indicator, together add up to a strong argument for increasing urban consumption of food and drink in the later fourteenth century. It is conceivable that their combined testimony might be the result of changes in the reporting or recording of information, but such changes might be expected to have left some trace in the records, either in the form of by-laws or in the wording of the court rolls. Administrative changes might also be expected to have caused sudden, discontinuous changes in the number of presentments. But the best of the available series, that of brewers who broke their assize, has more the continuous and fluctuating character that would be expected from relatively slow economic change. The case for an economic interpretation of the evidence – which is supported by other aspects of Colchester's economic record – is stronger than one based on administrative changes which can neither be defined nor chronologically located.

An increase in total consumption of food and drink in the town, and probably in the liberty as well since Colchester's population was so large a proportion of the whole, is to be explained in part by an increase in the living standards of townsmen. Wage earners stood to gain so much from the labour shortages following the Black Death that the government promptly introduced legislation to control wage increases. Wages rose, nonetheless, even though prices fell. The daily wage of a skilled man in the decade 1400–9 would buy about half as much again as that of such a man in the years 1360–9,[33] and it is to be expected that some of this increased purchasing power would go into drink. The growth of the cloth trade also increased the incomes of groups other than wage earners. Conceivably the whole increase in brewing activity could have been the result of individuals drinking more. It would have taken only a doubling of average consumption between 1360 and 1410 to achieve the recorded increase in activity.

However, industrial development is likely to have meant that the population of Colchester had more opportunity to increase than that of the country as a whole. In this case some of the increased brewing activity of the period would need to be attributed to an increase in the number of drinkers. The poll tax assessment of 1377, which lists inhabitants of Colchester over the age of 14, other than churchmen and beggars, is the

---

[33] Postan, *Essays on Medieval Agriculture*, p. 199, Table 10.2; Brown and Hopkins, *A Perspective of Wages and Prices*, p. 28.

best source of information on the town's population at any time before
the sixteenth century. The list has 1,441 men, 1,475 women and 38 of
unspecified sex.[34] Colchester's archives provide an opportunity to test the
quality of the poll tax list, which cannot be taken on trust,[35] but
unfortunately the tests give no clear result. The poll tax was assessed some
time after the grant of the tax in parliament late in February 1377, and
probably before the death of Edward III on 21 June,[36] and the surviving
list of taxpayers is therefore contemporary with a surviving court roll of
the year 1376/7.[37] However, there are severe deficiencies in the evidence
both because the court roll is incomplete and, more seriously, because both
in the poll tax list and in the borough court records men and women are
very imperfectly identified. In the tax assessment heads of families were
given both their Christian and surnames, but wives, children, lodgers and
servants often were not; John Keek had a wife, not named, and 11 servants
listed as 'vnus, duo, tres...'.[38] This means that, particularly among the
poorer and dependent sectors of the population the tax list gives little scope
for identifying individuals who might occur in the court rolls. Even heads
of households cannot always be identified because of the absence of
addresses in either source; two John Smarts are listed in the poll tax
assessment, and the most that can be said is that John Smart the miller
was probably one of them.[39] In the circumstances an elaborated attempt
to match court roll and poll tax evidence would be too indecisive in its
results to repay the labour involved.

Table 6.2 draws together some of the more readily available evidence.
Lists of various Colchester townsmen and women from the court rolls are
compared with the poll tax list to determine how many of them are named
there. Not surprisingly in most of the different categories there are some
who cannot be identified from the poll tax list. At least 5 per cent of this
is likely to be of no significance. Besides the already mentioned obstacles,
it may be added that some absences from the poll tax list will be explained
by deaths which occurred between the compiling of the court record and
the making of the assessment.[40] Intervening marriages also hamper the
comparison since single women are no longer identifiable when they crop
up in the poll tax list as housewives. It is unlikely that the poll tax list was

---

[34] P.R.O., E.179/107/54. My total is one fewer than that of the assessors
[35] Postan, 'Medieval Agrarian Society in its Prime: England', p. 562.
[36] In describing the account as a record *de eodem subsidio regi concesso anno lj°*, the assessors
imply that there had been no change of monarch. Had Edward III been dead one would
expect at least *regi Edwardo*.
[37] CR 18.   [38] P.R.O., E.179/107/54, m. 9r.
[39] *Ibid.*, mm. 8r, 9r.
[40] A death rate of 44 per thousand each year would account for a loss of 2 per cent over
six months. Moreover, deaths of male householders complicate the identifying of their
widows, who are not identified as such in the assessment list.

Table 6.2 *Names from Colchester court rolls compared with the poll tax assessment of 1377*

	Number identified	%
120 brewers of ale, 19.i.1377	105	88
9 bakers, 13.v.1377	8	89
7 vintners, 19.i.1377	7	100
6 millers, 19.i.1377	6	100
11 common forestallers, 19.i.1377	8	73
9 wanderers by night, 19.i.1377	7	78

Sources: P.R.O., E.179/107/54; CR 18.

as imperfect as the poorest of these results suggests or as good as the best of them. It looks as if the proportion unrecorded was higher in less respectable social groups. Probably the under-representation of the adult population was somewhere between 5 and 20 per cent, implying a total of $3,323 \pm 222$ adults. This is already higher than Rickword's estimate of the total population at the beginning of the century. Children under the age of 14 probably constituted between 35 and 45 per cent of the total population,[41] implying that the town had in all $5,608 \pm 837$ inhabitants.[42] After 1377 the population is likely to have continued to grow for at least 30 years, but there is no census-like material from the early fifteenth century from which the extent of the increase may be measured. Between 1375–7 and 1412–14 brewing activity rose by 91 per cent. Assuming that half of this resulted from rising levels of personal consumption[43] and half from growing numbers, a central estimate for Colchester's population at the latter date would be 8,160. This would suggest that the town may have been over twice as large as it had been before the Black Death.

Ways in which population grew cannot be closely analysed. Natural growth was held down, as it was everywhere in the later fourteenth century, by recurrent periods of high mortality. Colchester was again struck by plague in 1361 – 'the second plague', as it is termed in the Oath Book – and there seems to have been high mortality in 1369, 1375, 1380,

[41] Postan, 'Medieval Agrarian Society in its Prime: England', p. 562. A proportion of 35–40 per cent was normal in early fifteenth-century Tuscany: D. Herlihy and C. Klapisch-Zuber, *Les Toscans et leurs familles* (Paris, 1978), p. 375.
[42] The estimates of Macpherson (4,432), Cutts (4,500) and Russell (4,432) all fall appreciably below the range proposed here: D. Macpherson, *Annals of Commerce, Manufactures, Fisheries and Navigation* (4 vols., London, 1805), i, p. 583; E. L. Cutts, *Colchester* (London, 1897), p. 127; Russell, *British Medieval Population*, p. 142.
[43] Brown and Hopkins, *A Perspective of Wages and Prices*, p. 28.

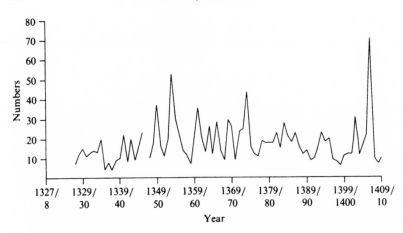

Figure 6.2 Numbers of new burgesses enrolled, 1327/8–1409/10

1384, 1387 and during the four years from autumn 1390 to autumn 1394.[44] None of these later peaks of mortality approached the severity of the earlier crises of 1348–9 and 1361, but they show that Colchester was subject to the same demographic misfortunes which, in the country as a whole, prevented the recovery of population to the level it had attained in the early fourteenth century. It is accordingly likely that the growth of Colchester's population after 1349 is attributable to the beneficial effects of immigration into the town. The importance of immigration is suggested by evidence in the Oath Book concerning the number of new burgesses elected from year to year, which was consistently higher in the later fourteenth century than it had been during the 1330s and 1340s (Figure 6.2).[45] The facts of immigration are imperfectly reflected in these figures, since not all immigrants became burgesses and not all new burgesses were recent immigrants. The fact that the number of new burgesses rose higher after 1350 than before, in spite of recurring epidemics, nevertheless suggests that the level of immigration was also higher, particularly if account is taken of the increasing opportunities at this time for the employment of newcomers as servants and wage earners, who would not have sufficient status to be elected burgesses.

The Oath Book lists permit some comment on the origins of new burgesses during the period after 1383/4, when it became normal to record each new burgess's place of origin.[46] Since it is not clear whether this meant

---

[44] OB, fos. 45r–63v. The years in question are those when the Oath Book registers an exceptionally high number of wills.

[45] The increase is not in itself evidence of population growth: Dobson, 'Admissions to the Freedom of the City of York', pp. 16–18.

[46] OB, fo. 57v.

the new burgess's last place of residence or the place where he was born – or, as is quite possible, sometimes the one and sometimes the other – a close analysis of these details would not be a very profitable exercise. But it is worth observing that of the 295 new burgesses between 1390/1 and 1409/10[47] whose origin is stated only 16 were from large towns – four from London, two from Bristol, one each from Canterbury, Salisbury, Gloucester, Northampton, Ipswich, Great Yarmouth, Norwich, Nottingham, Lincoln and York. A further 42 were from the bigger local market towns of Essex and East Anglia,[48] and 11 more were from substantial market towns in other parts of the country.[49] Even so, this means that over three-quarters of the new burgesses were village people by origin, who had moved to a centre where economic prospects would be better. In most cases immigrants were probably men who had brought with them some skill and some capital relevant to urban life. An occupational survey of newcomers is not possible, but there are enough examples to show that Colchester was recruiting tradesmen from village society. Between 1390/1 and 1409/10 there were weavers from Higham, Copford, Langham, Gestingthorpe, Stisted and from Exning in Suffolk. There was a barber and a peltmonger from Aldham, a carpenter from Maplestead, a smith from Copford, a butcher and a barber from Stoke by Nayland, a plumber from Rainham, a baker from Great Baddow, a tailor from Walton on the Naze, and a fuller from Weeley.

Although Colchester's growth depended upon some migration from neighbouring villages the number from any one village was small. Between 1390/1 and 1409/10 the borough enrolled nine new burgesses from Ardleigh, eight from Wivenhoe, and six from Stoke by Nayland,[50] but even these figures are exceptionally high because of the size and proximity of the villages in question. In very few cases did a village supply more than a couple of burgesses during this period, and even if an allowance is made for immigrants of wage-earning status the picture will not be much altered. It is unlikely that any increase in immigration into Colchester can have greatly affected the size of village populations in the surrounding countryside.

[47] OB, fos. 61v–73v.
[48] These are defined as markets listed in A. Everitt, 'The Marketing of Agricultural Produce', in J. Thirsk, ed., *The Agrarian History of England and Wales, iv: 1500–1640* (Cambridge, 1967), pp. 468–75.
[49] Potton (Beds.), Chertsey (Surrey), Ludlow (Salop), Wells and Wiveliscombe (Somerset), Kimbolton and St Ives (Hunts.), Watford (Herts.), Newark (Notts.), Great Limber (Lincs.), Sandwich (Kent).
[50] OB, fos. 61v–73v.

7

Credit and wealth

I

Colchester's growth of trade and industry during the later fourteenth century brought about major changes in the composition, level and distribution of wealth. The assessment of movables in 1334, on which the borough continued to be taxed, soon became grossly unrepresentative of the real state of affairs. Not all the implications of these changes can be observed, for want of evidence concerning the distribution of wealth. But some new features of life in the town are sufficiently in evidence to be worthy of comment, particularly the expansion of credit and the growth of the merchant class.

A glance at the growing bulk of Colchester's court rolls is enough to demonstrate the expansion of business during the years following the Black Death.[1] The total number of pleas brought to the courts increased by about five times between the mid 1350s and the early 1380s. More revealing than mere totals, however, is an analysis of litigation by types of plea. In the mid 1350s about one half of all pleas brought to court were for trespass – a broad category including all civil cases arising from assault and damage to property. The subsequent increase in the number of such pleas was no more than might be expected in the wake of rising urban population. Meanwhile, the number of pleas of other kinds increased more rapidly, so that by the early 1380s pleas of trespass accounted for less than one fifth of the total. Table 7.1 shows the number of pleas of different types in those years during the later fourteenth century for which reliable totals can be counted. The greatest increase was in the number of pleas of debt. In 1353/4 the number was no more than it normally had been during the earlier fourteenth century,[2] but by 1382/3 it was over 10 times greater, and it remained at or above this level for the rest of the century. Although it

---

[1] See the list of court rolls on pp. xvi–xix.　　　　[2] See Table 1.1.

Table 7.1 *Pleas brought to Colchester borough court, 1351/2–1399/1400*

	Debt	Broken Contract	Detention of Chattels	Account	Trespass	Other	Unknown	Total
1351/2	12	5	1	0	42	1	1	62
1353/4	32	9	8	0	72	2	4	127
1356/7	61	5	9	0	51	1	2	129
1359/60	125	37	14	1	106	1	2	286
1366/7	243	35	25	0	81	3	0	387
1372/3	173	36	12	0	100	1	0	322
1378/9	395	44	6	0	83	0	4	532
1381/2	467	49	19	2	113	3	1	654
1382/3	402	23	25	1	84	0	2	537
1384/5	481	41	23	0	92	6	0	643
1387/8	654	58	41	6	113	2	4	878
1398/9	435	31	23	57	116	6	0	668
1399/1400	349	37	17	33	107	3	9	555

Source: CR 9–12, 15, 16, 19, 21, 22, 24, 26, 30, 31.

is possible that part of the increase resulted from some unrecorded victory of the Colchester franchise courts over the ecclesiastical court of the archdeacon of Colchester, this interpretation can carry little conviction. Litigation for debt was a minor part of the business of archdeaconry courts in the fourteenth century.[3] It is unlikely that the effects of administrative changes of this sort would have spread themselves over at least 25 years. Moreover, Colchester's experience was not unique; an increase in the number of pleas of debt occurred in Clare and Sudbury, both outside the archdeaconry of Colchester.[4]

An explanation of this increase which may be dismissed from the outset is the argument that increasing numbers of pleas of debt between 1353/4 and 1382/3 resulted from a crisis of confidence in the economy. These years initiated a permanently higher level of litigation for debt in Colchester, and it is difficult to imagine any sort of crisis which could have had such an effect. A crisis of confidence would have initiated a temporary process of adjustment, and no increase of litigation for debt would have lasted more than a few years. If associated with the onset of economic contraction, a crisis would have led to a lower level of indebtedness and, presumably, a lower incidence of litigation. A permanent increase in litigation must be the result of a permanent increase in the level of indebtedness. The most that can be explained by crises is the occurrence of peaks of litigation in certain years. The high number of pleas of debt before the courts in 1387/8 demonstrates a credit crisis then, probably induced by disruption in the Baltic trade and by political upheaval in England.[5]

Even if not a response to a crisis of confidence, increased indebtedness could conceivably represent a solution to new monetary problems of the age. From about 1363 minting activity in England declined because of decreasing inflows of bullion into the kingdom, and this trend was exacerbated by bullionist conflicts with the Duchy of Burgundy after 1388. Perhaps there was some reduction in the monetary stock of the realm.[6] Townsmen might, in such circumstances, especially in periods of growing trade, escape some inconveniences of the monetary system by giving credit. Many debts would cancel out in the course of time, and the need for currency would be thereby circumvented. As a general explanation of Colchester's experience the argument is unacceptable on a number of

[3] B. L. Woodcock, *Medieval Ecclesiastical Courts in the Diocese of Canterbury* (Oxford, 1952), p. 89.

[4] P.R.O., S.C.2/203/38–50, 54 – 7, 59–65, 112–15; S.C.2/204/3–7, 10–13.

[5] Schulz, *Die Hanse und England*, pp. 43–8; A. Tuck, *Richard II and the English Nobility* (London, 1973), pp. 117–33.

[6] T. H. Lloyd, 'Overseas Trade and the English Money Supply in the Fourteenth Century', in N. J. Mayhew, ed., *Edwardian Monetary Affairs (1279–1344)*, B.A.R., 36 (Oxford, 1977), pp. 116, 117, 122; Munro, *Wool, Cloth, and Gold*, pp. 47, 50–1.

counts. Growth of credit was particularly rapid during the 1350s, when the output of English mints was even higher than it had been in the 1330s and 1340s. By contrast, there was no increase in the level of indebtedness between 1385 and 1410, when continued increases in Colchester's internal and external trade were contemporary with declining mint output and increasing complaints about scarcity of money.[7] The only period when sharply rising credit coincided with a decrease in minting activity would appear to be the 1370s. In these years, however, the supposed cause was insufficiently powerful to have accomplished the observed effect; it remains doubtful whether during the 1370s there was in fact any decline of the stock of money in circulation or any felt shortage of coin.[8]

A permanent increase in litigation for debt is more likely to have been caused by a permanent increase in indebtedness directly related, in some way, to economic development. In part it was a direct consequence of an increasing number of transactions of all sorts, since with an increase in transactions came an increase in defaults. Often indebtedness arose without any intention on the creditor's part to give credit. John Kyng of East Street was prosecuted in 1396 for wool bought the previous year for which he should have paid immediately, and he eventually acknowledged the debt in court.[9] The most frequent circumstances in which indebtedness increased without any development in the system of credit, and without any intention on the creditors' part to extend credit, were in transactions where some element of waiting was present as normal custom. Such were rent contracts and wage contracts in which payment followed at some accepted interval after the use of the property or services concerned.

Rents of all sorts multiplied in Colchester in the later fourteenth century, bringing men and women of all social categories to defend themselves before the bailiffs. House rents were sometimes claimed in this way,[10] and no doubt the number of houses on lease increased with the growth of urban population. However, the association between indebtedness and economic expansion is better illustrated from other types of property. The multiplication of taverns and shops created new rents. In 1399 Stephen Flisp, a merchant and vintner of Hythe,[11] was prosecuted for the rent of a tavern for the quarter between Christmas 1398 and the following Easter. Flisp said the landlord had agreed not to charge him rent for this quarter because he had ceased to occupy the tavern, and an inquest jury believed him.[12] Hugh Love the fuller[13] had a weaker case when in 1398 he was prosecuted for the rent of a mill at Hythe, and he had eventually to acknowledge the

[7] Munro, *Wool, Cloth, and Gold*, pp. 60–1, 190.
[8] Lloyd, 'Overseas Trade', p. 117; Munro, 'Monetary Contraction', pp. 97–8, 104.
[9] CR 24/7r, 16r.
[10] *E.g.* CR 24/7; CR 29/6r.
[11] CR 30/1r, 10r, 16r; OB, fo. 72v.
[12] CR 30/21d, 23d.
[13] See Chapter 5, p. 77.

debt.[14] Not all rents derived from fixed properties such as these. One of the largest debts claimed in 1395/6 was £51 16s 0d for a ship which Robert Longejohan had leased about the beginning of August 1391 on the understanding that the rent would be paid the following Michaelmas.[15] At the other extreme, one of the smaller debts of the year was 10d for a spinning wheel leased by the wife of Richard Taillour, a poor townsman.[16]

Indebtedness for wages brought some of the poorer inhabitants of the borough and its environs to court as plaintiffs. John Ive was successfully prosecuted for debt in the autumn of 1398 by David Bartelmew, a former employee. Bartelmew said he had lived in Ive's house in Head Ward and worked for him from Midsummer Day to the beginning of August, a period of five and a half weeks, and that he should have received 13s 0d when he left.[17] Many labour contracts, like this one, were of only short duration, and these seem to have been particularly prone to cause trouble. A similar case is that of Richard Hykeman who worked briefly for a fuller about mid September, 1398. When he moved on his employer owed him 5s 0d for his work and a further 1s 0d for carrying cloths to various fairs. The money was supposed to have been paid within a month, but the employer defaulted.[18] Indebtedness for wages was the more common in the fourteenth century because of the poor economic standing of many employers. John Coverour was prosecuted for debt in 1399 both by George Molle and by Stephen Scofeeld, both of whom established that they were owed money for working on roofs. Normally Coverour would have been amerced by the court on both charges, but these amercements were pardoned on account of his poverty.[19] This is presumably the nub of these cases as of many others; when small businessmen failed to meet their obligations because of bad luck or bad judgement their workers stood to lose alongside their other creditors. From these cases, as in those relating to rent, it can be seen how an increase in indebtedness would occur in the course of economic expansion without any change in business practices. Growing wage dependence, even if of a casual character, accompanied Colchester's development from the 1350s, and the very casualness of much employment increased the risks of misconduct on the part of both employers and employees.

The importance of commercial growth as a cause of the upsurge of indebtedness after 1351/2 is confirmed by the mounting number of pleas of broken contract and detention of chattels, both of which were responsive to changing levels of trade. But this will not explain the whole phenomenon. Although the number of transactions increased, and no doubt did so faster

---

[14] CR 30/7d, 10d.   [15] CR 29/16d.
[16] CR 29/6r, 7r.   [17] CR 30/5d, 8r.
[18] CR 29/5d, 7r; CR 30/18r, 20d.   [19] CR 30/14r, 15d, 19r,d.

than the size of Colchester's population, it is unlikely to have grown tenfold or fifteenfold between the mid 1350s and the 1380s. It is significant, in this context, that indebtedness increased in Sudbury and Clare, which had not experienced Colchester's industrial and commercial expansion. An additional cause of rising indebtedness was an increased willingness on the part of townsmen to allow credit in the normal course of their daily business. Such credit was often only for a few days or weeks, but it occurs in a very great number of those lawsuits which came to be pleaded in court and whose details were accordingly recorded in the court rolls. This greater availability of credit in local trade was encouraged by the growth of profits and wages during the decades following the Black Death; more money was available for lending. In Colchester's case the growth of credit was also encouraged by a high level of expectations resulting from the profitability of trade in woollen cloth.

Credit in the later fourteenth century did not depend on new commercial practices, and in fact much of it was based on word of mouth. Alongside the growing use of more sophisticated written instruments of credit there was a burgeoning of informal, friendly and undocumented credit which might lead to clashes of will and opinion in the moothall. At the lowest levels of retail trade Colchester men gave credit to customers known to them, often keeping no exact record of when debts were incurred or even, in some cases, of the terms on which they were to be repaid. An extreme instance is that of counter credit in the taverns. John Prentis the vintner allowed one of his customers to run up debts for wine over a period of about four months in 1393. The wine was sometimes served by him and sometimes by his son, so there was plenty of room for error and misunderstanding.[20] Most tradesmen probably operated with fixed terms for repayment, expecting their customers to settle their accounts by each quarter day or by some more appropriate date. John Merseye the butcher, who sold meat on credit to his regular customers in Colchester market, had Christmas and the beginning of Lent as two of his days of reckoning.[21]

These examples of credit in retail trade could be paralleled in various contexts. They can be supplemented with even more numerous and varied examples of credit at the pettiest levels of wholesale trade and trade in raw materials. In 1395, for example, Roger Barker successfully prosecuted Reginald Brakle for the price of leather sold in Lent 1394, which should have been paid for on 28 April. A further debt was due for leather sold in mid August 1395, which should have been settled on 8 September.[22] In both cases credit had been extended for only a few weeks, and this was common. Sometimes credit was allowed only on part of a sale. About 12

[20] CR 29/2d, 4d.
[21] CR 29/22d, 24r,d, 25d. [22] CR 29/3d, 6r.

March 1396 John Welles sold 40 quarters of barley to John Aylmar the
brewer and his wife. They paid £5 down and were given until Michaelmas
to pay the rest.[23] Tradesmen who dealt regularly with each other kept
some kind of running accounts, and in these cases days of settlement were
probably not closely predetermined. In some instances this gave grounds
for a complex of claims and counter-claims which could only be settled
by arbitration. About Christmas 1397 there was such an attempt to settle
out of court disputes between John Abel of Mile End and William Hervyle
of Ardleigh, though it failed, first because the arbitrators could not agree,
and later because Hervyle would not accept the decision of an impartial
mediator appointed by the arbitrators.[24]

Besides debts arising from various forms of trading, there is evidence
of frequent money-lending in Colchester, usually of an informal character
and for only a short period. Early in 1396 John Arwsmyth prosecuted
William Dod for 3s 0½d which he had lent him for seven days, and Stephen
Richard prosecuted Thomas Doune for 16s 8d which he had lent him for
repayment immediately afterwards.[25] In most examples of money-lending
nothing like pawn-broking nor usury was involved. Most loans were
unsecured, and in most cases it may be surmised that the borrower was
personally known to the lender.[26] It was not unusual for money-lending
to occur as an element in a complex of claims of other sorts, showing that
the lender and borrower had business dealings independent of the loan.
In February 1396 John Smyth of East Street was prosecuted for a debt
of 12s 9½d arising from a loan of 5s 0d and a delivery of 6,000 lath nails
worth 7s 9½d.[27] A few months later John Acliff was found to owe 7s 10d
of which 6s 0d was the rent of a barn in West Bergholt for three terms and
the rest was owed for ale sold and cash lent.[28] It is also common to find
that debts were repaid in forms other than money, either by prior
agreement or, probably more commonly, as a result of later discussion.
In August 1392 John Budde lent £1 to John Burdy on the understanding
that he should work for him for that sum.[29]

Alongside the expansion of credit of this informal character there was
also a marked increase in the number of debts backed by some written
instrument. Only two types of instrument require particular discussion, the
recognisance and the letter obligatory, both of which were much the same
everywhere in the kingdom. The recognisance was a direct offshoot of the
availability of local justice in borough courts and of the existence of court
rolls as a legal record.[30] Most Colchester examples were the result of

---

[23] CR 30/5r, 13r.   [24] CR 31/17d.   [25] CR 29/10d, 13r,d, 14r.
[26] The situation was similar in country areas: Hilton, *The English Peasantry*, p. 47.
[27] CR 29/16d.   [28] CR 29/24d.   [29] CR 29/4r, 6d.
[30] T. F. T. Plucknett, *Legislation of Edward I* (Oxford, 1949), pp. 138–43.

litigation; the debtor recognised in court his liability for the debt of which he was accused, and thereby put beyond question the plaintiff's right to recover the disputed sum. In these instances the making of a recognisance was usually combined with amercement of the debtor by the court. In a number of cases, however, recognisances for debt were recorded in the court rolls at the request of the parties concerned in exchange for a fee paid to the town clerk. The advantage of this procedure to creditors was that should a debt be not duly repaid the debtor's liability would be already an acknowledged fact within the cognisance of the court. This type of instrument, directly recorded in the court rolls amidst the normal business of the courts,[31] is much more in evidence than recognisances drawn up as separate and private documents.[32] The letter of obligation differed from the recognisance of debt in that it was a privately authenticated document, drawn up at the moment when a debt was contracted, whose terms would not be on record in court unless the debtor defaulted and had to be prosecuted, whereupon the letter of obligation would be produced as evidence by the prosecution.[33] The advantage of such an instrument was that the creditor had greater freedom where to sue for his claim; he carried his security with him, whereas a recognisance in Colchester court rolls could serve as a security only in the borough courts. This meant that the letter of obligation was more appropriate to transactions involving debts to creditors who were not burgesses of Colchester, since burgesses had in any case no choice where they should sue their fellow burgesses.[34] Presentation of such a document in court automatically led to a decision in the plaintiff's favour unless there were special circumstances surrounding it to which the defendant wished to allude.

It would be surprising if the larger and more formal debts on record in Colchester did not carry some return to the lender for the credit he had made available. However, the suits in which this aspect of development is most clearly apparent were not pleas of debt but pleas of account, which rapidly became more numerous during the 1390s.[35] The chief explanation for this is directly related to the expansion of credit in the borough. The advantage of the plea of account was that a plaintiff did not have to sue for the particular commodity he had sold or the sum he had lent; he sued for that together with some profit due to him, on the grounds that the

---

[31] In some towns enrolments of this sort were kept separate from the record of legal proceedings: Postan, *Medieval Trade and Finance*, p. 3; G. H. Martin, *The Early Court Rolls of the Borough of Ipswich*, Department of English Local History Occasional Papers, v (Leicester, 1954), p. 18.

[32] Varieties of recognisance are discussed in Postan, *Medieval Trade and Finance*, pp. 35–40.

[33] *Ibid.*, pp. 29–35.

[34] Burgesses were forbidden to sue fellow burgesses concerning such contracts outside the liberty of the borough: *Cal. Chart. R.*, i, p. 410; CR 4/12r, 13r.   [35] See Table 7.1.

recipient had been the plaintiff's agent. The plea of account thereby sanctioned a canonically satisfactory means of avoiding usury while profiting from the lending of money or stock. Robert Priour the butcher received 13 steers worth £13 4s 0d from Hugh Vows about 10 August 1398 'in order to trade with them to Hugh's gain and profit from the aforesaid day and year until the Christmas following'. He was then obliged to render account to Vows for the steers together with the trading profit earned on them. Priour alleged that he had met his obligations; that the two men had met in William Dyche's tavern in Head Ward, together with John Proval, whom Vows had chosen to be the auditor between them, and that there they had agreed on a settlement.[36] If this was the normal procedure in such cases they were clearly not usurious in character, since the creditor's profit depended upon arbitration. Loans of money were made in what appears to be essentially the same way. For example in 1396 Richard Petrisburgh the butcher[37] brought a plea of account against Thomas Thormad his agent on the grounds that the latter had recently received 15s 0d from Petrisburgh to be employed for two days on Petrisburgh's behalf and then to be accounted for.[38]

A number of pleas of debt, broken contract and account brought to court in Colchester every year involved men from other towns and villages. Sometimes both plaintiff and defendant were from other towns; a situation might arise when merchants trading together at the Colchester fairs agreed to settle up in the borough on some future occasion. Table 7.2 gives evidence from three years at the turn of the century for which the court rolls are complete. The total number of pleas of debt brought to court in the borough in each of those years is compared with the number in which the plaintiffs or defendants were outsiders, and the number in which the action was entirely between outsiders. The final column shows the number of pleas in which outsiders were associated with Colchester people in prosecuting or defending pleas of debt. From this evidence it can be shown that only 14.5 per cent of pleas of debt brought to court in Colchester in this period involved litigants described as outsiders. Even allowing for some failures of the clerk to describe outsiders as such, the proportion of such pleas would probably not exceed one fifth of the total. The Colchester courts were primarily concerned with indebtedness between inhabitants of the liberty of the borough. This shows that the level of such litigation *per capita* was high both by modern standards and by the standards of the contemporary countryside.[39] In the late 1370s there was annually at least one plea of debt for every eight adult residents of the borough. This

---

[36] CR 31/16r, 17d.
[37] See Chapter 10, p. 142. [38] CR 29/21r.
[39] *E.g.* Dewindt, *Land and People in Holywell-cum-Needingworth*, pp. 250–1.

Table 7.2 *Pleas of debt involving outsiders in Colchester courts,*
1398/9–1400/1

	Total number of pleas of debt	Pleas of debt by outsiders	Pleas of debt against outsiders	Pleas of debt between outsiders	Pleas of debt involving outsiders
1398/9	435	25	22	8	2
1399/1400	349	22	35	5	0
1400/1	357	20	17	6	3
Total of three years	1,141	67	74	19	5
Percentage	100	5.9	6.5	1.7	0.4

Source: CR 30, 31, 32.

suggests that indebtedness and credit was a more pervasive feature of urban life than it was of rural society.

Some evidence may be brought to bear on the size of the sums involved in this local litigation. In the middle of October 1385 Michael Aunger introduced the practice of systematically recording the sums of money claimed in new pleas of debt.[40] For subsequent years the record is very full, and although in occasional instances the sums in dispute went unrecorded, the main imperfections in the evidence are the result of damage to the rolls rather than of clerical laxity. Table 7.3 shows the evidence for two years in the late fourteenth century whose rolls are in good order. The first of these, 1387/8, was a year of financial crisis when the number of pleas of debt was the largest on record, but the quality of Aunger's recording was nevertheless so high that the size of the claim is unrecorded or unclear in only 20 cases. The year 1398/9 was more normal. In fact the size of claims was very similar in the two years, the main difference being that in 1387/8 the number of claims for under 5s 0d was larger than in 1398/9 as a proportion of the total. This is partly the effect of the poorer quality of recording in 1398/9; the claims whose size is unrecorded probably included a disproportionately large number of small debts. However, the main reason for the difference is that in a year of crisis many small claims would be brought to court which would have been allowed to ride in years of normal trade. These differences do not disguise the essential feature of debts contested in the borough courts. The range in 1387/8 was wide, from £392 to 4d, but the latter sum was closer than the former to the median

[40] CR 25/4r, 5r.

Table 7.3 *The size of claims in Colchester borough courts*

| | Number | | Percentage of total | |
	1387/8	1398/9	1387/8	1398/9
£1 *and above*	176	145	26.9	33.3
£5 and above	49	42	7.5	9.7
£4 to £4 19.11¾	15	5	2.3	1.1
£3 to £3 19.11¾	15	3	2.3	0.7
£2 to £2 19.11¾	34	34	5.2	7.8
£1 to £1 19.11¾	63	61	9.6	14.0
	176	145	26.9	33.3
Below £1	458	251	70.0	57.7
15s. to 19.11¾	34	33	5.2	7.6
10s. to 14.11¾	67	48	10.2	11.0
5s. to 9.11¾	131	81	20.0	18.6
below 5s.	226	89	34.6	20.5
	458	251	70.0	57.7
Uncertain	20	39	3.1	9.0
	654	435	100.0	100.0

Source: CR 26, 30.

value of claims, which was 7s 6d. In 1398/9 the range was narrower, from
£72 16s 0d to 4d, and the median claim was higher, at 12s 6½d. But the
conclusion to be drawn is the same; the courts functioned chiefly for the
recovery of small sums. Despite the differences between town and country
in the level of indebtedness, the normal size of debts was very similar to
those contested in manorial courts.[41] The small size of many claims shows
how cheap litigation was; in 1387/8 34 pleas of debt were for sums of 1s 0d
or less. The existence of the borough courts, for all their imperfections,
must have favoured the expansion of local credit in the later fourteenth
century at a time when economic circumstances made this expansion
opportune.

II

In several respects the growth of credit in Colchester after 1350 affords
direct evidence of increasing personal wealth among the town's inhabitants.
In part it was the consequence of the accumulation of property and the
multiplication of rents. In part it illustrates a form of investment, with
townsmen deliberately holding wealth in the form of claims against others.
Increasing credit-worthiness, too, was encouraged by general increases in

[41] Hilton, *The English Peasantry*, pp. 46–7; E. Clark, 'Debt Litigation in a Late Medieval
English Vill', in J. A. Raftis, ed., *Pathways to Medieval Peasants* (Toronto, 1981), p. 252.

personal wealth, which made it more feasible to distrain debtors in order to recover sums of money lent to them. Increasing wealth was probably characteristic of most groups in Colchester in this period, and the social range of creditors in the borough courts was broad. But one group, the merchants, was in the forefront both of the generation of credit and the acquisition of wealth, becoming in the process more prominent in the records of the borough.

Increased litigation for debt meant that from the 1350s more men described as merchants occur in the court rolls than ever before. Although merchants had no distinct legal status, the development of law relating to debt had been so intimately associated with their needs that, in this context, merchant status was considered peculiarly charmed.[42] The rolls for 1356/7 state the occupations of 70 men, of whom 50 were merchants, 3 were merchant fullers, 1 a merchant skinner and 1 a merchant mercer.[43] In the later Middle Ages the term merchant was reserved for men primarily engaged in wholesale trade,[44] but embraced those operating in a small way in local fairs and markets as well as those who bought and sold overseas or in other regions of the kingdom. An artisan engaged in the wholesale disposal of manufactures might be described as a merchant, and often was, so that 'merchant fuller' properly described a man who organised both the fulling and the marketing of cloth. Self-styled merchants in later fourteenth-century Colchester were accordingly a heterogeneous group, only a minority of whom were ever involved in overseas ventures.[45] For most of them the merchant's calling was a humdrum matter of buying and selling within the vicinity of the town. The greater number of merchants recorded in Colchester's later fourteenth-century court rolls needs, therefore, to be handled gingerly as evidence for a growth of the merchant class, both because the increase depends so much on burgeoning litigation and because the term merchant covered such a miscellany of social categories.

There are other grounds, however, for supposing that the merchant class was growing in this period both in numbers and in wealth. It is implied both by the growth of the cloth industry and by the accompanying growth of the town. Even if the organisation of the cloth industry gave scope chiefly to those who combined commerce with the exercise of a craft, this must have implied an increase in the number of men who could legitimately describe themselves as merchants. The provisioning of the town, and its supply with manufactures from other parts of the kingdom, created further

---

[42] Plucknett, *Legislation of Edward I*, pp. 136–48; T. H. Lloyd, *Alien Merchants in England in the High Middle Ages* (Brighton, 1982), pp. 14–16.
[43] CR 11.
[44] Thrupp, *The Merchant Class*, p. 6.
[45] In 1397–8, towards the peak of Colchester's commercial expansion, only 27 Colchester merchants occur in the customs accounts: P.R.Q., E.122/193/33, fos. 11v–17r, 24r–25r.

opportunities for petty mercantile enterprise. In this restricted sense, therefore, the greater number of merchants occurring in the court rolls as a result of increased litigation for debt is a faithful mirror of reality. Meanwhile, and more importantly for the matter of this chapter, economic development enabled some families to accumulate wealth through trade, and in this way it brought about more than simply an increase in the number of small traders. The number of merchants who were men of substance grew, and this had implications for the place of merchants in town life, since there were now more merchants wealthy enough to command authority in the affairs of the community. In this respect Colchester shared the experience of other towns (notably York) whose trading activities increased during this period.[46]

In 1349 urban govenment in Colchester received a shock from which it did not revive until the 1360s. Because of the loss of experienced men in the Black Death, novices assumed responsibilities which would not otherwise have come their way. A dozen men were elected bailiff for the first time between Michaelmas 1350 and Michaelmas 1359. Moreover, this new group in turn suffered heavy losses in the pestilence of 1361. Not until the 1360s did a group of reliable and recurring bailiffs emerge, with John and Robert atte Ford, Alexander le Cogger and William Reyne as its favourites. Similar discontinuity was evident in Colchester's parliamentary representation.[47] A closer examination of the new cohorts of bailiffs and parliament men supplies a cogent reason for regarding the Black Death as a turning point in Colchester's social history; it accelerated a social change in the composition of the borough's ruling group which was being brought about by economic change. The bailiffs elected during the 1350s and 1360s were not all self-made men; George Fordham was the son of a former bailiff;[48] Alexander le Cogger was married to William Buk's grand-daughter;[49] Richard le Dyer was probably the grandson of John le Dyer, a former bailiff.[50] There were probably other links with the past. However, the main point of interest with the bailiffs of this period is the prominence of merchants amongst them. The former rôle of landowners and clerks in borough administration was being undermined by the growth of mercantile wealth. There was no conflict of class interests here; the change reflected the opportunities for trade in Colchester and the emergence

---

[46] J. N. Bartlett, 'The Expansion and Decline of York in the Later Middle Ages', *Ec.H.R.*, 2nd ser., xii (1959), pp. 24–6.

[47] OB, fos. 41r–49r; *Return of Names*, pp. 150–82.

[48] CR 7/8r.

[49] Buk's daughter married William Hunt: CR 17/6d. In 1375 the couple held two-thirds of Buk's former property in West Mersea, the other third being held by Alexander le Cogger and his wife in dower: *Essex Fines*, iii, pp. 39, 176. Cogger also had property in Colchester which had been Buk's: OB, fos. 168v, 169v.

[50] John le Dyer had a grandson called Richard: CR 3/5r.

of a larger group of responsible merchants than had been available in the 1330s and 1340s.

No itinerant trader could assume the obligations of a bailiff, for the office required its incumbent to be on call throughout his period of service. The sort of man who became bailiff during the 1360s was engaged in trading which permitted him to be resident in the borough. If he engaged in overseas trade it was in those trades where routines were so well established that consignments of goods could be freighted in ships captained by others. A number of bailiffs combined wholesale trade with some retailing; of the eleven men who were elected bailiff between 1360/1 and 1371/2, six occur as retailers of wine.[51] At other times bailiffs are found handling imports of iron[52] and dyestuffs.[53] Henry Bosse,[54] Richard Drory[55] and William Mate[56] were involved in textiles – Bosse as a wool merchant, Drory probably as a clothier, Mate as a clothier and hosier. Richard le Dyer maintained his family's long-standing interest in trade; in 1356 he took up the lease of a vacant stall in the market place.[57] Both Alexander le Cogger's name and his connection with Buk suggest participation in overseas trade; so, too, does his ownership of a tavern in the centre of town.[58] In short, probably all the bailiffs elected between 1360 and 1372 were active in commerce. Colchester's representatives in parliament were chosen from the same group, with one notable exception. John Hall, who attended more parliaments than any other burgess during these years,[59] was a lawyer; he was frequently employed as an attorney in the borough courts,[60] and was engaged for legal work by neighbouring landlords.[61]

In medieval society merchants commonly put some of their savings into land to secure against bad luck, to provide for relatives and old age and to enhance their social status.[62] Families which grew wealthier through trade and industry must have increased their investable savings, and so had

---

[51] John Lucas (CR 14/1r, etc.), George Fordham (CR 10/1r, etc.), John atte Ford (CR 9/1d, etc.), Robert atte Ford (CR 11/1d), William Reyne (CR 16/1d, etc.), John Keek (CR 12/11d).

[52] William Reyne: CR 18/20r *bis*.

[53] William Reyne: CR 20/17r; John atte Ford: CR 21/51r.

[54] See below, n. 68.

[55] Drory sued John Arnold, fuller, in 1373 and sued John Dyer, dyer or fuller, in 1374. He was sued by Hugh Love, fuller, in 1379: CR 16/8d; CR 17/6r; CR 19/16r. For the occupation of John Dyer, see CR 17/4d, 14r and for Hugh Love see CR 18/21r.

[56] CR 11/3r.

[57] OB, fo. 43v.   [58] CR 25/13d, 16r.

[59] *Return of Names*, pp. 163–88.

[60] CR 8/10d *bis*; CR 9/8r; CR 10/7r *bis*, 12d, 13d, etc.

[61] Hall had some tie with the Sutton family, who allowed him a quarter of wheat from Langenhoe demesne in 1378/9 and 1380/1: E.R.O., D/DC 2/14d; D/DGe M200d. He acquired land on behalf of the abbot of St Osyth in the 1370s; *Essex Fines*, iii, p. 162; *Cal. Pat. R.*, *1377–81*, p. 541.

[62] Thrupp, *The Merchant Class*, pp. 118–30.

more opportunity to buy land. However, Colchester merchants in the later fourteenth century were more interested in investments of other kinds. Before the Black Death the frequent association of land-ownership and high rank in the borough has been illustrated in Chapter 2. During the later fourteenth century it becomes harder rather than easier to find burgesses with country estates. Between 1350 and 1375 there was an increase in the number of final concords relating to messuages in Colchester without land attached to them. A number of other fines relate to properties in the suburbs – 30 acres of John Graunger's in 1352, 12 acres of William Reyne's in 1355 and 30 acres of land with some wood belonging to Adam Waryn in 1359.[63] But there is only a single example of a man described as of Colchester with lands outside the liberty; in 1360 Thomas atte Asshe had a title to lands in Theydon Garnon and Theydon Mount.[64] Colchester's leading burgesses – those elected to high office in the borough – do not occur in the fines as landowners as they had done before 1350. The evidence here, therefore, is that Colchester landowners were fewer than they had been, and that land ownership was less characteristic of the borough's office-holders.

The poverty of evidence relating to ownership of land by Colchester burgesses reflects the peculiar economic circumstances of the age. During the 1350s and 1360s, when opportunities for investment in Colchester were outstandingly promising because of the growth of the cloth industry, the rural economy was in disarray on account of rising costs and uncertain markets. Profits in agriculture were much more risky than they had been before the price depression of 1337–43 and probably lower than they had been in the later 1340s. It was accordingly more advantageous to Colchester merchants to reinvest their profits in the growth of the urban economy. This would account in part for the rapid growth in credit during these years. There is some independent evidence that the purchase of land became less attractive than urban investments in that between 1340 and 1370 there was a sharp increase in the prominence of urban properties relative to land in the Essex final concords. During the 1330s landless messuages were the object of 5.9 per cent of Essex fines, but by the 1360s the proportion had risen to 14.4 per cent. The total number of fines concerning land had in the meanwhile declined.[65] This must mean that in Essex during these years the attractiveness of urban property had increased relative to agricultural land. Investment in commerce and industry, meanwhile, was probably even more profitable than investment in urban property.

Other features of urban society in these years point in the same direction.

[63] *Essex Fines*, iii, pp. 105, 112, 126.   [64] *Ibid.*, iii, p. 130.
[65] Britnell, 'Burghal Characteristics of Market Towns', pp. 150–1.

Families which before the Black Death had no great involvement in commerce had by 1370 produced prominent members of the merchant class. Switching into trade in these years was more common than escape from it. In the early fourteenth century the leading member of the Bosse family had been Hubert, landowner, cultivator of the soil and councillor of Colchester Abbey.[66] In the 1360s the family's principal figure was Henry Bosse the merchant, who had land adjoining East Street and probably elsewhere,[67] but whose interests were not primarily agricultural. He occurs in Langenhoe manorial accounts buying up the wool clip in 1370,[68] and was clearly taking advantage of new commercial opportunities. At some point he acquired a plot near the quay at Hythe.[69] He was one of those who, in the late 1360s or early 1370s, built new mills to meet the growing demand for flour in the borough.[70] By these and other schemes he maintained and enhanced the prestige of his family. In 1377 he had one of the four largest households in Colchester; he paid poll tax for himself, his wife and eight servants.[71] A similar movement into trade is apparent in the history of the Ford family.[72]

With the establishment of a new urban élite, and the return of more hopeful expectations in agriculture during the 1370s, wealthier townsmen became more prominent in local landed society. As before the Black Death professional lawyers and estate agents were conspicuous in this respect. In 1375 John Hall obtained a title to extensive properties in Sproughton, Stonham Aspall, Mickfield, Cowlinge and Mildenhall (Suffolk) and Steeple (Essex).[73] William Penne, who was retained by the Sutton family as an estate official,[74] had lands in Ardleigh, Elmstead and Thorpe le Soken in 1376 and 1377.[75] From this time, too, successful merchants invested in land more frequently. Thomas Fraunceys acquired William Buk's former estate in West Mersea.[76] Early in the fifteenth century Stephen Flisp possessed 149½ acres in Boxted, Wormingford and in Great and Little Horkesley, and Thomas Godeston had 230 acres in Ramsey.[77] The third quarter of the century stands out, in retrospect, as a temporary phase of dislocation, and in the final quarter a more normal structure of wealth was being restored.

[66] See Chapter 2, p. 33.
[67] CR 11/10r.
[68] E.R.O., D/DC 2/13d.
[69] OB, fo. 162v.
[70] See Chapter 6, p. 87.
[71] P.R.O., E.179/107/54, m. 1r.
[72] References to Robert and John atte Ford as merchants will be found earlier in this chapter and in the next one. An earlier John de la Ford, bailiff in 1314/15 (LB, fo. 180r,v) owned rents and lands in Colchester but is not known to have engaged in commerce; CR 1/1d, 12r; CR 2/1d; *Essex Fines*, ii, p. 231.
[73] *Essex Fines*, iii, p. 177.
[74] Penne's horse was fed at Langenhoe in 1383/4 when he went there 'to take the bailiff's account': E.R.O., D/DE1 M225d.
[75] *Essex Fines*, iii, pp. 148, 178, 183.
[76] *Ibid.*, iii, p. 176.
[77] *Ibid.*, iii, pp. 244, 245.

But Colchester had been transformed in the meanwhile. As a result of the growth of its cloth trade the town had experienced a commercial revolution. It retained its earlier function as a local market town, but the level of income and employment had now become dependent upon more distant markets. Credit institutions in the borough were still unsophisticated, but the operation of credit in everyday affairs had greatly increased. Merchants there were small fry in comparison with those of Europe's major cities, but they had increased in numbers and wealth to the point of taking the leading share of local government.[78] These were the repercussions, in a small town, of economic developments more usually studied in large ones, and their capacity to modify urban society rapidly and profoundly is unambiguous. It is now time to develop this conclusion further by examining ways in which the government of the borough changed after 1350. Constitutional changes, too, were ripples from the social upheavals in larger towns which had shaped the characteristic urban environment of medieval Europe.

---

[78] For an exceptionally detailed analysis of trading interests in the government of a small English borough during this period, see Kowaleski, 'The Commercial Dominance of a Medieval Provincial Oligarchy', pp. 363–78.

8

Government

I

Besides transforming the social composition of Colchester's ruling group, economic development simultaneously multiplied the tasks to be performed by elected officers; the income of the community increased, more pleas were brought to the borough courts and policing the town became more time-consuming. The casual ways of the early fourteenth century were no longer appropriate to the duties involved. And then, also, as Colchester's fame and fortune grew, civic pride took a share in recommending some types of reform and repudiating certain survivals from the past. So within a generation of the Black Death much had changed in the normal government of Colchester, and the constitutional history of the borough supplements the economic evidence to the effect that this was a period of innovation in response to new and higher expectations.

In 1372 the greater part of the burgesses of Colchester swore to observe a new set of ordinances, known as the New Constitutions, whose object was to reform the government of the borough and its electoral system.[1] The stated reasons for the reform, which are rehearsed in the preamble to the New Constitutions, were financial. For a long time, it was said, the town's income both from rents and from fines had been spent entirely at the will of the bailiffs, to the community's loss. The object of the New Constitutions was accordingly to keep a check on this expenditure. It was observed that the total of rents and fines amounted to a great sum each year.[2] Marginal entries to the court rolls show that in 1372/3 the income from fines and amercements was about £50, and a surviving rental of 1387/8 shows that the community's income from rents was then £13 2*s* 2*d*,[3] so the framers of the New Constitutions may be supposed to have been

---

[1] OB, fos. 22v–23v. See R. H. Britnell, 'The Oath Book of Colchester and the Borough Constitution, 1372–1404', *Essex Archaeology and History*, xiv (1982), p. 96.
[2] OB, fo. 22v.   [3] CR 16; OB, fos. 158r–170r.

thinking in terms of an expenditure of about £60 as in need of closer supervision than it had received in the past. Why financial reform should have seemed so necessary in 1372 cannot be closely explained, but two reasons may be suggested, one relating to the real facts of the case, the other suggested by current attitudes to problems of this type.

In the first place, then, one element in the recent experience of the ruling group was an increase in the sums of money at their disposal. Total fines and amercements can be calculated for the year 1351/2 when they were about £40,[4] implying that an increase occurred during the 20 years before 1372. In the preamble to the New Constitutions the fines and amercements in question are described as outrageous, meaning presumably that they were considered large rather than that they were improperly assessed.[5] The level of rents received by the community is also likely to have risen in the mid fourteenth century. In 1321 the burgesses had successfully petitioned Edward II in parliament to allow them to increase the income of the borough by developing waste spaces in the town.[6] This had permitted an increase in the community's income from rents, and a number of newly established rents from vacant plots are in evidence during the 1330s and 1340s.[7] Additions made to the rental of 1387/8 to be found in the Oath Book show the income from this source increasing still in the late fourteenth and early fifteenth centuries, so that by 1414 total receipts from property rents had reached about £17 15s 0d.[8] But this income probably increased more between 1322 and 1372 than during the following 50 years, and its growth may have been indirectly facilitated by the Black Death. In rural society one of the effects of plague epidemics was that property fell into the hands of manorial lords for want of heirs. By Edward II's tolerance the community of Colchester had put itself in the position of a manorial lord with respect to properties in the town which fell vacant in this way.

A second reason for financial reform in 1372 was a revival of public concern about the accountability of financial officers, which was a main theme of English politics during the 1370s and 1380s. A new phase of war with France beginning in 1369 brought with it not a rallying of country behind court but a growth of suspicion and conflict. There was evident weakness at the centre of government on account of Edward III's senility, and the military ventures of the Black Prince and John of Gaunt did

[4] CR 9.
[5] OB, fo. 22v. The word *outraiouse* is taken from current statutes, *e.g.* 25 Edward III, 2, preamble and 37 Edward III, c. 8: *Statutes*, i, pp. 311, 380.
[6] *Rot. Parl.*, i, p. 397. This petition had contemporary parallels from Cambridge and Lincoln: F. W. Maitland, *Township and Borough* (Cambridge, 1898), p. 83; F. Hill, *Medieval Lincoln* (Cambridge, 1948), p. 242.
[7] OB, fos. 30v–40r; CR 4/12d; CR 5/3r, 6d; CR 6/6d, 10r; CR 7/2d, 3r.
[8] OB, fos. 161r, 163r, 164r, 165r, 168r, 170r.

nothing to bring back the days of Crécy and Poitiers. The February parliament of 1371 initiated a period of discontent with the handling of financial affairs by the king's ministers. The main point at issue, the power of clerics in the government of the realm, was not a matter relevant to the internal affairs of boroughs, but the issue of accountability, having returned to the forefront of national politics, was likely to raise questions in local government as well.[9]

The new form of government established special officers to handle borough income and account for it and instituted an annual audit of their accounts. Two receivers, later known as chamberlains, were to be elected every year to take custody of the borough treasury. No documentation from their office has survived earlier than the late fifteenth century, but the receivers' duties are adequately known from other texts. They had responsibility for collecting the borough's income from all sources, or for co-ordinating its collection by others. Rents of property and the annual sums due from leases of borough assets of other sorts were from 1372 payable to them. Profits of jurisdiction, too, having been collected by the sergeants of the court, were delivered to the receivers in exchange for indentures or tallies. The receivers had no power to authorise expenditure by the community, though at least one of them had to be present on a new financial committee, the committee of auditors, which was competent in this matter. This absence of independent executive authority ensured that the receivers were subordinate to the bailiffs and auditors in the day-to-day execution of their duties. No man who had served as bailiff was eligible for the office, so that receivers were bound to be outweighed in experience and authority by the bailiffs and auditors, for whose posts there was no such restriction. The receivers had to prepare an account of receipts and expenses to be rendered annually on the Monday before the Nativity of the Virgin, a date which would always fall in the first week of September. On the Monday following they handed over the balance of their account to the receivers elected for the following year, drawing up a tripartite indenture, one part of which they kept themselves, the other two going to the new receivers and the bailiffs. The chamberlains' office must have been capable of handling the regular issue of indentures or tallies for payments into the treasury as well as drawing up an annual account.[10] This work would not have engaged a clerk in full-time activity, however, and there was no provision for special clerical assistance to perform it, so that the common clerk of the borough must have been responsible for such clerical duties as the receivers required.

The ratification of borough accounts, scheduled to take place annually

[9] B. Wilkinson, *The Later Middle Ages in England, 1216–1485* (London, 1969), pp. 151–2; M. McKisack, *The Fourteenth Century, 1307–1399* (Oxford, 1959), pp. 384–5.
[10] OB, fos. 22v, 23r; RPB, fo. 6r.

the Monday before the Nativity of the Virgin, was a public affair which reputable burgesses were free to attend if they wished, but the audit was principally the concern of eight elected auditors. The responsibilities of these eight were not restricted to this one occasion; they served through the year as a financial committee of the council which, with the bailiffs and receivers, decided the financial expenditure of the borough and supervised the efficiency of the sergeants in collecting borough incomes. The audit was their final task in the year, and it might take some time. The New Constitutions provided that after the rendering of the accounts on the Monday, the audit should continue from day to day until they were satisfactory.[11]

Financial administration accordingly required the election of 10 new borough officers. But the New Constitutions did not stop there, since they also provided for the creation of a borough council. This went beyond any requirements of financial reform. From the cream of Colchester's wit and wisdom the bailiffs and auditors were to choose 16 men to make up the full council. The 2 bailiffs and 24 councillors (8 auditors and 16 others) were to decide concerning everything affecting the borough and to issue by-laws. There were to be at least four council meetings a year. Burgesses other than councillors had no right of access to these meetings, and if they had anything to suggest they had to proceed by handing a written bill to the bailiffs. They were liable to imprisonment if they tried to create a stir before the bailiffs in court about any matter concerning the common interest. These provisions demonstrate the craving for a more formal system by which to conduct borough affairs. There was nothing, however, to prevent bailiffs from putting questions to a more open assembly of burgesses if they chose to do so.[12]

Furthermore, the system of elections was formalised in 1372 in such a way as to restrict the element of popular participation. The whole community was responsible for electing four men of substance and good conversation who had never been bailiffs, one for each ward of the borough, but that was the limit of the open election. The four men so elected then chose 20 others of the better and more substantial burgesses who had never been bailiffs to form an electing committee of 24 in all. It was this committee which, after having been sworn to lay aside love, hate, bribery and private interest, elected the bailiffs, receivers and auditors.[13] The government of the borough was probably no more oligarchic as a result of this change than it had been before, since it was nothing new for the good of the community to be identified with the good of its more substantial members or for elections to be dominated by relatively wealthy

---

[11] OB, fo. 22v.
[12] OB, fo. 23r.   [13] OB, fo. 22v.

burgesses. But the New Constitutions made it less likely that elections should be used as a battleground for private feuds and factions.

The concern for financial control, though it governed some provisions of the New Constitutions and provided an acceptable justification of their necessity, was clearly not the only consideration at work. In addition to the expressed intent to make the bailiffs accountable there were other motives, amongst them the burgesses' desire to multiply the number of elective officers and so emulate the institutions of larger and more famous towns. The concern with the dignity of the borough which the New Constitutions exhibit was aroused by the growth of Colchester's wealth and status. Leading burgesses were aware of the lustreless character of the existing constitution and of the precarious consensus on which it rested. The New Constitutions did nothing to change the power structure in the borough and cannot be related to any conflict of interest within the ruling group there, but they had implications for the development of political life and proved a turning point in the maturing of the merchant class. In the early fourteenth century the apex of responsible officialdom in Colchester had been very narrow, since below the rank of bailiff, elective posts were either menial or of only momentary importance. The New Constitutions created 26 honourable offices to be filled every year, and so allowed a big increase in the number of those who participated in the pomp and ceremony of official occasions. Beneath any more mundane explanations for the changes of 1372 may be seen this more fundamental one; a wider spread of office-holding in the borough was a fitting adaptation to an increase in the number of burgesses of substance.

The development of formal borough constitutions of the type which Colchester adopted in 1372 had an English tradition of over a century behind it, and only Colchester's small size had prevented the adoption of some similar constitution at an earlier date. Systematic comparison is difficult because of the scarcity of detail concerning borough constitutions in medieval England. The Colchester New Constitutions are one of the earliest such documents to have survived, and comparable information concerning systems of election and the criteria for office-holding are rarely available from other towns at this time. Enough is known, however, to be certain that the type of constitution devised in 1372 had numerous analogues amongst the larger towns, whose adoption of elected councils according to a variety of patterns had been a development of the thirteenth century. Ipswich presented the burgesses of Colchester with a nearby example of exceptional antiquity, but it did not constitute a model which they chose to imitate; the council at Ipswich was one of only 12 men. Councils of 24 are reported from Lincoln (1219), Northampton (*c.* 1260), Leicester (1264), Great Yarmouth (1272), Winchester (1275), Exeter (1296) and Norwich (*c.* 1340).[14] Indirect systems of election were certainly extant in the thirteenth and early fourteenth centuries, though the relationship of Colchester's system to those in other towns is unknown. The most distinctive feature of the Colchester system was the elevation of the 8 auditors above the rest of the 24. The fact that the auditors, together with the bailiffs, chose the remaining 16 to make up the council, and that the auditors met more frequently than the rest of the council to keep a check on money matters, meant that from the beginning the council had a clearly defined inner circle.[15] This detail was not copied from any known borough constitution and seems to represent an original point of design. By contrast, the regulations concerning financial organisation were nothing unusual. The desirability of separate financial officers and an annual account was accepted in Lincoln by the end of the thirteenth century and in Oxford, York, King's Lynn, Exeter, Cambridge, and doubtless elsewhere, by the mid fourteenth century. In the later Middle Ages it became much more widespread.[16]

II

Amongst Colchester's leading burgesses the acceptance of the New Constitutions inaugurated a period of exceptional civic pride, so that the broader consequences of reform were greater than the letter of the text would imply. Several new schemes changed the appearance of the moothall. In 1373/4 some new covered stalls, vaulted over and with rooms above them, were constructed beside the entrance to the moothall and finished off with laths and plaster of Paris. In the same year steps were newly built at the entrance to the moothall – marble in front, on the south side, and tiles at the rear, on the north side. Within the hall the seats, stools and other furnishings were redecorated. The civic feeling behind these changes is conveyed by the account of them in the Red Paper Book, which comments that they would impress travellers favourably and enhance the honour of the town. The new stalls, it says, would gladden the hearts of the people of Colchester and its neighbourhood because the rents due from them would be a perpetual source of new income for the community. The author considers the improvements as an act of veneration for a building handed down from past generations as the borough's record repository and law court. 'In fact this building may be called the Colchester community's

---

[14] Tait, *The Medieval English Borough*, pp. 270–9; Hill, *Medieval Lincoln* p. 294; A. S. Green, *Town Life in the Fifteenth Century* (2 vols., London, 1894), ii, pp. 364–5.
[15] *Cf.* Tait, *The Medieval English Borough*, pp. 335, 337. This study does not take sufficiently into account the distinct rôle of the eight auditors from the beginning.
[16] *York City Chamberlains' Accounts, 1396–1500*, ed. R. B. Dobson, Surtees Society, cxcii (Durham, 1980), pp. xviii–xix.

house of Justice and Honour since, just as the head is essential to the body of every living soul, so is this hall the head and honour of the whole community of Colchester.'[17] The imagery and the Latin might be faulted, but the sentiments behind them would have done justice to something grander than market stalls and marble steps.

The biggest civic building programme of the later fourteenth century was undoubtedly the restoration of the town walls, an operation in which pride mingled with a concern for public security. During the 1370s it had become obvious that the English government could not protect coastal towns against direct assault from the French. The most serious raids had occurred on the south coast in 1377 in the course of a co-ordinated campaign by French and Castilian shipping, and the ancient port of Rye had been captured and burned at their hands.[18] Town walls were potentially more than an ornament. In 1382 the burgesses of Colchester were exempted for five years from sending members to parliament in view of their expenses in enclosing the town. This exemption was extended in 1388 and again, though only for three years, in 1394.[19] In fact Colchester still returned members to most parliaments during these years, perhaps because this too was a point of status for the burgesses.[20] Work on the walls began about 1382, when it was observed that 'of late the bailiffs and community have been continuously having the stone walls of the town repaired, as is sorely needed'. Because John Hamptone and his wife had a house up against the walls by East Gate they were required to move it, and were given a building plot for the purpose.[21] Provision was also made for the wall's future maintenance. In 1394 a plot next to the wall near North Bridge, at the end of what is now St Peter's Street, was leased out by the bailiffs and community 'with conditions respecting repair of the stone wall there', probably simply to ensure proper access. In a lease of a plot inside the wall by North Gate in 1398 it was stipulated that the bailiffs and community should in perpetuity have access 'to inspect and repair the town wall whenever and as often as they please'.[22] The community did more, in fact, than restore the ancient stonework. Archaeological investigations have established the location of seven out of eight bastions which were added to the walls between 1382 and 1421.[23] No attempt was made, however, to extend the circuit of the walls to embrace any of the suburban housing which had grown up outside them.

In a second respect, too, enthusiasm for the community's sake was stirred up in the 1370s; the period was an important one in the development

[17] RPB, fo. 9r.
[18] Tuck, *Richard II and the English Nobility*, pp. 14–15.
[19] *Cal. Pat. R.*, *1381–5*, p. 214; *Cal. Pat. R.*, *1385–9*, p. 505; *Cal. Pat. R.*, *1391–6*, p. 379.
[20] *Return of Names*, pp. 212–52.   [21] OB, fo. 56v.
[22] OB, fos. 64r, 66r.   [23] Crummy, *Colchester: Recent Excavations*, p. 34.

of new sources of income. A number of these – the leasing of the moothall cellar as a wool market, the reorganisation of the cloth fairs, the provision of a crane at Hythe, the construction of new stalls by the moothall – have already been mentioned in other contexts,[24] but they do not exhaust the list of financial innovations. One feature of the 1373 elections was a successful attempt to raise the income due from the lease of customs and tolls. Although it may sound unlikely that the appointment of a farmer of tolls and customs should have been decided by the character of the man rather than by how much he would pay for the lease, this was indeed the case in the fourteenth century. The tolls were leased for £35 each year to meet the obligations which Colchester owed to the Crown, and confidence on this score was worth more than a possible few pounds of extra income. Raising the income from the lease did not compromise this principle because there was no question of making the lessee's appointment dependent upon his capacity to pay more. In 1373, after Augustine Plomer had been appointed farmer of the tolls and customs by an electing jury of 24, one of the bailiffs, in granting him the lease, persuaded him to pay an additional £5 towards the repairs at the moothall. Plomer found guarantors for this extra sum, but it was not strictly an augmentation of the rent. The following year Plomer promised £6 13s 4d in a similar manner after his election.[25] Simultaneously there was a burst of enthusiasm for increasing the community's income from rents, though this was simply to continue an interest in evidence for over 50 years. Tenants with strong stomachs were found for some plots of land by the castle ditch which had been used as a tip for night soil and rubbish, and perhaps also as a latrine. A plot at Hythe which Geoffrey Dawe had used for 17 years was converted into a tenure paying rent to the community, and some old leases were renewed at higher rents.[26]

A third aspect of the civic enthusiasm of the 1370s concerns chiefly the town clerk and his record-keeping activities. The chronicle account of the events of the 1370s refers to the moothall as the place 'in which the more important records of the community are brought together',[27] and this interest in the records was a bond between the clerk appointed in 1372[28] and his successor Michael Aunger, who was town clerk from 1380 to 1398.[29] Both were men who took pride in the borough archive and its

---

[24] See also Chapters 4 and 5, pp. 69–70 and 72–3.   [25] RPB, fos. 6v, 9v; CR 17/1d.

[26] RPB, fos. 7v, 8r, 10r.   [27] RPB, fo. 9r.

[28] The handwriting of this clerk prevails in CR 16–19 and in CR 20/1–24. It is identical with that of the chronicle account of Colchester between 1372 and 1378 (RPB, fos. 5r–11r) and of some other texts in the Red Paper Book.

[29] Aunger's hand in the court rolls predominates from the time of his election as a burgess in June 1380: CR 20/24r. His resignation may be tentatively dated to Michaelmas 1398; his handwriting occurs in the main heading of the rolls of 1398/9 and in a few places later, as if he was helping a new successor: CR 30/1r.

capacity to perpetuate the memory of matters other than routine business. The two surviving registers of the borough were started in the last quarter of the fourteenth century, within a short time of each other. The Red Paper Book opens with the chronicle of the years 1372–8, which constitutes the main source of evidence for the constitutional events of the 1370s. It was probably copied there between June 1377 and June 1380,[30] and this is accordingly the most likely time for the Red Paper Book to have been started. The Oath Book was begun as a memorandum book for texts relating to the town clerk's business, probably between 1380 and 1395.[31] These were not the only borough registers in use. Another one must have been kept for the recording of ordinances made by the borough council, and it is likely that a new volume for this purpose was started soon after the establishment of the council in 1372, though none has survived.[32] The two extant registers contain only a very imperfect record of council activity during the late fourteenth century, but they supply important testimony to the civic enthusiasm of this period. The two clerks who spanned the years from 1372 to 1398 and who started the surviving registers were the only ones who ever showed an interest in writing chronicles of local events. The clerk from 1372 to 1380 was the major practitioner of the art, as the probable author of the chronicler of the years 1372–8, and certainly as its copyist. Michael Aunger took from this text into the Oath Book the account of the 1372 elections as well as the text of the New Constitutions,[33] and he wrote various other items in chronicle style during his period as town clerk, both in the Red Paper Book and in the Oath Book.[34] The notion that happenings in Colchester were a fit subject for literary exercises disappeared during the 1390s, and after Aunger's retirement clerks were satisfied to transcribe the texts of formal documents.

Against this interpretation of the mood of Colchester's leading burgesses in the 1370s and 1380s it may be argued that it draws heavily from the chronicle of 1372–8, which survives only in the Red Paper Book. Had earlier registers of the borough survived they would perhaps have contained similar accounts of earlier periods. And even if the chronicle of 1372–8 had no precedent in Colchester's archival history, it perhaps reflects a single

---

[30] The bailiffs' oath as recorded in the chronicle requires them to swear fealty to King Richard: RPB, fo. 5v.

[31] Britnell, 'The Oath Book', pp. 96–7.

[32] A register called the Black Paper Book existed in the 1390s: OB, fo. 46r.

[33] OB, fos. 22v–23v. This is the beginning of the chronicle. It is missing from the text in the Oath Book.

[34] These include an account of the decision to increase the number of sergeants from three to four in 1380 (RPB, fo. 12r), an account of the Peasant's Revolt (RPB, fo. 257v), a record of revised court procedures introduced in 1388 (RPB, fo. 12v) and a note of the dispute about elections in 1394/5 (RPB, fo. 12r; OB, fo. 24r).

clerk's taste for bombast rather than the prevailing thoughts of his contemporaries. Against the first supposition there are two arguments. The first is that, though the Red Paper Book contains a number of quotations from earlier borough records relating to matters of continuing interest, none of them is in chronicle form. The second is that chronicle accounts of events in small towns are uncommon, and that the Colchester chronicle of 1372–8 is unusual both for its length and for the civic spirit it describes.[35] It is improbable that such compositions should have been a normal activity of fourteenth-century Colchester town clerks. And even if the chronicle expresses no more than an individual point of view, there stands behind the rhetoric a sequence of events which speak for themselves. When the author's glosses are set aside there remains a considerable amount of factual detail, much of it confirmed in other sources, concerning events which would not have happened except as a result of enthusiasm backed by prosperity.

Of any corresponding criticism of these changes, and of their meaning for members of the community without wealth or power, the records are silent. There must have been an antagonistic view. Nevertheless, despite some attempts to represent Colchester as a hotbed of rebellion in 1381, the evidence does not amount to much. John Ball's transitory associations with the town had little effect there; he spent his time stirring up the county, and his following among townsmen was small.[36] On 13 June insurgents from Manningtree, on their way to meet the young king at Mile End, assembled at Colchester in order to join a contingent from the borough.[37] But whereas men of Manningtree, North Weald Bassett, Thaxted, Broxted, Chelmsford and other Essex villages made their mark in the capital, those of Colchester kept a low profile.[38] In the borough and its environs the mood was tense during the summer months. St John's Abbey was invaded and records were removed; some Flemings were murdered in Colchester; the moothall was burgled on Sunday, 16 June and some rolls and other records were taken; no judicial sessions were held for five weeks.[39] Michael Aunger confessed to alarm in his best Latin; as town clerk and custodian of the court rolls he was a target for the rebels, and his brief account of the revolt

[35] S. Reynolds, *An Introduction to the History of English Medieval Towns* (Oxford, 1977), p. 179.

[36] The slenderness of any connection between John Ball and Colchester is demonstrated by B. Bird and D. Stephenson, 'Who was John Ball?', *Essex Archaeology and History*, viii (1976), pp. 287–8.

[37] A. Réville, *Le Soulèvement des travailleurs d'Angleterre en 1381* (Paris, 1898), pp. 216–17.

[38] A. Prescott, 'London in the Peasants' Revolt: A Portrait Gallery', *The London Journal*, vii (1981), pp. 127–9.

[39] CR 21/1d, 4r; Réville, *Le Soulèvement*, pp. 217–18. For a rather different assessment of these events, see B. Bird, 'The Rising of the Commons, 1381', *Colchester Historical Studies*, Colchester Local History Research Group, i (Colchester, *c*. 1980), pp. 2–4.

was written 'in very great fear both for himself and for his friends'.[40] Yet none of the borough officers suffered any harm, and any damage done to the court records was slight, since all the rolls back to 1327 survived to be indexed in the Oath Book during the 1390s.[41] The court roll of 1380/1 escaped the hands of the rebels to perish at the hands of some later clerk or antiquarian.[42] At no stage in 1381 could any great number in Colchester be effectively roused, and in the final rally of the Essex rebels, when a band came to mobilise the townsmen, no entreaties, threats nor arguments were of any avail.[43] In the event Colchester came through the revolt lightly, perhaps because complacency was not confined to the small ruling group.

III

Like any written constitution, the Colchester New Constitutions of 1372 had their teething troubles. The chief point of difficulty appears to have been the grafting of the new system on to the old pattern of electing town clerk, sergeants and toll collectors, since the Constitutions were more precise concerning the number of borough officers to be elected than they were concerning the time or mode of election. The new electing committee of 24 was expressly charged with electing the bailiffs, receivers and auditors, but there was no statement about when the elections should be held. In the matter of electing clerk, sergeants and toll collectors the Constitutions were silent, though the existence of these officers was assumed. It is clear enough from details in the Red Paper Book what happened in the years following the adoption of the New Constitutions; a single jury was responsible for electing bailiffs, receivers, auditors, clerk, sergeants and a toll collector, this being the electing jury of 24 whose composition was provided for by the Constitutions. However, there were two election days on which this jury was active. An account of the elections of 1372 shows that the jury was sworn in on 13 September (the Monday after the Nativity of the Virgin) and that the bailiffs were elected the same day. All the other officers were elected three weeks later on 4 October (the Monday after Michaelmas), which was the day of the Michaelmas lawhundred when the bailiffs formally assumed their office. The form followed in 1373 was the same as the year before.[44] It is surprising to find

[40] RPB, fo. 257v.
[41] The index to the court rolls was probably started during the years 1395–8: Britnell, 'The Oath Book', p. 98. Since writing that article I have found that the clerk who began the index (OB, fos. 29v–34r) occasionally assisted Aunger in the years 1392–6: CR 27/19r, 20r, 23d; CR 28/36r, 38d; CR 29/13d, 24d.
[42] The court roll of this year was indexed as usual: OB, fo. 55r,v.
[43] Thomas of Walsingham, *Historia Anglicana*, ii, p. 19.
[44] OB, fo. 23v; RPB, fos. 5r, 6r,v. In the Red Paper Book a record of the receivers' election on the second day was later erased (fo. 6v), presumably after 1394/5.

the receivers being elected on the second election day, in view of the
constitutional requirement that the old receivers were to hand over their
cash balances on the Monday after the Nativity of the Virgin, and it was
probably because of this anomaly that in 1374 and in subsequent years
the committee elected the receivers on the first election day.[45] By 1381 the
election of auditors was also brought forward,[46] with some administrative
advantages; the third part of the tripartite indenture which would normally
go to the incoming receivers was handed to the auditors if no new receivers
were elected.[47] The election of auditors on the first election day would also
have made it easier to prepare the formation of a council on the second.
The only jury elections to take place on the Monday after Michaelmas were
now the ones which had always been held then, namely those of the town
clerk, the three sergeants and the toll collector. At some point, most
probably between 1387 and 1392,[48] there was a move towards appointing
a new electing jury of 24 for the second round of elections. After some
unpleasantness between the supporters of rival interpretations of the
Constitutions, the practice of appointing a second electing jury was
established in 1394/5. The text of the Constitutions was so obscure on this
point that a formal alteration was unnecessary, and instead the bailiffs
opted, in the presence of the council and community, to condemn the
writings of foolish clerks who had misrepresented the New Constitutions.
They ordained that in future the sergeants and other officers to be elected
on the Monday after Michaelmas would be elected by a new jury chosen
from the more respectable burgesses present on the day.[49] This revised
procedure had the advantage of eliminating the need to recall a jury of
24 men after three weeks, and was accordingly a way round the inevitable
problem of absenteeism. There is no other obvious reason for the change.
The wrangling behind the ordinance of 1394/5 is accordingly to be
explained as a conflict between those who revered the practices of the 1370s
for tradition's sake and those who saw no obstacle to making a helpful
change in procedure where the Constitutions were silent. It was the
traditionalists who lost.

The New Constitutions transformed the government of Colchester, but
did not preclude subsequent changes, and their text was never inviolable.
The Oath Book copy was amended on a number of points of terminology
by John Brouneswold, the town clerk of *c.* 1415–23, to bring it in line with
normal usage. Even before this Thomas Rypere had rewritten the New
Constitutions in a form described as 'Correction and Amendment of the

[45] RPB, fos. 9r, 10v.   [46] CR 21/1 (attached schedule).
[47] OB, fo. 23r.
[48] Britnell, 'The Oath Book', p. 97.   [49] OB, fo. 24r; RPB, fo. 12r.

New Constitutions', rearranging the words and phrases of the original text in order to facilitate their exposition, and this redaction was itself the object of subsequent alteration.[50] The surviving texts are accordingly good evidence that the New Constitutions were the start of a long history of constitutional tinkering. However, since the major developments attested by these scribal amendments belong to the fifteenth century, discussion of them may be postponed until a later chapter.

IV

The prominence of merchants in Colchester so evident in the unsettled conditions of the 1360s was maintained after the New Constitutions were in force. The 10 elections between 1391 and 1400 may be taken to illustrate the situation which had resulted. In these elections a total of 12 men were chosen as bailiffs, 6 of them more than once.[51] Four of the 12, John Seburgh, Thomas Fraunceys, John Dyer and Stephen Flisp, occur in the customs records of 1397–8 as overseas merchants.[52] John Seburgh, who was elected bailiff four times during the decade,[53] was Colchester's biggest exporter of cloth. Seven of the 12, John Christian, John Seburgh, Thomas Fraunceys, John Dyer, William Mate, Thomas Clerk and Stephen Flisp, are listed as sellers of cloth in the ulnage accounts of 1394–7.[54] Ten of them were presented in Colchester lawhundreds as vintners – all, that is, except William Reyne and William Mate.[55] Even the former of these two men, for whom no active trading activity can be found in the 1390s, does not really escape from the generalisation that bailiffs in this period were primarily occupied in trade; he was an old merchant at the end of both his trading career and his active politics.[56] A similar preponderance of merchants is in evidence in the social composition of the council. This may be shown from the list of those elected in 1395,[57] which is about contemporary with the best ulnage accounts and with the best customs accounts of the later fourteenth century. Of the 24 councillors elected that year, 20 occur in the ulnage accounts as sellers of cloth, most of them a

---

[50] OB, fos. 22v–23v, 26v–27r.
[51] OB, fos. 62r–67r.
[52] P.R.O., E.122/193/33, fos. 11v, 12r,v, 13r, 14r,v, 15r, 17r, 24v, 25r.
[53] In 1391/2, 1394/5, 1396/7, 1399/1400: OB, fos. 62r, 64r, 65r, 67r.
[54] P.R.O., E.101/342/9, mm. 1r–3d, 8r–10r, 11r.
[55] Ralph Algar (CR 25/1d, etc.), John Christian (CR 28/1r), Thomas Clerk (CR 25/1d, etc.), John Dyer (CR 31/2r), Stephen Flisp (CR 27/14d, etc.), John atte Ford (CR 28/1r), Simon Fordham (CR 25/1d, etc.), Thomas Fraunceys (CR 27/14d, etc.), Thomas Godeston (CR 31/11r, etc.), John Seburgh (CR 25/1d, etc.).
[56] See Chapter 7, p. 111.
[57] CR 29/2r.

number of times.[58] Ten of these 20 also occur in the borough court rolls as sellers of wine on various occasions between 1385 and 1405.[59] Eight councillors occur in the customs accounts of 1397–8 as engaging in overseas trade, and they include two men who do not occur in the ulnage accounts.[60] From this handful of sources an active interest in trade may be demonstrated for almost all the members of the council, and it is unnecessary to labour the point. It may be noted, however, that sometimes the council included men whose background was different. John Hall was on the council in 1381/2, and no doubt valued for his learning in the law.[61]

Some further generalisations can be made concerning membership of the council. Table 8.1 shows the extent to which elections threw up the same men year after year. In each year the outgoing bailiffs were re-elected as auditors in the new council; it looks as if this was a matter of course. The table does not show the almost equal regularity with which bailiffs were elected from members of the outgoing council, often from those who had been auditors the year before. The council in this way gave almost permanent office in the administration of borough affairs to members of the community who were of the status to be elected as bailiffs. Of the 12 men who were elected between 1391 and 1400, seven were elected as either bailiffs or councillors in 1387, seven in 1395, nine in 1398, nine in 1399, and seven in 1400. Not all councillors were past or future bailiffs; at least half of those in any documented year never served as bailiffs at any stage of their careers. However, Table 8.1 shows how secure even these men were in their status if they wished to retain it. The main body of the council lost only three or four members each year, so that its composition changed only gradually. Both in 1384 and in 1398 three-quarters or more of council members had been on the council, or serving as bailiffs, four years earlier.

Though there was no ruling on the matter in the New Constitutions, the two borough receivers were not in practice elected as councillors. The office was intended as a subordinate one, and the Constitutions specified that former bailiffs were not eligible for it.[62] Receivers were not required to be changed annually, so that the office might be the making of a long career in the service of the community, as it was for Seman Clerk, who was

---

[58] Robert Aldwene, Michael Aubre, Stephen Baroun, John Best, Augustine Bonfaunt, Henry Bosse, Hugh Bokenham, Thomas Clerk, William Cotel, John Christian, Stephen Flisp, Thomas Fraunceys, John Gernoun, William Morton, John Pake, Alexander Pod, Simon Rodebright, John Seburgh, William Snook, Robert Wyght: P.R.O., E.101/342/9, mm. 1r–3d, 8r–10r, 11r.

[59] Thomas Clerk, John Christian, Stephen Flisp, Thomas Fraunceys and John Seburgh (as in n. 55) together with Stephen Baroun (CR 26/28r), John Best (CR 25/42r, etc.), William Cotel (CR 29/1d, etc.), John Pake (CR 30/16r, etc.), William Snook (CR 27/14d, etc.).

[60] John Best, Stephen Flisp, Thomas Fraunceys, William Morton, John Pake, John Seburgh, Simon Slade, Robert Wyght: P.R.O., E.122/193/33, fos. 11v–17r, 24r–25v.

[61] CR 21/1 (attached schedule).   [62] OB, fo. 22v.

Table 8.1 *Continuity of membership on Colchester Council, 1381–1400*

	1381	1384	1385	1387	1395	1398	1399	1400
Number of councillors elected	24	24	24	24	24	24	24	24
Bailiffs of the year before	2	2	2	2	2	2	2	2
Councillors of the year before	?	?	20	?	?	?	19	20
Bailiffs of 2 years before	2	1	1	2	0	2	2	1
Councillors of 2 years before	?	?	?	18	?	?	?	17
Baliffs of 4 years before	2	2	2	2	2	2	1	2
Councillors of 4 years before	?	17	?	?	?	16	?	?

Sources: CR 21/1 (attached list); CR 24/2 (attached list); CR 25/2r; CR 26/2d; CR 29/2r; CR 30/2r; CR 31/2d; CR 32/1r; OB, fols. 52v–67r.

probably a receiver continuously from 1385 or 1386 until 1400.[63] The burgesses did not, however, create a formal *cursus honorum* by such regulations. Some receivers were appointed following a spell on the council; Michael Aubre left the council to become a receiver in 1398[64] and William Snook did so in 1400.[65] Others, however, came to the office by other routes; Andrew Beche, who was elected a receiver in 1400 had not been on the council in the two preceding years, nor in earlier years for which council lists survive.[66] Service as receiver held no great promise of higher office in the borough. A receiver could expect to be elected to the council on his retirement from the office,[67] but his chances of being elected bailiff were unaffected. Of the seven receivers between 1385 and 1400 whose names are recorded only one was ever elected bailiff subsequently.[68]

Past service on the council was not an absolute requirement for election as bailiff; Thomas Godeston was elected bailiff in 1398 without having been on the council in the previous year or in any earlier recorded year.[69] There were no written or unwritten rules about the sequence of steps by which a man attained the dignity of highest office. In practice, however, for most townsmen who took an interest in borough politics, membership of the council was the most important route to a position of authority. New auditors seem normally to have been chosen from those with some

[63] CR 25/2r; CR 26/16r; CR 28/2r; CR 29/7d; CR 30/2d, 3r; CR 31/2d.
[64] CR 30/2r, 3r. He is listed as a councillor in CR 29/2r.
[65] CR 32/1r. He is listed as a councillor in CR 31/2d.
[66] CR 32/1r. Cf. CR 30/2r; CR 31/2d.
[67] *E.g.* John Curteys in 1386 or 1387 (CR 25/2r; CR 26/2d), William Mate between 1396 and 1398 (CR 29/7d; CR 30/2r), Seman Clerk in 1400 (CR 31/2d; CR 32/1r).
[68] William Mate, a receiver in 1395/6, was elected bailiff in 1397: CR 29/7d; OB, fo. 65v.
[69] OB, fo. 66r.

experience on council, and bailiffs were often chosen from men who had
been auditors, so that, without any definite rules about the sequence of
offices, there were certain regularities which are of interest for the
development of Colchester society after the New Constitutions were
adopted. Of the earlier stages in a man's career, by which he might gain
the rank of councillor, Colchester evidence is silent.

A final question concerning merchants and the government of Colchester
is the extent to which public service was a matter for real choice rather
than a duty which residence in the borough enjoined upon the wealthy or
the elderly. As regards the wealthy, it can be shown that the respectable
merchant population was appreciably larger than the number of heads of
families on the town council. Some prominent merchants of the 1390s –
Thomas Saxlingham,[70] Stephen Munde,[71] Adam Barbour,[72] for example –
do not occur in any council list, were never chosen as bailiffs and seem
to have shirked political and administrative involvement. The long service
of some men as councillors, and the frequent election of others as bailiffs,
was thus offset by widespread non-participation. Both for council membership and for the office of bailiff there was a preference for middle-aged
and older men, but at least half the 36 men who became bailiff for the first
time between 1350 and 1399 lived for 15 years or more, and five lived for
more than 30 years. Men of the fourteenth century who reached adulthood
could not normally expect to live to be more than 50 years old;[73] it is
therefore likely that Colchester men could reach the highest office in the
borough in their late thirties or early forties. A mercantile career cannot
have been very time-consuming. Taken all together, the evidence shows
that the administration of the community in the fourteenth century did
not depend upon onerous rotas or inescapable obligations. Juries elected
men who were willing to be elected and who were thought to be suitable
candidates on the strength of their wealth and personal qualities. If a man
was repeatedly re-elected as bailiff, like John atte Ford or Thomas
Fraunceys, it was presumably because he liked the job and was thought
to be good at it.

---

[70] Saxlingham engaged in foreign trade, exporting cloth and importing wine: P.R.O.,
E.122/193/33, fos. 11v, 13r, 14v, 24v, 25r. He retailed wine in Colchester: CR 27/14d,
etc.

[71] Munde also engaged in overseas trade: P.R.O., E.122/193/33, fos. 15r, 24v *bis*, 25r. In
the ulnage accounts he occurs as a seller of cloth: E.101/342/9, mm. 9r, 10r. He retailed
wine in the borough: CR 29/1d, etc.

[72] Barbour's overseas trade is recorded in P.R.O. E.122/193/33, fos. 13r,v, 14r. He is
prominent in the ulnage accounts: E.101/342/9, mm. 8d *bis*, 9r, 10r, 11r *ter*. He, too,
retailed wine: CR 27/14d, etc.

[73] Herlihy and Klapisch-Zuber, *Les Toscans et leurs familles*, p. 203.

9

Economic regulation

I

The growth of Colchester's population and industry in the later fourteenth century was accompanied by an expansion of every type of marketing institution. Trade through Hythe greatly increased,[1] as did trade in foodstuffs and raw materials through the central town markets. The wool trade can be shown to have grown,[2] and so can the meat trade. In 1359 'all the butchers of Colchester' numbered 13, but in 1400 'all the butchers of the town of Colchester' numbered 21. There was also an increased influx of butchers from other places coming to sell meat in the market on Saturdays.[3] Meanwhile there was growth in the informal trade between burgesses which took place in private homes and elsewhere. New shops were built;[4] new taverns were opened, so that by 1400 there were between 15 and 20 of them;[5] new inns were established for the benefit of visiting travellers, until by 1400 there were at least 13.[6] All these types of rendezvous occur frequently in litigation for debt as scenes of bargaining and exchange.[7] The growth of trade inevitably increased the work involved in enforcing the statutes relating to prices and measures, preventing illegitimate trade by non-burgesses, and carrying out the various traditional duties involved in regulating the market.

Of all the traditional concerns the one which loomed largest in this context was the enforcement of the Statute of Forestallers. This was a mounting problem, but in order to see the circumstances it is necessary to make some social distinctions. Throughout the fourteenth century the courts continued to amerce the sort of petty forestaller who had been the normal victim of this legislation before the Black Death. Lawhundred

---

[1] See Chapter 4, pp. 69–70. [2] See Chapter 5, pp. 72–3.
[3] CR 12/1d; CR 31/19r. [4] OB, fos. 166r, 167r.
[5] OB, fo. 167r; CR 31/1d; Appendix, Table 2. [6] CR 31/18r.
[7] *E.g.* CR 29/24r, 26d (transaction in William Reyne's tavern); CR 31/12r, 15r, 25d (transactions in John Aylmar's inn).

reports regularly contained lists of 'common forestallers of victuals' whose offences were numerous enough, but also minor enough, not to require specific details. The charge was generally one of trading before the market opened or intercepting produce on its way in. The number of people involved was never so large as in the second decade of the fourteenth century and showed no upward movement as urban consumption increased.[8] Probably the growth of incomes in the victualling trades made it easier to make a living without resorting to time-consuming and disreputable practices, and this type of forestalling must have seemed increasingly less of a problem to the townspeople. After 1412, though individuals continued to be charged with particular offences of this sort, the practice of drawing up lists of common forestallers was abandoned. The routine aspect of law enforcement had ceased to matter.

This did not mean, however, that the burgesses were indifferent to the principles involved; in fact they had become more genuinely concerned with the effects of forestalling than perhaps at any time in the past. This was chiefly because of their increased dependence upon water-borne supplies of victuals through Hythe, which accounts in part for the increasing value of tolls and other dues there. In the fish trade Hythe had always been the main source of supply, but towards the end of the fourteenth century water-borne grain was also becoming vitally important for the community. It is likely that supplies of grain through Hythe were growing more rapidly than those from more local sources. Much of the barley required for the brewing of ale came from coastal regions which specialised in this particular crop.[9] Among the plaintiffs in Colchester courts in 1400/1 were John Styward of Winterton, on the Norfolk coast, and John Horn of South Ferriby, on the southern shore of the Humber estuary, both claiming debts for barley sold at Hythe a few years before. Another suitor, John Stoklee of Bramford, near Ipswich, claimed a debt for barley sold in his home village.[10] A lawhundred jury in 1410, vigilant to protect the rules of trade at Hythe, had occasion to make observations concerning shiploads of barley brought by one Swillyngton from the North Country and by a certain Fraunesys of Kent.[11] Although barley and malt were the principal cereals to be transported from afar,[12] wheat too travelled long distances when prices were high. In 1407 a burgess was sued for £3 5s 0d, the cost of 6½ quarters of wheat sold at 8s 0d a quarter with an additional 13s 0d for their freight from Holland.[13]

The ease with which men with sufficient capital could intercept produce

[8] Appendix, Table 4.   [9] Britnell, 'Utilization of the Land'.
[10] CR 32/2d, 8d, 20d.   [11] CR 37/14d.
[12] Barley and malt were sold at Hythe more frequently than any other cereal: *e.g.* CR 31/3r, 4d, 14r, 21d.   [13] CR 36/27d.

approaching Hythe by sea was the most serious gap in Colchester's policing of local trade. The Colne estuary, as far south as Westness, was within the liberty of the borough; once goods had entered this area it was an offence to negotiate privately for them either on the water itself or on the banks. But nothing was simpler than for men to set out in boats from Hythe to meet incoming ships. Trade took place 'on Colne water',[14] and 'in a remote spot in the water of the liberty of Colchester'[15] or, more explicitly 'on the water opposite Wivenhoe church' in 1382,[16] 'on the water at Wodesende' in 1385,[17] 'on the sea at Hythe' in 1396.[18] The shores of the estuary were sometimes the location for illegal dealing as at Old Heath in 1373.[19] The commodity most frequently involved in these transactions was fish on its way to Hythe in fishing vessels, but from time to time the town's dependence upon sea-borne supplies of wheat and barley exposed it to forestalling of an identical kind. Both fish and grain were of so great an importance in the victualling of the borough, and the consignments of produce which could be intercepted on the river were so large, that the urban authorities tended to penalise those involved with exceptional severity. Richard Paccard was amerced 13s 4d in 1352 for intercepting grain between Hythe and Westness. In 1382 John Squerel of Alresford was amerced £1 for forestalling barley. John Mabbesone and Robert Horkeslegh were each fined 16s 8d in 1400[20] on two charges of forestalling victuals and other merchandise. These were not penalties to impose on petty misdemeanours. Colchester was not alone in experiencing these problems in the late fourteenth century. Forestalling was such a problem at Great Yarmouth, the chief centre of the herring fishing, that a royal ordinance was issued in 1357 to suppress it, and the purchase of herring at sea was expressly prohibited.[21]

Moreover, particularly between about 1390 and 1410 forestallers devised devious ways of obtaining large consignments of goods without even having to endure the discomforts of the estuary. In 1406 Stephen Flisp and John Plomer, both members of the borough council, were accused with others of conspiring to undermine the system of trade at Hythe. When a ship arrived with goods for sale, the master or his servant was obliged to go to the moothall for a bill. If the goods were imported on contract for particular burgesses, the bill would specify this and other burgesses would have no rights in them. If, however, the goods were not promised then the master of the ship agreed with the bailiffs to advertise them to the burgesses

---

[14] CR 24/19r.
[15] CR 32/9r.
[16] CR 21/30r.
[17] CR 24/19r.
[18] CR 29/11d.
[19] CR 16/6d.
[20] CR 9/6r; CR 21/30r; CR 31/19r.
[21] Ordinacio facta de allece vendito: *Statutes*, i, p. 353.

at a certain price, and a public announcement to this effect was made by
the town beadle, presumably in the market place outside the moothall.[22]
The tactic of Flisp, Plomer and their associates was to waylay the captain
of an incoming ship before a bill had been obtained from the moothall.
Once settled in a tavern with a drink the offenders would talk the captain
into agreeing to a conspiracy. He should say, if anyone were to ask, that
the goods were brought to Hythe on commission, and he should obtain
a bill to that effect from the moothall. Thereafter the burgesses would have
no right to a share in the cargo at Hythe, and the authors of the conspiracy
could gain control of the whole consignment.[23] The most blatant example
of forestalling in this period, however, involved men of rather less
eminence who began careers of systematic forestalling about the year 1392.
Their activities centred on William Holbeche's inn, where they met
fishmongers coming to Colchester market from outside the borough. The
conspiracy came to light in 1399 and provoked an outrage.

All the lawhundred jurors furthermore implore the worshipful bailiffs of Colchester
that they should cause John Caunceler and John Beneyt to revert and return to
their former crafts, which they have now abandoned for some time, because never
before has the liberty of Colchester known such gross forestallers as they are of
all kinds of fish coming to the town of Colchester, to the very great harm of
everyone, and so all unanimously implore that it be put right.[24]

Such an outburst is unusual, and implies an exceptional degree of concern.
The jurors, it may be observed, were appealing to a principle of statute
law that craftsmen should choose a trade and stick to it.[25] Caunceler's
career as an engrosser was unchecked by such opposition either in 1399
or later.[26]

II

Between 1351 and 1390 English towns were subject to a spate of royal
statutes regulating aspects of their everyday life. These new laws were in
part a reaction against the upward movement of labour costs and the
associated improvement of living standards in the lower ranks of society.
Wages and conditions of employment,[27] the treatment of beggars,[28]

22 CR 31/19r; CR 35/14d.
23 CR 35/14d. For the status of Flisp and Plomer, see CR 34/1r; CR 35/1r.
24 CR 30/16r,d.
25 37 Edward III, c. 6: *Statutes*, i, p. 379. The attempt to place a similar restraint on
merchants was soon abandoned: 37 Edward III, c. 5; 38 Edward III, 1, c. 2: *Statutes*,
i, pp. 379, 383.
26 CR 31/1d, 11r, 19r; CR 34/2r, 11d; CR 35/26d; CR 36/2r; CR 38/13r, 23r,d; CR 39/2d.
27 23 Edward III, cc. 1–5; 25 Edward III, 2, cc. 1–5; 34 Edward III, c. 9; 12 Richard II,
c. 4; 13 Richard II, c. 8: *Statutes*, i, pp. 307–8, 311–12, 366–7, and ii, pp. 57, 63.
28 23 Edward III, c. 7; 12 Richard II, cc. 7, 8: *Statutes*, i, p. 308, and ii, p. 58.

freedom of occupation,[29] victuallers' profits and the prices of foodstuffs,[30] standards of dress,[31] the cleanliness of waterways and town streets[32] were all at various times the objects of parliamentary discussion and intervention. In the same period there was a reiteration of older measures to regulate forestalling,[33] the use of standard weights and measures,[34] the dimensions of cloths manufactured,[35] the price of bread,[36] and other matters. During most of its period of growth, therefore, Colchester experienced a multiplication of rules imposed from outside, designed to restrain the freedom of individuals to make contracts with others and to allocate their time and money as they pleased.

These laws made little impact upon the normal policing activity of the borough courts. Those which were regularly enforced there were peripheral to governmental concern with prices and wages. The punishment of men who polluted the river, the wells and the streets became a more frequent part of lawhundred business after the Statute of Cambridge in 1388,[37] and from 1392 it was normal to amerce innkeepers who had been baking.[38] But economic controls are little in evidence. Legislation against artisans who followed two crafts was invoked only as a desperate measure against troublesome forestallers.[39] The bailiffs' powers to regulate the migration of labourers were exercised only occasionally, to ensure that there should be enough hands at harvest time.[40] And the prevention of excessive prices according to the provision of the Statute of Labourers was attempted only in periods of shortage, as in 1410, when a burgess was reported for raising the price of wheat by buying up stocks in the countryside for a penny a bushel above the current market price.[41] More usually lawhundred juries stuck to the time-honoured rules they knew, punishing offences against the assizes of bread and ale, enforcing the Statute of Forestallers, and from time to time intervening to stop the price-raising conspiracies of bakers, millers, butchers and other groups.[42]

[29] 37 Edward III, cc. 5, 6; 12 Richard II, c. 5; 13 Richard II, c. 12: *Statutes*, i, pp. 379–80, and ii, pp. 57, 65.
[30] 23 Edward III, c. 6; 25 Edward III, 2, c. 5; 37 Edward III, c. 3; 13 Richard II, c. 8: *Statutes*, i, pp. 308, 313, 378–9, and ii, p. 63.
[31] 37 Edward III, cc. 8–14: *Statutes*, i, pp. 380–2.
[32] 12 Richard II, c. 13: *Statutes*, ii, pp. 59–60.
[33] 25 Edward III, 3, c. 3; 6 Richard II, 1, c. 11: *Statutes*, i, p. 315, and ii, pp. 28–9.
[34] 25 Edward III, 5, c. 9; 34 Edward III, cc. 5, 6; 13 Richard II, 1, c. 9: *Statutes*, i, pp. 321, 365–6, and ii, pp. 63–4.
[35] 25 Edward III, 3, c. 1; 12 Richard II, c. 14; 13 Richard II, 1, c. 10: *Statutes*, i, p. 314, and ii, pp. 60, 64.   [36] 13 Richard II, 1, c. 8: *Statutes*, ii, p. 63.
[37] CR 30/10r, 16r and later.   [38] CR 27/28d and later.
[39] CR 30/16d.   [40] CR 16/3d.   [41] CR 37/14d.
[42] CR 22/4d; CR 31/19r. The unveiling of a conspiracy of bakers by an *ex officio* inquest is recorded in CR 29/15r.

The slight importance of newer economic controls in the normal operations of the bailiffs and the lawhundred court does not mean that Colchester was untouched by them. The court rolls themselves show how the Statute of Labourers, the most substantial single piece of economic regulation, impinged upon the development of private litigation in labour disputes. A new feature of the 1350s was the plea of broken contract 'against the statute', in which an employer attempted to show that a former employee had offended against the Statute of Labourers by abandoning his employment before his contract had terminated.[43] This form of action had the advantage over an ordinary plea of broken contract that the verdict was less capable of being turned by a conspiracy of the defendant's supporters. A case brought to court late in 1359 established that in pleas of broken contract of this kind the defendant was not entitled to wager his law with the help of his friends but had to abide the judgement of a jury.[44]

However, the established agencies for the enforcement of the new laws are wholly unrepresented in the everyday records of the borough community, and it is necessary to turn to the public records for the purpose. One relevant set of documents, the ulnage accounts, has already been examined in another context. Besides collecting subsidy and ulnage on each cloth, the ulnager enforced any relevant statutes and confiscated cloths not in accordance with the law. The bailiffs accordingly had no occasion to touch this matter, and the only lawhundred reports relating to the cloth industry concern offences, such as fraud, which had not been created by statute.[45] The ulnager's duties in Colchester were in fact never greatly concerned with industrial regulation since russets continued to be made to a variety of traditional specifications which were not governed by statute.

The Statute of Labourers was the concern of another special commission. In March 1351, soon after its enactment, a commission of the peace was appointed with powers to enforce it, and from 1368 this became a normal responsibility of justices of the peace.[46] Since Colchester did not at this time have a separate commission of the peace, it became part of the county of Essex for this purpose. The town officers were responsible only for collecting the fines. This led to a constitutional crisis in 1352, when the Colchester bailiffs and sub-collectors refused to collect and pay over the full sum of £84 7s 7d which had been charged in fines for offences against the statute. The bailiffs and sub-collectors were for a while imprisoned on

---

[43] B. H. Putnam, *The Enforcement of the Statute of Labourers during the First Decade after the Black Death, 1349–59* (New York, 1908), pp. 162–4.

[44] CR 12/6r: the plea was abandoned.

[45] CR 17/7r; CR 20/18d; CR 26/28d.   [46] 42 Edward III, c. 6: *Statutes*, i, p. 388.

this account. The issue was complicated by the unfortunate circumstance that the money was supposed to be handed to Lionel de Bradenham as one of the collectors of taxes for Essex.[47] Besides the slight to the borough's administrative independence which this implied, Bradenham was an old enemy of the burgesses; he had probably been involved in John Fitz Walter's harassment of the burgesses in 1343, and had engaged in some bullying on his own account in 1350.[48] The enforcement of the statute in Colchester having begun in disaster, its subsequent success was chequered. The surviving justices' rolls of 1377–9 do not record any labourers' fines from the borough.[49] If, as seems likely, the county justices had difficulty in assessing fines in Colchester, and, as is certain, the statute was not normally regarded by lawhundred juries, then the threat of private prosecution for breach of contract must have remained the main instrument for the control of labour. This would imply that the statute affected wage rates in the borough only indirectly, if at all, and that most of the time its capacity to oppress townsmen was slight.

This judgement appears, then, to be characteristic of most aspects of new legislation affecting the borough community between 1351 and 1390. Important though this was as a period when statute law branched out in new directions, it cannot be claimed that the economy and society of Colchester were much affected except in a few points of detail.

III

The community of the borough had powers to make by-laws for itself. The New Constitutions of 1372 expressly provided that the council should be able to make ordinances for the common profit of the burgesses, and it is clear that it did so from the Red Paper Book chronicle of the next few years.[50] Unfortunately too few texts have survived from the later fourteenth century for it to be possible to analyse the scope of this legislative activity or to assess its originality. But much of the economic regulation required was an easy development of what had gone before, and may be interpreted as a response to economic growth in Colchester. In this category come, most obviously, the various ordinances relating to the conduct of trade and the holding of markets. Marketing arrangements at Hythe were the object of some tighter regulations, to judge from some novel references in 1406 to an ordinance 'that if any goods are brought by anyone to Hythe in ships, they should be exposed for sale by day and not at night', and

---

[47] L. R. Poos, 'The Social Context of Statute of Labourers Enforcement', *Law and History Review*, i (1983), pp. 43–4.

[48] *Essex Sessions*, ed. Furber, p. 181.

[49] *Ibid.*, pp. 137–77.   [50] OB, fo. 23r; RPB, fos. 6r, 8r,v, 9r.

to another ordinance 'that when any wares or victuals come to Hythe, each and all of the burgesses claiming a share may have shares according to the quantity of the cargo'.[51] These were founded on principles already operative before the Black Death,[52] and probably derived from the need to spell out the rules more clearly as the volume of incoming trade increased. Other ordinances relating to Hythe must have been required to regulate the new wharfing and handling facilities which the community developed there in the later fourteenth century. Tighter regulation of the wool trade in 1373 and of the cloth fairs in 1374,[53] though these were ordinances establishing new institutions, were also derived directly from older principles of legislation, designed to ensure both that trade should be as open as possible and that the community should derive some financial benefit from it. These regulations serve to show, in fact, that the community maintained a tight grip on the established principles of urban marketing, which were thought to be necessary to protect the welfare of burgesses against non-burgesses and against monopolists from among their own number.

The policing of the market shows little sign of development along more formal lines during the later fourteenth century. Some trades which were heavily regulated were expected to appoint wardens to see that the rules were observed and to report misdemeanours to the bailiffs. The two meat wardens, who are already on record from 1311, were allowed a third of all the meat and skins they confiscated in the course of their duties.[54] As consumption grew in the later fourteenth century the responsibilities of meat wardens became more onerous, and they were more often in default after 1380 than earlier.[55] The rules they had to enforce were nevertheless the same as ever; butchers must not sell meat as fresh after a set period, they must not share carcasses between them, they must not sell dog meat from their ordinary stalls, and so on.[56] Wardens were also appointed at least as early as 1336 for the supervision of the leather trade,[57] and these too had the power to confiscate improperly tanned leather. In 1367 one of these wardens of untanned leather, as he was called, was reported at the Hilary lawhundred for corruptly having sold some leather he had seized in the course of duty.[58] These supervisory officers in the meat and leather trades constituted a rudimentary form of craft organisation, since they were chosen from year to year from the practitioners of the craft they supervised. But their duties were narrowly defined in terms of enforcing market regulations on the community's behalf, and their sworn loyalty was to the community as a whole rather than to the members of their craft.

---

[51] CR 35/14d.   [52] See Chapter 3, pp. 36–7
[53] RPB, fos. 6v, 7r, 8r,v.   [54] CR 1/5r; CR 11/4d.
[55] CR 24/19r; CR 29/20r; CR 30/1r; CR 31/19r; CR 32/9r; CR 33/20d.
[56] *E.g.* CR 30/16d; CR 31/19r.
[57] CR 5/1r.   [58] CR 15/6d.

There cannot have been similar officers in many other trades in view of the absence of reference to them in the court rolls.

Among industrial craftsmen there is no sign of regulatory organisation before the first decade of the fifteenth century. Even apprenticeship rules were as yet unformulated, a circumstance favourable to the growth of the cloth industry during its years of expansion.[59] Men could switch into new occupations in the time it took them to learn new skills from someone willing to teach them. This in turn implies that the scope of the community's own economic legislation was narrow. In the absence of craft organisations the disciplining of offenders against craft regulations must have been a matter for the borough courts, as it was in the meat and leather trades when wardens neglected their duty. But in fact lawhundred reports of the years 1350–1410 contain hardly anything of the kind which is new. Few of the regulations enforced there went beyond the community's statutory obligations, and even here, as has been shown, the structure of law enforcement did not require the bailiffs to change their ways very much. On the whole it seems to be true that as long as the urban economy was capable of expansion ruling groups in Colchester saw little need for restrictive by-laws.[60]

However, industrial growth could itself generate problems which called for regulation, and the earliest hints of a tighter industrial structure occur at the high point of Colchester's industrial development rather than after it. In May 1407 the court rolls record the election of two supervisors and masters of the weaver's craft to serve for a year following. The new officers swore to perform faithfully the duties of their position as laid down in the common constitutions made for the craft.[61] Details of these constitutions have not survived, but it is likely that they had just been introduced; both the timing of the election in the middle of an office year and the overt reference to written constitutions suggest that this was a new departure. Later elections were not recorded in the court rolls at all. If these regulations in fact belong to this extraordinary year, they cannot have been prompted by any experience of adversity. A similar caveat concerns some clauses in an ordinance of 1411/12 designed to protect textile workers within the liberty of the borough. Employers were required to use fixed weights in giving out wool to be spun and were forbidden to pay weavers in truck. They were also forbidden to take wool for spinning outside the liberty, a measure designed to prevent their seeking cheaper rural labour at the expense of urban spinsters at a time of full employment.[62] The difficulties facing employers and workers at this time were not those of stagnation or decay.

---

[59] See Chapter 16, p. 239.
[60] Hibbert, 'The Economic Policies of Towns', pp. 181–2.
[61] CR 36/23d.   [62] RPB, fo. 13r,v.

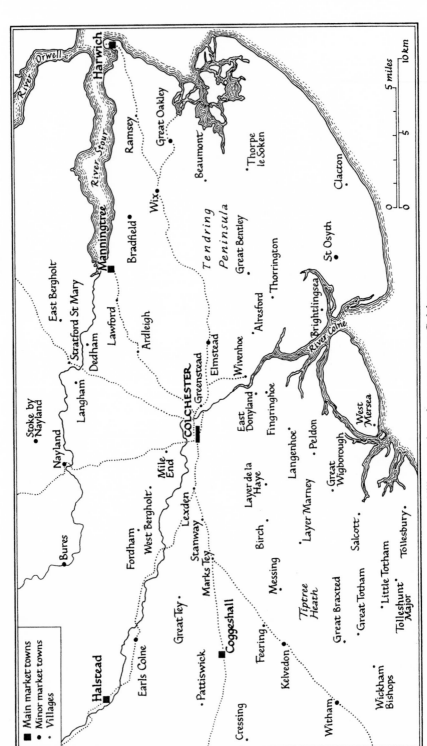

Villages and market towns near Colchester

10

Town and country

I

Colchester's growing requirements during the fourteenth century inevitably impinged upon local landlords and their tenants in a variety of ways. Rising population and standards of living there increased the consumption of grain, malt and meat, while expansion of industrial output implied greater sales of wool and leather in the market place. The evidence of both the cloth industry and the food trades suggests that during this period Colchester's development counteracted the debilitating effects of recurring epidemics upon agricultural production, since the town was quick to recover from the disaster of 1348 and continued to expand its demands beyond the point of mere recovery. By the first decade of the fifteenth century purchases of wool and malt, if not of bread grain and meat, were surely at least double what they had been during the 1340s. But the capacity of this urban development to benefit local agriculture was weakened by other changes affecting agricultural trade. To the extent that lines of supply lengthened as the town grew, the effects of that growth were spread over a wider area and the advantages for neighbouring villages were reduced. And insofar as population declined in the countryside as a result of recurrent epidemics, increases in Colchester's demand were likely to be offset by a contraction of rural trade.

The significance of the first of these considerations has already been shown in the context of Colchester's expanding trade through Hythe, one of whose major components was cereals.[1] The wool trade was similarly wide-ranging. Colchester's supply was not restricted to the marshlands of the Colne and the Blackwater. A purchase of white wool from a seller from Southminster is on record from 1403[2] and the frequency of trade with the southern Essex marshlands is further suggested by the prominence of wool

---

[1] See Chapter 9, p. 132.
[2] CR 34/4r.

141

merchants from Billericay in the moothall wool market during the years 1405–7.[3] Other supplies were drawn, as in the fourteenth century, from East Anglian pastures to the north. A seller of wool from Bury St Edmunds occurs suing for debt in the borough in 1400.[4]

Sources of butcher's meat, even at the time of Colchester's greatest medieval prosperity, were mostly local. Butchers from surrounding villages and towns – Dedham, East Bergholt, Stratford St Mary, Lawford, Manningtree – frequented the Saturday meat market in 1406, bringing with them carcasses from their own sources,[5] and stock raisers from surrounding villages also came to town to sell their animals there.[6] Alternatively, Colchester's own butchers set out to buy beasts in neighbouring villages, both those with markets and fairs and those without, like Elmstead, Great Wigborough, Peldon and East Bergholt.[7] The recorded activities of the butcher Richard Petrisburgh well illustrate this feature of the meat trade. He is found buying a cow in Stanway in the autumn of 1398.[8] In July 1401 he bought ewes at West Bergholt,[9] and in October 1402 he bought cows in Earls Colne.[10] He was at Stratford St Mary in November 1403 buying beasts of some kind.[11] But even meat supplies were responsive to opportunities outside the immediate market region. In 1404 Petrisburgh owed money for ewes bought in 'Aston', which may be the Aston near Stevenage.[12] And he engaged in a yet more distant venture in 1394, when his agent bought cows and steers on his behalf in Ely.[13] Big cattle fairs were capable of attracting an interest from many miles away – in this instance 67 miles by the route through Halstead, Haverhill, Linton and Cambridge. Petrisburgh denied that he had received the animals, which illustrates the problem with this sort of transaction.

The major development to offset Colchester's impact on the surrounding countryside was meanwhile a crisis in rural population. Even during the first decade of the fifteenth century, when the stimulus of Colchester market should have been greater than ever, all the signs of depopulation were to be found not far away; six tenements were ruinous at Wivenhoe in 1400,[14] as were three belonging to Bourchier Hall in Tollesbury in 1405.[15] Three houses in Thorrington were in ruins in 1401.[16] At Langham in 1406, five

[3] CR 35/2r, 13d, 26r; CR 36/1d, 11r.
[4] CR 32/9r.
[5] CR 35/14r, 26r; CR 36/2r, 11r.
[6] *E.g.* John Cony of Great Oakley: CR 35/5r, 7d.
[7] CR 33/29d (Elmstead); CR 35/8d (Great Wigborough); CR 30/18r, CR 34/13r (Peldon); CR 30/7r (East Bergholt).
[8] CR 31/7r.
[9] CR 34/15d.
[10] CR 33/6d.
[11] CR 34/26r.
[12] CR 34/5r, 6r.
[13] CR 29/25d.
[14] E.R.O., T/B 122.
[15] E.R.O., D/DK M75, m. 1r.
[16] E.R.O., T/A 167/1.

tenements were ordered to be repaired and another to be taken into the hands of the lord of the manor because they were ruinous and waste, and a tenant there was authorised to demolish a redundant dwelling house.[17] In Earls Colne there were five ruinous tenements at Whitsun 1408, some of which had been abandoned for several years.[18] The decline of rural population, even if accompanied by increasing standards of material comfort for the majority, had caused the loss of facilities which it was no longer profitable to maintain. At Langenhoe the value of the manorial grain mill was gradually increased to the point where, by 1413/14, it fell not far short of its level before the Black Death, the village being sufficiently close to Colchester to benefit from the growth of market demand there (Table 10.3). Farther away, where circumstances were less favourable, milling activity declined until mills were abandoned, as at Feering in 1359 and Kelvedon in 1396.[19] At Bourchier Hall a mill which survived to the mid 1350s had disappeared by 1403.[20] These instances imply that bread consumption in the villages was lower than it had been in the early fourteenth century.[21]

Declining rural population was, in fact, the primary influence upon the area of arable cultivation in the Colchester region during this period, though manors fared differently in this respect. The evidence of manorial demesnes is inevitably the clearest. At Wivenhoe, the closest documented manor to Colchester, the cultivated demesne was still in 1425/6 as large as it had been a century earlier, but at Langenhoe, though land had accumulated in the lord's hands for want of tenants, the sown acreage of the demesne was lower during the early fifteenth century than had been normal in the early fourteenth.[22] At Bourchier Hall, farther away from Colchester, the effects of agrarian recession were more marked, for here the demesne cultivated during the first decade of the fifteenth century was only about three-fifths of what it had been in the earlier 1340s.[23] On Westminster Abbey's manors of Kelvedon and Feering the contraction of demesne arable farming is demonstrable from a particularly fine series of manorial accounts; the sown acreage at Feering declined by 15 per cent between the 1340s and the early fifteenth century,[24] while at Kelvedon the

[17] E.R.O., D/DE1 M1, court held Tuesday in Whit week, 7 Henry IV.
[18] E.R.O., D/DPr 66, m. 10r.   [19] W.A.M., 25680r, 25870r.
[20] E.R.O., D/DK M86, m. 8r,d; D/DK M88d, 89d, 90r.
[21] *Cf.* A. Clark, 'Serfdom on an Essex Manor', *E.H.R.*, xx (1905), p. 483; K. C. Newton, *The Manor of Writtle* (Chichester, 1970), pp. 79–80. I am also indebted to Dr L. R. Poos for showing me his tithingpenny figures in advance of their publication.
[22] E.R.O., T/B 122; Britnell, 'Production for the Market', p. 386.
[23] Britnell, 'Agricultural Technology', pp. 62–3.
[24] On average 395.3 acres were sown between 1341 and 1348 (four years averaged) and 334.1 acres between 1400 and 1404 (five years averaged): W.A.M., 25662d, 25664d, 25744d, 25748d, 25752d, 25758d; P.R.O., S.C.6/841/8d, 9d, 10, m. 1d.

sown acreage declined by 34 per cent.[25] The downward movement of demesne cultivation ran parallel to a decline in the cultivation of tenant lands. Table 10.2, recording grain received by the manorial officers at Feering from the rectory there, gives some indication of the alteration during the 20 years after the Black Death, and Table 10.8 shows that there was further decline by the early fifteenth century.[26] A steep downturn in the value of Pattiswick Rectory tells the same tale.[27]

Contraction of arable husbandry during the later fourteenth century was combined with changes of practice which were partly influenced by market demand, partly by the conditions governing supply. Feering Rectory shows one of these developments, for the decline of cereals cultivation there had been compatible with increasing barley production. The same policy was adopted on Feering's demesne lands, where barley's share of the sown acreage increased from less than 1 per cent in the 1340s to 7.6 per cent between 1401 and 1404, and at Kelvedon the growth of barley husbandry was similar.[28] The same development on the demesnes at Bourchier Hall and Langenhoe shows that this was no peculiarity of Westminster Abbey estates.[29] Barley's greater importance in this period is explained by increased demand for barley malt. Consumption of ale had increased with rising standards of living, but barley malt had simultaneously replaced oats in the brewing industry as drinkers chose to be more discriminating. Oats were still malted around Colchester in the later fourteenth century,[30] but it was going out of favour, which accounts for some of the regression of oats cultivation. This was by far the most important change in cropping patterns during the later fourteenth century, and in part it must reflect the growth of brewing in Colchester and some other towns.

Another development in agrarian practices during these years illustrates the surplus capacity which farmers had at their disposal once cereals cultivation had contracted. Particularly on soils of poorer quality crop

---

[25] Here the sown acreage averaged 280.0 acres in 1345 and 1347 but only 185.3 acres between 1400 and 1402 (three years averaged): W.A.M., 25824d, 25825d, 25876d, 25878d, 25880d.

[26] Tables 10.2 and 10.8 do not record directly comparable information. The quantities in Table 10.2 are those passed from the rectory to the demesne barns after deduction of a small amount for the wages of tithe collectors. The figures in Table 10.8 are gross receipts at the rectory. Most of the difference, however, is owing to reduced gross receipts.

[27] The rent declined from £9 6s 8d in the 1340s to £3 13s 4d in 1406/7 and 1407/8: W.A.M., 25662r, 25664r, 25760r, 25761r.

[28] As above, nn. 24 and 25.

[29] For Bourchier Hall, see Britnell, 'Agricultural Technology', p. 65. At Langenhoe barley accounted for less than 1.0 per cent of the sown acreage in the 1340s, then for 6.1 per cent in 1404/5 and 8.3 per cent in 1413/14: E.R.O., D/DE1 M220d, 221d, 222d, 228d; D/DGe M201d.

[30] E.g. on Wix Priory's demesne at Wix, where in 1384/5, 87 quarters of oats were malted but only 71 quarters 1 peck of barley; P.R.O., S.C.6/849/16, m. 2.

rotations became more variable, so that individual parcels of land were rested more frequently. This is capable of illustration only from the wheatlands south and south-west of Colchester, and not from the ryelands of the town's immediate environment, where rotations were more flexible even in the earlier fourteenth century; no manor from the ryelands has left a sufficiently long series of manorial accounts. But from wheatlands which were well within Colchester's area of market supplies[31] there is evidence from several demesnes. Before the Black Death the crop courses in this region were well defined, even though it was common to allow additional periods of rest to parts of the land which would not bear cultivation in two years out of three.[32] In the early fifteenth century, however, rotations were much slacker than they had been, to the point where on marshland manors it becomes difficult to identify any three-course division of the cultivated lands.[33] Even on Westminster Abbey demesnes rotations had become more irregular, partly because fields were more commonly divided up between cropping courses, and partly because the assignment of lands to particular courses was less permanent. In Kelvedon, for example, Brodefeld was the core of the winter-sown course in 1395/6 and of the spring-sown course in 1396/7, and it was then fallowed in 1397/8, all according to tradition. In 1398/9 this field was again sown with wheat, though less was sown here than three years earlier. But in 1399/1400 it was fallowed and another called Reyelond was newly ploughed up for oats. Brodefeld was then brought back into cultivation in 1400/1, when 88½ acres were sown there with peas and oats; its place in the sequence of crops had been shifted a year through a characteristically flexible handling of the rotation scheme.[34]

Output of wool and meat had been less adversely affected than that of grain by the economic changes of the later fourteenth century, and on most demesnes the number of animals had increased. At Kelvedon the number of fleeces produced averaged 147 in the 1340s but 188 during the years 1400–2,[35] and at Feering the number had increased from 143 to 173 between the 1340s and 1400–4.[36] There was perhaps some increase, too, in the number of fleeces from Bourchier Hall. Here dairying also expanded, and there were more young cattle on the manor, under the stimulus of

[31] W.A.M., 25866r, 25868r.

[32] Britnell, 'Agriculture in a Region of Ancient Enclosure', pp. 46–52; *idem*, 'Agricultural Technology', pp. 58–9; *idem*, 'Production for the Market', p. 384.

[33] Britnell, 'Agricultural Technology', pp. 64–5; *idem*, 'Agricultural Techniques in Eastern England'.

[34] W.A.M., 25868d, 25870d, 25872d, 25874d, 25876d, 25878d.

[35] Both figures are averages of three years: W.A.M., 25824d, 25825d, 25827d, 25876d, 25878d, 25880d.

[36] Both figures are averages of five years: W.A.M., 25662d, 25664d, 25665d, 25744d, 25748d, 25752d, 25758d; P.R.O., S.C.6/841/8d, 9d, 10, m. 1d.

higher demand for meat and dairy produce.[37] At Feering the dairy herd was twice as big in the opening years of the fifteenth century as it had been before the Black Death, and at Kelvedon there were 30 cows at the latter date where there had been none at all in the 1340s.[38] Pasture farming developed on small tenements as well as on demesne lands. The size of tenant flocks trespassing on the demesne at Bourchier Hall rose steeply after the Black Death. A culprit with 100 sheep is in evidence there in 1365 and one with 120 in 1371, but larger flocks are known from the early fifteenth century; Richard James had 160 sheep in the lord's pastures and growing oats in 1408, and Nicholas Alfryth had 140 sheep in his wheat in 1410.[39] It is not difficult to explain such increases in terms of higher meat consumption and growing manufactures.

Partly because of the vigour of urban and industrial development, but more because of the proximity of the coast, commercial opportunities remained sufficiently good around Colchester to delay the decisive abandoning of direct demesne management by landlords.[40] The manor of Tolleshunt Major was still administered directly in 1397/8,[41] and Bartholomew Bourchier held in hand the neighbouring manor of Bourchier Hall in 1400/1, 1403/4 and 1405/6.[42] On the northern side of Tiptree Heath, Westminster Abbey's manor of Feering was leased out in 1372/3 and then for most of the time between 1373 and 1393 on two consecutive leases of nine years, but it was then in the abbot's hands until Michaelmas 1404 or shortly after. Kelvedon was leased out between 1386 and 1390 but then held in hand by the abbot until 1402, when it was put on lease for seven years.[43] The demesne at Layer Marney was in hand in 1408/9, 1412/13 and 1413/14 but not subsequently.[44] Langenhoe, on the western bank at the mouth of the Colne was administered directly by the Sutton family in 1409/10 and 1413/14,[45] and Wivenhoe, on the eastern bank, was similarly administered in 1425/6.[46] To the north of Colchester the prioress of Campsey Ash apparently kept in hand much of her demesne land in Dedham until 1409,[47] and the de Vere demesne at Earls Colne was not finally abandoned until 1418.[48] These examples suggest that the balance

[37] Britnell, 'Agricultural Technology', pp. 57, 63–4.
[38] P.R.O., S.C.6/841/8r,d, 9r,d, 10, m. 1r,d, 11d; W.A.M., 25662d, 25664d, 25748d, 25752d, 25758d (Feering). W.A.M., 25823d, 25824d, 25825d, 25827d, 25878d, 25880d (Kelvedon).
[39] E.R.O., D/DK M75, mm. 5d, 12d; D/DK M76, mm. 4r, 5r.
[40] For a local estate without these advantages, see Holmes, *The Estates of the Higher Nobility*, p. 92.   [41] P.R.O., S.C.6/848/13.   [42] E.R.O., D/DK M87–90.
[43] W.A.M., 25710–19, 25714–22; P.R.O., S.C.6/841/11 (Feering). W.A.M., 25853–6, 25882 (Kelvedon).
[44] P.R.O., S.C.6/1246/2, 3, 4.   [45] E.R.O., D/DE1 M227, M228.
[46] E.R.O., T/B 122.
[47] P.R.O., D.L.30/58/729, m. 18r,d.   [48] E.R.O., D/DPr 67, m. 8r,d.

Table 10.1 *Piece rates at Kelvedon in 1344/5 and 1401/2*

	Mowing 1 acre of meadow *d*	Harvesting 1 acre of wheat *d*	1 acre of oats *d*	Threshing 1 quarter of wheat *d*	1 quarter of oats *d*
1344/5	6	4[a]	3[a]	2½	1
1401/2	7	7	6	4	2

[a] With 1 loaf, commuted in 1398 for 1*d*.

Source: W.A.M., 25824r (1344/5), 25872r (1397/8), 25880r (1401/2).

of advantage between direct administration and leasing was a fine one in the later fourteenth century, and that the case for leasing became irresistible only in the first quarter of the fifteenth.

Through the later fourteenth century landlords retained the habits of vigilance and commercial acumen which they had acquired in more favourable times. As few concessions as possible were made to changing circumstances, and those concessions which had to be made were reversed if the opportunity presented itself. Many such victories were won in years of partial recovery from epidemics, proving that attention to detail was a landlord's best policy. However, from the vantage point of the year 1410 it could be shown that a good deal of ground had already been ceded, and that rural institutions were already greatly changed since the eve of the first outbreak of plague.

First of all, and furthest from any conceivable power of landlords to check, was the changing structure of prices and wages. Auditors might still quibble about wages paid to ploughmen or labourers,[49] but the conspicuous changes in money wage rates which had come about as an immediate result of the Black Death had proved to be of permanent effect.[50] Grain prices during the years 1397–1406 were some 38 per cent higher than in the years 1337–46, and wool prices were about 13 per cent higher,[51] but wages had risen appreciably more. Table 10.1, recording how piece rates had risen at Kelvedon between 1344/5 and 1401/2, indicates that the main ones were more than 50 per cent higher. The wages of ploughmen had also increased. In the 1340s ploughmen in north-eastern Essex usually received a subsistence wage amounting to between 34½ and 39 bushels of bread grain during

[49] *E.g.* W.A.M., 25868r (mowers), 25876r, 25878r, 25880r (ploughmen).
[50] N. Ritchie (née Kenyon), 'Labour Conditions in Essex in the Reign of Richard II', reprinted in E. M. Carus-Wilson, ed., *Essays in Economic History* (3 vols., London, 1954, 1962), ii, pp. 91–2.
[51] T. H. Lloyd, *The Movement of Wool Prices in Medieval England, Ec.H.R.* Supplement vi (Cambridge, 1973), pp. 41–2.

the course of a year together with a stipend of sown acres from the demesne (one acre of wheat and one of oats).[52] On some manors, instead of this stipend in sown acres they received the sum of about 5s 0d.[53] At the end of the century the subsistence wage payment was much as it had been, except that the proportion of wheat might be larger,[54] but it was more common to give a cash stipend, and the level of payment was appreciably higher than 5s 0d. At Tolleshunt Major in 1397/8 a plough-holder received 16s 0d a year and two drivers received 13s 4d and £1 respectively.[55] At Kelvedon in 1401/2 a holder received 13s 4d and a driver 12s 0d according to the estate auditors, though alterations to the account at this point imply that the man on the spot had had to pay more.[56] A holder at Bourchier Hall received 13s 4d in 1405/6.[57] Taking account of the change in grain prices, a stipend of 13s 4d represents an increased cost to the landlord of about 63 per cent in the ploughman's total annual wage. It may be added that such increases were by no means peculiar to the Colchester region and do not appear to be greater than those occurring elsewhere in England.[58]

Changes in wage rates did most to benefit poorer families in medieval villages, whose income depended upon the employment available. Wealthier families, however, also stood to benefit at their landlord's expense, because of the greater supply of available land.[59] Landlords were as yet reluctant to make permanent changes in the terms of tenure of customary holdings.[60] Some labour services continued to be performed;[61] lords continued to exact heriots, and expected villeins to pay merchet when they married their daughters, as at Wivenhoe, Langham and Feering;[62] the

---

[52] E.R.O., D/DC 2/11: *cf*. D/DE1 M220–3 (Langenhoe); E.R.O., D/DK M86, mm. 4d, 5r,d (Bourchier Hall); W.A.M., 25825, 25827 (Kelvedon); P.R.O., S.C.6/841/6, 7 (Feering); E.R.O., D/DU 19/27 (Kelvedon Hall).

[53] E.R.O., D/DU 40/75–7 (Carbonels in Wix); P.R.O., S.C.6/845/29, 30 (Pontes in Bulmer).

[54] *E.g.* at Bourchier Hall, where the proportion of wheat in servants' allowances increased from 30 per cent in 1340/1 and 1341/2 to 76 per cent in the years 1403/4 and 1405/6: E.R.O., D/DK M86, mm. 3d, 4d; D/DK M88d, M89d. *Cf*. C. Dyer, *Lords and Peasants in a Changing Society: The Estates of the Bishopric of Worcester, 680–1540*, Past and Present Publications (Cambridge, 1980), pp. 142–3.

[55] P.R.O., S.C.6/848/13r.

[56] W.A.M., 25880r.

[57] E.R.O., D/DK M89r.

[58] Dyer, *Lords and Peasants*, pp. 142–3; R. H. Hilton, *The Economic Development of some Leicestershire Estates in the Fourteenth and Fifteenth Centuries* (Oxford, 1947), pp. 140–3 and Appendix 6.

[59] Z. Razi, *Life, Marriage and Death in a Medieval Parish: Economy, Society and Demography in Halesowen, 1270–1400*, Past and Present Publications (Cambridge, 1980), pp. 147–50.

[60] A late example (1434) is in E.R.O., D/DPr 68, m. 16d.

[61] K. G. Feiling, 'An Essex Manor in the Fourteenth Century', *E.H.R.*, xxvi (1911), pp. 334–5.

[62] E.R.O., T/B 122 (Wivenhoe); E.R.O., D/DE1 M1, court held Tuesday in Whit week, 7 Henry IV (Langham); P.R.O., S.C.2/171/79, mm. 14d, 15r, 16d (Feering).

spinsters of Dedham still in 1405 paid *chyldwyt* for their illegitimate children.[63] But when customary holdings could not be tenanted on the old terms, as was increasingly the case from the 1390s, landlords leased them out, necessarily foregoing labour services and other servile dues. And this created attractive opportunities. At Kelvedon in 1405/6 Robert atte Thorne took out a lease for 12 years of an agglomeration of properties totalling well over 50 acres, some former customary land, some former demesne, paying a rent of £1 18s 0d all told.[64] Such accumulations of formerly separate tenures in the hands of single tenants became a distinctive feature of village economies in the fifteenth century.

There were rural families, meanwhile, whose main ambition was to break with their past. Some migrants, as previous discussion has suggested, were rural artisans, but others came from the upper ranks of the tenantry. At Earls Colne in 1408 four of the lord's tenants were reported to have removed themselves.[65] The lord's interest had been roused by abandoned houses in the village. One absconder was John Crudde. William and John, sons of Gosselin the reeve, were two others, a tenement called Gossethereves having passed into other hands some years previously.[66] Thomas son of Robert Stephen was the fourth, and his father's tenement was ruinous by 1411.[67] Further enquiry located William Gossethereve as a weaver in St Giles's parish, Colchester, and established further that he had a sister Agnes living in Holy Trinity parish there. Thomas son of Robert Stephen was found to be living in Sudbury in the home of a bladesmith, together with his brother John.[68] These migrants are unlikely to have been from the ranks of the pauper families of the village. Each family was associated with land. Gosselin the reeve, to judge from his name, had been a manorial officer, and Adam Crudde, who was himself responsible for dilapidated premises,[69] had once been the lessee of Earls Colne Priory demesne lands.[70] The circumstances of the runaways is not clear, but they are unlikely to have been all without opportunities for subsistence in the village. In such families the stigma of serfdom still contributed to individual discontent and encouraged young people to look for opportunities elsewhere. Those from Earls Colne did not have far to look in the early years of the fifteenth century.

II

These contrasts between the 1340s and the early 1400s should not be taken to imply that agricultural changes all proceeded smoothly in the same

[63] P.R.O., D.L.30/58/729, mm. 7d, 12r.
[64] W.A.M., 25884r, 25885r.
[65] E.R.O., D/DPr 66, m. 10d.
[66] *Ibid.*, m. 6d.
[67] *Ibid.*, m. 17d.
[68] *Ibid.*, m. 11r.
[69] *Ibid.*, m. 11r.
[70] E.R.O., D/DPr 13r.

Table 10.2 *Average annual net receipts of tithe corn from Feering Rectory (bushels)*

Years[a]	Wheat b.	Rye and maslin b.	Legumes b.	Barley b.	Oats b.
1331–47 (9)	419	6	73	–	178
1348–51 (4)	261	5	53	–	92
1352–5 (4)	297	12	107	–	135
1367–72 (6)	321	–	69	22	189

[a] Number of years averaged in brackets.
Sources: W.A.M. 25659–25700 (manor rolls); P.R.O., S.C.6/841/6–9.

direction. Landlords faced different problems, or faced the same problem differently. Moreover, during the 60 years after the Black Death years of crisis for landlords alternated with periods of progress. The 1350s and 1360s were decades of partial recovery and initial reorientation, not seriously interrupted by the less severe epidemic of 1361, and between about 1370 and 1385 signs of recovery were more convincing still. Then the years from about 1385 to 1410, which saw a reversal of the rising trends of earlier years and a widespread abandonment of agricultural resources, initiated the severe agrarian crisis of the early fifteenth century.

After 1348 the restructuring of wage rates was extremely vigorous despite legislation designed to control it. During the 1350s and 1360s wage earners became used to the idea that they could improve their lot through frequently recontracting, so that both in town and country the enforcement of existing contracts became a more prominent function of the law courts.[71] Prices rose during these two decades, especially those for wool, and both because of higher wages and because of relatively higher wool prices lords and tenants enlarged their sheep flocks on land abandoned from arable husbandry. The consequent increase in wool production supplied the local cloth manufacture.[72] The quantity of grain harvested remained lower than it had been before the Black Death, despite some slow revival. At Feering, although there was as yet no contraction of the cultivated area of demesne land, there was a severe reduction in tithe receipts, and even by the end of the 1360s wheat receipts were still 23 per cent below below their level

[71] Putman, *The Enforcement of the Statute of Labourers*, pp. 160–5.
[72] The number of fleeces produced on Kelvedon demesne rose from 147 on average in the 1340s to 220 in 1376 and 273 in 1377: W.A.M., 25824d, 25825d, 25827d, 25829d, 25831d. At Feering the number rose from 143 in the 1340s to 171 during the six years 1367–72: W.A.M., 25662d, 25664d, 25665d, 25687d, 25689d, 25691d, 25693d, 25695d, 25697d; P.R.O., S.C.6/841/8d, 9d.

in the 1330s and 1340s (Table 10.2). This suggests that the output of the village was significantly below its former level. Where soils were poor and exceptionally sensitive to changes in the profitability of cereals husbandry the decline could be spectacular, as at Bourchier Hall.[73] The contraction of arable husbandry probably explains why the rent received by the abbot of Westminster for Pattiswick Rectory declined from £9 6s 8d in the 1340s to only £5 during the 1360s.[74]

During the 1350s and 1360s landlords were often successful in re-establishing their former structure of tenures, though they were obliged to resort to temporary expedients in years of crisis.[75] Customary rents were more easily restored than contractual ones, which were often lower in these decades than in the 1340s despite the intervening increase in prices. At Bourchier Hall a tenement called Peldonislond, formerly leased for £1 10s 0d was leased in 1356/7 for £1 4s 0d. At Feering the rent from a property called from Blaveneys, leased for £5 6s 8d in 1345/6, had fallen to £2 12s 8d in the 1360s.[76] Landlords' income from customary rents was protected partly by the sanction which custom bestowed upon existing rents and partly by rising prices, which alleviated the burden on tenants.

The 1370s was the best decade of the later fourteenth century for landlords around Colchester. High wool prices, as well as high wheat prices until 1376,[77] had a beneficial effect upon the level of contractual rents, which were revised upwards as leases fell in.[78] At Feering the rent from Blaveneys was first raised from £2 12s 8d to £2 19s 4d in 1372 and then to £3 3s 4d in 1384. The rent from Pattiswick Rectory was raised from £5 to £6 13s 4d in 1372, and in 1374 the rent of a tenement called Thornes was raised from 8s 0d to 9s 0d.[79] Similar rent increases are in evidence at Kelvedon between 1376 and 1382.[80] Recovery was not simply a matter of rent levels. Tithe receipts at Feering register some increase in the output of cereals (Tables 10.2 and 10.8), and mill receipts at Langenhoe suggest an increase in milling activity (Table 10.3). At Kelvedon the four quarters of wheat rendered by the mill in the early 1380s, though still greatly below the level of the 1340s, was the highest recorded payment for many years.[81]

[73] Britnell, 'Agricultural Technology', p. 62.
[74] W.A.M., 25662r, 25664r, 25683r–25686r, 25688r, 25690r, 25692r.
[75] Feiling, 'An Essex Manor', p. 335; Holmes, *The Estates of the Higher Nobility*, p. 90.
[76] E.R.O., D/DK M86, mm. 1r–4r, 8r (Bourchier Hall); W.A.M., 25664r, 25680r–25686r, 25688r, 25690r, 25692r (Feering).
[77] Lloyd, *The Movement of Wool Prices*, p. 41.
[78] *Cf.* Feiling, 'An Essex Manor', p. 335.
[79] W.A.M., 25698r, 25701r, 25703r, 25714r.
[80] The rent of two crofts in Wodefeld was raised in 1376 (W.A.M., 25831r). Other increases were obtained for 24 acres in Pourtesfeld in 1379 (25829r, 25837r) and a pasture close called Cherchmed in 1382 (25843r).
[81] The mill had been allowed to fall into disrepair by the late 1370s (W.A.M., 25829d, 25831d, 25833d, 25835d, 25837d) but was repaired in 1380 and leased (25839r).

Table 10.3 *The rent from Langenhoe Mill, 1324/5–1413/14* (*bushels*)

	Wheat b.	Rye and maslin b.		Wheat b.	Rye and maslin b.
1324/5	64	104	1378/9	40	80
1338/9	64	112	1380/1	48	80
1342/3	64	112	1381/2	48	80
1344/5	72	120	1383/4	48	80
1347/8	75	136¾	1387/8	48	80
1369/70	28	60	1396/7	50	86
1370/1[a]	32	64	1413/14	64	96

[a] From 1370/1, 2s 0d was received for the fishing rights in the mill pond.
Source: E.R.O., D/DC 2/11d–14d, 16d; D/DGe M220d; D/DEl M220d–226d, 228d.

Table 10.4 *Toll and pickage from Wix fair, 1381–1402*

	s	d		s	d
1381	6	1	1390	5	8
1383	5	3	1391	3	0
1385	3	3	1393	3	4[a]
1386	2	8	1394	3	8
1387	1	5½	1401	5	11
1388	4	11	1402	4	5
1389	4	1			

[a] This figure is from an account roll. The court rolls says 5s 4d.
Source: P.R.O., S.C.2/174/19, mm. 1d, 3r, 4d, 7r, d, 8d; S.C.2/174/20, mm. 1r, 2r, 10r; S.C.2/174/21, m. 1r; S.C.2/174/22, mm. 4d, 7r; S.C.6/849/15r, 20r, 21r.

Rural population was unaffected by any upheavals during these years, and wages at Feering and Kelvedon, the best local series, held steady at the rates achieved during the 1350s and 1360s.[82] Some of the good fortunes of local landlords in this period may be ascribed to industrial growth in Colchester (and probably elsewhere) in the context of well sustained rural demand.

From the later 1380s, and particularly during the 1390s, the scene changed once more. Economic evidence suggests that the plague epidemic attributed by chroniclers to 1390–1[83] was severe around Colchester,

[82] Compare, for example, W.A.M., 25829 and 25949.
[83] J. F. D. Shrewsbury, *A History of Bubonic Plague in the British Isles* (Cambridge, 1971), pp. 137–8; Hatcher, *Plague, Population and the English Economy*, p. 59.

Table 10.5 *The price of a fleece from the demesne flocks at Langenhoe and Kelvedon, 1370–1402*

| | Langenhoe | | | Kelvedon | |
| | Wethers and ewes | Hoggets | Wethers | Ewes | Hoggets |
	d	*d*	*d*	*d*	*d*
1370	9	6			
1376			8½		7
1377		.	8½	8	
1378			10	10	7
1379	8	6	10	10	
1380			8½		
1381	8	7	6		6
1382	7	6	7		5
1383			7ᵃ		
1384	7	6	8		8
1386			7		7
1388	5	4			
1391	5½	5½	6		
1392			6		
1393			5		
1394			6		
1395			7		5
1396			7½		
1397	6				
1398			5		
1399			6		
1400			6½		
1401			6½		
1402			6½		

ᵃ The fleeces were sold by weight, but the average price was 7.13*d*.

Sources: E.R.O., D/DC 2/13–16; D/DE1 M224–6; D/DGe M200; P.R.O., S.C.6/842/24; W.A.M., 25829–25880.

affecting adversely the trade and agriculture of the region. At Wix the prioress's receipts of toll and pickage from the fair registered first a crisis in 1387, which may be related to the credit crisis in Colchester in 1387/8,[84] and then the high mortality of the early 1390s (Table 10.4). Wool prices fell, as Table 10.5 shows, and wheat prices were also lower after 1385.[85] Rents, predictably, tended to fall. The rent of Pattiswick Rectory, already reduced to £5 6*s* 8*d* in 1382, fell further to £4 in 1399 and to £3 13*s* 4*d* about 1406.[86] The rent of Thornes in Feering fell from 10*s* 0*d* in 1393 to 8*s* 0*d*

[84] See Chapter 7, pp. 100, 107.   [85] Lloyd, *The Movement of Wool Prices*, p. 42.
[86] W.A.M., 25711r, 25745r, 25760r.

Table 10.6 *Cropping on the demesne of the prioress of Wix at Wix, 1381/2–1393/4*

	Wheat ac.	Rye ac.	Legumes ac.	Barley ac.	Dredge ac.	Oats ac.	Total ac.
1381/2	89	49	42¼	38¾	–	150	368½
1389/90	73	33	46	45	–	85	282
1391/2	84	32	43	23	7	75	264
1393/4	57	24	30¼	12½	24	108	255¾

Source: P.R.O., S.C.6/849/15d, 19d, 20d, 21d.

Table 10.7 *Average annual acreages sown on demesnes at Kelvedon, Feering and Langenhoe, 1370–1404 (number of years averaged in brackets)*

	Kelvedon ac.	Feering ac.	Langenhoe ac.
1370–4	?	361.2 (5)	134.0 (1)
1375–9	266.9 (4)	345.5ᵃ (5)	123.8 (1)
1380–4	252.1 (5)	351.5ᵃ (4)	131.2 (3)
1385–9	259.4ᵃ (5)	358.1ᵃ (5)	118.0 (1)
1390–4	232.5 (5)	345.8ᵃ (5)	134.8 (1)
1395–9	198.7 (5)	265.7 (3)	105.0 (2)
1400–4	185.3 (3)	334.1 (5)	115.3 (1)

ᵃ Averages marked with an asterisk include several years when the demesne was leased; the average includes the recorded sown acres for which the tenant accounted annually.
Sources: W.A.M., 25693–25758, 25829–25880 (manor rolls); E.R.O., D/DC 2/13–16; D/DE1 M224–6; D/DGe M200, 201; P.R.O., S.C.6/841/10, m.1; S.C.6/842/24.

in 1397, 6*s* 8*d* in 1399 and to 5*s* 0*d* in 1403, and that of another tenement there called Denescroft fell from 8*s* 0*d* in 1382 to 6*s* 8*d* in 1391, 6*s* 0*d* in 1393 and to 4*s* 0*d* in 1403.[87] At Kelvedon four crofts leased for 12*s* 6*d* in 1376 were let again for only 10*s* 0*d* in 1384, then for 8*s* 0*d* in 1390, and the rent was further reduced in 1404 when they were leased together with another field.[88] The rent of Huntesland in Wix, which had been 12*s* 0*d* a year in the early 1380s, was reduced to 10*s* 0*d* in 1393 after several years in abeyance.[89] It was in this period, too, that the efficacy of

[87] W.A.M., 25726r, 25736r, 25745r, 25757r (Thornes); 25711r, 25720r, 25721r, 25726r, 25757r (Denescroft).
[88] W.A.M., 25831r, 25847r, 25857r, 25883r.
[89] P.R.O., S.C.6/849/15r, 16 (attached collector's account), 19r–21r.

Table 10.8 *Annual average tithe receipts at Feering and Kelvedon Rectories, 1376–1404 (number of years averaged in brackets)*

	Wheat b.	Rye and maslin b.	Legumes b.	Barley b.	Dredge b.	Oats b.
Feering						
1382 (1)	454	3	235	153	–	174
1393–8 (4)	196	–	75	99	9	122
1399–1403 (5)	132	1	50	60	5	123
Kelvedon						
1376–85 (9)	271	12	83	125	36	234
1390–1401 (12)	229	3	74	131	12	145

Sources: W.A.M., 25713–25759, 25832–25881 (rectory accounts); P.R.O., S.C.6/841/10, m.2.

custom as a shield for landlords began to fail conspicuously, and the number of leasehold tenures increased more rapidly as the ability of landlords to let tenements on the old terms diminished.[90]

Falling prices and rents were accompanied by reductions in agricultural output, particularly in that of cereals. This is apparent on manorial demesnes with appropriate documentation (Table 10.6 and 10.7) and also in the declining tithe receipts at Feering and Kelvedon (Table 10.8). At Kelvedon the early years of the fifteenth century were even more depressed than the 1390s. Moreover, continuing investment in sheep flocks to compensate for declining returns in arable husbandry ultimately had adverse consequences for the price of wool, so that towards the end of the century some landlords were induced to reduce their pastoral activities. At Langenhoe demesne flocks were augmented by 240 wethers sometime between 1388 and 1395, so that sales of wool increased considerably. Here, too, perhaps because of Colchester's close proximity, the rent of a pasture called Dagefen was increased from £1 in 1387/8 to £1 3s 0d in 1396/7.[91] However, the demesnes at Feering and Kelvedon, which had earlier

[90] As at Langenhoe (E.R.O., D/DC 2/16r; D/DE1 M228r) and at Feering (W.A.M., 25723r–25736r). A turning point about 1390 occurred in the policy of many estates: B. Harvey, *Westminster Abbey and its Estates in the Middle Ages* (Oxford, 1977), pp. 268–9; Dyer, *Lords and Peasants*, pp. 147–9; R. A. L. Smith, *Canterbury Cathedral Priory* (Cambridge, 1943), pp. 190–4; J. A. Raftis, *The Estates of Ramsey Abbey*, Pontifical Institute of Medieval Studies, Studies and Texts, iii (Toronto, 1957), p. 265; F. M. Page, *The Estates of Crowland Abbey* (Cambridge, 1934), pp. 152–3.

[91] E.R.O., D/DE1 M226r,d; D/DC 2/15r,d, 16r. The number of fleeces sold rose from 502 on average (maximum 530) between 1370 and 1388 to 714 in 1397: E.R.O., D/DC 2/13d, 14d, 16d; D/DE1 M224d–226d; D/DGe M200d.

Table 10.9 *Receipts at Wivenhoe for pannage, avesage and for pigs slaughtered by villeins*

	Pannage		Avesage		Pigs slaughtered	
	s	d	s	d	s	d
1381	0	0	3	5	1	10
1382	6	6		?	1	7½
1385	0	0	3	10	1	9
1386	0	0	2	6	1	2
1389	6	1	3	3	1	5½
1391	4	1	1	11	1	6
1393	0	0	1	9	1	7
1394	5	8	1	6	1	5½
1395	14	4	3	7	1	5
1397	10	7	2	4	1	5
1398	7	10	1	6	1	4
1399	0	0	1	10	1	1½
1400	0	0		4		7½
1401	0	0	1	10	1	8
1404	10	4	2	2		7
1405	0	0	1	11	1	8
1407	0	0	1	9		6
1408	11	4	1	5	1	4
1412	0	0		11		11½
1413	2	11		11	1	7½

Source: E.R.O., T/B 122; D/DHt M88.

increased their flocks, did so no longer. The number of fleeces produced at Feering rose from an average of 171 (1367–72) to 190 (1394–8), but then declined once more to 173 (1400–4), while at Kelvedon the number decreased from 261 (1376–86) to 221 (1391–9) and then again to 188 (1400–2).[92] Other aspects of animal farming even close to Colchester felt little benefit from developments there. At Wivenhoe the lord of the manor was entitled every January to pannage (for the pasturing of pigs in his woods, when it was deemed that there were enough acorns), to avesage, otherwise called *grasaves* (for pasturing pigs in the lord's stubble) and to a levy of ½d every time a villein slaughtered a pig for his larder.[93] Table 10.9, showing the changes in these receipts between 1381 and 1413,

[92] For Feering, W.A.M., 25687d–25697d, 25727d–25735d, 25744d–25758d (manor rolls); P.R.O., S.C.6/841/10d. For Kelvedon, W.A.M., 25829d–25849d, 25857d–25874d, 25876d–25880d (manor rolls).

[93] For the definitions given here, see E.R.O., T/B 122, courts held Wednesday after Epiphany 16 Richard II and Wednesday after Epiphany 22 Richard II.

indicates contraction rather than growth in those for avesage and villeins' bacon. All told, the agrarian evidence implies that the advantageous effects of Colchester's economic development during the 1390s and early 1400s were more than outweighed by the widespread consequences of falling demand in the countryside.

III

Colchester's growth during the late fourteenth century was clearly inadequate to confer many significant benefits upon the agriculture of the region. Within a very few miles of the town market landlords may have been in a better position to withstand the adversities of the 1390s and early fifteenth century. The abbot of Colchester was acquiring land and enclosing it between about 1404 and 1413, and thereby provoked conflict with the burgesses.[94] But even so close as Wivenhoe and Langenhoe there are signs of economic contraction at this time. Colchester's share of marketed agricultural produce must have increased between the 1340s and the early 1400s, and yet the years of rapid urban development during the late 1390s and early 1400s were years of pronounced agricultural depression.[95]

There are several inferences to be drawn from these observations. First, and perhaps least ambiguous, is the absence of symbiosis in the economic development of town and country. The urban economy had responded to commercial opportunities over long distances, chiefly in overseas markets. The rural economy was more governed by local changes in demand, and Colchester was not a big enough town to determine the current local trends. Changes in agriculture were here much the same as elsewhere in Essex. This conclusion is one of general relevance to medieval England, where very few towns were sufficiently large to dominate local market demand.

A further inference concerns the consequences of rural crises for the urban economy. Because Colchester was not dependent on local demand for its development there were ways in which the town stood positively to gain from rural depression. One of these was the release of prime water-power resources for fulling, which was a feature of the 1350s and 1360s. Cheap water power was probably a major factor in Colchester's industrial performance in the immediate aftermath of the Black Death. The same advantages were enjoyed by rural industry; a water mill at Feering was converted for fulling about 1361, perhaps for the fullers of Coggeshall.[96] In the immediate vicinity of Colchester the later growth of population put pressure on water supplies again, so that fullers and bakers had to make

---

[94] CR 33/12d, 20d and later; CR 38/1d, 13r and later; CR 39/5r,d, 18d, 32r and later.
[95] *Cf.* J. L. Bolton, *The Medieval English Economy, 1150–1500* (London, 1980), p. 229.
[96] W.A.M., 25677r, 25682r.

longer journeys as the town grew, but they did not have to go far. There
was plenty of surplus water power in the vicinity by 1410. A further way
in which the urban economy benefited from agrarian crisis was through
the cheapening of wool supplies. The contraction of arable acreages
immediately after the Black Death freed considerable reserves of land for
waste or pasture, and the same pattern was repeated to a lesser degree
during the 1390s. The movement of wool prices has been examined by Dr
Lloyd, who observes that during the late Middle Ages wool prices were
lower relative to cereals prices than they had been earlier, partly because
landlords invested in sheep at very low rates of return in order to use land
that would otherwise be idle.[97] Two of the major phases of growth in
Colchester (1351–6, 1398–1406) correspond to periods of exceptionally low
wool prices. Finally, it is probable, too, that agriculture released capital
and labour for developing urban activities. Not all medieval villagers were
content to stay at home accumulating unwanted tenements, and the
depression at the end of the fourteenth century and the opening of the
fifteenth was conspicuous for an increased level of peasant mobility.[98]
When prices of grain and wool were low the attractions of urban
employment were greater both for small landowners and for labourers. The
great influx of new burgesses into Colchester in the early fifteenth century,
notably in 1406/7, which was a year of exceptionally low agricultural
prices, was a response to agrarian depression as well as to industrial
opportunity. At this point disillusionment with agriculture as a means to
prosperity interacted with the resentment provoked by dependent personal
status to launch an exceptional number of countrymen into urban pursuits.

[97] Lloyd, *The Movement of Wool Prices*, pp. 22–4, 29.
[98] J. A. Raftis, *Tenure and Mobility: Studies in the Social History of the Medieval English
Village*, Pontifical Institute of Medieval Studies, Studies and Texts, viii (Toronto, 1964),
p. 153.

SURVEY, 1350–1414

In spite of heavy losses of population at the time of the Black Death, Colchester immediately entered a new phase of industrial and commercial growth. Colchester merchants increased their trade to Gascony and opened up new relations with the Baltic, exporting local russets in exchange for wine, fish, salt, continental manufactures and other commodities. In the last decades of the fourteenth century even the Mediterranean world offered markets for Colchester cloth through the agency of Italian exporters in London. Cloth output increased to satisfy these expanding markets, creating new employment in the town. This, with its secondary repercussions, brought about an expansion of urban population from below 3,000 immediately after the Black Death to perhaps over 8,000 by the end of the century. The growth of cloth production was accompanied by increasing levels of internal trade in the town and by an even more considerable expansion of credit. The merchant class became rapidly larger. Colchester's good fortune in these years was not unique; the growth of urban industry and trade had parallels elsewhere, notably in Coventry[1] and Salisbury,[2] and the older and larger towns of York[3] and Norwich[4] also enjoyed an industrial upsurge in this period. Nearer at hand, other market towns and industrialising villages were showing features of industrial development, such as at Hadleigh in Suffolk and Thaxted in Essex.[5]

The years between 1380 and 1430 have been described as a golden age of English urban civilisation, despite the simultaneous decay of many small market towns.[6] In Colchester urban self-confidence was at its height between 1372 and c. 1414. In the former year the borough adopted a new form of government to elect finance officers (receivers) to provide for an

---

[1] C. Phythian-Adams, *Desolation of a City: Coventry and the Urban Crisis of the Late Middle Ages*, Past and Present Publications (Cambridge, 1979), pp. 33–5.
[2] Bridbury, *Medieval English Clothmaking*, pp. 66–82.
[3] Bartlett, 'The Expansion and Decline of York', pp. 23–7.
[4] Bolton, *The Medieval English Economy*, p. 252.
[5] K. C. Newton, *Thaxted in the Fourteenth Century* (Chelmsford, 1960), pp. 26–7.
[6] Phythian-Adams, 'Urban Decay', p. 167.

annual audit of the accounts and to establish a council for formal deliberations about the affairs of the community. This event, which greatly increased the number of wealthy burgesses elected to office, heralded a surge of civic patriotism. The moothall was ornamented and the sources of borough income were increased. A literary account of events in Colchester between 1372 and 1379, the most unusual medieval record to have survived in the borough, clearly conveys a spirit of enthusiasm amongst the ruling group. The men elected to public office during the later fourteenth century were almost all merchants, in strong contrast with the period before the Black Death, but the form of election gave a rôle to lesser tradesmen in the process of government. Though there was some increase in economic and social regulation, not all statutory measures were vigorously enforced, and the town government was modest in its use of by-laws to control industry and trade. There were no craft gilds, and burgesses were very free in their choice of employment. It was perhaps because of high employment and light controls that there was little support amongst townsmen for the revolt of 1381. Several economic indicators suggest that Colchester achieved a peak of population in the period 1406–14, and the latter date may be taken as a terminal point for the golden age.

Though Colchester, and a few other cloth towns in the nearby countryside, grew during the later fourteenth century, the surrounding villages suffered depopulation. Colchester must have considerably increased its importance in local agricultural trade; its share of population within an eight-mile radius of the borough increased from perhaps one tenth to one quarter between the early fourteenth century and the early fifteenth.[7] But because the loss of numbers in the countryside greatly outweighed Colchester's increase, and because the borough's lines of supply became more extended, urban growth was not able to save local agriculture from the characteristic features of late medieval contraction. There was some recovery of output and rent levels between 1350 and *c.* 1385, and some of this must be attributed to Colchester's expansion, particularly during the 1370s and early 1380s. But though urban demand continued to expand, agriculture entered a phase of severe recession during the late 1380s and 1390s. From this it is apparent that Colchester's economic performance was not the main determinant of prosperity in the surrounding countryside. Indeed there was a more powerful causal relationship working in the opposite direction. The town's manufacturing industry and trade stood to gain from rural crisis, which liberated manpower and capital, especially when rural crisis was accompanied by falling prices of raw materials.

[7] Assuming, that is, that the population of Colchester doubled while that of the surrounding countryside declined by about 40 per cent.

PART III

Change and decay, 1415–1525

11

Colchester cloth and its markets

I

Having earlier established a dual structure of trade, southwards to Gascony and eastwards to the Baltic, Colchester merchants continued to profit from these routes in the early fifteenth century. Trade with Bordeaux revived after the crisis of 1407 and was following its old course in 1413/14, dominated by merchants from Colchester itself. A customs account of that year also shows Colchester men importing herrings from the Baltic.[1] But the 30 years following 1407 brought little opportunity for merchants to increase their sales abroad, either directly or through the mediation of foreign merchants. England's cloth trade, having contracted suddenly in 1402, did not regain its former level until the 1420s, and even in the years 1430–4, the number of cloths exported was about the same as in 1395–9.[2] Colchester's traditional markets were in the doldrums. Gascony, suffering from depopulation, wartime devastation and monetary disorder, showed as yet no sign of economic recovery.[3] In Prussia the defeat of the Teutonic Knights at Tannenberg in 1410 initiated a new era of invasion, depopulation and commercial disruption during the course of which the market for cloth contracted.[4] Total exports of English cloth by non-Hanseatic aliens increased by 13 per cent between 1406/7–1415/16 and 1426/7–1435/6, but this was because of developments at Southampton; it is unlikely that they benefited the export of Essex cloths by Italian merchants.[5]

The 10 years between about 1415 and 1425 were, in fact, a period of dislocation in Colchester's industrial history. In the face of difficulties in traditional markets the *decena* of russet, which had served the town so well

[1] P.R.O., E.122/51/40, mm. 1d, 2r, 3r,d.
[2] Munro, 'Monetary Contraction', pp. 138, 151.
[3] Boutruche, *La Crise d'une société*, pp. 223–31.
[4] F. L. Carsten, *The Origins of Prussia* (Oxford, 1954), pp. 102–3, 120–2; Renken, *Der Handel der Königsberger Grossschäfferei*, p. 104.
[5] Carus-Wilson and Coleman, *England's Export Trade*, pp. 89–94.

Table 11.1 *Prices of russets in Colchester, 1407–54*

| | Price of a pannus integer | | | |
	s	d	Year	Reference
duo panni integri de gray russet	46	0	1407	CR 36/20d
vnus pannus integer de tany russet	50	0	1415	CR 40/15d
vnus pannus integer de tany russet	46	8	1416	CR 40/9r
vnus pannus integer de tany russet	46	0	1416	CR 40/42r
duo panni integri coloris de grey russet	50	0	1419	CR 42/9r
vnus pannus integer coloris de grey russet	51	0	1419	CR 42/27r
vnus pannus integer de tany russet	42	0	1422	CR 43/22d
vnus pannus integer de grey russet	40	0	1423	CR 47/17d
iiij^{or} panni largi de tany russet	43	4	1423	CR 47/25d
vnus pannus largus de broun russet	40	0	1424	CR 45/9d
quatuor panni lanei largi, viz. ij russet nigri et ij russet grisei	49	0	1424	CR 48/29d
j pannus largus de tawny russet	40	0	1426	CR 47/15r
vnus pannus largus de grey russet	38	0	1428	CR 49/11r
vnus pannus largus coloris grisei	40	0	1430	CR 50/27r
viij panni lanei integri coloris de grey	42	6	1430	CR 50/34d
vnus pannus largus de tany	46	8	1431	CR 51/16r
vnus pannus largus coloris de grey russet	32	0	1432	CR 51/26r
duo panni lanei largi coloris grisei	40	0	1435	CR 56/21d
iij panni lanei integri russeti nigri	40	0	1437	CR 55/20r
vnus pannus de tany largus	40	0	1438	CR 57/6d
vnus pannus laneus vocatus a tany	40	4	1454	CR 66/23d

during its years of rapid growth, was abandoned in favour of larger cloths of a more diverse character. A *decena* of broad tawny russet was fulled in 1413, and from the same year is a record of three *decena* of russet having been sold in the borough.[6] But after that the term *decena* rapidly disappeared from the borough records. When shorter cloths occur later in the century they are either called dozens or their length is given in yards; they were usually straits.[7] The new standard in Colchester was the 'whole cloth' of 24 × 2 yards, equivalent to two former *decene*.[8] Whole cloths of russet sold for about twice the price of *decene*, which meant that until 1419 they would fetch between £2 6s 0d and £2 10s 0d (Table 11.1). The transition to these new dimensions was not the direct consequence of the

[6] CR 39/23r, 38d.
[7] CR 47/9r; CR 49/7d; CR 50/10d, 34d; CR 52/18r.
[8] CR 64/5r, 9r; CR 69/20r.

more rigid assize of cloth introduced by statute in 1410 and 1411, since though the length of Colchester cloths was now in conformity with the assize, their width still deviated from it.[9] It seems, rather, than in order to compete in a world of tighter markets, Colchester manufacturers found it advantageous to conform more closely to the normal English standard.

About 1419 the cloth industry in Colchester was struck with depression. Prices fell by over 10 per cent, so that during the 1420s a whole cloth of russet sold for between £2 and £2 3s 4d (Table 11.1). There was a sharp fall in the Gascon wine trade after Michaelmas 1418 following 10 years of particularly active exchange,[10] and trade in the Baltic was threatened by rising Anglo-Hanseatic jealousies during the years which followed.[11] Colchester manufacturers viewed the new crisis as more than a temporary disruption, and within a few years it was apparent that Colchester cloth was changing its nature yet further. Alongside traditional russet cloths, selling at £2 or so, manufacturers gradually introduced a new range of superior fabrics costing half as much again (Table 11.2). For a start, they increased the output of musterdevillers, known in Colchester as 'musterdelers', which were modelled on the fine greys of Montivilliers.[12] Another area of development was the manufacture of blue cloths, dyed in the wool in woad.[13] The standard technique later became known as dyeing 'with fourpenny hue'.[14] These remained a staple of Colchester industry all through the fifteenth century, representing a rapprochement to the style of fabric made in Lavenham.[15] Indeed, in 1470 William Spring was commissioned in Colchester to dye blue 100 *lb* of wool on behalf of John Spring of Lavenham.[16] The major success of Colchester enterprise, however, came towards the end of this period of trial with the cloths called new greys and murrey greys. These first occur in 1437, when a fuller contracted, so it was later alleged, to work two woollen broadcloths 'one of newegreyes, the other of blue'.[17] By the 1440s these cloths had established themselves well; a Colchester 'grey' was more likely to be such a fabric than a more traditional russet. Russets did not disappear from the scene, but references to them after the late 1430s are outnumbered by those

---

[9] Bridbury, *Medieval English Clothmaking*, pp. 69, 109.
[10] James, *Studies in the Medieval Wine Trade*, pp. 108–9.
[11] Postan, *Medieval Trade and Finance*, pp. 257–8; Dollinger, *The German Hansa*, p. 303.
[12] Mollat, *Études*, item 5, p. 409; *O.E.D.*, under musterdevillers.
[13] For the dyeing of wool blue (*in colorem blodium*) see CR 45/17r; CR 47/17d; CR 49/6r, 9d; CR 50/6r, 27d, 28d. That this implied a woad dye is clear from CR 77/15d.
[14] CR 76/26r; CR 77/15d.
[15] D. Dymond and A. Betterton, *Lavenham: 700 Years of Textile Making* (Woodbridge, 1982), pp. 16–17. Blues were also a speciality of Coventry: E. M. Carus-Wilson, 'The Oversea Trade of Late Medieval Coventry', in *Économies et sociétés au Moyen Âge: Mélanges offerts à Edouard Perroy* (Paris, 1973), p. 372.
[16] CR 75/7d.   [17] CR 55/29r.

Table 11.2 *Prices of musterdevillers, blues, new greys and murrey greys in Colchester, 1422–67*

	Implied price of a *pannus integer*		Year	Reference
	s	d		
duo panni coloris de murrey	73	4	1422	CR 44/22r
iij panni coloris de vesse et de musterdelyre	66	8	1422	CR 44/22r
vnus pannus integer de musterdeler	66	8	1422	CR 45/4d
vnus pannus integer de blyw vesse	80	0	1423	CR 44/13r
vnus pannus integer de musterdelyre	60	0	1424	CR 45/8d
vnus pannus integer de musterdelyr	53	4	1425	CR 46/7d
j pannus largus coloris blodii	63	4	1426	CR 47/16r
vnus pannus longus coloris vocati vesse	75	0	1427	CR 50/6d
vnus pannus laneus integer de musterdeler	80	0	1434	CR 52/4r
vnus pannus laneus integer de blew vesse	66	8	1437	CR 55/20r
dimidius pannus de musterdeler	60	0	1439	CR 56/39d
vnus pannus de musterdeler	73	4	1439	CR 57/9r
vnus pannus laneus largus coloris de musterdelyr	66	8	1440	CR 59/3d
vnus pannus laneus de musterdevelers continens in longitudine xxiiij virgas et in latitudine duas virgas	80	0	1444	CR 60/16d
vnus pannus laneus de veteri grey continens in longitudine xxx virgas et in latitutdine duas virgas	53	4	1444	CR 60/16d
vnus pannus laneus de nouo grey continens in longitudine xxiiij virgas et in latitudine duas virgas	80	0	1444	CR 60/16d
vnus pannus laneus coloris blodii continens in longitudine xxvj virgas et in latitudine duas virgas	80	0	1444	CR 60/16d
quinque panni lanei vocati murrygreyes	60	0	1445	CR 66/9r
vnus pannus laneus largus vocatus a mustedelier ⎱ vnus pannus laneus largus vocatus a newgrey	70	0	1449	CR 69/20r
vij^{tem} panni lanei vocati murrigreyes	66	8	1449	CR 64/5r
vnus pannus laneus vocatus a newegrey	66	8	1452	CR 65/7d
vnus pannus largus vocatus a newegrey	53	6	1452	CR 68/7d
vnus pannus laneus vocatus a vesse ⎱ vnus pannus laneus vocatus a murregrey	59	2	1452	CR 72/26r
vnus pannus laneus de mustirdelier	73	4	1456	CR 68/7d
sex panni lanei vocati murrygreyes	41	8	1458	CR 68/22r
duo panni lanei de greyes	63	4	1458	CR 68/22r
duo panni lanei largi vocati murrigreys	66	8	1459	CR 69/20d
vnus pannus laneus vocatus a new murrygrey	60	0	1462	CR 72/4r
sexdecim panni lanei largi vocati newe murrygreyes	62	6	1462	CR 72/29d
vnus pannus laneus vocatus a vesse	85	0	1463	CR 72/23d
duo panni lanei vocati musterfeleys ⎱ duo panni lanei vocati newegreyys	60	0	1463	CR 72/23d
vnus pannus laneus vocatus a grey	73	4	1466	CR 73/36r
tres panni lanei vocati musterlerys	87	9	1467	CR 73/36r

Note: all the above cloths except the *dimidius pannus* (whose price has been doubled for inclusion in the list) are counted as *panni integri*, though the group of cloths recorded from 1444 shows that they were not all exactly the same length.

to musterdevillers, blues and new greys. The implication is that more skill and better materials went into Colchester's typical products, and it is likely that the importance of mechanical fulling was reduced in consequence.[18] References to fulling by water mills are rarer in the mid fifteenth century than in the 1390s and early 1400s, and this may not be wholly because of the more laconic forms of legal recording favoured by fifteenth-century town clerks.

These developments were not peculiar to Colchester. In the late Middle ages the commercial fortunes of superior fabrics were generally rising at the expense of inferior ones. Many smaller towns in the Low Countries had already abandoned their local traditions in order to imitate the draperies of Ypres, Ghent and Bruges.[19] In northern Italy the silk industry was being taken up in new centres, and earning high profits for a few entrepreneurs, at a time when the woollen industry was sluggish.[20] There are general explanations both from supply and demand conditions why this should have been so. On the demand side, the severe reduction of rural and urban populations since the Black Death, together with a greatly increased concentration of property ownership, meant that the market for cheaper cloths had contracted and that for dearer cloths had expanded. These changes ultimately had the effect of reducing the demand for old-fashioned russets among laymen and the religious orders alike. Meanwhile, on the supply side, rising costs of transport and commercial risk were a deterrent to enterprise in cheaper fabrics in whose final price these elements were proportionately larger than they were in the price of luxury cloths.[21] Neither of these explanations will very immediately explain the course of development in Colchester, whose switch to new styles of cloth was not associated with turning points in the history of either real incomes or transport economy. But both marketing problems and the constraints of transport costs were relevant to the town's problems. Traditional russets had been among the cheapest cloths to enter international commerce, and their diffusion in Europe in the later fourteenth century had been determined by the low cost of shipping them in bilateral trade to Danzig, Bordeaux or to Mediterranean ports. The range of possible markets was narrowly restricted, and when those markets were depressed, as a consequence of depopulation and devastation, there was

[18] Mollat, *Études*, item 5, pp. 417–18.
[19] Munro, *Wool, Cloth, and Gold*, p. 2.
[20] G. Luzzatto, *An Economic History of Italy from the Fall of the Roman Empire to the Beginning of the Sixteenth Century*, trans. P. Jones (London, 1961), pp. 159–61; M. F. Mazzaoui, *The Italian Cotton Industry in the Later Middle Ages, 1100–1600* (Cambridge, 1981), pp. 132–6.
[21] H. A. Miskimin, *The Economy of Early Renaissance Europe, 1300–1460* (Eaglewood Cliffs, 1969), pp. 91–2; Munro, 'Monetary Contraction', p. 119.

little that Colchester's merchants could do to direct their cloth to new ones. Improving the style of cloth so that it would pay to take it further, while still using traditional skills in dyeing, was perhaps the only way out of this particular corner.

In the short term Colchester's adaptation to new circumstances must be judged a success. Throughout the first half of the fifteenth century Colchester cloths were able to retain a distinctive position in established overseas markets and even to gain a few pockets of new trade. In the Baltic the town continued to be known for its greys, and these, with kerseys, were the two English fabrics for which demand was found to be most reliable.[22] In 1426 a burgess of Danzig lost 36 kerseys and two whole grey Colchester cloths which were stolen by Scandinavians, and in 1427 another Prussian was robbed of a black hooded cloak of Amsterdam cloth lined with Colchester grey.[23] Colchester's newer styles found a ready market in this part of the world; a consignment of cloth sent by Andreas Bonnemann from Colchester to Danzig in 1453 included four blues and 'two fine greys of the new colour'.[24]

Until the middle of the century much of this trade remained in the hands of Colchester men. In the spring of 1438, following an interlude of Anglo-Hanseatic conflict, Colchester was amongst the towns petitioning the Grand Master of Prussia for freedom to trade in his lands, and three years later Thomas Kymberley of Colchester was a moving spirit among those merchants frequenting Danzig who wanted the English government to investigate conditions of trading there. Kymberley with John Trewe and John Edrich of Colchester, told of losses inflicted on them by Germans in 1439, from which it appears that wheat and flax were among the commodities brought back from Colchester in exchange for cloth.[25] Some of Colchester's trade to Danzig in the later 1430s was handled through a resident factor, Henry Brook, whose brother was a clothier in Dedham. In 1438 Colchester petitioned the borough of Danzig on Brook's behalf because he had suffered the confiscation of 36 Colchester cloths.[26] It was through contact with Danzig in particular that Colchester cloth remained a staple item in the drapery trade of Prussia. Between 1433 and 1449 citations of Colchester cloth prices in Danzig records are frequent enough

[22] L. K. Goetz, *Deutsch-Russische Handelsgeschichte des Mittelalters*, Hansische Geschichtsquellen, new ser., v (Lübeck, 1922), p. 284.

[23] *Hanserecesse von 1431–76*, ed. G. von der Ropp (8 vols., Leipzig, 1876–92), i, no. 381 (item 38) and no. 543 (item 18) pp. 283, 479.

[24] *Hansisches Urkundenbuch*, ed. K. Höhlbaum and others (11 vols., Halle, 1876–1916), viii, no. 244, p. 176.

[25] *Hanserecesse von 1431–76*, ed. von der Ropp, ii, nos. 222, 538, 644 (par. 41–4), pp. 178–9, 456–7, 545–6.

[26] *Hansisches Urkundenbuch*, ed. Höhlbaum and others, vii(1), no. 329, pp. 161–2.

to supply one of the best series for any sort of cloth there.[27] From Prussia cloths travelled inland to east-central Europe, as in 1444 when the head of the Diesbach-Watt-Gesellschaft establishment at Cracow reported the receipt of a small pack of Colchester cloth which had reached him by way of Warsaw.[28] Colchester cloth was also a regular component of Hanseatic trade with Russia.[29]

In Gascony inroads were made into inland markets in competition with imported cloths from Normandy. Colchester greys entered the Toulouse drapery trade in the earlier fifteenth century, having not been known there previously, and around 1430 they competed there with greys from Auffay, Montivilliers and Rouen.[30] These were probably musterdevillers or new greys whose quality was more closely akin to that of the Norman cloths.

Even in the Mediterranean there may have been Colchester fabrics among the *panni di Sex* which Italian merchants continued to export until at least 1450. These cloths are mentioned in Damascus in 1424 and 1442. In 1438 they sold in Constantinople, and they were known in Alexandria in 1441.[31] The Venetians, who were increasingly dominant in the trade routes of the eastern Mediterranean, also exported Essex cloths to Tana on the Black Sea.[32]

The main events in Colchester's overseas trade, however, involved merchants from the Rhineland, and it was this connection which, more than any other, explains the town's ability to share in England's surge of cloth exports in the late 1430s. Already from 1427 the port of Ipswich became the most important outside London for the shipment of cloth by Hanseatic merchants. During the following ten years Hanseatic exports registered there were subordinate in quantity to those of native Englishmen. In 1437, however, Hanseatic activity there greatly increased and immediately overshadowed all other. It continued to do so for 31 years.[33] The suddenness of these changes, both the enhanced German presence in 1437 and its reduction after 1468, implies that they were the outcome of policy decisions on the part of Hanseatic merchants, those most concerned being

[27] T. Hirsch, *Danzigs Handels- und Gewerbsgeschichte unter der Herrschaft des Deutschen Ordens*, Preisschriften hrsg. von der fürstlich jablonowski'schen Gesellschaft zu Leipzig (Leipzig, 1858), pp. 243, 251.

[28] H. Ammann, *Die Diesbach-Watt-Gesellschaft: ein Beitrag zur Handelsgeschichte des 15 Jahrhunderts* (St Gallen, 1928), item 129, p. 42.

[29] Goetz, *Deutsch-Russische Handelsgeschichte*, p. 284.

[30] P. Wolff, *Commerces et marchands de Toulouse (vers 1350–vers 1450)* (Paris, 1954), pp. 237–42.

[31] *Documenti per la storia economica*, ed. Melis, nos. 35, 93, pp. 194, 318; Ashtor, 'L'Exportation de textiles occidentaux', p. 343.

[32] E. Ashtor, *Studies in the Levantine Trade in the Middle Ages* (London, 1978), item 6, pp. 17–23; *idem*, 'L'Exportation de textiles occidentaux', p. 344.

[33] Carus-Wilson and Coleman, *England's Export Trade*, pp. 88–103.

Table 11.3 *Wine imports and cloth exports through Ipswich (annual averages). 1410/11–1524/5*

	Wine imports (tons)	Cloth exports (no. of cloths)			
		Denizen	Hanseatic	Alien	Total
1410/11–1435/6	229	1,186	597	23	1,807[a]
1436/7–1449/50	206	2,011	2,509	43	4,563
1450/1–1467/8	107	454	1,415	23	1,893[a]
1468/9–1495/6	53	363	212	10	585
1496/7–1524/5	?	1,466	4	57	1,527

[a] Totals in these years do not equal the sum of the parts because of rounding.
Sources: E. M. Carus-Wilson and O. Coleman, *England's Export Trade, 1275–1547* (Oxford, 1963), pp. 90–116; M. K. James, *Studies in the Medieval Wine Trade*, ed. E. M. Veale (Oxford, 1971), pp. 109–16.

from Cologne. Cologne in the mid fifteenth century was the largest city in Germany, and her merchants were conveniently placed to be the principal intermediaries between north-western and central Europe. The chief commodity they obtained from the western termini of their trade was woollen cloth, which they bought in many varieties to supply both the Rhineland and markets farther afield. The fairs of Frankfurt were a channel through which cloths passed to merchants from southern and central Europe. More than any other German merchants, those of Cologne knew what was available in England and what would sell in Germany.[34]

The revival of German exports of cloth from England in 1437 followed the signing of a treaty with the Hanseatic League on 22 March that year whereby six years of mutual hostilities and interrupted trade were brought to an end. The two parties were encouraged to settle their differences by the outbreak of war between England and Burgundy, which disrupted the normal commerce of both English and Germany merchants in the Low Countries. But the Germans' enthusiasm for the treaty was furthered by the irresistible attraction of English cloths in European markets.[35] When trade was restored it was instantly at a level higher than ever before, and the attention which the Germans paid to East Anglian cloths is evident

[34] F. Irsigler, 'Kölner Wirtschaft im Spätmittelalter', in H. Kellenbenz, ed., *Zwei Jahrtausende Kölner Wirtschaft* (2 vols., Cologne, 1975), i, pp. 275–6; Amman, 'Deutschland und die Tuchindustrie Nordwesteuropas', pp. 49–50.
[35] Schulz, *Die Hanse und England*, pp. 83–6; Postan, *Medieval Trade and Finance*, pp. 261–4.

Table 11.4 *Cloths exported from Colchester and Ipswich,*
29.xi.1458–29.ix.1459

	Denizen no.	Hanseatic no.	Other alien no.
Ipswich	432	123	0
Colchester	167	1,114½	0
	599	1,237½	0
'Ipswich'	599	1,237	0

Note: the units are *panni curti sine grano*. Straits, of which there are only a few, are counted as half cloths. Other cloths are not included.
Sources: P.R.O., E.122/52/42. The 'Ipswich' figures are those enrolled, as given in E. M. Carus-Wilson and O. Coleman, *England's Export Trade, 1275–1547* (Oxford, 1963), p. 100.

from the expansion of their exports through the port of Ipswich, which in some years approached, and once even exceeded, those through London.[36] This German interest, together with the revival in denizen trade which accompanied it, meant that trade through the port of Ipswich enjoyed a boom period between 1436/7 and 1449/50. Thereafter both denizen and Hanseatic trade contracted, but the continued activities of German merchants up to 1468 maintained the cloth trade at a higher level than that of the years before 1437 (Table 11.3).

II

Hanseatic trade through the port of Ipswich, which is better illustrated for the 1450s and 1460s than for earlier decades, was more closely relevant to Colchester's economic development than might be supposed. In their enrolled form English customs records do not distinguish between the different harbours which made up the port of Ipswich for purposes of customs administration – Ipswich, Harwich, Colchester and Maldon – and most of the surviving particulars of account, though stating the days on which ships arrived or departed, do not record where they did so. The counter-roll from 29 November 1458 to Michaelmas 1459, however, distinguishes unambiguously between Ipswich and Colchester,[37] and shows that Hanseatic exports through the latter greatly exceeded those through the former (Table 11.4). That this was no freak year is shown by

[36] Carus-Wilson and Coleman, *England's Export Trade*, p. 102.
[37] P.R.O., E.122/52/42.

Table 11.5 *Cloths exported from Colchester and Ipswich,*
18.xi.1462–10.vii.1463 and 29.ix.1465–29.xi.1466

	1462/3			1465/6		
	Denizen no.	Hanseatic no.	Other alien no.	Denizen no.	Hanseatic no.	Other alien no.
Ipswich	34	310	45½	79	377	16½
Colchester	67½	698½	5	79½	4,145½	28
Harwich	2½	8	0	0	0	0
	104	1,016½	50½	158½	4,522½	44½
'Ipswich'	106	1,022	51	159	4,525	43

Note: the units are as in Table 11.4.
Sources: P.R.O., E.122/52/45, 46, 47, 48; Carus-Wilson and Coleman, *England's Export Trade*, pp. 101–2.

the counter-rolls for 1462/3[38] and 1465/6,[39] whose evidence is summarised in Table 11.5. By good fortune these records permit comparison between a quiet year and an exceptionally busy one, demonstrating that it was in the latter instance that Colchester's pre-eminence was most marked. In 1465/6, a year whose exports of cloth by German merchants was exceeded only by those of 1446/7, they took 92 per cent of them through Colchester.

Not all the cloth exported through Colchester was of the town's own making. In 1458 Thomas Peverell of East Bergholt bound himself by letter obligatory to full four vesses and two new greys on behalf of Eberhard Kryt of Cologne.[40] A complaint by Henning Buring in 1468 records that he claimed debts in Dedham, Stratford St Mary, Stoke by Nayland and Lavenham as well as in Colchester.[41] As a result of such direct contact with inland villages and towns German merchants to some extent replaced those of Colchester in regional trade. By the years 1445–65 litigants from Suffolk are much less in evidence as debtors and creditors than they had been between 1390 and 1410. The court rolls of the later period, though more fully preserved than those of the earlier one, record no litigants in pleas of debt from Clare, Cavendish, Glemsford or Long Melford, only one each

[38] The counter-rolls for 1462/3 list separately receipts at Ipswich, Colchester and Harwich: P.R.O., E.122/52/45, 46.

[39] The collector's account of 29 September 1465 to 19 March 1466 has two sequences of receipts, the second of which is labelled *Colcestr'* in the margin: P.R.O., E.122/52/48, m. 3v. The counter-roll of 19 March 1466 to Michaelmas 1466 is similarly composed, and there is a marginal *C* at the appropriate place: E.122/52/49, m. 1r.

[40] CR 69/12r, 19d. A vesse was a local type of woollen cloth, apparently of a blue colour: *O.E.D.* under vesse, and see above, Table 11.2.

[41] *Hansisches Urkundenbuch*, ed. Höhlbaum and others, ix, no. 541, p. 413.

from Sudbury and Kersey,[42] and two each from Hadleigh[43] and Lavenham.[44] These eight places, which together supply the names of 58 litigants in debt cases from the period 1390–1410, have therefore only six recorded from 1445–65. Their cloth industries stood to benefit, like that of Colchester, from Hanseatic trade, but there was little associated advantage to Colchester middlemen. A similar state of affairs has been observed at Southampton, where again the activities of native merchants were restrained by the inland operations of foreigners.[45]

The styles of cloth exported by the Germans were representative of the wide variety of colours and sizes to be found in local workshops. An account of a cargo which had probably come from Colchester is available because early in 1460 some Frenchmen pillaged the contents of Peter Lobbe's ship when it was on charter from Bergen op Zoom to some German merchants. The vessel contained some of the cheapest English cloths, frieze, cogware and stockbridge, together with 110 vesses and about a dozen each of musterdevillers and blues. However, the most valuable part of the cloth was grey, the merchants distinguishing $188\frac{1}{2}$ grey cloths (three of which were used as wrappers) from $92\frac{1}{2}$ white-greys. These greys were mostly of the newer styles. Two of them were said to be of russet grey and one was 'of the old colour', but no such qualification is made concerning the rest. The $57\frac{1}{2}$ greys for which a separate valuation may be isolated were together valued at £172 9s 8d, and so averaged almost exactly £3 each.[46] Clearly, then, there was a place for Colchester's newer fabrics in the German market, and no doubt Hanseatic interest accelerated the change in this direction. In 1459 John Horndon contracted in Colchester to make for an English client two broadcloths called murrey greys 'like the ones he used to sell to merchants of the Hanse'.[47] And the importance of Colchester's own products in this trade is indicated in other ways. Cologne merchants recognised Colchester cloth as a distinct type, even if, as Eberhard Kryt's dealings in East Bergholt demonstate, they could obtain similar cloths elsewhere. In 1447, for example, the Cologne merchant Henchen van der Seligenstadt claimed Hanseatic privilege in London with respect to 17 grey Colchester cloths.[48]

[42] CR 64/24r; CR 66/28r.   [43] CR 70/12d; CR 72/21r.
[44] CR 67/24r; CR 71/21r.
[45] O. Coleman, 'Trade and Prosperity in the Fifteenth Century: Some Aspects of the Trade of Southampton', *Ec.H.R.*, 2nd ser., xvi (1963), p. 18.
[46] *Quellen zur Geschichte des Kölner Handels und Verkehrs im Mittelalter*, ed. B. Kuske, Publikationen der Gesellschaft fur Rheinische Geschichtskunde, xxxiii (4 vols., Bonn, 1917–34), ii, no. 243, pp. 113–14. *Cf. ibid.*, ii, nos. 231, 232 and 242, pp. 108–9, 112–13. Visits by Lobbe's ship to Colchester in 1462 and 1463 are recorded in P.R.O., E.122/52/43, mm. 1r, 2d; E.122/52/46, m. 3v.
[47] CR 69/20d.
[48] *Quellen*, ed. Kuske, i, no. 1160, p. 407.

The number of Hanseatic merchants who exported cloth from the quays at Hythe varied from year to year – 25 in 1458/9, 11 in 1462/3, 46 in 1465/6. The size of the shipments also varied with the level of trade. German activity depended partly on a system by which vessels were chartered to visit England in convoy on behalf of a group of merchants. On 6 March 1466 five ships took 1,625 cloths from Colchester, and on 1 July following four ships sailed together with 1,692½ cloths.[49] The Germans usually employed Dutch shipping,[50] so that in this respect the growth of their trade strengthened an already existing structure of communications across the North Sea. In 1465 Johann van A of Cologne and two fellow Cologne merchants contracted with a shipman from Bergen op Zoom that at the Whit Market in Amsterdam he should take on board woad, Gascon wine, yarn and linen for shipment to Colchester,[51] and on 26 October the same year the ship of Claes Noirt of Amsterdam left Colchester with cloth belonging to 11 Hanseatic merchants.[52] Those Germans whose trade was most frequent often shipped small consignments of merchandise in association with English and Dutch merchants.

The necessary means of organisation on the English side of the North Sea were provided by Germans resident in Colchester. Several names are on record, the main figure being Johann van A, who traded both on his own account and for others. He had become a burgher of Cologne in 1443, when in the service of Johann Rinck, and continued to act as Rinck's agent after coming to Colchester about four years later.[53] In 1459 he was closely associated with Hermann Rinck, and was probably acting as his factor.[54] Not surprisingly, van A was one of the more regular exporters of cloth through Colchester; his activity remained steady even in years when other German merchants passed Colchester by – 292 cloths in 1458/9, 323 in 1462/3, 242 in 1465/6.[55] On return journeys he imported oil, litmus, linen, dyestuffs and a wide variety of other exports and re-exports from the Low Countries. Not being a burgess of Colchester, van A must have restricted his business to wholesale trade in the town. After 16 November 1447, when

---

[49] P.R.O., E.122/52/48, fos. 7r–9r; E.122/52/49, mm. 1v–2r.

[50] Schulz, *Die Hanse und England*, p. 93.

[51] *Bronnen*, ed. Smit, ii, no. 1558, p. 1001. For evidence that Edelkind, one of the two merchants in question, came from a Cologne family see *Quellen*, ed. Kuske, ii, no. 451, pp. 195–6.

[52] P.R.O., E.122/52/48, m. 4r. Noirt's origin is identified from F. Ketner, *Handel en Scheepvaart van Amsterdam in de Vijftiende Eeuw* (Brill, 1946), p. 206.

[53] *Quellen*, ed. Kuske, i, no. 1160n, p. 407 and ii, no. 43, p. 21. For the extent of the Rinck enterprises, see Irsigler, 'Kölner Wirtschaft im Spätmittelalter', p. 292.

[54] In three ships of the Hanseatic convoy leaving Colchester on 24 July 1459, von A and Rinck were the only merchants to ship cloth through Colchester, and in the customs account relating to another ship of the convoy their names are adjacent: P.R.O., E.122/52/42, m. 3d.

[55] Sources as in Tables 11.4 and 11.5.

he first occurs in Colchester records as a litigant,[56] his name recurs through the 1450s and earlier 1460s. He returned to Cologne during the mid or later 1460s and in 1468 nominated his son, Johann van A the younger, together with Diederich Boele, to be his factors in England.[57] The activities of Johann van A the younger took him abroad with his merchandise for extended periods,[58] and it was perhaps for this reason that he committed his property in Colchester to another's keeping in 1470.[59] But he continued to trade there, and in 1476, 1477 and 1478 brought pleas of debt against Colchester burgesses, two of them in his father's name.[60] Another member of the family, Hermann van A, was still in Colchester in 1492, and so well at home there that he was reported to have opened a goldsmith's shop and to be in partnership with an Englishman; but this was a malicious rumour on the part of his fellow countrymen.[61]

III

By the 1490s, however, the German association with Colchester was of minor importance. The van A family had maintained the connection long after the majority of Cologne merchants had abandoned it. Colchester's trade with Germany never recovered from the breakdown of Anglo-Hanseatic relations in 1468 and the ensuing naval war.[62] In that year Colchester was still picked out in a letter from the Steelyard to the Englandfahrer in Cologne as a place where there were resident Germans, the other colonies in England being in London, Ipswich, Norwich, Boston and Lincoln.[63] There were still German residents, besides Johann van A, in the early 1470s; in 1470 Reynart van Lubberich of Cologne and Joris Tacke of Duisburg went from Colchester to attend a meeting of German merchants in London,[64] and in January that year two Cologne merchants in Colchester were instructed to inform the council at Cologne concerning their status as merchants or factors.[65] Those who remained continued to operate much as they had done in the past, though without the advantage

[56] CR 62/6d.
[57] *Quellen*, ed. Kuske, ii, no. 451, pp. 195–6.
[58] P.R.O., C.1/46/320.
[59] OB, fo. 102v. The interpretation to be placed on this type of transaction is discussed in *Calendar of Plea and Memoranda Rolls, 1413–37*, ed. Thomas, pp. xix–xxiii; *Calendar of Plea and Memoranda Rolls of the City of London, A.D. 1437–1457*, ed. P. E. Jones (Cambridge, 1954), pp. xxii–xxviii.
[60] CR 76/3r, 7r; CR 77/4r, 25r.
[61] *Hansisches Urkundenbuch*, ed. Höhlbaum and others, xi, nos. 518, 545, 548, 579, pp. 352–4, 364–5, 365–7, 381–2.
[62] Postan, *Medieval Trade and Finance*, pp. 280–7.
[63] *Hansisches Urkundenbuch*, ed. Höhlbaum and others, ix, no. 490, pp. 346–7.
[64] *Hanserecesse von 1431–76*, ed. von der Ropp, vi, no. 370 (item 2), pp. 364–6.
[65] *Hansisches Urkundenbuch*, ed. Höhlbaum and others, ix, no. 698 (item 3), p. 639.

of chartered convoys to ship their merchandise. Johann van A the younger wrote from Colchester to London in 1472 to send news of the arrival of a caravel in Colchester and of the safe crossing of three small ships from Colchester to Zealand.[66] Hanseatic cloth exports, however, were rapidly reduced to a trickle (Table 11.3). Moreover, references to Germans resident in Colchester become more sparse in the course of the 1470s, and the colony was no doubt shrinking during those years.

In the meanwhile, after a busy period in the late 1430s and the 1440s, the trade of Colchester's own merchants had suffered a severe decline. In 1449 the reopening of war with France – the final stage of the Hundred Years' War – caused the disruption of the wine trade with Gascony. Wine imports through Ipswich contracted sharply (Table 11.3). Trade with the Baltic was similarly interrupted for English merchants by Robert Winnington's capture of a Hanseatic fleet in 1449, an event which aroused bitter resentment in Lübeck. The Oresund was closed to English shipping, by an agreement with Denmark, and merchants frequenting Danzig had serious obstacles to overcome.[67] Even without the renewed outbreak of violent antagonism, however, the simultaneous loss of interest in the Baltic region by both the English and the Germans implies that Colchester cloth had no longer the competitive advantages there which it had enjoyed in the 1430s and 1440s. The profitability of exporting cloth so far was jeopardised by a decline in cloth prices which had no equivalent in the English home market or in the English manufacturer's costs. Between 1435–44 and 1465–74 the price of an ell of grey woollen cloth in Rostock, measured in terms of the quantity of silver for which it could be exchanged, declined by 37 per cent.[68] This decline is not to be explained by falling transport costs or rising productivity in the Baltic region; it was owing chiefly to a drain of bullion from the Baltic which adversely affected prices generally throughout the region.[69] So after abandoning trade with Prussia at the end of the 1440s, Colchester merchants had subsequently no commercial motives to restore it. As a result of the crises in both Gascon and Prussian trade, denizen activity in the port of Ipswich collapsed permanently from the high level of the 1440s (Table 11.3).

The low level to which Colchester's overseas enterprise had dwindled by the last decades of the century is shown by customs accounts of the period. Only one or two Colchester merchants continued to trade abroad.

[66] *Ibid.*, x, no. 111, p. 67.
[67] Postan, *Medieval Trade and Finance*, pp. 273–5.
[68] U. Hauschild, *Studien zu Löhnen und Preisen in Rostock im Spätmittelalter*, Quellen und Darstellungen zur Hansischen Geschichte, new ser., xix (Cologne, 1973), p. 197.
[69] R. Sprandel, *Das mittelalterliche Zahlungssystem nach hansisch-nordischen Quellen des 13.–15. Jahrhunderts*, Monographien zur Geschichte des Mittelalters, x (Stuttgart, 1975), p. 133.

William Smith alone continued to export cloth in the years 1481/2, 1483/4 and 1491/2, for which there are accounts; in return he imported iron and salt as well as miscellaneous products from the Low Countries.[70] Robert Barker, who in October 1491 imported a cargo of madder, woad, hand cards, metal ware and cloth, all imports from the Low Countries, was probably the eminent Colchester burgess of that name, but his overseas trading was not very vigorous.[71] There are no known Colchester importers of wine in these decades. The situation was no more lively in the early sixteenth century. An account of 1505/6 again records only one Colchester merchant paying customs duties on cloth, Thomas Christmas, and he exported only 11 out of 1,496 cloths shipped through the port of Ipswich that year. This account contains little evidence of an import trade by Colchester men, but William Smith, who brought in 35½ out of the year's total of 290¼ tons of wine, was perhaps the son of William Smith who had been active during 1480s.[72] A larger part of denizen trade than in the past was in the hands of Londoners, some of whom handled more business than any local men. In 1481/2 William Shore of London accounted for over one third of wine imports through Ipswich – it was, admittedly, a lean year – and he exported 61½ cloths, a number much the same as that for which William Smith was responsible.[73] In 1505/6 Henry Patiner of London exported 476 cloths through Ipswich, nearly one third of the year's total.[74]

With both foreign and denizen trade through Hythe in decay, Colchester's ability to export became more dependent on trade through London itself. This was not a unique experience in this period; the diversion of cloth exports from the Midlands through London was partly to blame for the contemporary decay of Boston and King's Lynn.[75] Contact between Colchester and the capital is sparsely documented and no magnitude may be assigned to the volume of trade. But it is recorded that in February 1528 John Boswell of Colchester, clothmaker, had three or four cloths for sale 'in a hall called Colchester Hall within Blackwell Hall'.[76] This illustrates the existence of a trade through London and implies that Colchester had

[70] P.R.O., E.122/52/58, mm. 5d, 6d, 11r; E.122/53/1, m. 1d; E.122/53/9, mm. 2d, 3r, 5d, 6r, 7d, 8r.

[71] P.R.O., E.122/53/9, m. 2r. Barker was a fuller and clothier: CR 76/27d; P.R.O., E.101/343/9d, 10d, 11r, 13d.

[72] P.R.O., E.122/53/17, m. 1d *bis*; OB, fo. 115r. The Oath Book reference is to 'William Smyth of Colchester, fuller, son and heir of William Smyth formerly of Hythe in the said town, merchant'.

[73] P.R.O., E.122/52/58, mm. 4r,d, 5d, 6r, 7r.

[74] P.R.O., E.122/53/17, mm. 1r, 4r.

[75] E. M. Carus-Wilson, 'The Medieval Trade of the Ports of the Wash', *Medieval Archaeology*, vi, vii (1962–3), p. 201; idem, 'The Oversea Trade of Late Medieval Coventry', pp. 378–9.

[76] *L. and P.*, iv(2), no. 4145, p. 1831.

Table 11.6 *Prices of russets and blues in Colchester, 1470–1529*

Description	Price s	Price d	Implied price of a cloth of 24 yards s	Implied price of a cloth of 24 yards d	Year	Reference
RUSSETS						
vnus pannus laneus integer russett' coloris et nouem virge panni lanei eiusdem coloris	80	0	58	2	1470	CR 74/16r
vna pecia panni lanei coloris de ronerussette continens in longitudine duodecim virgas	40	0	80	0	1473	CR 77/24d
xij virge panni lanei coloris de russat	36	0	72	0	1484	CR 81/28d
vnus pannus laneus coloris russet	80	0	80	0	1514	CR 86/4r
quatuor virge panni lanei lati coloris russet	21	4	128	0	1522	CR 97/5d
vna pecia panni lanei lati coloris russett continens ix virgatas	26	4	70	3	1525	CR 98/5r
vj virgate panni lanei coloris tawny	13	4	53	4	1527	CR 98/5r
BLUES						
vna pecia panni lanei continens octo virgatas coloris blodii	26	8	80	0	1525	CR 96/6d
vna longa pecia panni lanei coloris a brown blewe continens xxx^{ta} virgatas panni lanei	120	0	96	0	1527	CR 98/8r
vna pecia panni lanei lati coloris asur blew continens xxiiij^{or} virgatas	56	8	56	8	1529	CR 100/12d

some recognised niche within the main cloth market of the city. There were carrier services available for clothiers who had agents in London. In 1531 a carrier was commissioned to take a short azure cloth to London and to deliver it to William Cowpere at the sign of the Bell in Gracechurch Street.[77] The London outlet was potentially a source of new growth in the early sixteenth century following the commercial treaty with Burgundy in 1496. Cloth exports from the capital increased from an annual average of 36,995 (1489/90–1493/4) to 63,084 (1515/16–1519/20).[78] There was also an

[77] CR 100/18r, 21d.
[78] Carus-Wilson and Coleman, *England's Export Trade*, pp. 110–15.

increase in shipments through Ipswich at this period (Table 11.3). Nevertheless, it is uncertain how far Colchester contributed to this increase, and there is no evidence of economic development in the town during these years comparable to that in earlier periods of rising exports. On balance it is unlikely that the cloth industry experienced a new surge of output under the early Tudors.

References to particular cloths manufactured in Colchester after 1470 are few. Russets are the most commonly mentioned and supply the greatest number of prices, though few prices are stated for whole cloths and it is more common than in the past to find disputes about pieces of irregular length (Table 11.6). Qualities seem to have varied greatly, but it is plain enough that the normal russet of the early sixteenth century was a more expensive product that its forebear of a hundred years before. The upgrading of russets had begun at least as early as the 1450s. Towards the end of that decade manufacturers had launched a type called roan russet, imitating the greys of Rouen, which sold at a price of £2 12s 8d in 1459,[79] and by the early 1470s such fabrics were being made to sell at £4 (Table 11.6). Blues also occur in the early sixteenth century, and woad was the main component of Colchester's trade in dyestuffs.[80] No pattern of standard types emerges from this sparse evidence. Colchester had clung to its famous greys and brown, but the range of colours, qualities and sizes was diverse. To this extent Colchester cloth had become a less easily identifiable product in the course of the fifteenth century. The Lübeck toll books of 1492–6 may record the export of a few Colchester cloths from Lübeck to Riga and Pernau, but if so the name of the town was even more mangled than usual.[81] There is nothing in published sources of the late fifteenth century to suggest that Colchester cloth was as well known on the continent of Europe as it had been in former times.

IV

These developments in overseas trade through Colchester during the fifteenth century contributed to fluctuations in the income which the community of the borough derived from Hythe. There were two components to this income, first the water tolls on incoming cargoes, which were leased with the land tolls in the first decade of the fifteenth century but separately thereafter until 1439, and second the lease of harbour dues (wharfage, quayage, cranage, measurage and poundage, together with some harbour

---

[79] CR 70/5d. For roan as an equivalent of Rouen, see *O.E.D.* under roan, sb(3).
[80] CR 85/8d, 13r; CR 89/7r; CR 95/4r, 10r; CR 96/4r, 18d.
[81] F. Bruns, 'Die Lübeckischen Pfundzollbücher von 1492–1496', *Hansische Geschichtsblätter*, xiii (1907), pp. 473, 478.

buildings). From Michaelmas 1439 these two leases were amalgamated. The extant figures[82] suggest that in the first decade of the century the community's annual income from these two sources averaged £55 but that there followed a period of lower receipts between 1412 and 1423. Initially this was because a large residential property formerly included in the lease was now taken out of it, but the steep drop in income from the quays in 1419 cannot be accounted for so easily. It may be a facet of the depression which affected Colchester's traditional exports at this time, though there is no equivalent dip in the records of cloths exported through Ipswich.[83] From the mid 1420s, however, the movement of income from Hythe corresponded more closely to that of cloth exports, and receipts recovered to a level of £52 between 1434 and 1447. After that they declined gradually to the late 1450s and then more rapidly in the early 1460s. The community's income there settled around £35 during the 1470s and 1480s, but then fell yet further. The lowest figures on record are from the first two decades of the sixteenth century, when the value of Hythe to the community was only £24. The lease was raised at Michaelmas 1521, but only to £28, and it was still at this level in 1541. These figures accordingly confirm the severe decline in trading activity at Hythe in the later fifteenth century which is implied both by the abandonment of adventuring amongst Colchester men and by the withdrawal of foreign merchants.

[82] Appendix, Table 5.
[83] Carus-Wilson and Coleman, *England's Export Trade*, pp. 91–2.

12

Industry

I

The opportunities which presented themselves to Colchester's cloth manufacturers during the 50 years after 1412 did not permit continuous growth, but it is likely that cloth output in the borough did not reach its peak until the 1440s. The recorded leases of the wool market imply that the level of activity attained in 1411/12 and 1413/14, when the rent stood at £9 6s 8d, was not surpassed until the 1440s, when in at least one year it reached £12.[1] That was in 1443/4, a year of exceptionally heavy cloth exports through Ipswich.[2] The intervening years were a period of lower rents, particularly during the early 1430s. The recovery of the late 1430s and the 1440s was a direct consequence of the coming of German merchants from 1437, and the high level of trade in the 1440s was unlikely to have survived the waning of their interest. After 1449, unfortunately, the lease of the wool market was amalgamated with that of overland tolls, but the combined rent in the 1470s was still the same as the sum of the two separate rents in 1448/9, and this implies that the wool market was probably valued at £8 a year.

The evidence of the wool markets is complemented by that of the ulnage accounts. Table 12.1 shows the number of cloth sales ascribed to Colchester during the years 1461–78 and compares it with the available figures from the 1390s. The busiest period of cloth sales was in June and July when the cloth fairs were held,[3] and this explains why so few cloths were sealed in the borough between October 1398 and May 1399. But the documented period of 194 weeks in the 1390s included seven fairs, which is proportionately about right.[4] The comparison between the 1390s and the 1460s

---

[1] CR 59/1d.
[2] Carus-Wilson and Coleman, *England's Export Trade*, p. 96.
[3] See Chapter 5, p. 80.
[4] William Geldrich's commission of 1394 for Essex was timed to begin on the first day of Colchester's St Mary Magdalen fair: P.R.O., E.101/342/9, m. 1r.

Table 12.1 *Cloths paying subsidy and ulnage in Colchester 1394–9 and 1461–78*

	No.	Weekly average
20.vii.1394–30.xi.1395	849¾	
30.xi.1395–29.ix.1397	2,170	
22.x.1398–5.v.1399	166¼	
194 weeks, 1394–9	3,186	16.4
3.iii.1461–18.iv.1462	1,784	30.2
1466/7	1,204	23.2
1467/8	1,393	26.8
1468/9	1,390	26.7
1469/70	1,297	24.9
1471/2	1,388	26.7
1473/4	1,366	26.3
1476/7	1,389	26.7
1477/8	1,389	26.7

Note: the units are *integri panni lati*, each equivalent to two *decene*.
Source: P.R.O., E.101/342/9, mm. 1r–3d, 8r–10r, 11r; E.101/342/13, E.101/342/21, back membrane; E.101/343/4, m. 3; E.101/343/5–7, 9–11, 13, 14. Note that E.101/343/13 is the foot of E.101/343/8 and that E.101/343/14 belongs with E.101/343/2.

suggests that sales were considerably higher in the latter period. Average weekly sales were 84 per cent higher in 1461–2 than in the 1390s and even in the late 1460s they were 63 per cent higher. This increase was within the range of what was perhaps achieved between 1399 and 1412, when the rent of the wool market was raised by 75 per cent.[5] But if trade in local cloths had contracted since the peak of Hanseatic exporting before 1450, then sales during the 1440s must have been appreciably more than 84 per cent above the level of the 1390s, and this again implies that the 1440s was the period of greatest activity in Colchester's textile trade. In retrospect, Colchester's industrial history may be told as a series of bursts of acceleration separated by years of stagnation or depression. The main phases of growth were probably 1351–6, 1375–80, 1398–1412 and 1437–47, each of which carried output to a higher level than before.

The fossilisation of the ulnage statistics of the 1470s and the subsequent dearth of quantitative evidence relating to the production or sale of cloth means that no independent account of changing cloth output can be attempted. It is likely that, notwithstanding the increased exports of cloth

[5] Appendix, Table 5.

Table 12.2 *Distribution of cloth sales between men paying subsidy and ulnage in Colchester, 1461–71/2*

Number of panni integri sold	3.iii.1461–18.iv.1462	Number of sellers				
		1466/7	1467/8	1468/9	1469/70	1471/2
5 or fewer	1	15	0	3	3	0
5¼ to 10	1	14	3	3	13	1
10¼ to 15	3	7	7	6	2	1
15¼ to 20	2	6	4	6	6	1
20¼ to 25	5	5	2	7	4	4
25¼ to 30	2	7	3	3	8	6
30¼ to 35	0	0	1	0	3	4
35¼ to 40	0	11	5	6	7	7
40¼ to 45	2	0	1	4	3	7
45¼ to 50	2	0	4	4	2	4
Over 50	13	2	9	5	2	3
Uncertain	7+	0	0	0	0	0

Note: the units are *integri panni lati*, each equivalent to two *decene*.
Source: as Table 12.1.

from England during these years, Colchester's cloth industry contracted between 1468 and 1524. However, this judgement is inferred from other economic evidence yet to be examined. The only shred of quantitative evidence in its support is that the combined rent of overland tolls and the wool market was at its lowest recorded level in 1484/5, which is the latest year for which the lease is recorded.

II

The internal organisation of Colchester's cloth trade was transformed during the fifteenth century through the concentration of entrepreneurial activities in fewer hands. In the 1390s, as an earlier chapter has shown, most sellers of cloth in the town were small operators who sold fewer than 20 *decene* a year.[6] Table 12.2 shows the changed scene of the later fifteenth century, as it appears in the ulnage accounts. Even if the distribution of sales in 1466/7 was more accurately represented than that of later years, the trade was controlled by a number of men much smaller than that in the 1390s. There were still in the 1460s and 1470s independent clothmakers who sold cloth on their own account. No single craft dominated the trade;

[6] See Chapter 5, pp. 78–9.

sellers of cloth included fullers,[7] dyers,[8] shearmen[9] and a number of weavers.[10] But these details simply show that Colchester's textile crafts contained a heterogeneous body of workmen. The entrepreneurs among them were a small minority. Most weavers sold no cloth, to judge from the ulnage accounts, and depended upon other men for their employment.[11] The same differences are found within the other textile crafts at this time; the majority of known dyers and fullers did not sell cloth,[12] and may be assumed to have worked on contract. The rising level of industrial concentration implies that by the 1470s wage dependence was more characteristic of clothmaking than it had been a hundred years earlier.

Industrial concentration remained in the 1470s less advanced in Colchester than in Lavenham. In 1477/8 the top quartile of sellers accounted for 36 per cent of all sales in the former, 79 in the latter. The leading Lavenham merchants were bigger operators than any in Colchester; Thomas Spring, William Spring and William Jacob all in 1477/8 sold at least twice as many cloths as Colchester's major seller, William Smith.[13] But Colchester probably moved towards a higher degree of industrial concentration during the last quarter of the century, when it became common for Colchester's wealthier townsmen to describe themselves as clothmakers. The earliest bailiffs known to be called by this term were Richard Plomer, bailiff in 1484/5 and 1487/8,[14] Richard Harvy, bailiff for a few weeks in 1487,[15] John Thursk, bailiff in 1495/6[16] and Thomas Christmas II, bailiff in 1497/8.[17] It rapidly became more usual to designate wealthy entrepreneurs as clothmakers than to assign them to any particular craft. The principal Colchester clothmakers were involved in the process of manufacture at all stages. By his will, proved in 1520, Thomas Christmas left an ell of linen worth 6*d* 'to euery of my spynners that of olde longtyme haue contynued withine' and he left 6*s* 8*d* each 'to euery of my tenauntes that be my fullers, wevers and shermen'. An appended

---

[7] Robert Barker (CR 76/27d) and John Martin (CR 73/38r): P.R.O., E.101/343/9r–11r, 13d.
[8] William Hunt (CR 72/29r) and John Thomas (CR 73/39r): P.R.O., E.101/342/21, back membrane; E.101/343/14r.
[9] John Sewhale (CR 71/5d): P.R.O., E.101/342/21, back membrane.
[10] John Clerk (CR 71/17r), John Shipman (CR 72/15d): P.R.O., E.101/343/13d.
[11] *E.g.* John Sendout (CR 71/7d), John Crudde (CR 71/25r), John Carter (CR 72/11r), John Sonde (CR 72/12r), John Tassell (CR 72/21r), Robert Sorell (CR 72/21r).
[12] *E.g.* Edmund Fuller (CR 71/2d), Robert Smith (CR 71/12d), both dyers; Robert Sayer (CR 71/3d), John Nicole (CR 71/3d), John Colman (CR 71/25r), Thomas Felde (CR 72/17d), all fullers.
[13] P.R.O., E.101/343/11r.
[14] OB, fos. 107v, 108r, 109r.
[15] OB, fos. 109r, 112r.
[16] OB, fos. 111v, 112r.
[17] OB, fo. 112v; *L. and P.*, i(1), no. 1803(2), pp. 821–2.

memorandum lists only five weavers and two shearmen, but Christmas may be supposed to have employed other men who were not tenants.[18] Clothmakers also commanded local water mills. Thomas Christmas' father had had leases of a grain mill and fulling mill at Hythe, and of another grain mill and fulling mill called Lexden Mills.[19] He himself had on lease Newbridge Mill in West Bergholt, which had previously been leased by another clothmaker, Richard Harvy.[20] Control of fulling mills meant that an entrepreneur could be more sure of getting cloths finished as and when he wanted them. Having organised the manufacture of cloth, it was the clothmaker who then arranged for its carriage to London, if that was where it was destined to be sold.[21]

Concentration of industrial entrepreneurship was a feature of all the clothmaking centres of Essex and Suffolk during the later fifteenth century and the early sixteenth,[22] and by the 1520s and 1530s employment in the industry was in their gift. The Duke of Norfolk's correspondence shows him in 1528 summoning clothiers to meet him, one or two from each clothmaking town, to allay their fears of impending crisis in trade with Flanders, and to persuade them, in the interests of public order, to maintain a normal level of employment.[23] A complaint by the weavers of Hadleigh, Lavenham, Colchester and other nearby towns in 1539 registers that the petitioners felt wholly dependent upon rich clothiers for their work, and that the clothiers had agreed on a fixed price for weaving cloths. Householders with families were at a disadvantage, it was alleged, because 'the clothiers haue their loomes and weyvers and also their fullers dailie workyng within their owne howses'.[24]

In part the concentration of enterprise in the Colchester textile industry was a consequence of industrial regulations introduced to protect the quality of Colchester cloth. In 1418 the town clerk registered in the court roll some 'Constitutions and Ordinances of the Fullers' Craft'.[25] A transcript of such a document, in a later fifteenth-century hand, is preserved in the Red Paper Book,[26] and the language of the text, which is in English, is compatible with an early fifteenth-century date. The transcriber has taken the document's title from the margin of his original and spread it through the text in an unintelligent fashion, so that the first

[18] P.C.C., Ayloffe, 28.
[19] OB, fo. 110r; *Cal. Pat. R., 1494–1509*, p. 60.
[20] E.R.O., D/DMa M2, mm. 5r, 8r; D/DMa M3, m. 20r.
[21] *L. and P.*, iv(2), no. 4145, p. 1831.
[22] B. McClenaghan, *The Springs of Lavenham* (Ipswich, 1924), pp. ix–xi; G. A. Thornton, *A History of Clare, Suffolk* (Cambridge, 1928), pp. 181–4.
[23] Unwin, *Studies in Economic History*, pp. 267–8.
[24] *Tudor Economic Documents*, ed. R. H. Tawney and E. Power (3 vols., London, 1924), i, pp. 177–8.
[25] OB, fo. 77r.   [26] RPB, fos. 23v–24v.

paragraph is headed *Constituciones*, the second *Et Ordinaciones*, the third *Artis Fullonum* and the fourth *Ville Colcestrie*. In 1419 and 1425 men were reported by lawhundred juries for activites of the sort proscribed by the ordinances.[27] These considerations put the identification of the Red Paper Book text with that of 1418 beyond reasonable doubt. The object of these ordinances was to restrict entry into the textile crafts. The fullers started from the premise that shoddy workmanship was undermining Colchester's reputation and that 'the sale of clothe of this towne makyng is lickly to be lost for defaute of gouernaunce', perhaps because Colchester's shift towards cloth of better quality was calling for higher standards of skill. It was ordained that in future no journeyman should full any cloth on his own initiative, whether in his employer's house, his own home or elsewhere. A journeyman should engage in fulling, from this time, only if he were employed by a master fuller and if his master granted him permission to do so. Concern for the future is also to be seen in the laying down of terms for apprenticeships. Weavers and fullers should be apprenticed for at least five years and no one should engage in these crafts without an apprenticeship. It was an explicit intention of these rules to prevent weavers from fulling their own cloth. The ordinances created a more profound gulf between masters and their employees than any which had existed before this time, and in so doing put further dampers upon entrepreneurship in the cloth industry.

Even in the absence of such regulations, however, the characteristic unit of enterprise in clothmaking would have grown larger, as it did throughout the industry. Men who commanded access to raw materials and fulling mills were able, already in the 1390s,[28] to operate as employers of other men, and probably produced at a low unit cost. Larger enterprises were also at an advantage in marketing cloth through London, which counted for more after the Hanseatic merchants' withdrawal in 1468. In good years clothmakers could build up their business, but it may have been in poor years that their low costs gave them the greatest advantages over smaller men. The declining number of cloth sellers during the 1460s and 1470s suggest a retreat of small entrepreneurs at a time when profits were harder to achieve.[29] The weavers' petition of 1539 alleges that the concentration of industrial control in the hands of clothiers was associated with rising unemployment and falling wages, which, if true, is hardly compatible with any sort of industrial upsurge. The phenomenon of industrial concentration is often accepted uncritically as evidence of industrial growth. In itself, however, it indicated neither growth nor contraction of total employment, but was a long development caused by the gradual accumulation of wealth in the hands of particular families.

[27] CR 41/13r; CR 45/25r; CR 46/2d.
[28] See Chapter 5, p. 77.

III

In the 1390s, as an earlier chapter showed, Colchester was one of the main cloth markets in the eastern counties, and probably the biggest. For over 60 years after 1399 no further comparisons can be made for want of ulnage accounts, and when such records became available again in the 1460s and 1470s they are very different from those of the 1390s. Comparisons between counties and between individual towns and villages become easier, since Essex, Suffolk and Norfolk, together with Cambridgeshire and Huntingdonshire, were in the hands of a single ulnager – William Whelpdale, from Easter 1465 to Christmas 1469,[30] John Flegge from Christmas 1469 to at least Michaelmas 1478.[31] The accounting period was standardised from 1466 to the normal office year from Michaelmas to Michaelmas.[32] This was all the result of a recent administrative reform.

Surviving ulnage accounts from the early 1460s reveal administrative chaos in which the possibilities of continuity from year to year were slight. Individual centres of trade had their own receivers who rendered account for irregular periods. An account of John Levyngton, receiver for Colchester, covers the period from 3 March 1461 to 18 April 1462, and one of John Farmer, receiver for Lavenham, runs from 1 December 1463 to 20 November 1464.[33] The surviving ulnage accounts of 1464–5 are a bundle of individual receivers' accounts sewn together. They cover different periods, but mostly end at Easter 1465, and each relates to a single town or group of towns in Essex, Suffolk or Norfolk.[34] No attempt was made to draw all these accounts together into a single record for each county or for the region as a whole. At Easter 1465 the system was overhauled. William Whelpdale, an experienced and trusted receiver of royal revenues,[35] drew up a summarised account for Essex, Suffolk, Norfolk and the city of Norwich from 14 April 1465 to the following 1 August.[36] Then for the period from 1 August 1465 to Michaelmas 1466 he compiled detailed accounts for each county, of which those for Suffolk and Norfolk survive.[37] He divided the accounting year into two terms, Easter and Michaelmas, with separate totals for each. The following year he again drew up accounts for each county but abandoned the division of the year – this time a single office year – between two terms. Only the Suffolk account survives, and though the totals are similar to those of the year before there seems so far

---

[30] P.R.O., E.101/342/24, m. 8; E.101/342/25, 26; E.101/343/1, 2, 4–6.
[31] P.R.O., E.101/343/7–11. [32] P.R.O., E.101/343/2.
[33] P.R.O., E.101/342/21, m. 2 and back membrane. Details of the Lavenham account are printed in Dymond and Betterton, *Lavenham*, p. 65, but the document is there dated to 1424–5. For the correct date, *cf.* E.101/342/24, m. 10r, and E.101/342/25, m. 5r.
[34] P.R.O., E.101/342/24.
[35] *Cal. Pat. R., 1461–7*, pp. 111, 113, 224, 386, 387, 472.
[36] P.R.O., E.101/342/24, m. 8r. [37] P.R.O., E.101/342/25, 26.

to have been no stereotyping.[38] Then in 1467/8, for the first time, an annual account was compiled for the whole region of Whelpdale's concern,[39] and again the totals seem to be independently derived, even though some individual payments were rounded up to multiples of ten. This last practice is associated with an increase in the sums collected, and presumably represents some device for tugging the total more closely into line with what it should have been. Not all the increase between the early and later 1460s was the consequence of better administration; some was the consequence of recovery from economic crisis in the early 1460s.[40] But the very fact of the increases undermines the most severe points of criticism which have been directed at the later ulnage accounts of Edward IV's reign.[41] During the 1460s the accounts show the same strong administrative hand as is to be found in other branches of royal finance at that time,[42] and the accounts of Whelpdale, if not a perfect mirror of reality, were at least the fruit of an attempt to make them so.

By comparison with the accounts of the 1390s the most striking feature of the 1460s and 1470s is the prominence of Suffolk, where the annual number of sealings had about doubled from the estimated number in the 1390s.[43] By contrast the number in Essex and Norfolk showed little change – perhaps a slight increase in the former and a slight decrease in the latter. However, Colchester remained the largest centre of the trade in the three counties. The increase in sales there between the 1390s and the 1460s had been sufficient both to maintain its status at the head of the table and to maintain its share of the eastern market, so that as in the 1390s about one sixth of the cloths sold in the three counties were sealed there. As this implies, Colchester had expanded its trade at the expense of other centres in Essex (Table 12.3). Braintree's cloth trade had contracted sharply, while Chelmsford and Maldon had dwindled to insignificance. The only minor centre in Essex to have appreciably increased its number of sealings was Dedham, Colchester's near neighbour.[44] In Norfolk the same pattern is to be observed. The number of cloths sealed in Norwich had increased[45] but trade had declined in King's Lynn,[46] and sales of cloth

---

[38] P.R.O., E.101/343/2.   [39] P.R.O., E.101/343/4.

[40] The number of cloths sealed in Lavenham in 1463–4 was much lower than in 1461–2: P.R.O., E.101/342/21, m. 2r,d; E.101/342/24, m. 10r.

[41] Carus-Wilson, *Medieval Merchant Venturers*, pp. 279–91.

[42] B. P. Wolffe, *The Royal Demesne in the English History: The Crown Estate in the Governance of the Realm from the Conquest to 1509* (London, 1971), pp. 143–80.

[43] 5,981½ cloths were sold during 194 weeks in 1394–7, implying about 1,600 a year on average. For a contrast with 1468/9 see Thornton, *A History of Clare*, p. 153.

[44] See Table 5.2.

[45] The number of sealings rose from 400 during a period of 59 weeks in 1398–9 to 488½ in 1467/8: P.R.O., E.101/343/12, m. 2r; E.101/343/4, m. 4r.

[46] Numbers contracted from 249 cloths in 59 weeks of 1398–9 to 162 cloths in 1467/8: P.R.O., E.101/343/12, m. 1r; E.101/343/4, m. 1r.

Table 12.3 *Cloths paying subsidy and ulnage in Essex markets* 1467/8

	Cloths of assize
Colchester	1,393
Coggeshall	324
Dedham	322
Braintree	210
Chelmsford	46
Springfield	28
Thaxted and Saffron Walden	27
Maldon	17
Woodham Ferrers	15
St Osyth	12
'Bekyrley'	4
Watham (Holy Cross)	1

Source: P.R.O., E.101/343/4, m.3.

in Great Yarmouth, North Walsham, Hingham and some other centres, only small in the 1390s, were not worth the ulnager's attention in the 1460s.[47] Similar analysis of the Suffolk trade is impossible for want of details about the location of trade in the 1390s, but in view of the experience of Essex and Norfolk it is improbable that the considerable growth of trade here had been evenly shared among the cloth markets of the county. The chances are that growth in one or two markets had been exceptionally rapid, with Lavenham as the leader. In 1467/8 over one fifth of all the sealings in Suffolk were registered in Lavenham, and Lavenham was second only to Colchester as a market for cloth in the eastern counties.[48]

The conclusion to be drawn from ulnage accounts is that Colchester entrepreneurs had managed well between the 1390s and the 1460s. Trade in Lavenham and Hadleigh had probably grown more rapidly, but taking the region as a whole there is nothing in the supposition that small rural centres were in a more favourable position. The converse was the case; smaller centres had lost ground to a few larger ones. If, in spite of this relative success, Colchester's cloth output was no greater than in the second decade of the fifteenth centry, it is unlikely that smaller and less favourably endowed boroughs were enjoying industrial growth.

The court rolls of Sudbury give no direct indication of the performance of the cloth industry since the collection of custom on looms there was no longer recorded after 1405,[49] and no item of leet jurisdiction bore

---

[47] These markets do not occur in the fifteenth-century accounts.
[48] P.R.O., E.101/343/4, mm. 1–4.   [49] See Table 5.3.

specifically upon practices in the cloth trade. But other indicators suggest economic contraction in the early decades of the fifteenth century. Administrative changes perhaps account for an extraordinary drop in the number of brewers after 1442, but a general decrease in the food trades between the 1390s and the 1430s is implied by the downward movement in the number of brewers, butchers, bakers and regrators simultaneously. Evidence of litigation for debt suggests a severe reduction of credit operations between the 1390s and the 1420s. No count of the total number of pleas is practicable, but it is a straightforward enough matter to count those which terminated before they had run their course, either because the plaintiff had failed to appear in court to prosecute his case or because the defendant had settled out of court.[50] On the evidence of these indicators the economy of Sudbury was contracting in the early fifteenth century and showed no subsequent recovery. The number of cloths sold there in 1467/8 was only 318, less than a quarter the number sold in Colchester.[51]

Clare, too, experienced a contraction of brewing and baking during the first third of the century and a rapid reduction of litigation for debt in the 1420s and 1430s,[52] signifying a reduction in credit. Some confirming comment concerning economic depression in Clare in 1425 comes from an enquiry held at the lord of the manor's behest. The bailiffs had sought a reduction in the amount of rent they were supposed to collect, and the lord wanted their case to be examined. The jury reported that 11 market stalls could not be let.[53] A further observation on the state of trade concerns Wentford fair, which had formerly been held at the feast of the Nativity of the Virgin in September. This fair had not been held for three years – not, that is, since 1421 – because nobody went to trade there.[54] Many medieval fairs were only precariously profitable, but the abandonment of this one, taken in conjunction with all the other evidence of the court rolls, is good evidence for a contraction of trade. With the exception of the number of bakers in Clare, none of the main economic indicators recovered the level of the early fifteenth century, and it is unlikely that the cloth trade in Clare can have been greater in the 1460s than in the 1390s. Only 69 cloths were sealed there in 1467/8.[55]

It is not possible to investigate how the developments of other cloth markets in eastern England compared with that of Colchester between the 1470s and the 1520s. Most accounts of the region represent this period as the zenith of industrial prosperity, though the terms in which such a judgement may be expressed are invariably and necessarily vague. For

---

[50] P.R.O., S.C.2/204/13–20.
[51] P.R.O., E.101/343/4, m. 2r.
[52] P.R.O., S.C.2/203/65–72.
[53] P.R.O., S.C.2/203/67, m. 3d.
[54] For this fair, see Thornton, *A History of Clare*, pp. 177–8.
[55] P.R.O., E.101/343/4, m. 2r.

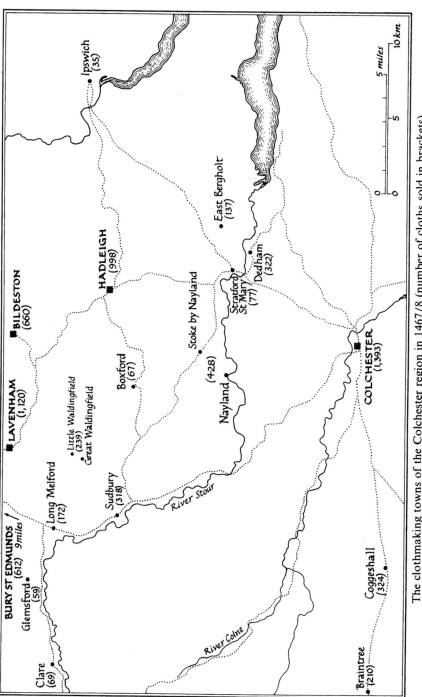

The clothmaking towns of the Colchester region in 1467/8 (number of cloths sold in brackets)

Source: *P.R.O., E.101/343/4.*

George Unwin the Suffolk industry 'attained its full development' by the middle of the sixteenth century and declined thereafter.[56] Another view is that 'the end of the fifteenth century and the beginning of the sixteenth saw the Suffolk trade at its height', and that by the mid sixteenth century the trade was declining.[57] The best account of Lavenham's cloth industry speaks of Lavenham's heyday in the 1520s, and surmises that the town reached the peak of its prosperity in that decade.[58] In Essex, too, this was a golden age in Eileen Power's eyes.[59] By all interpretations the period between 1467/8 and 1518 (when Thomas Paycocke of Coggeshall died) or 1523 (when Thomas Spring III of Lavenham died) was one of industrial growth in the cloth towns and villages of the region.

Some scepticism is in order, in the absence of any figures relating to output or sales. It would be surprising, in the light of earlier developments, if all the clothmaking villages of the region were enjoying industrial growth. The argument to this effect is largely an unwarranted inference from evidence of an increasingly capitalist organisation. However, the fabled wealth of the Spring family,[60] the quantity of good housing of around this period still remaining and the building of the still surviving Corpus Christi guildhall supposedly during the 1520s[61] all encourage the supposition that industry and trade in Lavenham and its environs had continued to grow under the early Tudors. Perhaps in this period Colchester's cloth trade lost some of the status it had managed to retain until the 1470s.

[56] Unwin, *Studies in Economic History*, p. 268.
[57] McClenaghan, *The Springs*, p. 26.
[58] Dymond and Betterton, *Lavenham*, pp. 24–7.
[59] E. Power, *The Paycockes of Coggeshall* (London, 1920), pp. 8–9.
[60] John Skelton, *The Complete English Poems*, ed. J. Scattergood (Harmondsworth, 1983), no. 20, lines 933–52, pp. 302–3.
[61] Dymond and Betterton, *Lavenham*, p. 21.

13

Population

I

The history of English towns in the fourteenth century is one of strongly contrasting experiences. While many decayed under the impact of famines and epidemics, others, like Colchester, grew. In the fifteenth century, however, urban fortunes were more uniformly waning, and the early sixteenth century was the last phase in a long period of general urban contraction.[1] Colchester did not have any unique advantages in this context. The townsmen enjoyed easy access to the North Sea and Baltic trades, but in the middle and late fifteenth century urban decay was particularly marked in towns on or near the east coast.[2] Colchester was a centre of the new English cloth industry, but so were York, Norwich and Coventry, all of which had greatly shrunk from their former size by the 1520s. Coventry's population fell by about 40 per cent between 1440 and 1523.[3] Evidence already discussed suggests that water-borne trade through Hythe diminished after the middle of the century and that employment in clothmaking was probably below the peak level of *c.* 1412–14 for the rest of the fifteenth century except in some years between 1436 and 1449. The chances that Colchester experienced some contraction are therefore high.

The changing number of brewers, as reported by lawhundred juries, constitutes the most continuous evidence relating to consumption in the town (Figure 13.1). The number was greatest early in the fifteenth century, and then declined slowly. By 1522 the number of brewers amerced at the lawhundreds was much the same as it had been in the early fourteenth century. The rate of decline implied by these figures is nothing dramatic.

---

[1] Phythian-Adams, 'Urban Decay', pp. 164–9.
[2] *Ibid.*, pp. 167–8; Carus-Wilson, 'The Medieval Trade of the Ports of the Wash', p. 200; A. F. Butcher, 'Rent, Population and Economic Change in Late-Medieval Newcastle', *Northern History*, xiv (1978), pp. 73–5.
[3] Phythian-Adams, 'Urban Decay', p. 169; *idem, Desolation of a City*, pp. 35–9, 196–7.

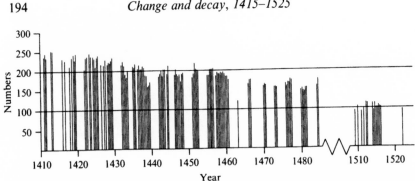

Figure 13.1 Numbers amerced in Colchester for brewing against the assize,
1410–1524

Table 13.1 *The greatest and smallest numbers of vintners presented for
breach of the assize of wine in a single lawhundred (by decades),
1390–1519*

Decade	Number of documented lawhundreds	Greatest number of vintners	Smallest number of vintners
1390–9	12	22	8
1400–9	16	20	1
1410–19	10	13	5
1420–9	17	19	4
1430–9	21	9	2
1440–9	19	17	3
1450–9	18	17	2
1460–9	11	12	2
1470–9	11	9	2
1480–9	9	11	3
1510–19	15	7	0

Source: Appendix, Table 2.

Between 1355–9 and 1405–9 the annual average increase in the number of
brewers was 1.6 per cent, but between 1410–14 and 1515–19 the average
decrease was 0.8 per cent each year, so that contraction proceeded at only
half the speed at which the number had increased during the years of
economic growth. However, the reliability of these figures as evidence of
consumption is open to doubt. Changes in income or relative changes in
price may have induced townsmen to substitute wine or beer for ale.
Alternatively, changes in the organisation of the brewing industry may
have increased the average output of brewers.[4]

[4] Hilton, *The English Peasantry*, p. 45; Dyer, *Lords and Peasants*, pp. 346–9.

The possibility that wine was substituted for ale can be ruled out as an objection. Reports on vintners by lawhundred juries supply minimum figures for the number of taverns operating in Colchester, and if the internal wine trade had increased greatly this number would have shown signs of increasing too. But in fact the number of vintners amerced was never greater than at the end of the fourteenth century and the beginning of the fifteenth (Table 13.1). Wine imports into Ipswich, as into England as a whole, declined during the fifteenth century,[5] and this is reflected in Colchester's internal wine trade. This evidence shows more erratic fluctuations and inconsistencies than that relating to brewing partly because trade was so dependent on circumstances affecting trade with France[6] and partly because the number of people involved was much fewer.

Imports of beer also decreased, but for a different reason. Particulars of customs from the 1390s show beer coming into Hythe from the continent to the extent of about 100 barrels in the year following 10 July 1397.[7] These accounts record no imports of hops. But in similar accounts from the late 1450s and early 1460s there are no recorded imports of beer at all, and instead hops were being brought in in large quantities.[8] Colchester men had not only acquired a taste for beer; they had started making it themselves, and had thereby eliminated the need for imports. In itself, however, this change does not affect the validity of the brewing statistics as an index of consumption since lawhundred juries began early in the fifteenth century to take beer into account. The earliest such report was at Michaelmas 1406, when five sellers of beer were amerced.[9] Some early beer sellers were of Dutch origin,[10] though most of them were English. The lawhundred juries gave ample testimony that these beer sellers themselves brewed the beer they sold; at the Hilary lawhundred of 1412, for example, 'the jury presents that Florencius Beermakere brewed and sold beer against the assize and proclamation' (i.e. he charged too high a price for it), and four others did the same.[11] This means that evidence relating to the number of beer brewers is as good as that for brewers of ale. This seems to solve the problem. The number of people amerced 'for beer' was as large in the first two decades of the century as it ever became.

[5] James, *Studies in the Medieval Wine Trade*, pp. 49–50, 57–9, 94, 108–16.
[6] *Ibid.*, pp. 39–50.
[7] P.R.O., E.122/193/33, fos. 13v, 15v, 16v *bis*, 25v. Imports of beer into Colchester amounted to 7 lasts and 16 barrels, a last being 12 barrels: *O.E.D.* under last, sb(2).
[8] P.R.O., E.122/52/42, mm. 1d, 2r, 3r; E.122/52/43, m. 1r. This development was widespread in the North Sea trading area: van der Wee, *The Growth of the Antwerp Market*, ii, p. 31; L. Delisle, *Études sur la condition de la classe agricole et l'état de l'agriculture en Normandie au Moyen Âge* (Évreux, 1851), pp. 483–4.
[9] CR 36/3r,d.
[10] Beer sellers included John Smyth 'Ducheman' in 1407 and 1411/12 (CR 36/11d; CR 38/2r, 13d), Clays Ducheman in 1411/12 (CR 38/2r, 13d, 24d), Agnes Smyth 'Ducheman' and William Alwyne 'Ducheman' in 1412 (CR 38/24d).   [11] CR 38/13d.

As many as six at a time were amerced at Hocktide 1412.[12] In later years the number was smaller, though there were often six in the 1470s.[13]

The argument that average units of ale production grew larger as a result of occupational specialisation during the fifteenth century is also debatable. There were never more than three or four men at a time in Colchester who called themselves brewers, and they first occur not when the number of brewers began to contract but in the years when it was expanding. John Aylmar, brewer, was already known as such in 1385.[14] William Wykham, brewer, became a burgess in 1388 and William Taseler, brewer, did so in 1389,[15] and these three brewers operated simultaneously in the late fourteenth century when the number of brewers was growing.[16] John Aylmar, who acknowledged Brewer as an alternative surname,[17] is a prominent figure in the borough records. Between 1392 and 1413 he occurs as the keeper of an inn in Colchester, no doubt the tenement in the market place in which he lived and for which he paid an annual rent of £4 to the community about 1410.[18] If the number of brewers continued to grow for 20 years from 1385, despite the activities of Aylmar and other specialised brewers, it is open to doubt whether the change in trend after 1414 can be explained by changes in industrial organisation.

The most effective argument against the use of the brewing figures concerns the organisation of beer making. The major brewers of the fifteenth century were specifically beer men. The first major beer brewer was Thomas Wode. He lived at Hythe, where he held a tenement from the community,[19] and he was considered a man of some substance, for he was granted the lease of tolls at Hythe for a number of years between 1435/6 and 1448/9.[20] He meanwhile gained control of beer brewing in the town; during the 1440s his wife was the only beer seller to be amerced.[21] The location of his premises perhaps suited him because many of his customers were Dutchmen and Germans from the ships, but it also enabled him to handle easily large quantities of imported barley. He was accused in 1440 of raising barley prices in Colchester by means of a consignment of 500 quarters shipped from Norfolk.[22] Later prominent beer brewers were immigrants from the Low Countries. One was Peter Herryson from Brabant, who became a burgess in 1454,[23] and who was alternatively called

---

[12] CR 38/24d.

[13] CR 74/2r, 14d, 23d; CR 75/2d, 10d, 19d; CR 76/2d, 11d.

[14] CR 24/36d, 37r.   [15] OB, fos. 60v, 61v.

[16] CR 30/10r,d, 16d; CR 31/2r.   [17] CR 34/2d, 11d, 22d; OB, fo. 77r.

[18] CR 27/28d...CR 39/1d; OB, fo. 170r.

[19] CR 49/1d; CR 50/1d; CR 51/1d.

[20] CR 53/1d; CR 54/1d; CR 55/1d; CR 62/1d; CR 63/1d.

[21] CR 59/3r, 11r, 17d; CR 60/14d, 22d; CR 61/12r, 19r; CR 62/3r, 11d, 18d; CR 63/3r, 8d, 15d.

[22] CR 57/15r.   [23] OB, fo. 96r.

Peter Bierman or Peter Bierbrewer.[24] He occurs in most of the lawhundred reports from Michaelmas 1455 to Hocktide 1471.[25] In 1460 the lawhundred amerced him because 'he throws the draff from his brewing beside his house in Hythe and annoys the king's subjects with the smell thereof'.[26] Another Brabanter, Edmund Hermanson, who became a burgess in 1465,[27] was a beer brewer in every surviving lawhundred report between Michaelmas 1466 and Hocktide 1485.[28] He became wealthy enough to endow one of Colchester's few chantries.[29] James Godfrey, who came from Gelderland, followed the same tradition. He became a burgess in 1515[30] and set up in Hythe[31] as a beer brewer.[32] In 1524 he was amongst the wealthiest 12 men in Colchester.[33] Beer brewing evidently depended on larger individual capitals than ale brewing, so that the number of brewers is no guide to the volume of beer production relative to that of ale.

It is reasonable to ascribe some of the decline in the number of ale brewers to competition from beer. Thomas Wode's success as a beer brewer in the 1430s and 1440s perhaps corresponded to the first inroads of beer drinking at the expense of ale. And the larger scale of operations in beer brewing would explain why the total number of brewers fell during these decades despite the temporary recovery of Colchester's trade and industry after 1437. However, not all the decrease in the number of brewers during the fifteenth century can be explained in this way. The evidence nowhere implies that there were more larger breweries in the 1520s than in the 1460s, or that the average size had increased. There is still room, therefore, for declining consumption as part of the explanation for the movement of the figures, particularly in the later part of the period when large breweries and a taste for beer were already well established features of the urban scene.

To some extent the evidence of brewing statistics may be supported with other information reported by lawhundred juries. It seems that the number of mills operating in the liberty declined during the fifteenth century. The horse mills which appeared in the 1390s are not mentioned subsequently, but there were still eight mills in operation as there had been during the 1370s and 1380s. The next change was that a windmill which had formerly belonged to Simon Fordham, probably the one built for William Reyne

[24] CR 71/1d, 2r.
[25] CR 66/2d…CR 74/23d. His widow occurs at Michaelmas 1473; CR 75/2d.
[26] CR 71/1d, 10d.
[27] OB, fo. 100v.
[28] CR 73/2r…CR 81/21d. Hermanson continued brewing through most of Henry VII's reign, but he was dead by 1504: OB, fol. 114v.
[29] Morant, *Colchester*, ii, p. 51.
[30] CR 86/21r.
[31] RPB, fo. 168v.
[32] CR 94/4d; CR 95/14r.   [33] P.R.O., E.179/108/162, m. 2.

about 1370, disappears from the records from 1414.[34] This was perhaps simply because the mill had become decrepit, though it may also be a consequence of some contraction in the demand for flour. Only seven mills were now working, and the number was normally at this level during the following 14 years. A new mill was constructed by the bailiffs and community about the year 1428. It was situated at Hythe, and was called Hythe Mill.[35] But at about this time Bourne Mill went out of action as a grain mill,[36] so that the total number of mills was unchanged, and seven mills were working still in the later 1430s[37] and through the earlier 1440s.[38] Then Hythe Mill disappears from the jury reports after Michaelmas 1448[39] so that only six mills are on record during the 1450s and 1460s.[40] During the 1470s town clerks abandoned the practice of recording the name of the mill which each miller occupied, and so made it impossible to keep track of the number of active grain mills from their records. There is confirming evidence from the Red Paper Book, however, that in 1489 the grain mill at Hythe, like the fulling mill there, was derelict, and that it had been so for some years past.[41] This series accordingly supports the case for supposing that there was some contraction of consumption in Colchester during the fifteenth century, though it does not help much with the chronology of decline.

Demand for meat in the fifteenth century benefited perhaps more than that for any other foodstuff from the improvement in real wages which had occurred since the mid fourteenth century.[42] The number of Colchester butchers occurring in different lists vary widely, however, so that any attempt to count them requires a certain amount of interpretation. On two

---

[34] Simon Fordham's mill first appears at Michaelmas 1395 (CR 29/1d) after the last appearance of William Reyne's mill (CR 28/28r). When last heard of this was 'Marjory Fordham's windmill' (CR 39/32r).

[35] A fulling mill at Hythe belonged to the community in 1398 and 1399: CR 30/2r; CR 31/2d. Later the community owned a grain mill there as well: RPB, fo. 188r. The grain mill dates from about 1428–9, when the abbot of Colchester complained about its construction: RPB, fo. 73r. Hythe Mill occurs as a grain mill in the court rolls in 1436: CR 53/12r, 20d.

[36] The mill occurs early in 1430 (CR 50/14d) and then disappears for 12 years.

[37] Lexden Mill, East Mill, Canwick Mill, Middle Mill, Hythe Mill, Hull Mill and a windmill: CR 56/28d; CR 57/2d, 15r, 22d. Hull Mill, which first occurs in 1437 (CR 54/11r), could be the Mill in the Wood, which disappears after 1435 (CR 52/20d).

[38] Lexden Mill, East Mill, Canwick Mill, Middle Mill, Hythe Mill, Hull Mill and Bourne Mill. The windmill disappears after 1440 (CR 57/22d) but Bourne Mill returns as a grain mill at Michaelmas 1442 (CR 58/2d).

[39] After CR 63/2d.

[40] Lexden Mill, East Mill, Canwick Mill, Middle Mill, Hull Mill and Bourne Mill: CR 65/2d, 11d, 18d.

[41] RPB, fo. 188r,v.

[42] C. Dyer, 'English Diet in the Later Middle Ages', in T. H. Aston, P. R. Coss, C. Dyer and J. Thirsk, eds., *Social Relations and Ideas: Essays in Honour of R. H. Hilton*, Past and Present Publications (Cambridge, 1983), pp. 213–14.

occasions the court rolls give a list of all the butchers. In 1400 'all the butchers of the town of Colchester', numbering 21, divided carcasses between themselves contrary to the regulations of the trade. And in 1452 'all the butchers within the town of Colchester', numbering 12, conspired to raise the price of tallow.[43] Unfortunately, despite appearances, these figures are not directly comparable. The number of butchers 'within the town of Colchester' probably signifies the number of butchers trading in the shambles on weekdays, and excludes those who traded from shops outside the walls. The total number of butchers remained higher than 12, since 20 butchers, all burgesses, were amerced in 1444 for keeping their meat too long.[44]

The only figures relating to butchers for which any sort of long view is possible are for butchers using the weekly markets. Here there is good evidence of contracting trade in the second quarter of the fifteenth century. There were 16 butchers 'living within the town' amerced in 1406 for bringing meat to market without hides 'through all weeks of the year, i.e on meat days'.[45] There were 15 butchers from the town amerced in 1420 because they left offal below the meat stalls in the highway, and so created a stench.[46] But by 1452 'all the butchers within the town' numbered only 12, as already shown above. The interpretation of this as the number using the weekly market is supported by some later evidence. Between 1466 and 1474 there were repeated amercements of butchers for failing to maintain a cart, whose purpose was to clear the market of refuse and carry it outside the walls. Presumably all butchers using the market were liable to contribute and all would be amerced if the cart was not provided. The masters of the butchers' craft head the earliest list. The number of butchers amerced on this account is shown in Table 13.2, and it implies that the number of butchers using the market had declined since the early fifteenth century. There was no subsequent revival. From Michaelmas 1517 it became usual to amerce the butchers under a cover-all charge of irregular conduct once a year, but no more than 10 were ever reported at once (Table 13.3).

The only statistical series to show any increase during the late fifteenth and early sixteenth centuries is that of the number of bakers amerced for breaking their assize.[47] After having shown little trend all through the fourteenth and fifteenth centuries the number increased sharply during the second and third decades of the sixteenth. This increase is so closely

---

[43] CR 31/19r; CR 64/20r.   [44] CR 59/10d.

[45] CR 35/14r. Eight other butchers amerced were from outside Colchester: two from Dedham, one each from Hythe, Lawford, Manningtree, Stratford St Mary, East Bergholt and Thorp le Soken.

[46] CR 42/23r. Four other butchers amerced were from outside Colchester: from Nayland, Stratford St Mary, East Bergholt and Thorp le Soken.   [47] Appendix, Table 3.

Table 13.2 *Butchers amerced for not maintaining their common cart,*
1466–74

	No.
Michaelmas, 1466	13
Hilary, 1467	12
Michaelmas, 1470	12
Hilary, 1471	12
Michaelmas, 1473	10
Hilary, 1474	10[a]
Hocktide, 1474	9[b]

[a] The names of two outside butchers are added to these ten.
[b] One outside butcher was also amerced.
Source: CR 73/2r, 18d; CR 74/1d, 14r; CR 75/1d, 10r, 19r

Table 13.3 *Butchers amerced for selling meat in secret places, not*
carrying skins to market and other offences, 1517–30

	No.
Michaelmas, 1517	10
Michaelmas, 1519	10
Michaelmas, 1521	9
Michaelmas, 1527	7
Michaelmas, 1528	8
Michaelmas, 1530	8

Source: CR 88/22d; CR 90/19r; CR 91/27r; CR 97/20r; CR 98/20d; CR 99/24d

associated with changes in administration and recording that it may be regarded as the result of a change in public policy rather than as evidence for an increase in baking. The bakers' inquests of 1515/16 are enrolled together at the end of the court roll instead of being interspersed as usual amongst other business,[48] and those of 1516/17 are not enrolled at all in the surviving court record. Then in 1517/18 and 1518/19 the bakers' amercements are recorded separately for each ward adjacent to the business of the lawhundreds.[49] The increase in the number of bakers reported was probably the consequence of a more relentless enforcement of the assize, either as an easy means to allay popular unrest about standards of living or to raise income for the community.

The largest number of recorded grain mills in operation was in 1392;[50]

[48] CR 87/23d.
[49] CR 89/2r–4d; CR 90/2r–4d.   [50] CR 27/28d.

the largest number of vintners amerced for breaking their assize was also in 1392;[51] the largest number of butchers amerced at once was in 1400;[52] the largest number of brewers amerced was in 1407.[53] The bunching of these years within the period 1390–1414 is surely not an accident. It was probably at this time that Colchester approached and attained its largest medieval population. In the 1440s the number of grain mills was only one fewer than it had been before 1414, and the number of butchers was still close to what it had been in 1400. The decrease in the number of brewers of ale was at least in part the result of more beer drinking. So it is likely that up to about 1450 any contraction in Colchester's population was slight. This tallies with the evidence of trade and industry to the effect that 1437–50 was a busy period even in comparison with the years before 1414.

Two estimates of Colchester's population are available from the early sixteenth century. One for 1524 may be hazarded from the evidence that 754 taxpayers in the liberty of the borough contributed to the subsidy of that year.[54] It is generally accepted that the subsidy returns give an incomplete count of actual households, the number omitted ranging from at least one third up to as high as two-thirds in some places. In Colchester the proportion omitted was relatively low, since in comparison with other principal towns – Norwich, Bristol, Coventry, Salisbury and Exeter – the number of taxpayers was large relative to the total tax payment. It is unlikely that the number of households excluded was as high as in Coventry, where between 50 and 55 per cent paid nothing.[55] If between one third and one half of all households were omitted in Colchester, and if there were on average four persons to each household, then the number of inhabitants in 1524 was of the order of $5,278 \pm 754$.[56] A second estimate may be made for 1534. In that year 1,135 men were listed in the Red Paper Book as having sworn, or not sworn, the succession oath following Henry VIII's marriage to Anne Boleyn.[57] Like the poll tax list of 1377 this count should include laymen over the age of 14,[58] but it also includes 52 clergy – 20 secular, 32 religious – who would have been omitted from the poll tax list. The adult male lay population had, by this reckoning, declined by one

---

[51] CR 28/1r.
[52] CR 31/19r *bis*.
[53] CR 36/21d, 22r.
[54] P.R.O., E.179/108/162.
[55] Phythian-Adams, *Desolation of a City*, p. 12; *idem*, 'Urban Decay', p. 170; Bridbury, *Economic Growth*, pp. 112–13.
[56] This estimate is intermediate between that of Doolittle (3,945) and that of Phythian-Adams (over 6,000). The former seems to me to allow too little for omitted households and the latter too much: I. G. Doolittle, 'Population Growth and Movement in Colchester and the Tendring Hundred, 1500–1800', *Essex Journal*, vii (1972), p. 33; Phythian-Adams, *Desolation of a City*, p. 12.
[57] RPB, fos. 161v–172r.
[58] McKisack, *The Fourteenth Century*, p. 396; G. R. Elton, *Policy and Police: The Enforcement of the Reformation in the Age of Thomas Cromwell* (Cambridge, 1972), pp. 225–6.

quarter since 1377. In view of the sensitive nature of the proceedings it is possible that under-registration was even greater in the list of oath takers in 1534 than it had been in the poll tax list. The small size of the recorded adult male population nevertheless suggests that it would be wrong to scale up early sixteenth-century estimates for Colchester to the extent necessary in some towns. Both the estimate for 1524 and the list of adult men from 1534 are compatible with a sizeable reduction of population since the early fifteenth century, perhaps by as much as one third.

II

Declining population in Colchester is associated with recurrent crises of mortality. There were epidemics in 1412/13[59] and 1420/1,[60] and probably in 1426/7, 1433/4 and 1439.[61] After a period of respite there was an exceptionally severe crisis in the early 1460s. The disruption in the brewing industry at that time has no parallel. There was no report on brewers at Michaelmas 1463, and an inquest *ex officio* held on 8 November reported only 124, a number one third below the average for the later 1450s. No attempt was made to amerce brewers at the Hilary and Hocktide lawhundreds of 1464.[62] Though there was some recovery from the low level of 1463, the average number of recorded brewers fell by one eighth between the later 1450s and the later 1460s. There was further severe loss of population during Henry VII's reign, to judge from the decline in brewing. At Bury St Edmunds there was a plague epidemic in the years 1499–1500 and another in 1509.[63] But crises of mortality are not enough to explain Colchester's contraction. The epidemics of 1348 and 1361 were more severe than any in the fifteenth century, and yet they occurred at the start of half a century of population growth in the town. Some circumstances affecting the economy's capacity to recover from epidemics must have changed during the fourteenth and fifteenth centuries. From the Black Death until about 1415 epidemics were so rapidly followed by recovery that population grew; between 1415 and about 1450 recovery was barely sufficient to

---

[59] The number of wills proved in the borough court (16) was the highest in any year since 1360/1: OB, fo. 74v. *Cf.* Shrewsbury, *A History of Bubonic Plague*, p. 143; Hatcher, *Plague, Population and the English Economy*, pp. 17, 57.

[60] 13 wills were enrolled: OB, fos. 78v, 79r.

[61] There are sharp dips in the number of brewers amerced in these years: Appendix, Table 1. The year 1439 was one of dearth. *Cf.* R. S. Gottfried, *Epidemic Disease in Fifteenth-Century England: The Medical Response and the Demographic Consequences* (Leicester, 1978), pp. 36–9, 47–8.

[62] CR 72/6d. At the Hilary lawhundred of 1464 no brewers were amerced, allegedly because all had brewed well: CR 72/11d. There was a widespread plague epidemic in the years 1463–5; Gottfried, *Epidemic Disease*, pp. 42, 49, 98–100.

[63] Gottfried, *Bury St. Edmunds*, p. 64.

maintain steady numbers; after 1450 recovery from epidemics was inadequate to prevent population from declining. It is unlikely that changes in the rate of natural population growth – as measured by replacement rates – can have been great enough to bring about these contrasts, and consideration of the way in which population grew in the earlier period readily suggests the alternative answer. A substantially lower responsiveness of immigration to demographic crises in the borough would be enough to slow down population growth, and even to bring about a decline in total numbers if the underlying pattern of natural replacement was unfavourable.

The distances over which Colchester drew new burgesses during the fifteenth century were still considerable. Of the 58 new burgesses elected between 1467/8 and 1476/7, both years inclusive,[64] only 18 originated from villages within 10 miles of Colchester. Of the others, 18 were from other parts of Essex and Suffolk, and 22 had been born even farther away than this. Not all these men will have moved directly to Colchester from their birthplaces, and for some of them life in the town was one episode of a migratory career. In fact the scattered origins of new burgesses testify not so much to Colchester's far-reaching attractions as to the normally high level of mobility among men of the trading classes, particularly in their early years.[65] In the same spirit Colchester's own youngsters often migrated to other towns, and especially to London, which was a magnet for them all through the fifteenth century.[66] Notwithstanding Colchester's capacity to attract migrants, the number of men applying to be burgesses declined. Figure 13.2 shows the number of new burgesses elected each year between 1399/1400 and 1524/5. This number, though not the same as the number of immigrants into the town, is the only available indicator of the town's capacity to attract newcomers, and its evidence is relevant to the total level of immigration if only because the total number of burgesses affected the total demand for servants and other employees. A few observations from the figures are relevant to Colchester's falling population. First, it is a clear implication of this evidence that the years when Colchester's power to attract new burgesses was greatest also show the largest increase in brewing activity. The largest number of new burgesses

[64] OB, fos. 101v–105r.
[65] Thrupp, *The Merchant Class*, pp. 206–19; A. F. Butcher, 'The Origins of Romney Freemen, 1433–1523', *Ec.H.R.*, 2nd ser., xxvii (1974), pp. 23, 27.
[66] Young men from Colchester were apprenticed in London: *Calendar of Plea and Memoranda Rolls, 1413–37*, ed. Thomas, pp. 76, 86; *Calendar of Plea and Memoranda Rolls, 1437–57*, ed. Jones, p. 90. Another resident from Colchester occurs in *The Medieval Records of a London City Church (St. Mary at Hill), A.D. 1420–1559*, ed. H. Littlehales, Early English Text Society, cxxviii (London, 1905), p. 183. For migrants to Sandwich, see Butcher, 'The Origins of Romney Freemen', p. 25.

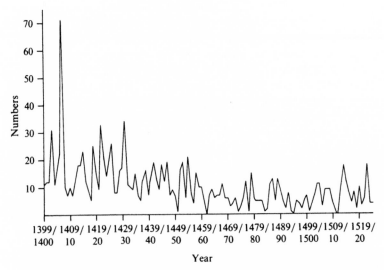

Figure 13.2 Numbers of new burgesses enrolled, 1399/1400–1524/5

ever created in a single year was 71 in the year 1406/7. This probably represents the peak of 10 years or so of exceptionally heavy immigration into the town, and it is surely no coincidence that a larger number of brewers was amerced at the Hocktide lawhundred of that year than in any other recorded court. A second observation is that numbers of new burgesses show a diminishing response to periods of high mortality. The number of new burgesses elected did not respond to epidemics as it had done to those of 1348 and 1361. This is particularly striking in the latter half of the fifteenth century. In spite of the epidemic of 1463–4, the later 1460s and earlier 1470s register less than half the number of new burgesses which had been normal in the first half of the century. Within the period charted in Figure 13.2 the number of new burgesses must have contracted more than the town's total population, and this suggests a reduced rate of immigration into the town. A final point, therefore, is that, so far from compensating for decreases in population caused by epidemic diseases, changes in the normal level of migration into Colchester may have reinforced the downward trend of the urban population.

The declining number of new burgesses may be satisfactorily explained by the change in Colchester's economic expectations. There was no attempt to deter new burgesses by any change of rules; throughout the fifteenth century a newcomer required four pledges and the entry fine he paid was usually £1 or £1 3s 4d.[67] But once the town had stopped growing,

---

[67] CR 33/4r, 14d, 21d; CR 34/3r, 4d, 9d, 15d; CR 81/3r; CR 82/4r, 8d, 9d, 11r.

and particularly once its trade was contracting, it lost its capacity to lure men away from their villages. There is no sign from the figures that the apprenticeship rules introduced in 1418 deterred applicants, but the growing concentration of enterprise may have done so later in the century since it reduced the chances of a newcomer with only a small capital being able to maintain his independence.[68] For men with no capital the considerations were different, but nonetheless tied to economic expectations in the borough. A wage earner's prospects depended upon wage rates and constancy of employment, and it was the latter which was likely to vary most in different phases of Colchester's history. If employment became more erratic, a decision to migrate to town as a way of making one's way in the world would become increasingly unlikely. Such considerations, which are compatible with what is known about trade and industry in Colchester, go far towards explaining a diminishing movement from country to town during the course of the fifteenth century.

[68] Men who became burgesses by virtue of birth within the liberty of Colchester did not pay an entry fine and were not entered in the court rolls either before 1420 or after: Morant, *Colchester*, i, p. 98. The Colchester figures are not, therefore, as imperfect as Dr Bridbury supposes: Bridbury, *Economic Growth*, p. 61. The examples quoted by Morant were recorded in the rolls only because it was sometimes necessary to scrutinise claims to burgess status by birth.

14

Credit and wealth

I

During the fifteenth century the style of legal recording in Colchester changed to the historian's disadvantage. From the 1430s it became unusual for clerks to give details of pleading in court, and the court rolls consequently become poorer as a source of economic information. It is rarely possible to distinguish between debts for wages, for rent, for purchases or for loans, and there is no longer the wealth of evidence relating to prices and commodities which is available for the years when Colchester developed most rapidly. Even the number of pleas of debt becomes more difficult to establish between 1442 and 1482 as a result of labour-saving reforms in the listing of new pleas.[1] The latter obstacle, however, may be overcome, and Table 14.1 shows changes in the number of pleas of debt between 1381/2 and 1524/5. The amount of litigation for debt, having reached a peak in the 1380s and 1390s, contracted sharply in the fifteenth century, particularly during the 1480s, so that the number of pleas of debt between 1491 and 1525 was only 30 per cent of what it had been at its highest point.

These figures greatly distort any changes in the level of Colchester's trade during the period they cover. This is not, however, because of any decrease in the efficiency of the courts. The surprising decline in litigation for debt between the late fourteenth century and the early fifteenth may in fact have been due to improvements in the courts' speed of operations which were introduced at a time of extraordinarily voluminous litigation in 1388. The right of a defendant to delay justice by essoining himself was greatly curtailed, and this perhaps encouraged debtors to settle more quickly.[2] The courts retained their proper authority throughout the fifteenth century. The routine business which they handled – involving very few actions

---

[1] Britnell, 'Colchester Courts and Court Records'.   [2] RPB, fo. 12v.

Table 14.1 *Average annual number of pleas of debt in Colchester borough courts*

Years[a]	No.
1381/2–1398/9 (5)	488
1399/1400–1411/12 (5)	379
1419/20–1435/6 (10)	305
1437/8–1448/9 (7)	311
1451/2–1466/7 (9)	262
1476/7–1481/2 (3)	255
1490/1–1524/5 (11)	144

[a] Number of years averaged in brackets.
Source: Appendix, Table 7.

relating to possession of property – was not the sort which affected the struggles for power in landed society and attracted the intervention of magnates. The officers of the court lost none of their power to enforce law and order and the due performance of private contracts within the bounds of the liberty. One indication of the esteem in which the courts were held is the percentage of pleas which, upon being initiated, were immediately settled out of court. This is roughly indicated between 1442 and 1482 by the number of pleas which, having been registered with the town clerk, were immediately resolved without taking up the courts' time; defendants were often jolted into making a private settlement. In the case of pleas of debt this proportion rose steeply in the 1470s and early 1480s. In the 1440s, 1450s and 1460s it was about one quarter – 29.2 per cent in the 1440s (average of six years), 25.6 per cent in the 1450s (average of six years), 25.4 per cent in the 1460s (average of three years). The average proportion for the three years 1476/7, 1477/8 and 1481/2 was 43.0 per cent.[3] This implies that the power of the courts to enforce contracts was more likely to have been increasing than waning in the later fifteenth century.

Perhaps the increasing concentration of enterprise in the hands of clothiers had some effect in reducing the number of transactions between townsmen, and so diminishing the likelihood of disputes for debt. But this could not explain much of the movement in Table 14.1. The cloth industry

[3] CR 59–80. Sometime between Michaelmas 1439 and Michaelmas 1442 the town clerk stopped listing all new pleas at the session to which they were first referred. When a plea was abandoned at this first session because it had been settled out of court, or because the plaintiff had made some procedural error, it was omitted from the initial list, and its termination was noted amongst the business of the court.

Table 14.2 *Size of claims of debt in Colchester courts in selected years,*
1398/9–1524/5

	1398/9 %	1419/20 %	1443/4 %	1463/4 %	1481/2 %	1524/5 %
£2 or above	19.3	22.4	30.7	34.2	26.6	12.8
£1 to £1/19/11¾	14.0	13.5	14.1	16.3	16.4	12.2
below £1	57.7	48.0	54.2	47.3	55.5	69.9
uncertain	9.0	16.1	1.0	2.2	1.6	5.1
	100.0	100.0	100.0	100.0	(100.0)	100.0

Source: CR 30, 42, 59, 72, 79, 95.

did not account for a large enough number of pleas to dominate the business of the courts, and the growing capitalist organisation of industry would not lower the number of transactions in the food trades or the number of rent and wage contracts. Furthermore, there was no significant change in the usual size of claims. Table 14.2 shows the evidence from a number of years spanning the fifteenth century whose documentation is adequate in this respect. These figures show that the character of the courts as an agency for recovering small sums remained unaltered.

There may have been further institutional reasons for declining litigation for debt which have nothing to do with changes in the level of credit. But the most likely explanation, particular after 1415, is that with the end of the phase of confident economic expansion in the later fourteenth century there was a reduction in indebtedness. A predominantly institutional explanation is unacceptable because the phenomenon was not confined to Colchester. It is to be found not only in the seigneurial boroughs of Clare[4] and Sudbury[5] in Suffolk but, even more starkly, in the Essex market town of Writtle.[6] It is impossible to assess just how much of the contraction was owing to a smaller number of transactions and how much to decreasing willingness to allow credit, but the two causes were not wholly independent. Tradesmen were less likely to accept risks in periods of uncertain trade, and in such circumstances they were likely to demand cash more frequently. Although its exact implications are uncertain, the evidence concerning litigation for debt adds to the probability that Colchester's trade contracted during the fifteenth century, and it increases the likelihood that the town was severely depressed in the early Tudor period.

[4] P.R.O., S.C.2/203/65–72.
[5] P.R.O., S.C.2/204/13–20.   [6] Clark, 'Debt Litigation', p. 251.

II

During the period of lower expectations after the cloth industry had passed its peak the forms of investment preferred by Colchester's wealthiest inhabitants underwent a gradual change. During the fifteenth century investment in clothmaking became less widely diffused. The tighter organisation of the industry in the 1470s, and the later adoption of the term clothmaker by a small group of employers, show that cloth had become more of a sectional interest. The woollen industry was less open to casual enterprise than that of the 1390s had been, and the proportion of burgesses who dabbled in clothmaking in the 1520s was lower than it had been during the 1390s. By this time the industry was structured into specialised rôles; there was a greater separation between entrepreneurs and employees and the ties of worker dependence had become stronger. Thomas Christmas, in drawing up his will, spoke of his employees in an unmistakably possessive tone.[7]

Another development was an increase in the share of real estate in the assets of Colchester's leading merchants and tradesmen. Landed property, having become a more prominent feature of mercantile fortunes during the late fourteenth century, remained so, and there are examples at all stages of the fifteenth. For example, John Trewe the merchant, whose will was proved in 1448,[8] accumulated enough property for his son to call himself gentleman.[9] But instances from the late fifteenth and early sixteenth centuries are particularly numerous, perhaps because poorer expectations of the future in urban trades induced merchants to opt for more traditional types of asset. Thomas Jopson the merchant, who had come to Colchester from Yorkshire,[10] bought land in Langenhoe and established a landed family; his grandson was to prosper in the service of the Crown and to take the lands of Colchester Abbey after its dissolution.[11] Nicholas Clere the clothier[12] and his son John acquired lands in Essex and Suffolk,[13] and the latter was described in 1510 as 'clothmaker or yeoman'.[14] Edmund Hermanson of Brabant, the beer brewer,[15] acquired enough land to endow a chantry.[16] Other estates were accumulated in the

---

[7] P.C.C., Ayloffe, 28.

[8] OB, fo. 93v. For his merchant status, see OB, fo. 91v.

[9] CR 65/21r; CR 67/15r, 17r, 19d.

[10] OB, fo. 99v. For his merchant status, see OB, fo. 111v; CR 82/20r.

[11] *Essex Fines*, iv, pp. 76, 82; Morant, *Colchester*, ii, p. 29, note B; idem, *Essex*, ii, p. 186 and note P; S. T. Bindoff, *The House of Commons, 1509–1558*, The History of Parliament (3 vols., London, 1982), ii, pp. 444–6.

[12] P.R.O., E.101/343/9d. 10d, 11r, 13d.

[13] Bindoff, *The House of Commons*, i, p. 651.

[14] *L. and P.*, i(1), no. 1803(1), p. 817.   [15] See Chapter 13, p. 197.

[16] Morant, *Colchester*, ii, p. 51.

early sixteenth century by Thomas Cock the whittawer[17] and John Makin the grocer.[18] The most striking case of merchants turning to land was that of the Christmas family. Thomas Christmas II, a merchant and draper,[19] acquired the manor of Down Hall in Bradwell near the Sea, the manor of Barnhams in Beaumont and other lands in Bradwell, the Sokens, Clacton, Fingringhoe, Layer de la Haye, Mersea, South Hanningfield, Birch, Copford and within the liberty of Colchester.[20] His son, John, acquired Rook Hall manor in Little Totham during his father's lifetime,[21] and about the time of his father's death in 1520 began to assume the title of esquire.[22] In 1524 he was by far Colchester's wealthiest inhabitant.[23]

Landownership was becoming more prominent in the borough for another reason, and seemingly an antithetical one. While urban merchants put their savings into land for the security and status that this brought them there were minor gentry coming into Colchester in order to augment their incomes. There was little to be said for being a gentleman if one could not live as one,[24] and an urban environment offered more opportunities to do so. A minority of gentlemen turned to trade. John Bishop[25] and John Boteler[26] were of this sort, and occur in the ulnage accounts of the 1460s and 1470s as major sellers of cloth.[27] Christopher Hammond, a new burgess in 1510, was a gentleman[28] who subsequently described himself on occasion as vintner or merchant.[29] Other gentlemen found professional legal and administrative work. Walter Wingfield, esquire, who also became a burgess in 1510, was the Earl of Oxford's surveyor at Wivenhoe.[30] William Mauncell, gentleman, who entered the burgage in 1515/16 became one of the principal attorneys in Colchester court.[31] The town clerk's office was taken over by gentlemen probably during the reign of Henry VII. William Teye, gentleman, was town clerk in 1510/11 and 1512/13.[32] He made way for the greatest figure in Colchester's history since the days of King Coel when, on 2 October 1514, Thomas Audley, gentleman, was

[17] *Essex Fines*, iv, pp. 206, 219. For his occupation, see CR 90/9d.
[18] *Essex Fines*, iv, pp. 134, 206; Bindoff, *The House of Commons*, ii, p. 560.
[19] OB, fos. 115r, 118r; CR 91/21d.
[20] P.C.C., Ayloffe, 28.   [21] *Essex Fines*, iv, p. 129.
[22] OB, fos. 122v, 125v.   [23] P.R.O., E.179/108/162, m. 1.
[24] *Paston Letters and Papers of the Fifteenth Century*, ed. N. Davies (2 vols. out of 3, Oxford, 1971, 1976), no. 292, i, p. 486.
[25] He occurs as a landowner in the 1450s (CR 66/1d, 2r, 11d) and as a gentleman in 1484 (CR 80/20r).
[26] John Boteler was described as a gentleman in 1454: *Cal. Close R., 1447–54*, p. 489.
[27] P.R.O., E.101/342/21, back membrane; E.101/343/4, m. 3r; E.101/343/5d, 9d, 10d, 11r, 13d.
[28] OB, fo. 116r.   [29] CR 85/8d; CR 86/22d.
[30] OB, fo. 116r; E.R.O. T/B 122, court held Wednesday after Epiphany, 23 Henry VIII.
[31] OB, fo. 118v; CR 101/2d, 4r,d, 7r, 10d, etc.
[32] CR 83/1r; CR 85/1r.

elected a burgess of Colchester and appointed to be town clerk jointly with John Barnabe.[33] From Michaelmas 1515 to Michaelmas 1532 Audley was sole town clerk, and at the latter date he was replaced by Richard Duke, gentleman.[34] Audley had rapidly ceased to depend on Colchester for his advancement, and his post became partly honorific, but he had nonetheless brought landed wealth into Colchester. His mother-in-law, Lady Elizabeth Barnardeston, was one of the wealthiest taxpayers in the borough in 1524.[35] The influx of gentry had a significant impact upon the structure of wealth and authority in Colchester. Of the thirty-two bailiffs elected between 1460 and 1499 five were gentlemen with no involvement in trade[36] and two more were gentlemen who had come to Colchester to involve themselves in the cloth industry.[37]

This shift towards landed wealth within the borough's ruling group did not, however, mean that the developments of the fourteenth century were reversed. The textile industry remained the greatest single source of wealth and authority in Colchester. Of the thirty-two men elected to be bailiffs of Colchester between 1460 and 1499 four described themselves as clothmakers,[38] three as fullers[39] and one as a shearman.[40] A further twelve appear in the ulnage accounts as sellers of cloth during the 1460s and 1470s.[41] Over half this leading group of burgesses had, therefore, an identifiable rôle in the making of cloth. Ten bailiffs were described as mercers or merchants (including four of the already mentioned sellers of cloth)[42] and another was a vintner.[43] In effect the situation was close to that of the late fourteenth century; of the 32 in question 25 can firmly be said to have belonged to the mercantile and clothmaking interest of the borough.

[33] CR 86/1r, 2d.   [34] CR 102/1r.

[35] Bindoff, *House of Commons*, i, p. 382; P.R.O., E.179/108/162, m. 7. For her lands in the liberty, see *Essex Fines*, iv, p. 141.

[36] John Breton (OB, fos. 111v, 113r), Richard Heynes (RPB, fo. 220r), Richard Markes (OB, fo. 112r), Thomas Stamp (*Essex Fines*, iv, p. 76), John Wright (OB, fos. 95v, 98v).

[37] John Bishop and John Boteler, discussed above, p. 210.

[38] Thomas Christmas II (*L. and P.*, i(1), no. 1803(2), pp. 821–2), Richard Harvy (OB, fo. 112r), Richard Plomer (OB, fo. 107v), John Thursk (OB, fo. 111v).

[39] John Bardfield (CR 81/9d, 11r), Richard Barker (*Cal. Pat. R., 1476–85*, p. 276), William Colchester (CR 57/6d).

[40] William Rede: CR 71/1d, 2r.

[41] John Bishop, John Boteler, Thomas Christmas I, Nicholas Clere, Matthew Drury, William Ford, Richard Halke, Richard Parker, John Seman, Thomas Smith, William Smith, Richard Weld: P.R.O., E.101/342/21, back membrane; E.101/343/4, m. 3r; E.101/343/5d, 6r, 7r, 9d, 10d, 11r, 13d, 14r.

[42] John Baron (CR 60/24d), John Boteler (CR 62/19r), Thomas Christmas II (OB, fos. 115r, 118r), William Ford (OB, fo. 103v), John Gamday (OB, fo. 108r), Thomas Jopson (CR 82/20r), Richard Parker (CR 72/19r), Thomas Smith (*Cal. Pat. R., 1476–85*, p. 291), William Smith (OB, fos. 103r, 104v), John Swayn (CR 72/19r).

[43] John Water: CR 71/2r, 11r, 16d.

The absence of ulnage accounts from the early sixteenth century makes it difficult to recognise those who sold cloth. Nevertheless a powerful textile interest can be identified in Colchester. Of the nineteen burgesses elected bailiff between 1510 and 1529, seven were men who described themselves as clothmaker[44] and five were merchants.[45] The subsidy list of 1524 supplies further evidence of the prominence of this group. Out of the 32 men and women in the top category of taxpayer, assessed on movable property valued at £40 or more, or an equivalent assessment on land, 13 were clothmakers, and this was the largest single category of taxpayers within this class.[46] Five more were merchants.[47] In the 1520s the cloth trade was still the most obvious source of personal wealth in Colchester.

III

The growing wealth of Colchester's trading classes in the late fourteenth and early fifteenth centuries had visibly raised the quality of housing and domestic comfort to be seen in the main streets of the town. Since the 1380s, if not earlier, the number of houses and shops with two storeys had increased, often by the addition of additional floors to existing structures; this involved the construction of supports which encroached on public rights of way.[48] The bigger town houses had gateways leading off the street, sometimes with rooms above them.[49] There was also a good deal of less conspicuous improvement in smaller properties. An inventory of John Pool's goods made soon after his death illustrates the character of a tavern and its landlord's private quarters in the year 1458.[50] The hall, his main living room, had wall hangings of Flemish manufacture, and the seats had coverings and cushions. There was a large folding table, a cupboard and a cage for a pet bird. This room was warmed from an open hearth with an iron fender. Because of his trade, Pool needed more sitting room than most; his house contained two parlours, one large and one small, with two

---

[44] Thomas Christmas II and John Clere (as above), William Bekett (OB, fo. 125r), Thomas Flyngaunt (CR 90/14Ad), John Neve (CR 94/4d), Richard Pakke (CR 94/4d), John Smalpece (CR 94/4d).

[45] Christopher Hammond and John Swayn (as above), John Colle (CR 85/7r), William Jopson (CR 83/6r), Ambrose Lowth (CR 84/13d).

[46] William Bekett, John Clere, Thomas Flyngaunt, John Neve, Richard Pakke, John Smalpece (as above), William Alfeld (CR 92/27r), Thomas Baker (CR 90/17d), Philip Heyward (CR 90/10r, 14r, 17r), John Maynerd (CR 91/15d, 17d), Robert Northon (CR 90/9d), Thomas Nothak (CR 93/8r, 11d), Henry Webbe (OB, fo. 130v).

[47] John Colle, Christopher Hammond, William Jopson, Ambrose Lowth (as above), John John (CR 74/16r, 18d; CR 78/10r).

[48] OB, fos. 158v, 165v, 166r, 167r, 169v; CR 30/1d; CR 31/1d, 11r.

[49] OB, fos. 163r, 165v, 166v; CR 27/28d.

[50] John Pool was regularly reported as a seller of wine by lawhundred juries between 1442 and 1458: CR 58/2d...CR 69/2r.

Table 14.3 *Taxation from the clothmaking parts of Essex and Suffolk in 1334 and 1524*

| | 1334 | | 1524 | |
	£	%	£	%
Colchester	17.4	4.1	215.9	14.2
Lexden Hundred	74.3	17.5	226.9	15.0
Hinckford Hundred	167.5	39.5	293.7	19.4
Cosford Hundred	45.2	10.6	163.4	10.8
Babergh Hundred	120.0	28.3	615.9	40.6
	424.4	100.0	1,515.8	100.0

Sources: The Lay Subsidy of 1334, ed. R. E. Glasscock, The British Academy: Records of Social and Economic History, new ser., ii (London, 1975), pp. 80, 88, 291; P.R.O., E.179/108/154, 162, 163; *Suffolk in 1524, being the Return for a Subsidy granted in 1523*, ed. S. H. A. Hervey, Suffolk Green Books, x (Woodbridge, 1910), pp. 1–46, 152–66.

trestle tables in the former and a small folding table in the latter. In both rooms the seats had cloth covers and cushions, and the large parlour had a chair specially made for a child. Tavern pots of various sizes, six wine glasses, six tavern towels, six candlesticks and other items of tavern equipment were kept in the buttery, together with a stall on which to set ale. This room also stored some items of silver – spoons and other tavern pieces – weighing in all 2¼ *lb*. In the kitchen the fireplace had bellows, spits and trivets, and the utensils available there included three pots, four pans, a frying pan and a 30-piece set of pewter vessels. Upstairs the chamber contained the best bed, with hangings of white linen powdered with ermine. With it were two feather beds, one of them for a child, and two mattresses on which servants slept. Each bed had a pillow and a pair of sheets, supplemented with a blanket or a quilt. The chamber also contained a trestle table with two benches and a spruce chest. The best garments included a sanguine gown with fur trimmings, a green gown and a gown of musterdevillers. By past standards this all represented a very decent standard of accommodation, and yet Pool was not a man of high standing in Colchester and there were many who were wealthier than he.[51]

In 1524 the concentration of wealth in Colchester's streets was demonstrably more accentuated than it had been in 1334. The contrast is most usefully illustrated in the context of the economic region in which Colchester was a marketing centre, the clothmaking parts of Essex and Suffolk. These may be defined for the purpose as the hundred of Colchester, Lexden and Hinckford in Essex and the hundreds of Babergh

[51] CR 68/28r,d.

and Cosford in Suffolk.[52] An adjustment needs making to the figures as received. Colchester and its four hamlets were taxed in 1334 at one tenth of the assessed value of movable wealth there while the country areas were taxed at one fifteenth, so the Colchester figure for 1334 has to be adjusted downwards by one third before it is added in. Table 14.3 shows the contrasts which emerge from this analysis and by how much taxable wealth in Colchester had increased relative to that in rural areas. In fact, Colchester's share of taxable wealth had risen from 4.1 per cent of the total in 1334 to 14.2 per cent in 1524.

The differences between 1334 and 1524 cannot be explained away.[53] It is true that the wealthy townsmen of 1334 were less heavily taxed than those two centuries later, but this would not have affected Colchester's position relative to neighbouring villages and towns at that date. In any case, Colchester's records do not suggest that there was a colony of exceptionally wealthy families there in the early fourteenth century. It is also true that in 1524 each taxpayer's obligations to the Crown were totalled and charged at one place, whereas in 1334 perhaps in some cases separate assessments were made in each village.[54] This change would have increased the proportion of taxes paid in towns with landowning inhabitants. But Colchester was no more a haven for landowners in 1524 than in 1334, and there is rather more evidence of mercantile fortunes being used to found landed families at the latter date than at the former. The group of clothmakers, so prominent in 1524, had had no equivalent two centuries before. The suggestion that Colchester was relatively wealthier than the surrounding countryside in 1524 than in 1334, and that this had come about through the development of the urban economy between these years, is therefore one with solid evidence in its favour. Its probability is increased when the details of tax assessments from nearby villages and market towns are examined in greater detail.

Table 14.4 lists the towns and villages, as defined for purposes of tax assessment, whose share of the total sum payable from the five hundreds of Colchester, Lexden, Hinckford, Babergh and Cosford increased between 1334 and 1524. They are listed in descending order of the proportion by which their shares increased, Lavenham heading the list because its share was seven times greater in the latter year than in the former. It is an

[52] The Essex assessments are P.R.O., E.179/108/154, 162, 163. Suffolk assessments are printed in *Suffolk in 1524, being the Return for a Subsidy granted in 1523*, ed. S. H. A. Hervey, Suffolk Green Books, x (Woodbridge, 1910).

[53] These differences are discussed more generally in Bridbury, *Economic Growth*, pp. 77–82, and in J. F. Hadwin, 'The Medieval Lay Subsidies and Economic History', *Ec.H.R.*, 2nd ser., xxxvi (1983), pp. 210–13.

[54] R. S. Schofield, 'The Geographical Distribution of Wealth in England, 1334–1649', *Ec.H.R.*, 2nd ser., xviii (1965), pp. 495–6.

Table 14.4 *Places increasing their share of the taxes raised in the
Hundreds of Colchester, Lexden, Hinckford, Babergh and Cosford
between 1334 and 1524*

	Percentage of total taxes paid	
	1334	1524
Lavenham*	1.7	11.9
Colchester*	4.1	14.2
Hadleigh*	2.0	7.0
Nayland*	0.7	3.9
Long Melford*	1.7	4.3
Bures	0.8	2.5
Dedham*	1.0	2.6
Wivenhoe	0.3	1.8
Boxford	0.6	1.6
Stoke by Nayland*	1.1	2.0
Rayne	0.4	1.3
Little Waldingfield*	0.6	1.4
Glemsford	0.9	1.7
Coggeshall with Markshall*	1.4	2.0
Wethersfield	1.5	1.8
Bocking	1.2	1.4
Bildeston*	0.7	0.8

Sources: as Table 14.3.

interesting list for two reasons. It is noteworthy that of the 119 places taxed[55] the number whose share of the tax burden increased significantly was only 17; Sudbury and Clare, it will be observed, were not among them. And secondly, the prominence of the main textile centres of the region is very striking. The 10 places marked with an asterisk were all credited with more than 100 cloths of assize in 1467/8. Of the other places in the list, Glemsford occurs in the ulnage accounts as a clothing village.[56] Bocking, another clothing village, was adjacent to Braintree and not distinguished from it in the ulnage accounts.[57] Just as the distribution of the textile trade was becoming more localised in a few centres between the 1390s and the 1460s, so over a longer time span the ownership of wealth was becoming

[55] Excluding Finchingfield, Stambourne and Great Yeldham, for which no figures are obtainable because of damage to the manuscripts. In other instances where no figure is available from the return of 1524 a sufficiently close equivalent is to be had from that of 1525: P.R.O., E.179/108/176, 241A; *Suffolk in 1524*, ed. Hervey, p. 161.

[56] *E.g.* P.R.O., E.101/342/24, m. 10r; E.101/342/25, m. 8r.

[57] Morant says of Bocking that 'part of it extends into what appears the heart of the town of Braintree': Morant, *Essex*, ii, p. 383.

more concentrated. The two processes were closely associated, as Table 14.4 shows, and it is reasonable to describe the relationship as one of cause and effect. Places which established and maintained a sizeable cloth industry in the later Middle Ages were able to increase their share of the region's taxable wealth. The strength of this relationship confirms the peculiar importance of clothmaking in Colchester's economic development between 1334 and 1524.

It is one thing to argue that wealth had accumulated in Colchester between 1334 and 1524 and another to suppose that this was the consequence of sustained economic growth. Evidence relating to different aspects of the borough's history between these years has suggested that growth was a feature of the late fourteenth and early fifteenth centuries, but that the hundred years before 1524 had experienced contraction of population, consumption, output and trade. If there appears to be some contradiction in the evidence here, it is illusory. The accumulation of wealth between 1334 and 1524 is compatible with economic contraction between *c.* 1414 and 1524 if the magnitude of Colchester's achievement before 1414 is taken into account. Between 1334 and 1414 the town's population had perhaps doubled, and urban incomes had surely increased faster as a result of higher wages and profits. The great increase in the level of indebtedness in the third quarter of the fourteenth century – implying that townsmen held more of their wealth in the form of credit – is complementary evidence of an extraordinary development of urban wealth in this period. The new prominence of merchants in Colchester in the later fourteenth century suggests an accompanying transformation in the structure of urban society. The class of property owners grew in numbers and wealth as profits were reinvested in trading capital, loans and urban property. All this was happening against a background of demographic crisis in the countryside, disinvestment in agriculture and the abandonment of demesne farming on many manors. Between 1352 and 1414 the changing wealth of Colchester and some other clothmaking centres relative to the countryside around them must therefore have been pronounced. The alteration in Colchester's status which is revealed by the subsidy roll of 1524 would have been apparent 100 years earlier.

Between 1414 and 1524 Colchester's new status in the region was maintained. This is not surprising in view of the gradual character of the town's contraction. Population, industry and trade were all as late as 1450 close to the level of 1414, and total income remained very much higher relative to the surrounding countryside than in 1334. A similar increase was still apparent in Colchester's share of the region's wealth. Particularly after 1450 economic contraction must have had some adverse consequences for property owners. Total trading capital probably contracted, as the level of credit seems to have done. But wealthier townsmen put savings into property to protect their position and, as in the countryside, individual fortunes accumulated to an imposing size even in the context of economic stagnation or decay. Average personal wealth was still in 1524 very much higher than two centuries before, and Colchester's population was larger. Relative to the surrounding villages, the town remained conspicuously richer than it had been.

15

Government

For 150 years after 1372 there was no fundamental rethinking of Colchester's administrative and electoral system. Changes were matters of detail. The extent and direction of piecemeal reform are nevertheless of interest for their relevance to social change, and make a necessary introduction to the major revisions of the years 1519–25. The history of government in the borough is best discussed with reference to the question of oligarchy. In his brief account of developments in Colchester, Tait saw the process as one of a progressively increasing concentration of power in the hands of an inner ring of burgesses,[1] a common enough theme in the history of the late Middle Ages, but one which has occasioned debate on a number of separate issues. It is questionable how far ruling groups in towns were cut off from the support and consent of their fellow townsmen. Evidence for increasing oligarchy should sometimes be interpreted rather as the codification of past practice, and even where a more oligarchical form of government was in fact established, the implications for burgesses' welfare need dispassionate scrutiny.[2] The detailed evidence from Colchester makes it feasible both to look at Tait's conclusion more closely and to investigate the wider issues.

At the core of the problem is the question of the part played by the commons in borough affairs. The commons, in this context, were not synonymous with the lower ranks of the burgesses; the term signifies all those burgesses who were neither bailiffs nor members of the council, and so must include the majority of tradesmen and property owners. At the start of the fifteenth century the commons had several legitimate avenues for the expression of grievances and the initiation of reforms. One of these was the ancient lawhundred procedure, which was used more vigorously

---

[1] Tait, *The Medieval English Borough*, pp. 322–3, 334–5.
[2] Reynolds, *English Medieval Towns*, p. 171.

in the fifteenth century than it had been in the fourteenth for expressions of opinion about how the borough ought to be administered. From the 1440s onwards there were frequent formal complaints against the chamberlains for failing to maintain public properties for which they were responsible.[3] The bailiffs also came in for occasional reproaches. They had not properly corrected a woman they knew to be a prostitute;[4] they had not adequately provided for the supervision of the central fish market.[5] These representations were inevitably restricted to certain areas of complaint, but they could be used in an attempt to initiate changes in administrative procedure. In 1438, and subsequently, 'the jury requested the bailiffs to appoint, at their discretion, supervisors of wool sales in the moothall cellar, for the common good, etc.'.[6] Besides this mode of complaint, which may have led to borough ordinances relating to markets, roads and dunghills, the commons were allowed to petition the bailiffs and council with particular recommendations for the common good. This was the way in which craft ordinances were introduced for the fullers and cordwainers.[7] Last, and surely least, the commons had some capacity to influence events through their part in elections. The commons chose four headmen, one from each ward, to constitute the core of the committee of twenty-four men who elected the bailiffs and eight auditors each year. The electing committee was made up of men who, for the most part, were not councillors, and the membership of these committees really did change fundamentally from year to year.[8]

Throughout the fifteenth and early sixteenth centuries the constitutional rôle of the commons was greater than the written rules implied. Under the terms of the New Constitutions the council was empowered to make 'hard and fast constitutions, always to be maintained',[9] but whenever it was desirable to proceed with some broader measure of assent, the council acknowledged the fact. The fullers' constitutions were ordained 'by assent of the bayllez and the discrete councell of the towne of Colc' and with all the masters of fullers craft withinne the towne and fraunchise'.[10] Ordinances of a constitutional character were put before public meetings, probably at lawhundreds or on election days. For example, some new regulations concerning elections introduced probably between 1438 and 1449 were established 'by the avys, acord and assent of the bailiffs of the seid burgh this tyme beyng, aldermen, counsell and comunes of the same'.[11]

---

[3] *E.g.* CR 61/18r; CR 72/11d, 19d.   [4] CR 64/11r.
[5] CR 73/18d.   [6] CR 55/31r.
[7] RPB, fo. 23v; CR 45/16d.
[8] The names of those serving on election juries were annually recorded near the beginning of each new court roll.
[9] OB, fo. 23r.   [10] RPB, fo. 23v.
[11] OB, fo. 24v. For the date, see below, p. 220.

Ordinances of 1447 concerning eligibility for office were made 'by the bailiffs of the town of Colchester, the aldermen and council of the said town and the greater part of the community of the same'.[12] The borough charter of 1462 added nothing to the powers of the council and did nothing to alter its policy in this respect. An ordinance of 1488/9 to prevent the careless keeping of pigs and to regulate the commoning of cows and bullocks was 'ordeyned, stabilesshid and ffinally determined by the baillefes, aldermen, consell and commonalte', and is followed by a list of 33 names of men who were present with the bailiffs, aldermen and council when the ordinance was made.[13] In 1489 the borough's policy towards the mills at Hythe was determined at a meeting in the moothall attended by 'the bailiffs with the aldermen of the borough and the greater part of the discreet men of the community of the borough'; a list of those assenting to it includes the eight aldermen and eighty others. On the same occasion an ordinance concerning the commoning of cows was made 'by the said bailiffs with the assent of the aldermen...and of the 16 of the common council of the town, and at the special request of all the persons named above'.[14] Any notion of oligarchy applicable to fifteenth-century Colchester must accommodate this attentiveness of the oligarchs to the opinions of the commons.

Needless to say, burgesses of Colchester were never all equals in the business of the community, and in one respect the distinctions of rank which mattered were made more explicit in the fifteenth century than they had been before. In this context the most interesting ordinance is one surviving in the Oath Book, copied there by John Horndon, who was town clerk between 1438 and *c.* 1449, concerning the annual election of bailiffs, chamberlains and aldermen.[15] It probably belongs to his period in office as clerk, and may certainly be dated to some time after 1430, since it takes its tone from a royal statute of that year.[16] On election days in past years, it was said, 'many troublez, parlous discordes and inconuenientes haue be founde by experience by cause of the multitude concurrent to such eleccions, presumyng and vsurpyng enteresse in the seid eleccions wher in dede they owe noon to haue'. To remedy this, restrictions were placed upon the electorate. The first stage in the proceedings was the election of a headman for each ward. It was ordained that in future the only people to attend these elections and have any say in them should be 'fremen of the seid burgh, sworn to the kyng and to the toun, inhabitauntes in the same, lyvyng by ther lyvelode, marchaundise or craftys, housholdyng in her own persone and namys, beryng also taxe and talage whenne they falle for their

---

[12] OB, fo. 145v.
[13] RPB, fos. 182r–183r, dated from OB, fo. 109v.
[14] RPB, fos. 188r, 190r.
[15] OB, fo. 24v.
[16] 8 Henry VI, c. 7: *Statutes*, ii, pp. 243–4.

partes, [and] lot and shot to all resonable eides in the same burgh'. Children, lodgers, apprentices and some categories of journeymen were explicitly excluded. Further restrictions concerned eligibility to be a headman or to serve on a jury of election. From now on no one should be chosen for these positions ' ofles thanne he haue of yerly lyvelode in rente xl s.'. Moreover, the electing committee of twenty-four was in future to contain at least six councillors. These restrictions on the electorate were not solely a means to reduce the dangers of disorder; the ordinance was a device to ensure that the right people were elected without dissension.

In its explicit adoption of economic criteria of suitability to elect borough officers this measure has all the appearance of a further step towards oligarchy. However, it is in fact more interesting as a comment upon the existing constitution than as an instrument of change. The freedom with which electing juries could elect councillors was already heavily circumscribed by strict expectations concerning who was and who was not suitable, and the ordinance concerning elections introduced no new principle into normal practice. It was primarily a reactionary measure against attempts from some quarter to upset the *status quo*. The objection to having the poorer sort of burgesses on electing committees was that it gave rise to 'sotill werkynges...to wilfull preferrement of some persones after blynded affeccions, wyth-oute due regard had to the weele of the seid burgh and the sad rule ther-of', which must mean that there had been attempts to get men elected who were unsuitable by the accepted criteria. This may be taken as evidence of active political aspirations at this period amongst less wealthy townsmen, and notably those without property. There had been some sort of workers' organisation in the borough in 1425, when a lawhundred jury reported that 'Nicholas Dawber is master and rules all the other labourers of the town of Colchester, and is accustomed to take an excessive wage against the Statute of Labourers, etc., and is accustomed to exhort all the rest to do likewise'.[17] It is more likely that the community was taking steps to prevent such a movement from having political expression than that it was really settling for a more oligarchic form of government.

II

A better argument for the increasingly oligarchic nature of government in Colchester is from evidence relating to the leading officers of the borough. Predictably, the number of such officers increased during the fifteenth century. From the first decade comes the first evidence for the appointment of four claviers, who kept the keys of the town chest.[18] These officers were elected annually by the jury which also elected the sergeants, the town clerk

---

[17] CR 45/25r.   [18] Morant, *Colchester*, i, p. 94.

and the coroners. In 1447 a charter of Henry VI established that the burgesses should have their own commission of the peace and elect four of their number to act jointly with the bailiffs for this purpose.[19] Such elections are first recorded at Michaelmas 1463, when the task was given to the jury charged with electing bailiffs, aldermen and chamberlains,[20] and it is likely that they were first instituted following the reception of Edward IV's charter of 1462. That charter had authorised the burgesses to elect a recorder to join the commission of the peace, and this new office also first appears at Michaelmas 1463, when John Grene was elected recorder and justice of the peace alongside the other justices.[21] However, this increase in numbers was matched by a parallel development of rules about eligibility for office, which meant that in fact most offices in the borough were passed around among a small group of burgesses. Of central importance in this respect was the way the status of the auditors changed during the fifteenth century.

Originally in 1372 the eight auditors were to act with the bailiffs and receivers as a financial committee to control the community's expenditure. Both for this purpose, and for the annual audit of accounts, they met separately from the main council, which sat only about four times a year.[22] From the beginning, therefore, the auditors constituted an inner group of councillors with more work and responsibility than the rest. Auditors stood for election every year and, after serving for a year of two, were likely to return to the status of ordinary councillors. Stephen Flisp, John Pake and William Mate were all elected auditors in 1398 and councillors in 1399. Then in 1400 Pake remained a councillor, Mate was re-elected as an auditor and Flisp was elected bailiff.[23] Such fluidity was compatible with a good deal of continuity from year to year. If the bailiffs and auditors for each year are considered as a group of ten, then seven members of the group elected in 1399 and six members of the group elected in 1400 had belonged to it the previous year. The latter figure was lower because two auditors had died in office earlier in the year.[24]

Shortly after the beginning of the century it was decided to call these officers aldermen rather than auditors. The change was made between Michaelmas 1400, when the eight were recorded in the court roll as auditors, and Michaelmas 1404, when they were recorded as aldermen. The title of the receivers was altered at the same time; they were now to be called chamberlains.[25] The rewritten version of the New Constitutions in the hand

---

[19] *Cal. Chart. R.*, vi, p. 84.
[20] CR 72/1r. This is the first roll to include any reference to sessions of the peace in its heading, but in fact it does not record any.
[21] CR 72/1r.   [22] See Chapter 8, p. 118.
[23] CR 30/2r; CR 31/2d; CR 32/1r.
[24] Simon Fordham and Thomas Clerk: OB, fo. 67r.   [25] CR 32/1r; CR 34/1r.

of Thomas Rypere, who was town clerk from 1407 to 1414, systematically replaces the *auditours* of the original text by *aldermen* and the *resceiuours* by *chamberleyns*.[26] Although the term auditors did not pass out of currency for some while,[27] it became unusual in the borough records after the opening years of the century. The change of name can at first, at least, have been no more than a way of acknowledging the dignity of the office. Colchester aldermen had little in common with the aldermen of London, where the office was attached to each ward of the city, entailed a variety of legal, administrative and conciliar functions and was held for life.[28] The aldermen of 1404 had no duties their auditor predecessors had not had before them. Nor was there any alteration in the way they were elected. Of the eight aldermen elected in 1404, four were re-elected in 1405, two were elected bailiffs and two became ordinary councillors.[29] The pattern was the same in 1406; there was still a flow of men in and out. Philip Neggemere was a bailiff in 1402/3, an alderman (probably) in 1403/4 and (certainly) in 1404/5, and an ordinary councillor in 1405/6.[30]

After 1400 distinctions between aldermen and ordinary councillors became more marked. One indication of change comes in the recording of Michaelmas elections in the court rolls. From Michaelmas 1400 it became the clerks' normal practice to start each year's new court rolls with a list of borough officers. The bailiffs were named in the roll's heading and the aldermen were listed underneath; then came the names of other elected officers, followed by those of ordinary councillors.[31] In this order of things the councillors came closer to the ephemeral juries of election, whose names were copied last of all, than to the bailiffs and aldermen. A growing distinction between aldermen and councillors is also evident in the use of a tripartite formula to describe the nature of authority in the borough. This was the type of evidence adduced by Tait to suggest that 'the distinction of status between the eight auditors and the other sixteen councillors ended in the separation of the auditors as aldermen before 1443'.[32] In the first decade of the century the council was considered as a single body. An incomplete ordinance probably of 1401/2 speaks of a petition addressed 'to the baillifs and to the xxiiij'.[33] The bailiffs licensed a footbridge at Hythe in 1407 'by the will and assent of the 24 of the council of the town for this year'.[34] A term used in 1424/5 to similar effect was 'general counseill'; some ordinances of that year were made 'by the ... baillifs and the general

---

[26] OB, fos. 26v–27r.
[27] RPB, fo. 66v (ordinances of 1424/5).
[28] Williams, *Medieval London*, pp. 30–4; Tait, *The Medieval English Borough*, p. 313.
[29] CR 34/1r; CR 35/1r.
[30] OB, fo. 68v; CR 34/1r; CR 35/1r.   [31] The first such list is in CR 32/1r.
[32] Tait, *The Medieval English Borough*, p. 335 (*cf.* pp. 323n, 337n).
[33] RPB, fo. 43r.   [34] CR 36/32d.

counseill of the said toun'.[35] By this time, however, a tripartite formula was becoming more common. The fullers' constitutions and ordinances of 1418 use a variety of phrases; they are made 'by assent of the bayllez and the discrete councell of the towne of Colc'', and 'by the bayles and the councell of the towne of Colc' aforeseid', but also 'by assent of the bayles, of the aldermen and by assent and graunt of the commune councell of the towne'.[36] The cordwainers' constitutions and ordinances of 1425 were made on petition to, and by consent of, the bailiffs, aldermen and councillors.[37] This formula did not eliminate the older ones; in 1455 an ordinance was made by the bailiffs 'and all the hool counseill of [the foreseid] toun'.[38] Furthermore, the number of surviving ordinances is not large enough to show what normal usage was. However, the appearance of the tripartite formula from about 1418 suggests that status distinctions within the council had become more formal. Another indication to the same effect occurs in the formula used in borough leases. Until 1422 the court roll record of leases of the wool market, tolls and harbour dues says simply that 'the bailiffs conceded and leased...'. From the Michaelmas of that year the phrase 'with the aldermen's assent' was added as standard form.[39]

The distinction between aldermen and other councillors was at some point in the first half of the fifteenth century acknowledged by a change in their formal dress. The history of civic livery in Colchester may be taken back to 1372, when the New Constitutions allowed that the bailiffs should receive only £2 10s 0d for their term of office, together with a robe, 'and that they be dressed in livery'.[40] No provision was made at this time for payment or robes to auditors or members of the council. In 1411/12 the giving of livery was extended to councillors, but they received only a hood, not a whole robe: '...each councillor shall have each year a hood, price 2s 0d, if he has come duly at the bailiffs' bidding in reasonable time without any false or inappropriate excuse. And if he fails to come he shall forfeit 6d of the price of his hood for each default.'[41] This created the distinction between those of the 'whole clothing' of the town and those of the 'hooding' of the town which occurs in an ordinance of 1447. But this ordinance, which tightened up the rules of eligibility for the office of alderman, demonstrates that by 1447 aldermen received full robes, and were therefore differently dressed from ordinary councillors. It was ordained that 'no man be chose in-to the hole clothyng to ocupie as aldirman, otherwyse of old tyme called auditour, but if he be at the tyme of the seid elleccion in the hodyng of lyuere of the seid toun'; in other

---

[35] RPB, fos. 65v, 66r.   [36] RPB, fos. 23v, 24r.   [37] CR 45/16d.

[38] RPB, fo. 245v.   [39] CR 43/1d. *Cf.* CR 42/1d and earlier rolls.

[40] OB, fo. 22v.   [41] RPB, fo. 13r.

words, service on the council was a prerequisite of election as an alderman.[42] There is no record just when aldermen were first allowed full robes. It may have been as early as the first appearance of their new title in the early years of the century. There is a shred of evidence in favour of aldermen being in full livery by 1414; Thomas Rypere amended his revised version of the New Constitutions to prohibit aldermen from taking the livery of any lord having property or seigneurial authority within the liberty of the borough, and he is unlikely to have added this memorandum after his period as town clerk. The provision would make good sense if aldermen were already of the full livery of the borough.[43] The likeliest sequence of events is that aldermen were given full robes about 1400–4 as a further token of their respected status, and that the decision to allow 'hooding' to the other councillors in 1411/12 was a subsequent development. Of the nature of Colchester's livery there is some hint from an episode in 1423 when the duke of Gloucester, then acting head of state, visited the borough. On this occasion a reception party rode to meet him, and those who went were instructed to supply themselves with 'a man's gown and a red hood for the honour of the town'. Seven burgesses were later amerced heavily for disobeying these instructions.[44]

The problem with the rising dignity of aldermen, which has all this evidence behind it, is to know what it amounted to in terms of constitutional change. Evidence for increasing distinctions between aldermen and other councillors relates much more to the forms and pageantry of office than it does to the realities of what aldermen actually did. The auditors of 1372 were already distinguished from other councillors by the clearest differences of function. Besides their control of expenditure, it was, after all, the bailiffs and auditors who nominated the other 16 members of the council. On the face of it the changes which have been described were merely giving formal expression to differences of status and function which had been there from the beginning. This is very close to the truth. Aldermen ceremonially distanced themselves from ordinary councillors, just as ordinary councillors distanced themselves from the rest of the community, thereby illustrating a taste for ritual and outward show which was everywhere characteristic of fifteenth-century civic patriotism.[45] It is all of a piece with the elaborate new borough coat of arms, affirming Colchester's association with St Helen, which is first in evidence in 1413.[46] Such things count for something in any form of government, but they make a poor guide to changes in political realities. None of Tait's evidence of a 'growing separation of the

[42] OB, fo. 146r.   [43] OB, fo. 26v.
[44] CR 43/20r. For the date of the duke's visit, see LB, fos. 298r, 300r.
[45] Reynolds, *English Medieval Towns*, pp. 179–80.
[46] J. H. Round, 'The Arms of Colchester', *T.E.A.S.*, new ser., v (1895), p. 247.

aldermen from the rest of the council' establishes that this was a matter of constitutional significance.

However, there is more to be said in favour of Tait's argument. In the later fourteenth century, as an earlier chapter has shown, it was already common for juries to elect bailiffs from the previous year's auditors. But they were not obliged to do so, and evidence from eight years between 1382/3 and 1400/1 shows that four out of the sixteen bailiffs had not been auditors the year before.[47] After 1400 it became unusual to elect as bailiff a man who had not just been an auditor (alderman); the evidence is clear because of the new practice of recording councillors' names near the start of each year's court roll. A parallel development affected the borough's coroners, whose appointment in the fourteenth century seems to have been irrelevant to the *cursus honorum* of borough officers. From Michaelmas 1437 the two coroners were chosen from the ranks of the aldermen.[48] These changes, by which the body of aldermen became a pool from which other borough officers were chosen, were formalised in 1447, after the reception of Henry VI's charter of that year. It was now ordained 'that from thys tyme forward no baillif, justice of the pees, coronere nor-clavyour be electe in-to eny of the seid offices but if he be at tyme of the eleccion of the hole clothyng of the seid toun'.[49] These developments restricted the choice of electing juries rather more than in the past and ensured that the grandeur of aldermen should be enhanced by tenure of other offices. There may have been some administrative advantage in restricting judicial office in the borough to men with experience at the top level of administration, and these changes might be represented as a measure of the seriousness with which the Colchester community acknowledged its obligations to the Crown. It is more likely, though, that the new rules derived from the implications of hierarchical structuring in the community, and that administrative benefits, if any, were a secondary consideration.

This was no instance of an urban patriciate closing its ranks. At least 8 out of the 15 men who were elected bailiffs between 1430 and 1449, and who constituted the main part of the body of aldermen during those decades, were immigrants to Colchester,[50] and such fluidity remained characteristic of the ruling group throughout the century; at least half the 32 men elected bailiff between 1460 and 1499 were newcomers.[51] Nor was

---

[47] CR 21/1 (attached schedule), CR 22/3d; CR 24/2 (attached schedule); CR 25/2r; CR 26/2d; CR 29/2r; CR 30/2r; CR 31/2d; OB, fos. 57r–67r.

[48] CR 55/1r.   [49] OB, fo. 146r.

[50] Walter Bonfey (OB, fo. 79v), John Odelyshoo (fo. 73r), Thomas Oskyn (fo. 68v), Nicholas Peek (fo. 89v), John Rouge (fo. 79v), John Steven (fo. 70r or fo. 72r), John Trewe (fo. 71v), Thomas atte Wode (fo. 79v).

[51] John Baron (OB, fo. 87r), John Boteler (fo. 93v), John Breton (fo. 109r), Matthew Drury (fo. 94r), John Gamday (fo. 98r), Richard Halke (fo. 96r), Richard Harvy (fo. 94v or fo. 101v), Richard Heynes (fo. 108r,v), Thomas Jopson (fo. 99v), Richard Markes (fo.

increased oligarchy a conspiracy of employers or rentiers; the mercantile and property-owning interest of fifteenth-century aldermen were already sufficiently safeguarded before 1400. From the 1460s the increased number of landowners among the aldermen[52] makes it inappropriate to think of them primarily as an urban employers' group, despite the increasingly capitalist organisation of the cloth industry. In fact, the progress of oligarchy did not represent the triumph of any particular interest group within the community. Oligarchic privileges were increased with the approval of the council and were compatible with the interests of a broad body of opinion. The restriction of high office to aldermen might be viewed as an enhancement of their dignity or a concentration of power, but in the circumstances, given the constitutional constraints upon individual officers, it was the dignity of aldermanic status which constituted its chief attraction. In particular, the oligarchic system ensured that aldermen held positions of authority recognised outside Colchester itself, in the community of the shire and in Westminster. The reason for giving such honours to rich men was chiefly to attach them to the interests of the community, as the councillors and those they represented understood them.

It is impossible to trace all the benefits of the oligarchic system either to the ruling group or to the community. But some, at least, of the ways in which the community benefited from its commitment to these men can be shown from the later fifteenth century. Amongst Morant's manuscripts are preserved a number of assessment books from the years 1488–1504 relating both to tallages for the community's own use and to the collection of fifteenths and tenths on behalf of the Crown.[53] These records illustrate one of the relationships between oligarchic privilege and obligation to the community. The assessment in 1488 for 'the confirmacion of our chartere' lists the names of 418 contributors from the parishes of the liberty. Of these only three paid more than 5s 0d – the abbot of Colchester (13s 4d on two properties), the abbot of St Osyth (6s 8d) and the lord of the manor of Lexden (6s 8d). Three more landowners, including the prior of St Botolph, paid sums over 2s 6d. The remaining assessments range downwards to payments of 2d a head in the lower ranks of urban householders. However, at the apex of the burgesses' contributions there stand 10 assessments at 5s 0d and 18 at 2s 6d. The two bailiffs for 1487/8 are among those who contributed 5s 0d, as are those of every year from 1480/1 to 1486/7. This implies strongly that the 10 burgesses assessed at 5s 0d were the bailiffs and

---

101r), Richard Plomer (fo. 94v), William Rede (fo. 93r), Thomas Stamp (fo. 105r), John Thursk (fo. 100r), John Upchar (fo. 101v), John Water (fo. 87r), Richard Weld (fo. 86v or fo. 95r), John Wright (fo. 97r).

[52] See Chapter 14, p. 211.   [53] B.L., Stowe 828.

aldermen of 1487/8, and that the 18 who paid 2s 6d included the common councillors.[54] This is a fair illustration of oligarchy going hand in hand with the assumption of financial responsibilities.

The same principle operated in the assessment of fifteenths and tenths when these were collected on behalf of the Crown. The assessors did not apportion the tax between households by attempting to evaluate goods and chattels, but instead employed some rough and ready scheme with no uniform principle. Gradations of wealth were somehow acknowledged, so that in 1488/9 and 1489/90 rich townsmen paid 15 times as much as the poorest. But the artificiality of the system is apparent from an identification of the leading taxpayers. Comparison between the surviving list of bailiffs and aldermen in 1489/90 and the contemporary tax assessment shows that each of these 10 men paid 2s 6d towards a half fifteenth and that no other burgess paid as much. The same principle operated in later assessments of a whole fifteenth, to which bailiffs and aldermen contributed 5s 0d.[55]

There are further examples, in these years, of leading townsmen putting their resources at the community's disposal, even if it was with the expectation of eventual remuneration. Those who served as members of parliament, for example, could not expect prompt repayment of their expenses. Thomas Christmas and Thomas Jopson were still in November 1490 owed £17 16s 0d and £13 respectively for attendance in parliament in 1489. Each was to receive an annuity of £1 6s 8d from a mill at Hythe until the debt was paid; they must, in short, wait 14 years and 10 years respectively for the final instalment.[56] Thomas Jopson's expenses at the parliament of 1491, of which £5 8s 6d were still owing in March 1494, were to be repaid from annual rents of 12s 9d; he would have to wait a further nine years for the final payment.[57] This system of repayment was an unhappy one, since it meant that the community was tying up its regular sources of income. It was less than ideal for the members of parliament concerned, who would have been better off with a lump sum promptly paid. The point is not, however, that the system caused hardship to the individuals concerned, but that it depended upon their being wealthy and forebearing. It depended, in other words, on just such an alliance of wealth and public responsibility as that achieved by the oligarchic tradition.

A final illustration of this point is the agreement made in December, 1489, whereby two aldermen, Thomas Christmas the elder and Richard

[54] *Ibid.*, fos. 48r–57v. The object of this aid is apparent from fos. 58r and 59v. *Cf. The Charters and Letters Patent granted to the Borough*, ed. W. G. Benham (Colchester, 1904), p. 56.
[55] RPB, fos. 188r–189r; B. L., Stowe 828, fos. 14r–42r, 83r–98r, 110r–125r.
[56] RPB, fos. 219v, 222r–223r. The correct sequence of RPB, fos. 218–23 is worked out in *The Red Paper Book of Colchester*, ed. W. G. Benham (Colchester, 1902), pp. 124–31.
[57] RPB, fos. 218r,v, 220v.

Barker 'to the honour of God and the borough, and moved with tenderness by the prayer of the community', undertook to build two mills at Hythe, one for corn and one for fulling, to replace two which had broken down, paying the community £2 13*s* 4*d* a year for the site. At the end of 20 years the mills were to be handed over to the community. The site was granted to the two men under indentures of 12 January 1490 and the mills were constructed, it was said, at great cost. When in March 1494 the lease was transferred to Richard Barker to hold in his own right it was renewed for a new period of 20 years in recognition of his expenses incurred in the project.[58] The tone of the documentation relating to this venture strongly suggests that entrepreneurship was subordinate to public spirit and that the profitability of the mills was far from assured.

In these last examples the private incomes of aldermen were compensating for the inadequacies of the community's own resources. The scope for such assistance increased during the fifteenth century as the community's regular income declined. The Hythe leases, water tolls, land tolls and wool market had fallen in value by about one third between the first decade of the fifteenth century and the mid 1480s.[59] Court revenues had fallen considerably more. It is not surprising if the community had some difficulty in maintaining its public life and obligations without occasional hitches, and it was to some extent the obligation of aldermen to help out at such times. The early developments of aldermen's privileges go back to better days, and it would not be true to say that a more oligarchic constitution was a response to economic difficulties in the community. But the development of oligarchic practices acquired a new justification in the context of economic contraction, when it became increasingly necessary for the borough to attract the interest of its wealthiest men.

The most vulnerable posts in the borough administration during the years of contracting income were those of the two chamberlains. Though they bore a heavy responsibility for making ends meet, their office lacked the distinction belonging to that of the bailiffs and aldermen. Until the 1460s men could be found to undertake the work for two years successively; this was the usual stint during the 1430s, 1440s and 1450s.[60] But the crisis of the early 1460s interrupted this pattern. In 1463 and 1466 only one chamberlain was elected, perhaps because it was impossible to find a second.[61] Then in the 1470s and early 1480s it again became the practice to appoint two chamberlains, and some served for more than one year.[62] But the system soon broke down permanently. Sometime after

[58] RPB, fos. 188r–189v, 218v, 219r, 221r,v; OB, fo. 110r.
[59] Appendix, Table 5.
[60] CR 53/1r and 54/1r; CR 55/1r and 56/1r; CR 58/1r and 59/1r; CR 66/1r and 67/1r; CR 70/1r and 71/1r.   [61] CR 72/1r; CR 73/1r.
[62] *E.g.* John Colyn in 1480/1 and 1481/2: CR 78/1r; CR 79/1r.

1487/8,[63] probably by 1489/90[64] but certainly by 1497/8,[65] the community abandoned the attempt to find two chamberlains each year and settled for only one. As a corollary it was understood that nobody should be expected to serve more than once. From this point onwards, therefore, a year's self-sacrifice as chamberlain became a normal step in the public career of leading burgesses. Chamberlains were chosen from members of the council, and a man's willingness to take the office was a touchstone of his goodwill to the community, not to mention his suitability for higher honours. As a new chamberlain had to be found each year it was something of a problem to keep the office going, and it could reasonably be expected that members of the borough council should feel obliged to take a turn, even when they had no aspirations to become aldermen.

It was not unusual, however, for councillors to refuse this hurdle in the early sixteenth century. Peter Borough declined the chamberlainship in 1510 and John Baddyng did so in 1511. Each was punished by a fine of £1 and loss of burgess status, the latter being promptly redeemed for a further £1.[66] This misconduct did not damage the men's status as councillors.[67] Subsequent offenders too were able to retain their place on the council.[68] But the penalty for non-compliance was made steeper. When Thomas Nothak was elected chamberlain at Michaelmas 1519 he refused the office and was fined £2.[69] John Mytch declined to be chamberlain in 1521 and was fined £3 6s 8d 'according to old custom'.[70] Thomas Ryveley did likewise when elected chamberlain in 1522. On that occasion the bailiffs and aldermen decided that in future anyone who refused to be chamberlain after having been elected should be fined £5, but that Ryveley, as a special concession, should be asked only for £3 6s 8d. They were influenced, perhaps, by the consideration that Ryveley had already earned goodwill by waiving debts owed to him by the community.[71]

III

Between 1519 and 1525 there was a series of new constitutional reforms. The circumstances in which they were introduced were very different from

---

[63] More than one chamberlain in that year is indicated by RPB, fo. 91v.

[64] That Thomas Christmas II was sole chamberlain in 1489–90 is suggested by B.L., Stowe 828, fos. 28r–42r. This account shows him as sole receiver of tax money, and concludes with a memorandum 'that Thomas Cristemasse hath accoumpte [d] for these ij halfe taxes afore, as it apperith in his accompt de anno sexto Henrici septimi'.

[65] OB, fo. 112v.

[66] CR 83/2r; CR 84/2r. See Dobson, 'Urban Decline', pp. 13–14; *York City Chamberlains' Account Rolls*, ed. Dobson, pp. xxxviii–ix; Kermode, 'Urban Decline?', p. 187.

[67] CR 84/1r; CR 85/1r; CR 86/1r.

[68] E.g. CR 92/1r; CR 93/1r, etc. (Thomas Nothak); CR 94/1r; CR 95/1r (John Mytch).

[69] CR 91/1r.

[70] CR 93/1d; OB, fo. 121v.   [71] CR 87/21r; CR 94/1d.

those of 1372 when the council and auditors were first introduced to Colchester, and it would not be appropriate to see them as a self-confident expression of merchant prosperity. These years followed a period when communal income probably declined even more rapidly than it had done between 1415 and 1485, and the burden of public office had increased. The responsibilities of wealthy burgesses were inevitably a source of friction within the ruling group, exacerbating other contemporary difficulties and deepening the differences between individuals. There was a bitter quarrel in the moothall in 1520 after William Debenham, a former bailiff and one of Colchester's resident gentlemen, had refused to accept election as an alderman. 'Thou hast said,' said Debenham to John Colle, one of the newly elected bailiffs, 'that I neuer dyd good to this towne, but I haue been as good to this town as euer thy kynnesmen hath bene to God. And [when] he was demaundyd by the same John Cole what he ment be that, [he] seyd they ware herytykes.'[72] There were also severe tensions between the ruling group, or certain members of it, and other sections of the population. The elections of 1514, when Audley was first appointed to office in the borough, were impeded by at least 40 rioters, who abused the bailiffs and other dignitaries.[73] And on the evening of 7 December 1516 one of the bailiffs was insulted on his way through the streets with cries of 'Down wyth the bayly, down wyth hym', and the town sergeant accompanying him was assaulted.[74]

On top of these internal problems came a severe increase in the burden of royal taxation. Throughout the late fourteenth and fifteenth centuries the upper ranks or urban society had been lightly taxed by former standards. When required to pay a tenth, Colchester had to find only £26 2s 9d,[75] and, as has been shown, the most that any individual had to pay was 5s 0d. Between 1514 and 1523, however, Wolsey's experimenting with subsidies enlarged the number of taxpayers and the amount which the wealthy had to pay. For the subsidy granted in 1523, and mostly collected the two following years, Colchester had to collect £215 18s 1d in 1524 and a similar sum in 1525. Most of the increased pressure was on property owners; the 354 wage earners assessed contributed only 5.2 per cent to the total, but the 32 taxpayers assessed on movables worth at least £40, or with an equivalent taxable value in land, were liable for 57.2 per cent. The wealthiest taxpayer, John Christmas, was required to pay £30, and the bailiffs and aldermen between them owed £70 10s 0d, the equivalent of over two and a half tenths.[76] Elsewhere in the eastern clothmaking district this level of taxation was enough to cause public disorder amongst clothworkers who thought that it contributed directly to unemployment.[77]

[72] CR 92/18d.
[73] CR 86/5r.
[74] CR 88/23r,d.
[75] RPB, fo. 252r; B.L., Campb. Ch. xxix, 10.
[76] CR 95/1r; P.R.O., E.179/108/162.
[77] Dymond and Betterton, *Lavenham*, p. 28.

But whatever the effects higher taxation may have had on mercantile investment, the consequences for public spirit were likely to be detrimental, especially if burgesses continued to think in terms of their taxes being paid on behalf of the town.

The first stage of constitutional reform was an enlarging of the council in 1519, probably to broaden the basis of consent to the financial management of the community. A proposal of this kind was already in the air in 1462. Edward IV's charter of that year authorised the making of by-laws and the levying of tallages in Colchester on the authority of a common council of 42 men including the bailiffs and aldermen; in addition to the 26 as established in 1372 there were to be 16 additional councillors, 4 from each ward, to be chosen by the bailiffs and aldermen.[78] But for over 50 years this provision was never put into effect. Until Michaelmas 1519 the court rolls each year record the election of 16 men to form a common council, and these were simply the members who, in accordance with the New Constitutions of 1372, joined the 8 aldermen to make a council of 24.[79] Only at Michaelmas 1519, for the first time, is there a list of the names of 16 men elected from each ward who constituted a second group of councillors.[80] Later rolls describe these additional councillors as having been elected by the bailiffs, the aldermen and the 16.[81] They did not form a second council; they are described at the election of 1524 and thereafter as having been elected to the common council to which their electors also belonged.[82] The intention behind this innovation was not to introduce more flexibility into office-holding in the borough; the new group of 1519 was re-elected to a man in 1520 and 1521. In 1522 the elections returned 15 of the original 16 supplementary councillors, and 13 of them were re-elected even in 1524.[83] The enlargement of the council served, therefore, to increase the number of burgesses who had an established foothold in office. The new councillors were not chosen in such a way as to provide a more representative cross section of Colchester society. Comparison with the subsidy list of 1524 shows that the second group of 16, like the first, were burgesses assessed on goods worth £10 or more, which means that they were from the wealthiest 16 per cent of the population.[84] This measure did not, therefore, preclude the desirability in some circumstances of seeking the consent of the commons to council decisions. On 31 March 1523 the levying of a rate 'to provyde x complete harnes, to be in a redynesse at all tymez to be at the kynges commaundment whan they shalbe requyred' was agreed in an assembly of aldermen, councillors and

[78] *Cal. Chart. R.*, vi, p. 150.
[79] *E.g.* CR 90/1r.
[80] CR 91/1r.
[81] *E.g.* CR 94/1r.
[82] CR 95/1r; CR 96/1r; CR 97/1r.
[83] CR 92/1r; CR 93/1r; CR 94/1r; CR 95/1r.
[84] P.R.O., E.179/108/162.

burgesses, following the election of Thomas Audley and Ambrose Lowth to represent the borough in parliament.[85] An ordinance of 1537 to enclose lands in the borough was made 'by the baylyffes, [alder]men, counseill and commonaltie' and there is a list of between 50 and 60 men other than aldermen and councillors who were present to give their consent.[86]

It was the new and larger council which inaugurated a second stage of constitutional reform, carrying the oligarchic principle yet further. On 30 September 1523 the right of electors to change the composition of the body of aldermen was formally curtailed. From now on

no person beyng electe and sworne to the offyce and rome of an alderman of the sayd borough shall in no wyse be amovyd or putt ffrom the same office and rome by the eligors of the sayd aldermen withoute the agrement, assent and consent of the baylyffes and aldermen of the said boroughe, or the most part of them.[87]

Sometime between late April and Michaelmas 1524 a more far-reaching reform was adopted to eliminate certain elections.[88] The second election day, when the town clerk, the sergeants, the claviers and the coroners were elected, was abolished outright. The election of claviers and coroners was transferred to the first election day when the bailiffs themselves were elected. The open election of sergeants, chamberlain and town clerk was to be discontinued; sergeants were instead to be nominated by the bailiffs and the chamberlain and town clerk were to be appointed for life by the bailiffs, aldermen and common council. The earlier ordinance relating to aldermen's tenure was reaffirmed.

The provisions made here for the chamberlainship would have raised the office to one of unprecedented dignity of status. It is uncertain, even so, how the bailiffs could hope to find a life tenant for an office with such a history of refusals. The proposed arrangement depended, perhaps, upon a wider sharing of financial responsibilities by the bailiffs and aldermen than in the past. At the same time the New Constitutions made a virtue of recent necessity in requiring the deliberately ineffectual election of a second chamberlain. When the bailiffs and aldermen were elected the electors were to nominate a member of the council of 24 as a chamberlain, but he would immediately be discharged upon payment of £1. Comparable use of an electoral system as a form of money raising is known from other English towns in this period, though not usually so explicitly as in the Colchester proposal of 1524.[89]

[85] RPB, fo. 27r.
[86] RPB, detached folio. See *The Red Paper Book*, ed. Benham, p. 166.
[87] RPB, fo. 30v.
[88] RPB, fos. 31v–32v. The constitutions are dated to 16 Henry VIII (22 April 1524 to 21 April 1525) in the time of John Makin and John Colle, bailiffs (5 October 1523 to 3 October 1524): OB, fo. 122v.
[89] Kermode, 'Urban Decline?', pp. 195–6.

This part of the new electoral procedure was not, however, to come into effect. The new regulations were initially intended to be implemented at Michaelmas 1524 and to be retained in following years if the bailiffs, aldermen and community thought it advantageous to do so. In fact they ran into difficulties. The new rules were not enforced until Michaelmas 1525, and then with the difference that the chamberlain and clerk continued to be elected annually. The device of appointing a second chamberlain was probably abandoned; certainly there are no names of discharged chamberlains in the court rolls. A single chamberlain was elected each year, as before. The other reforms, however, were adopted and remained operative in later years.[90] This revised constitution has a neatness which makes it a fitting point at which to halt the history of medieval constitutional development in Colchester. There was now to be a single electing jury whose remit ruled out any wanton change in the body of aldermen. Its task was primarily to allocate aldermen to the various offices which they alone could fill: two bailiffs, four justices of the peace, two coroners and two claviers. They had, in addition, to find a chamberlain from the ranks of those who were not yet aldermen. The only other elective officers, those of recorder and clerk, were sufficiently exalted and difficult to fill to preclude any sudden changes. The system ensured that only wealthier burgesses should ever attain to high office and that, having done so, they should enjoy a dignified security of status.

The sequence of events between 1519 and 1525 confirms that the oligarchic principle had the full approval of the wealthier families of Colchester and that it was compatible with older traditions of consultation and debate. The terms of the proposals of 1523 and 1524 demonstrate the importance of personal dignity in the progress of oligarchy; there was little reason for seeking to abolish the election of the sergeants, chamberlain and town clerk except that the whole business of election was considered to derogate from the dignity of these offices. The events of these years also support the view that the oligarchic system was particularly well attuned to the maintenance of town government in hard times. It is no accident that the new constitutions of 1523 and 1524 were introduced at a time when a recession in cloth exports and a steep increase in taxes were exacerbating the longer-term problems of the borough.

The success of the oligarchic system in committing the wealthy may be judged from the evidence of the 1524 subsidy list. Of the 32 wealthiest inhabitants of the borough 3 were women and 1 was an alien; there was no place for these in public office. But of the remaining 28 there were 22 in the current list of borough office-holders: 2 bailiffs, 8 aldermen and 12

---

[90] A second jury to elect coroners, claviers, sergeants and town clerk was formed at Michaelmas 1524 (CR 95/1d) but not in subsequent years.

councillors.[91] Four others, though not currently in office, had been bailiffs in past years. Eventually 18 out of the 28 were elected bailiff at some stage in their careers.[92] There was, too, a direct correlation between a man's wealth and the community's expectations of him. The leading 4 taxpayers in 1524 were each elected bailiff at least 4 times, and ultimately they had 21 years' experience in this office between them. The 4 taxpayers closest to them in wealth were all bailiffs at least once and accumulated 12 years in office between them. A wealthy man in Colchester, it seems, could hardly escape the trammels of public life, and the wealthier he grew the more involved he was likely to become. Because of the greater demands of the community, the heightened emphasis on sharing the burdens of administration, the increased number of offices to be filled and the larger number of seats on the council, it was harder to opt out than it had been in the fourteenth century. A rich man who wanted to enjoy his wealth without pageantry was better off living in a country village.

[91] CR 95/1r; P.R.O., E.179/108/162.
[92] Bailiffs are listed year by year in the Oath Book.

16

Economic regulation

I

Throughout the fifteenth century the old-established rules of marketing in Colchester remained in operation. In the central markets trading began with the ringing of a bell at a regular hour.[1] Transactions were monitored to ensure that individual vendors did not bid up prices, and tradesmen were punished if they attempted to sell above the price currently authorised.[2] Those in charge of cargoes coming to Hythe were expected to remain ignorant of current market conditions,[3] to obtain a bill from the moothall before offering goods for sale[4] and to sell them at a publicly proclaimed price agreed with the bailiffs.[5] Those buying up produce on its way to market were punished, whether they operated by sea or land. As in the fourteenth century fish was the commodity most frequently forestalled, with grain in second place. The main development in the enforcement of this legislation was that the community during the fifteenth century took account of forestalling in a wider variety of commodities, including, from time to time, butter,[6] eggs,[7] cheese,[8] rabbits,[9] onions,[10] garlic,[11] mustard seed,[12] salt,[13] vinegar,[14] tallow,[15] hides,[16] coal,[17] linen cloth,[18] earthenware,[19] rope[20] and bast.[21]

[1] CR 76/11r.   [2] CR 64/3d; CR 79/26d.
[3] CR 73/27r; CR 74/23r; CR 89/4d; CR 90/4d.
[4] CR 51/2d, 12r; CR 53/2d; CR 56/18r.
[5] CR 74/23r; CR 89/4r,d; CR 90/4r,d; CR 93/20r,d.
[6] CR 77/17d; CR 78/2r; CR 79/26r.
[7] CR 58/15r; CR 77/18r; CR 78/2r; CR 79/26r; CR 85/9r,d; CR 89/4d.
[8] CR 55/31d; CR 78/2r; CR 79/26r.
[9] CR 59/17r; CR 61/11r; CR 78/2r.
[10] CR 54/2d; CR 55/3r; CR 61/11r; CR 71/2r.
[11] CR 54/2d; CR 55/3r.   [12] CR 51/12r.
[13] CR 54/2d; CR 71/2r; CR 80/19d; CR 81/13r.
[14] CR 51/12r.   [15] CR 39/2d; CR 79/2r.
[16] CR 49/14d; CR 69/9r, 15r.   [17] CR 58/15r.   [18] CR 51/12r.
[19] CR 73/1d; CR 75/2r.   [20] CR 75/2r.   [21] CR 75/2r.

The problems of enforcing regulations against forestalling had mounted with the growth of Colchester's trade and its increased prominence in the region as a point of supply. Pedlars were coming into Colchester from as far afield as north-west Essex and southern Cambridgeshire in search of fish, and they were not particular about obeying market regulations.[22] The problem of forestalling by external merchants, who bought produce up on its way to Colchester and diverted it to other markets, was always present.[23] From time to time illegal markets were in operation on the confines of the liberty to meet the needs of these traders. Such a market at Fingringhoe, described in 1426 as 'newly started', specialised in oysters and mussels. It continued to trouble the burgesses until at least 1430.[24] A later illegal market at Rowhedge, which was frequently reported by lawhundred juries between 1466 and the 1520s, catered for all kinds of fresh fish.[25] Urban fishmongers had no interest in siding with the community in this matter, since they could supplement their livelihoods as go-betweens and middlemen, and it was common for fishmongers to be accused of selling to outside pedlars rather than to Colchester burgesses.[26] In these circumstances the Statute of Forestallers was no longer the main pillar of the community's defences, since Colchester men and other interlopers were operating in such a way as to by-pass the liberty of the borough altogether.

The law against forestalling became swamped for another reason. The community began to use lawhundreds more frequently for the enforcement of Edward III's statutes relating to prices.[27] These were altogether vaguer than the Statute of Forestallers in their definition of the offence they created, since they merely required that victuallers' prices should not be excessive in relation to prices in neighbouring markets. In many instances the price of victuals was already regulated by the assizes of bread and ale or by the normal rules of price determination in the town markets. But from 1424 onwards the community was more eager than in the past to punish butchers who sold meat at excessive prices, and in 1425 began the regular punishment of innkeepers who sold hay and other commodities at excessive prices in their inns.[28] The principle that prices should be reasonable was sometimes employed in other contexts as well, to punish sellers of grain[29] or fish.[30] There was accordingly more arbitrary amercement of urban traders for supposed misdemeanours during the fifteenth century than in earlier periods. This development cannot be related closely

[22] CR 45/25r. [23] CR 51/21d; CR 54/19d; CR 68/12d, 20r.

[24] CR 46/21r; CR 47/23r; CR 48/23r; CR 49/1d, 14d, 23r; CR 50/2d, 13d, 23d.

[25] CR 73/1d; CR 75/2r and so on up to CR 93/15r; CR 94/2d.

[26] CR 49/23r; CR 51/21d; CR 53/2d, 11d, 20r; CR 54/2r, 10r, 18d; CR 56/18r, 28d; CR 69/2r; CR 78/2r; CR 84/16r,d.

[27] See Chapter 9, p. 135. [28] CR 45/24r; CR 46/2r and subsequently.

[29] CR 55/2d. [30] CR 61/11r.

to any real problems in Colchester's economy, but it may be that the burgesses were in a mood for economic regulation following the collapse of the early fifteenth-century boom.

Partly because of more complex problems, partly because of a wider range of rules and regulations, the legal foundation of the community's activities became disconcertingly vague. By the middle of the fifteenth century the distinction between statutory obligations and by-laws was barely appreciated, and town clerks became more slipshod than in the past in their use of technical vocabulary. The term forestalling lost its connection with the Statute of Forestallers and became a general term to cover all sorts of activities. A man who bought grain in the market place and then sold it there at a higher price was said in 1438 to have forestalled it.[31] A merchant who in 1440 bought 500 quarters of barley in Norfolk at what was considered too high a price was said to have forestalled and regrated it there.[32] In 1467 three butchers were reported for forestalling because they bought meat in the market from outside butchers and then resold it.[33] Since those enforcing economic regulations could no longer identify correctly the rules they were implementing, it is reasonable to conclude that they cannot invariably have acted justly.

II

From 1413 the Colchester community abandoned its hitherto passive stance with respect to the regulation of labour. Although there are only a few cases, it is interesting to see that at this point lawhundred juries began to report workers who took excessive wages. In 1413 seven roof builders were amerced for taking $4\frac{1}{2}d$ or $5d$ a day as well as food,[34] and a labourer was fined in 1424.[35] Seven others were similarly punished in 1425, and it was implied that they had some sort of organisation.[36] Occasionally, too, the statutes were enforced to punish those who aided and abetted servants in breaking their contracts.[37] But these infrequent interventions can have had little effect upon the labour market, and they do not represent the community's main concern at this period. The main innovations arose from problems in the woollen industry, and were embodied in the fullers' regulations of 1418.[38]

In regulating their own craft the fullers persuaded the authorities of the need for general rules. For their own protection they established that in future no burgess should practise the crafts of weaving and fulling together. But the ordinances also require

---

[31] CR 56/4r. [32] CR 57/15r.
[33] CR 73/18d. [34] CR 39/3r.
[35] CR 44/11r. [36] CR 45/25r.
[37] CR 50/14r. [38] See Chapter 12, pp. 185–6.

that no man fro this day forward that is of eny other craft shall hold the craftes of wevyng and fullyng to-gedre ne none other hande craft but only the same craft that he was prentys of, savyng only they that haue continued by long tyme in the craftys of wefyng and fulling that it be lefull to hem to ocupie the same craftes as they haue done here before this tyme notwithstandyng this ordinaunce... And allso what man of eny other craft that doth the contrary of this ordinaunce agens the craft that he vsith that he pay to the motehalle xxs. and that as oft tymes as he is founde in that defawte.[39]

This regulation is firmly anchored in statute law. It had been a requirement of Edward III's statutes of 1363 that each craftsman should confine himself to one craft,[40] and lawhundred juries had since availed themselves of this principle when it suited them to do so.[41] However, the decision to apply the law so as to affect the organisation of urban industry was new in the second decade of the fifteenth century. This legislation was treated by urban authorities as permissive, to be made effective as and when they chose.[42] In spite of its statutory sanction, therefore, the council's decision to make a general ruling in 1418 – when the problem in hand concerned only the fulling of cloth – has real significance as further evidence that the fullers were not alone in wanting a more restrictive structure of employment.

It is an implied consequence of these new ordinances that in future no one should work as a fuller who had not served an apprenticeship in the craft. And in this matter, too, the ordinances of 1418 were a major new development in the regulation of labour. Terms of apprenticeship were not laid down by statute, and the townsmen had to be guided by the practices of other towns, which varied considerably. Under cover of regulating their own craft the fullers secured the enactment 'that no man take none apprentices of the craftes of wefyng ne of fullyng nor of none other craft within the ffraunchise of this towne lasse than the terme of v yere'.[43] A general regulation concerning the duration of apprenticeships could not have been introduced in this manner had there been any significant degree of craft organisation in the borough at the time; the fullers were pioneering new developments in craft organisation. This is shown yet more clearly by the general requirement that the commencement of new apprenticeships was to be a matter of public record; masters in all crafts were obliged to have article of apprenticeship enrolled by the town clerk.[44] Enrolment of apprenticeships was becoming a normal feature of English towns. The fact that in Colchester's case this was introduced in the early days of craft

[39] RPB, fo. 24r.
[40] 37 Edward III, c. 6: *Statutes*, i, pp. 379–80.
[41] CR 30/16d; CR 33/20d.
[42] Lipson, *The Economic History of England*, i, pp. 357–9.   [43] RPB, fo. 24r,v.
[44] From 1424 onwards there are references to a Liber de Probacionibus Seruiencium in which such contracts were recorded: CR 44/15d, 25d; CR 53/18d.

organisation suggests that the object was more to guard against fraud than to enforce municipal control over the crafts.[45]

The fullers' regulations illustrate the tendency, when conditions of employment deteriorate, for men to become more restrictive in their trading policies as a means of self-protection.[46] But since the cloth industry was currently responding to adverse circumstances by raising the quality of its standard products, the tightening up of terms of employment in 1418 was not purely defensive. Colchester merchants and clothiers were having to establish the reputation of cloths which required more careful manufacture than their old russets, and they were predictably concerned about current standards of workmanship. If the quality of cloth from Colchester was unreliable this would affect its reputation and marketability; it was for this reason that urban authorities everywhere regulated their cloth industries, particularly when finer cloths were in question. The importance of clothmaking in Colchester's economy, the unregulated way in which the industry had grown so far and the particular problems of adjustment in the early fifteenth century all made the introduction of new rules a matter of general concern. The regulation of the cloth industry at this point in the town's development was not the start of a rising tide of protective measures either in textiles or other industries. There is no record of any further attempt to control employment in clothmaking in the period before 1525, and no other industry has left any comparable code of new practices. The Red Paper Book, it is true, preserves the text of some regulations relating to leather workers, amongst other tradesmen, and these imply a deliberate attempt to prevent occupational overlapping between tanners, whittawers, cordwainers and curriers.[47] But this text was known in Northampton and in Coventry, where it was called the Statute of Winchester,[48] and its status is ambiguous. It cannot be assumed to have any significance for the course of change in Colchester.

III

Much of the industrial regulation in evidence from the fifteenth century had nothing to do with the wish to protect employment. Statute law in the fourteenth century had set precedents for many types of intervention by the community where public interest required it, and the fifteenth

---

[45] Lipson, *The Economic History of England*, i, pp. 322–3.
[46] Hibbert, 'The Economic Policies of Towns', pp. 209–12.
[47] RPB, fos. 16v–18r.
[48] *Records of the Borough of Northampton*, ed. C. A. Markham and J. C. Cox (2 vols., Northampton, 1898), i, pp. 344–9; *The Coventry Leet Book or Mayor's Register*, ed. M. D. Harris, Early English Text Society, cxxxiv, cxxxv, cxxxviii, cxlvi (4 parts, London, 1907–13), pp. 395–401.

century saw a considerable increase in the amount of detailed regulation founded on these earlier principles. Sometimes fifteenth-century concepts of the public interest were a good way removed from those of modern legislators. In 1424/5, for example, the prices at which whittawers could sell their leather was fixed in the public interest, but if they resented this measure the whittawers must have felt the more keenly the added requirement 'that euery swych white tawyer with-outen grutchyng be redy and wel willyd to seruen the peeple whan they haue nede to her craft, on peryll that may fallen there-of, etc.'.[49] But other extant industrial regulations from Colchester accord well enough with modern principles of legislation. The same ordinance which regulated the prices charged by whittawers also took steps to prevent the pollution of the river by the washing of hides there. Tanners and whittawers were prohibited from doing so in future, and it was ordered that each craftsman should wash his hides 'only in his owne water vpon his owne ground' and that the pits in which he did so should not drain into the river.[50] This wholesome by-law was simply a gloss on the Statute of Cambridge. Another unobjectionable category of industrial regulation, with centuries of tradition behind it, concerned the standardisation of weights and measures, either to prevent fraud or to prevent other inconveniences to consumers. By an ordinance of 1411/12 the weights by which wool was doled out to spinners were fixed by reference to standard leaden weights to be sealed and kept in the moothall. A larger weight of $4\frac{1}{2}$ *lb* was to be used as one stone and a smaller weight of $2\frac{1}{4}$ *lb* was to be one 'werk'.[51] By 1452 there was a similar standard for doling out wool to combers. It was then the custom that any inhabitant of the town exercising the craft of clothmaking who wished to put out wool to be combed or spun in households other than his own should use a weight of 5 *lb* called a 'kembyngston' for women combing the wool and another of $4\frac{1}{2}$ *lb* called a 'spynnyngston' for women spinning. The bailiffs claimed the right to imprison and fine employers convicted of exploiting women by using overlarge weights.[52] The policy here was designed to prevent fraudulent practices by employers. As an example of regulation to prevent gross inconvenience there is an ordinance of 1424/5 concerning tilemakers, who were under criticism because they made their tiles from moulds of different sizes 'none of hem acordaunt to other'. The council fixed the size of tiles to be made in future according to a standard to be kept in the moothall.[53] Regulation of terms of employment was sometimes necessary to prevent fraud and discontent. In 1411/12 it was ordained that no weaver should be compelled to take merchandise or foodstuffs for his wages, and that he was to be paid in gold or silver if he so desired.[54]

[49] RPB, fo. 66r.   [50] RPB, fo. 65v.   [51] RPB, fo. 13r.
[52] RPB, fo. 81v.   [53] RPB, fo. 66r.   [54] RPB, fo. 13v.

Sunday trading was a further matter for regulation by by-law. This has more to do with changing standards of Christian devotion amongst laymen than with any economic change.[55] Such is the subject matter of the only surviving set of craft ordinances other than the fullers'. It dates from 1425, only seven years after the fullers', but differs from theirs in almost every conceivable way. The shoemakers, it is said, had come to the Hilary lawhundred requesting by written petition that certain constitutions and ordinances should in future apply to all shoemakers in the liberty, and that they should be enrolled in the borough court rolls. All this was granted. The ordinances have entirely to do with the suppression of Sunday trading. In future no shoemaker shall sell his wares, or cause them to be sold, on a Sunday; no master of the craft shall send his wares on a Sunday to be sold in rural areas outside Colchester; shoes must be got ready by Saturday so that customers do not need to fetch them on Sunday; no shoemaker shall do any sewing on Saturday nights.[56] These rules had parallels in other trades, either by some ordinance of general scope or by a series of craft ordinances. In 1425 a cutler and his two servants were reported by a lawhundred jury to have worked on Sundays and other feast days 'against the ordinance and proclamation of the town' and the same jury reported a woman for selling linen and other merchandise on Sundays.[57]

IV

The increasing amount of industrial regulation during the fifteenth century, both to protect employment and to prevent abuses, had the effect of increasing the number of supervisory offices in the borough and widening the stratum of those with publicly recognised authority. The enforcement of rules concerning craftsmen and their work was delegated to the crafts themselves, and the development of craft organisation was a feature of the growth of regulation.[58] This is well demonstrated both by the fullers' ordinances of 1418 and by those of the cordwainers of 1425.

Until 1418 the fullers had had no craft organisation at all, for a major part of their reform was to create such an organisation for the future. It was provided that master fullers – those, that is, who operated on their own capital and credit rather than for wages – should meet annually in the chapel of the Holy Cross on Michaelmas Day to elect two governors or overseers who would supervise the fulling of cloth in the borough and

[55] For more mundane explanations, see Green, *Town Life*, ii, p. 148, and Lipson, *The Economic History of England*, i, pp. 334–5.
[56] CR 45/16d.   [57] CR 45/15r.
[58] The function of craft gilds as agencies of borough government has long been recognised: Green, *Town Life*, ii, pp. 135–6; W. J. Ashley, *An Introduction to English Economic History and Theory*, 4th edn (2 vols., London, 1906, 1909), ii, pp. 87–9, 94–5.

impose penalties upon offenders. Each year the new governors were to be presented to the bailiffs 'at the next hundred day that is holden in the common halle of the towne after ther eleccion', and there they were to take an oath of office. The names of new masters were to be reported on the same occasion.[59] The rôle of craft organisation in the enforcement of regulations is here well illustrated by the procedures made available to those who should in future suffer from poor craftsmanship at the hands of members of the fullers' craft. In effect the masters and governors of the craft were constituted a court for the purpose of attending to complaints and finding a remedy. Those with complaints were to bring the badly fulled cloth to the masters and governors, who would evaluate the damage done to the cloth. The offending fuller would be prohibited from fulling until he had settled with the complainant or made such amends as the masters and governors directed.[60] Early in 1419, only a few months after these ordinances were enrolled, Robert Doget was reported by a lawhundred jury for breach of borough regulations concerning the cloth industry, and the nature of the charge shows that the fullers' ordinances had come into effect.[61]

The novelty of craft organisation in Colchester is confirmed by examination of the cordwainers' ordinances of 1425. These contain no provision for the creation of a craft constitution such as that of the fullers, and any information to be had about the cordwainers' organisation has to be taken from circumstantial evidence in the text. The cordwainers had a common fund, since a cordwainer who traded on Sundays was to forfeit 3s 4d 'to the commune of the artificers of the aforesaid craft' as well as a like sum to the community of the borough. But the ordinances say nothing to imply that the craft had elected officers. They describe those in authority in the craft as 'masters', as in the provision that a persistent rebel against the ordinances shall be presented before the bailiffs 'by those who are masters of the craft at the time'. But the term 'master' is also used simply to mean an employer, as in the requirement that no cordwainer 'whether master or servant' shall sew on a Saturday night.[62] Probably the membership of this craft was too small to justify the election of officers, so that the craft did not need any constitutional apparatus. There is supporting evidence for this supposition from later in the year. When on 7 May some offenders were reported to the bailiffs at a hundred court, the procedure followed was an interesting one. Four cordwainers reported two others.

To this court came John Andrew, John Mendham, John Pyryton and Robert Hunte, masters of the art of cordwainers of Colchester town, and they took their oath to perform and fulfil to the best of their ability all the constitutions and

[59] RPB, p. 23v.
[60] RPB, p. 24v.
[61] CR 41/13r.
[62] CR 45/16d.

ordinances of the aforesaid craft, etc. And they present that Thomas Smyth, cordwainer, against the form and tenor of these ordinances sold his wares...on Easter Day and on other Sundays. Likewise they present that John Reed...went out of Colchester to Maldon fair with his wares...on Sunday the feast of the Annunciation of the Blessed Virgin Mary last past.[63]

There are two interesting features of this incident – the swearing in of the masters and the nature of the charges they had to report. The bailiffs were used to acting on 'presentments' of offenders, but they always received such reports from men who were sworn to tell the truth. The lawhundred jury was the main case in point, but in inquests *ex officio* a jury was also involved. Where, as in the case of the fullers' craft, there were elected officers, they took their oath of office before the bailiffs at the beginning of their term. Accordingly, when four masters of the cordwainers' craft turned up with presentments to make it was only proper to swear them in. The form of the oath suggests that the men had not already been sworn in as officers of the craft and that the oath on 7 May was a procedural necessity for this reason. This implies that in 1425 the cordwainers had no elected officers such as the fullers had. Another feature of the presentments, the nature of the charges, is also relevant to the status of this craft. Having sworn to respect the constitutions and ordinances of their craft the four cordwainers reported offences against the ordinances whose text is extant and no others. There are a number of reasons why this might be so, the likeliest being that these were the only constitutions they had. The organisation of the cordwainers, to judge from both these features of their appearance in court, was still at an amorphous stage.

There is no reason to suppose that Colchester's crafts progressed beyond this point, or that they all developed so far. Crafts with small numbers of members could manage their affairs informally, and Colchester had no elaborate cycle of mystery plays to impose the need for co-operation between townsmen within a gild structure. The only surviving list of the crafts is in the Oath Book, and was written there sometime between 1428 and *c.* 1434. It has to do with liability to pay tolls to the community, but its significance is not explained. And though the list has 43 different crafts, including such minority interests as bellmaking and parchment making, it does not include fulling or weaving, so that it cannot be taken as a list of crafts with some sort of organisation.[64] The most that can be claimed is that from about the 1440s come signs that an increasing number of crafts had elected officers. Such elections are often recorded in the court rolls, though clerks did not strive after completeness. The roll of 1448/9 records the swearing in at the Michaelmas lawhundred of two masters of the

[63] CR 45/27r.
[64] OB, fo. 8v. The list is in the hand of John Hayward, the town clerk, and this supplies the date.

clothiers' craft and two masters of the shearmen's craft.[65] The roll of 1451/2 records the oaths of two masters of the wax chandlers' craft, and that of 1456/7 records that of four supervisors of the curriers' craft.[66] In this context the terms 'master' and 'supervisor' were about synonymous.

Regulation of non-manufacturing trades had been so thorough in the fourteenth century that there was little more to be done. There was no increase in the amount of regulation here comparable to that affecting industry. From the meat trade comes an early – and, for Colchester, rare – allusion to conditions of craft membership. Robert Doget was alleged to owe 6s 8d which had been paid on his behalf at Michaelmas 1412 for freedom of the butchers' craft.[67] It suggests that the butchers were more organised at the time than the main manufacturing interests, presumably because of the large number of regulations affecting the trade. Later developments were very much matters of detail, like the requirement from about 1466 that they should keep a common cart.[68] Nevertheless, non-manufacturing trades were developing in line with industry to the extent that the number of supervisory officers increased. Besides the wardens of untanned leather and the meat wardens, who occur in fourteenth-century sources, there were analogous officers for the fish trade. The court rolls record the election at Michaelmas 1443 of two supervisors of the fish market in the market place and two supervisors of the fish market at Hythe.[69] They also note the election at Michaelmas 1448 of an officer called the measurer of woad.[70] There are some indications that this marketing organisation of the trades was becoming assimilated to that of the craft gilds. The wardens of untanned leather occur in the 1440s as the 'supervisors of the tanners' craft', 'supervisors of badly tanned leather'[71] and, less politely, as 'masters of the craft of badly tanned leather',[72] implying that they were equivalent to the officers of a craft gild. The meat wardens occur normally after 1418 as the masters (or 'masters and supervisors') of the butchers' craft,[73] a title analogous to that of the officers of an industrial craft.

In Colchester, then, as in large towns, the experience of economic stagnation and contraction was a factor affecting the growth of industrial regulation and the multiplication of crafts. But economic changes were not the sole cause of these developments. Even the imperfect Colchester evidence suggests the importance of two other factors in the development of craft organisations. One was the introduction of a variety of regulations necessary for the well-being of an urban society. The assimilation to craft organisation of other older systems of economic regulation was another.

[65] CR 63/3r.
[66] CR 64/3d; CR 67/2d.
[67] CR 39/28r.
[68] See Chapter 13, pp. 199–200.
[69] CR 59/3r.
[70] CR 63/3r.
[71] CR 59/3r; CR 60/2d.
[72] CR 58/2r.
[73] CR 41/2r.

17

Town and country

I

Colchester's growing dependence upon supplies from a distance during the later fourteenth century, when consumption in the borough was growing, seems to have become even more accentuated in the first half of the fifteenth. For certain agricultural products the low costs of water transport, coupled with economies of bulk trading and a growth of expertise amongst Colchester's merchants, ensured that large consignments came from outside the local marketing region. A major source of grain for Colchester was the east coast of Norfolk, where the intensive cultivation of barley was a long established feature of agricultural economy.[1] As it happens, manorial accounts have survived from one of the manors in this region which supplied Colchester with malt in the first half of the fifteenth century, namely Ormesby Hall in Ormesby St Margarets, which belonged to the Clere family.[2] The recorded sales, shown in Table 17.1, add considerably to the evidence of the grain trade available from Colchester's own archives. Evidently a number of burgesses at this time went to Norfolk for malt, and one of them had made it a habit. Purchases were made when prices were low as well as when they were high, demonstrating that this was no emergency trade limited to years of dearth.

Ormesby's accounts do not provide direct evidence for Colchester's own grain supplies, since Colchester buyers may have sold in other markets, just as buyers from other ports provisioned Colchester. But the magnitude of Colchester's dependence upon Norfolk is revealed in the special conditions of 1439, a year of nationwide dearth, when royal licences were required for shipments of grain. A licence to export 1,000 quarters of wheat and barley from Norfolk and Suffolk granted early in the year was

---

[1] R. H. Britnell, 'The Pastons and their Norfolk' (forthcoming).
[2] P.R.O., S.C.6/939/1 to S.C.6/941/2. Later accounts give less detail because the demesne was leased.

Table 17.1 *Sales of malt from Ormesby Hall to Colchester men,*
1434/5–1452/3

Year	Buyer	Quarters bought	Price per quarter s d	
1434/5	a merchant of Colchester	60	3	8
	a crayerman of Colchester	31	3	9
1436/7	a crayerman of Colchester	60	3	0
	a crayerman of Colchester	60	3	0
	divers merchants of Colchester	67½	3	0
1437/8	John Snow of Colchester	46½	5	4
1443/4	a crayerman called Wylde of Colchester	10	2	2
1446/7	Wilde of Colchester, crayerman	10	2	0
1449/50	John Wylde of Colchester	40	2	4
	a crayerman of Colchester	45	2	6
1452/3	John Hervy of Colchester	60	1	8
	a man of Colchester	20	2	6

Source: P.R.O., S.C.6/939/10r–12r; S.C.6/940/5r, 7r, 9r, 11r.

expressly to victual the town and the abbey. Two licences from early in
December the same year together authorise shipments of 1,500 quarters
of barley and other grain. Licence for a further 160 quarters from Great
Yarmouth was granted early in 1440.[3] Dependence upon Norfolk barley
at this time is apparent in Colchester's own records. In 1440 it was reported
at the Hilary lawhundred that Thomas Wode the beer brewer had bought
up over 500 quarters of barley in Norfolk, and in doing so, as the
lawhundred jury supposed, he had engaged in forestalling, since he had
paid 1s 8d a quarter more than the price prevailing in the market place.[4]
It is true that in 1439 barley prices were higher than usual in Norfolk, most
of the crop at Ormesby having sold at 6s 0d and 6s 8d a quarter,[5] but if
the prevailing price in Colchester was really lower than this Wode's
purchases could have harmed no one but himself. The jury's accusation
is an instance of popular prejudice ranged against a prominent middleman
at a time of high grain prices. It implies that Norfolk was a principal source
of supply and that the price of barley in Colchester, for better or worse,
was determined by the quality of the Norfolk harvest.

[3] *Cal. Pat. R., 1436–41*, pp. 239, 351, 355, 362.
[4] CR 57/15r.   [5] P.R.O., S.C.6/940/1r.

Wool was also shipped along the coast, notably from Kent, whose coarse fleeces were similar in quality and price to those of Essex and Suffolk.[6] Thomas Marsh of London was authorised to ship 6,000 fleeces to Colchester from Faversham in 1427 and 10,000 in 1429. In 1436 John Cook of Colchester was licensed to bring 25 sacks of wool from Sandwich; this was equivalent to about 6,500 fleeces. And again in the summer of 1441 licences were granted for the shipment of 11,000 fleeces from Kent, most of them to be shipped in barges across the Thames estuary from Higham to Tilbury and then carried to Colchester overland.[7] It is commonly reckoned that there were 260 fleeces to a sack, and that each sack of wool would make $4\frac{1}{3}$ standard cloths of assize.[8] This would imply that the largest recorded consignment of Kentish wool would make no more than $183\frac{1}{3}$ of Colchester's whole cloths. This was not a large share of the borough's cloth output, but Kent was not the only distant source of wool. There were supplies from Suffolk and the coast of East Anglia. In 1437, for example, white wool was sold for the Colchester market by a man from Woodbridge.[9] There were also deliveries from elsewhere in England by way of major wool markets, perhaps for cloths of better quality. Two carriers were retained for four days in July 1452 to carry wool from London to Colchester.[10]

If as a result of improved mercantile organisation, changing industrial requirements, or both, Colchester was deriving more of its supplies from afar, this would help account for a puzzling feature of litigation in the borough courts. The 56 villages situated 8 miles or less from Colchester market, but beyond the bounds of the liberty of the borough, provide the names of 182 litigants in debt cases between 1390 and 1410, when there are rolls for 11 years, but there are only 60 to be identified from the same villages in the period 1445–65, when there are rolls for 12 years.[11] From 25 of these villages there is no recorded litigant for debt in the later period, though only three failed to produce at least one during the earlier one. These figures cannot be converted into quantitative statements concerning the changing volume or direction of trade. Even the smallest of these villages continued to trade with Colchester in the mid fifteenth century; Layer Marney has no recorded involvement in debt in Colchester between 1445 and 1465, but the manor accounts show that a Colchester butcher was among those who bought beasts there in the years 1445–8.[12] It is

[6] E. Power and M. M. Postan, eds., *Studies in English Trade in the Fifteenth Century* (London, 1933), pp. 363 (n. 33), 367 (n. 56); Lloyd, *The Movement of Wool Prices*, p. 71.

[7] *Cal. Pat. R., 1422–9*, pp. 457, 525; *Cal. Pat. R., 1429–36*, p. 493; *Cal. Close R., 1435–41*, pp. 418, 420. Colchester merchants were regular traders in Romney: Butcher, 'The Origins of Romney Freemen', p. 19.

[8] Carus-Wilson and Coleman, *England's Export Trade*, p. 13; Bolton, *The Medieval English Economy*, p. 301.   [9] CR 55/21r.   [10] CR 65/13r.

[11] CR 27–37; CR 61–72.   [12] P.R.O., S.C.6/845/12r; S.C.6/1246/17r.

difficult, however, to interpret the court roll evidence except in terms of fewer transactions between Colchester and the countryside. And the severity of the implied contraction, which is out of all proportion to changes in internal trade or in the total number of pleas of debt, might be explained by the growth of transactions over long distances.

A change in the sources of Colchester's basic supplies might also explain a problematic decline in the lease of land tolls between the 1420s and the 1440s at a time when the value of water tolls was rising. These tolls were described in 1520 as 'the pety lande toll and custume vsed before tyme to be taken at the iiij gates of the same towne of and for horses, cartes, woodes, corne, pakkes and other thinges commyng of the same towne, goyng from it or passyng to and fro thorough the same towne of Colchester'.[13] Burgesses were free of tolls, and even resident non-burgesses paid no tolls on purchases for their own households,[14] but the income from land tolls would respond to changes in the level of sales by non-burgesses and of purchases by non-residents. Price changes would not directly affect the level of the community's receipts, since all the dues were fixed ones; changes in income from tolls should correspond broadly to changes in the volume of overland trade. The level of this income was at its peak between 1398/9 and 1406/7 when the land tolls were leased together with the water tolls for £40. At this point the land tolls were valued at between £18 and £20. Between 1413/14 and 1428/9 the lease was for £16, between 1434/5 and 1442/3 it was £12 or £13 and between 1443/4 and 1448/9 it was £10. Thereafter the land tolls were leased with the wool market, so that there is no separate figure, but it is likely that there was no great reduction during the 1450s and 1460s.[15] Eventually, however, the downward movement reasserted itself, and Thomas Christmas's will offered the community an annuity of £4 on condition that the tolls should be abolished altogether. This fivefold reduction in the value of land tolls since 1400 does not represent the proportion by which overland trade had declined, since the lease had to allow for the high costs of administering the collection of these dues. Administrative overheads probably took a large and rising share of the total receipt. But the figures seem to imply a contraction of trade with the surrounding countryside, which might in part be a result of a decline in urban consumption but which may also be the result of more goods coming in by sea.

Because of the diffuse pattern of Colchester's trade in agricultural produce, the effects of any contraction of consumption during the more depressed phases of the town's fifteenth-century history did not fall only

---

[13] P.C.C., Ayloffe, 28.
[14] OB, fo. 8r.
[15] Appendix, Table 5.

upon the immediate neighbourhood. They must often have been imperceptible, since Colchester was too small a town for its fortunes to have made much difference to distant suppliers. It is true that Norfolk agriculture was adversely affected by contractions in the demand for ale and beer, probably between 1414 and 1440 and certainly during the 1460s and 1470s,[16] but this region supplied ports and towns all along the east coast, including London, so that Colchester's individual contribution to the problems of barley growers was a minor one. To the extent that regional specialisations had developed in medieval England it is impossible to assess the independent effect of any one town.

II

The impact of Colchester's economy on the local rural economy must have been more apparent than on that of Norfolk or Kent, since local farmers would have traded regularly in the urban market or with visiting burgesses. Whether because burgesses went farther afield for supplies, as it seems in the first half of the fifteenth century, or because of decreasing total demand, as particularly in the latter half, Colchester's economic development had a dampening effect upon the demand for agricultural produce. Change in the villages themselves was more neutral in its impact before 1450 and probably over the century as a whole. Though there were repeated crises caused by epidemics, any long-term changes in population after 1414 were slight. The evidence from Colchester's immediate vicinity is poor, but the demographic evidence from Writtle may be matched by sources rather nearer Colchester (Table 17.2). At Witham the common fine from the main centre of population around the market was a fixed sum, but a varying amount was received from the inhabitants of Chipping Hill and Cressing, where males over the age of 12 paid 1*d* each year.[17] In Boreham residents on the lord's fee paid $\frac{1}{2}d$ a year.[18] If the stability these figures suggest was characteristic of the countryside around Colchester, then once again the town differed from the country in the effects of its development upon agricultural output. But, in contrast with the fourteenth century, falling numbers were now more characteristic of the town than of the countryside.

To isolate the effects of urban change from other influences on local agriculture is nevertheless impossible. Urban decay in Colchester was slow, and its impact upon estates round about was never dramatic enough to have induced any common pattern of development. In addition, other local circumstances favouring or discouraging investment had an autonomous impact upon rural prosperity. Variations of experience between different villages were to be expected, and it is instructive to observe how local these

---

[16] Britnell, 'The Pastons'.
[17] E.R.O., D/DBw M99, m. 2Ad.
[18] P.R.O., S.C.2/171/30, m. 1r.

Table 17.2 *Number of males liable for common fine on certain Essex manors, 1400–99 (number of years averaged in brackets)*

Years	Writtle	Boreham	Witham (Chipping Hill)	Cressing
1400–9	248(4)	55(9)	–	–
1410–19	204(8)	52(3)	–	–
1420–9	–	51(5)	23(7)	40(6)
1430–9	–	50(8)	25(9)	43(9)
1440–9	198(2)	48(8)	21(3)	42(3)
1450–9	222(3)	51(5)	–	–
1460–9	221(10)	–	–	–
1470–9	223(6)	–	–	–
1480–9	208(1)	–	–	–
1490–9	258(2)	–	–	–

Sources: K. C. Newton, *The Manor of Writtle* (Chichester, 1970), p. 80; P.R.O., S.C.2/171/30–3; E.R.O., D/DBw/M99, M100.

might be. Some villages fared particularly badly, notably those in the heathlands, whose poor soils deterred tenants and whose populations enjoyed no compensating growth of industrial employment. Of the estates of the earl of Kent in 1467/8, those which had declined in value since the late fourteenth century included the manor of Great Braxted on the edge of Tiptree Heath.[19] Other villages, however, experienced good fortune all of their own because of industrial growth or for some other reason. Two villages near Colchester, Dedham and Wivenhoe, are known to have been particularly fortunate inasmuch as they belonged to the small group of settlements in the clothmaking region of Essex and Suffolk whose share of taxable wealth increased between 1334 and 1524.[20] Both villages have fifteenth-century manorial records from which some features of their development may be identified.

Dedham, which is documented by court rolls of the lordship of Campsey Ash Priory, was a clothmaking village, whose manufactures were much the same as Colchester's; in April 1430 a servile smallholding there was sold on condition that the purchaser should pay 'six whole woollen cloths called *russettes*', and early the following year another smallholding was surrendered in exchange for 'six whole woollen cloths of russet called *holbrodclothis*'; in 1441 some tenements were sold on payment of 'two pieces of new woollen cloth of russet colour, each 28 yards long and two yards wide'.[21] It is no coincidence that these references came from the years

[19] M. W. Beresford and J. G. Hurst, *Deserted Medieval Villages: Studies* (London, 1971), p. 187; *The Grey of Ruthin Valor*, ed. R. I. Jack (Sydney, 1965), p. 28.
[20] See Table 14.4.   [21] P.R.O., D.L.30/59/730, mm. 9d, 10d, 16d.

when Dedham's cloth industry was supplying the markets of the Baltic through Henry Brook's activities in Danzig,[22] and the village may also have benefited from Sir John Fastolf's attentions over many years.[23] During the 1430s and 1440s land values in Dedham rose, and the entry fines paid to the prioress of Campsey Ash by new tenants taking up customary holdings were capable of being increased. For example, two crofts containing about eight acres called Gonetesland paid 4s 0d in 1433 when acquired by Nicholas Lovekyn and William Wodegate, but 6s 8d when Nicholas's son was admitted as the next heir in 1449.[24] The upward movement of land values is also suggested by increases in the prioress's income from some demesne leases. Much of the demesne was leased out in parcels from Michaelmas 1409,[25] and a number of these leases were later renewed on steeper terms when the opportunity presented itself. A close and adjacent meadow called Lorebregge, for example, were leased in 1409 for 10 years for 16s 8d. By 1436 the rent had been raised to £1, and in November that year it was further raised to £1 2s 0d.[26] At some point about the middle of the fifteenth century this upward tendency came to an end, probably because Dedham shared Colchester's unfortunate experiences in the cloth trade of the continent, and by the final quarter of the century the movement of rents and entry fines had been reversed. Having enjoyed unusual prosperity and growth before 1450, Dedham then presents exceptionally unambiguous evidence of economic decline. Entry fines from Gonetesland fell from 6s 8d when Stephen Lovekyn was admitted in 1449, to 3s 0d when his son took it over in 1481, and 3s 4d when it changed hands the following year. When John Hadleigh obtained the holding in 1489 he paid a fine of 5s 0d, but his daughter paid only 1s 6d when she inherited it in 1508–9. As late as 1537–8 it changed hands at an entry fine of only 2s 8d.[27]

Wivenhoe's circumstances were very different from Dedham's because at no time was the village a centre of the textile industry. Being only two miles away from Colchester market, the manor was perhaps affected more than most by the movement of demand in Colchester, and yet the rural economy even here had its own determinants of depression and recovery, which differed from those of the region as a whole. In the mid 1420s, before Colchester's economy had registered any pronounced decline, Wivenhoe

[22] See Chapter 11, p. 168.
[23] C. A. Jones, *A History of Dedham* (Colchester, 1907), pp. 19–25; K. B. McFarlane, *England in the Fifteenth Century: Collected Essays* (London, 1981), p. 162; E. M. Carus-Wilson, 'Evidences of Industrial Growth on some Fifteenth-Century Manors', in *idem*, ed., *Essays in Economic History* (3 vols., London, 1954, 1962), ii, pp. 160–2.
[24] P.R.O., D.L.30/59/730, mm. 11Ar, 21r. *Cf.* Carus-Wilson, 'Evidences of Industrial Growth', p. 166.
[25] P.R.O., D.L.30/58/729, m. 18r,d.
[26] P.R.O., D.L.30/58/729, m. 18r; D.L.30/59/730, m. 12d.
[27] P.R.O., D.L.30/59/731, fo. 6v; D.L.30/59/732, m. 9r; D.L.30/59/734, m. 11r.

was showing the signs characteristic of most other villages in the region. In 1425 the lord had trouble in finding tenants for his mill, his fisheries, his garden and his pastures. The rent of Battleswick declined during the course of the 1420s. By 1455/6, though there had been recovery in some elements of manorial income – the rents of the mill and of Battleswick were higher than in the 1420s – there had been deterioration in others. Here, however, the later fifteenth century was a period of recovery; the lord's total income from lands and cottages, without the demesne lands, rose from £25 14s 9d in 1455/6 to £33 14s 3½d in 1509/10. The increase in rents, which was most pronounced between 1470/1 and 1492/3, may be traced in the history of some individual properties. Dairy farming was one of the strengths of the manor, but the lord was also increasing his revenues from the rabbit warrens which were established, and had perhaps expanded, upon the sandy soils of his demesne. Wivenhoe's revival during these years is largely attributable to the earls of Oxford themselves. Having acquired the property earlier in the century they made it a family residence. Tile works were built and a forge was erected, partly in order to supply building operations at the manor house and for the requirements of the stables there. An elegant home needed many servants and services. It required, too, appropriate facilities for the recreation of its owners, and to this end Wivenhoe Park was established some time between Michaelmas 1502 and 1509; the lord abandoned some crofts and warrens which had earlier been leased.[28] Wivenhoe families may also have benefited from the weakening of Colchester's control over the fish trade during the fifteenth century. In the 1460s the practice of marketing fish in the Colne estuary opposite Mersea Stone had become so frequent, to judge from the recurrent but ineffectual amercement of those responsible for it, as to have become a routine. Buyers came from afar to circumvent Colchester's market controls, and included pedlars from Cornard, Bures St Mary and Thaxted as well as Seman Whitefoot, Colchester's most notorious forestaller of the fish at the time.[29]

With such vagaries of experience affecting villages so close to Colchester, it is not surprising that the rural consequences of changes in the urban economy are obscured and overlain by developments whose origins were different. An analysis of general characteristics of local farming in the fifteenth and early sixteenth centuries can nevertheless show how far they are consistent with a pessimistic view of the main direction of change.

[28] E.R.O., T/B 122.
[29] CR 68/12d, 20r; CR 69/1d, 9r, 15r.

Table 17.3 *Rents of Colne Priory from rectories and mills near*
Colchester, 1374/5–1441/2

	1374/5			1424/5			1425/6			1428/9			1441/2		
	£	s	d	£	s	d	£	s	d	£	s	d	£	s	d
Gt Bentley Rectory	13	6	8	11	0	0	11	6	8	10	13	4	11	0	0
Messing Rectory	13	6	8	8	0	0	8	0	0	8	0	0	7	6	8
Colneford Mills*a*	4	6	8	3	0	0	3	0	0	3	0	0	2	16	8

a Two mills, Piersesmelne and Asshmelne were leased in 1374/5. In later years there was
 only one mill, called Colneford Mill.
Source: E.R.O., D/DPr M13–18.

III

Some accounts of Colne Priory from between 1374/5 and 1441/2 give
details of two rectories and some mills leased in the Colchester region. The
former derived their income from tithes and the latter from mill tolls, so
that the movement of these rents is a crude indicator of changes in local
output and consumption. Despite a simultaneous fall in the price level, the
figures unambiguously imply a contraction of the local rural economy
between 1375 and 1425, and then a period of relative stability at this lower
level of economic activity between 1425 and 1442 (Table 17.3). Surplus
building sites and land which was little used remained throughout this
period, and later, a normal part of the village scene. Five tenants in
Thorrington in 1437 were ordered to repair ruined buildings.[30] At Langham
in 1438 five tenements with the timber growing on them were ordered to
be seized by the servants of the lord of the manor because no one wanted
to live there.[31] In 1439 the lands of four tenements were lying waste in Earls
Colne, and the tenants were amerced.[32] In the course of time cottages fell
down or were demolished, and only the memory of their former sites
remained. Agricultural land was subject to similar dereliction. Periodic
cropping and grazing usually prevented the permanent reversion of
farmland to waste, but periods of temporary abandonment were not
uncommon, and here and there nature regained footholds once lost. A
piece of land called Bushettes in Witham was granted by copy of court
roll in 1418–19 on condition that the tenant should eradicate the brambles
there, but in 1430 the task was still to be done.[33] Two crofts called

[30] E.R.O., T/A 167/1.
[31] E.R.O., D/DE1 M1, court held Monday the morrow of the Exaltation of the Holy Cross,
 17 Henry VI.
[32] E.R.O., D/DPr 68, m. 20r.   [33] E.R.O., D/DBw M99, m. 5r.

Table 17.4 *Fleeces produced and sold on the demesne at Layer Marney*

	1408/9	1411/12	1412/13	1413/14	1444/5	1445/6
Produced	569	769[a]	644	804	136	31
Sold	512	692	580	724	123	28

[a] 692 fleeces remained at Michaelmas 1412.
Source: P.R.O., S.C.6/1246/2d, 3d, 4d, 16d, 17d.

Cokefeldcroft and Morellescroft in Layer Marney, previously leased for
2s 0d and 3s 4d respectively, were in the hands of the lord of the manor
for want of a tenant in 1444/5, becoming overgrown with brambles and
bushes, so that when a tenant was found in 1445 the rent had to be lowered
to 3s 0d a year for the two.[34]
    These details imply that the pastoral sector of local agriculture did not
invariably take over resources abandoned from cropping. The state of the
market discouraged farmers from expanding their output of meat, dairy
produce, leather or wool. Profits of sheep farming were too low to ensure
the survival of demesne flocks even on manors whose demesnes remained
intact. At Layer Marney during the 30 years after Michaelmas 1414 wool
production on the demesne was curtailed to less than a quarter of its
former level (Table 17.4). At Wivenhoe the demesne flocks were sold when
the demesne lands were leased out in 1426, and though the demesne lands
were again directly managed in 1455/6 there was no accounting for sheep.
Pastures, like arable lands, were often understocked or untenanted. At
Wivenhoe in 1426 demand for grazing was so reduced that there was
herbage in demesne crofts which nobody wanted and receipts from tenants
pasturing on demesne pastures were disappointingly low the following
winter. The account of this manor in 1455/6 still shows excess capacity
on the pastoral side of manorial economy; meadowland at Cockaynes
could not be let, and though the demesne was directly managed there were
no receipts from sales of pasture and herbage.[35]
    A lower intensity of land utilisation reduced both the economic im-
portance of rights of common and the vigilance of those possessing them.
Colchester court rolls contain many complaints about the interruption of
common rights during the fifteenth century, mostly between 1400 and 1415
and again between 1450 and 1465. However, the area of land to which
burgesses had access for commoning diminished during the course of the
century. In 1489 there was a new dispute with the abbot of Colchester, this

[34] P.R.O., S.C.6/1246/7r–12r, 14r, 16r, 17r.
[35] E.R.O., T/B 122.

time concerning commoning on the abbot's enclosure called Marylands;[36] the bailiffs and burgesses woke up to the fact that some 400 acres of land upon which they had once commoned had been bought up piecemeal by the abbey, and that ancient rights were being disregarded.[37] On their manor of Greenstead, too, the abbot and monks were reducing the number of claims to common rights simply by acquiring tenements to which such rights attached. A note in the abbey's register written about 1400 lists 13 tenements with rights of common on Cross Heath and Parson's Heath, and allocates to each the number of animals permitted, the total being 438 sheep, 51 cattle (*bestie*), 8 pigs and 2 horses or oxen (*grossa animalia*). Against seven of the tenements it is noted in a later hand that they had come into the abbot's hands, and the combined stint of these lands was over half the total.[38] The abbot of Colchester's responsibility for reducing the amount of commoning in the liberty was partly deliberate, partly accidental, but either way its repercussions were of less consequence than they would have been in an age when land was more scarce. A declining need for commons was experienced all through the region. At Wickham Bishop on the southern side of Tiptree Heath the lord of the manor received payments for pannage and avesage of pigs in his woodland, and though his receipts varied sharply from year to year, partly because of variations in the quality of acorns, there was a gradual downward movement both in the number of tenants exercising common rights and in the number of pigs.[39] It was in the context of reduced demand for common rights that in 1535 the burgesses of Colchester acquired Kingswood from Henry VIII and resolved to convert it from common land to severalty, each occupier paying rent to the community of the borough.[40]

Land values in the Colchester region did not generally recover at any time during the hundred years after 1425, and contractual rents tended to decline, though this was neither universal nor rapid. The rent of the demesne and rectory at Kelvedon, leased together at £20 a year for 15 years from Michaelmas 1409, had fallen to £13 6s 8d by Michaelmas 1441, and was still at that level at the time of the Reformation.[41] The demesne and rectory at Feering, leased at £40 for 21 years in 1405, were down to £25 a year by 1535.[42] In Earls Colne, 14 acres of former demesne land, leased for 16s 0½d a year in 1418, were rented at only 13s 4d a century later.[43] More disconcerting than such reductions in contractual rent were the difficulties

---

[36] LB, fo. 277r,v.　　　[37] RPB, fo. 211r.　　　[38] LB, fo. 157v.

[39] P.R.O., S.C.2/174/7–11.

[40] RPB, detached folio: *The Red Paper Book*, ed. Benham, p. 166.

[41] W.A.M., 25888r, 25889r, 25890r; Harvey, *Westminster Abbey and its Estates*, p. 342n.

[42] P.R.O., S.C.6/841/11r, 12r; Harvey, *Westminster Abbey and its Estates*, p. 341n.

[43] This assumes that 13 acres 3 roods leased at 1s 2d an acre in 1418 were the 14 acres recorded in 1522; E.R.O., D/DPr 67, m. 8r; D/DPr 71, m. 14d.

landlords faced in collecting their dues. In periods of acute difficulty tenants ran up arrears which it was well nigh impossible to recover even with all the apparatus of manorial courts which lords had at their disposal. The 1460s and 1470s were a period of depression in the agriculture of eastern England and such problems were then rife.[44] At Bourchier Hall in Tollesbury the court compiled lists of tenants owing arrears in 1464 and again in 1469. Lords had to maintain constant vigilance in order to keep track of what was owing to them, and even large rents might remain uncollected for years if the bureaucratic procedures of estate management went awry.[45] Landlords' problems, especially on large estates, were exacerbated by periodic lapses of managerial efficiency.

Circumstances became no easier for landlords in the late fifteenth and early sixteenth centuries. On the manor of Dales in Lawford during Henry VII's reign the lord was frequently not taking heriots from tenants who owed them.[46] Here, as on the manor of Faites in Dedham,[47] and at Earls Colne,[48] entry fines were paltry. The state of affairs early in the sixteenth century at Stoke by Nayland, a clothmaking village, is illustrated by an account of the duke of Norfolk's lands there from 1514/15. Most rents there, to a total of £125 0s 4½d, had not recently changed, but a property called Bachous, lately leased for £6 a year, now rendered £5 6s 8d. The bailiff himself leased Stoke Hall lands for £3 6s 8d instead of the £4 13s 4d for which they had lately been leased, and this because no one else would take the lease at a higher rent. He was unable to find a tenant for the fishery, which had lately been worth 8s 0d a year. The only note of an increase of rent in the account relates back to Michaelmas 1505, when the rent of some lands called Petites had been raised from £2 6s 8d to £2 13s 4d. Although, therefore, the duke's income had altered little within accounting memory, the movement of rents was still, if anything, downward.[49]

As for the rents of Colchester's own houses, fields and pastures, the chief determinant here was likely to be the town's economic performance, which means there is little scope for optimism concerning the hundred years before 1524. From the accounts of the duke of Norfolk's estates in 1514/15 already cited there survive some details concerning rents in Colchester which are fully in accordance with the evidence of urban consumption from the borough records. A property called the Dyhow(s)e, lately at rent for £2 had found no tenant that year, and so rendered nothing. The New Inn with two tenements, recently leased for £8 10s 0d, was now leased for five years at a rent of only £8 a year. Four other urban properties, including

[44] Britnell, 'The Pastons'.
[45] E.R.O., D/DK M78, mm. 1d, 2r; D/DPr 71, m. 14d.   [46] P.R.O., S.C.2/173/14.
[47] E.R.O., D/DC 14/14, m. 14d.
[48] E.R.O., D/DPr 70.   [49] B.L., Add. Roll 215, m. 1r,d.

an inn called the Swan, were leased to various tenants for a combined total of £5 8s 0d, their rents not having altered recently to any significant degree. There was also a field called Synchden, lying next to North Street and containing 30 acres, which was on a seven-year lease. The old rent was £1 10s 0d, and to this had been added at some stage an increment of 9s 0d. However, the account of 1514/15 acknowledged receipt of £1 6s 8d and the remaining 12s 4d was written off as a matter of course. The combined rent on these properties, embracing commercial premises, residential accommodation and arable land, had fallen by $17\frac{1}{2}$ per cent within accounting memory. Not a single rent had been raised successfully during this period.[50] On this showing the movement of rents from the duke's urban property was more steeply downward in the early sixteenth century than that of his rents in the nearby countryside.

IV

From the late fourteenth century landlords' policies of estate management were designed to safeguard their incomes, but to do so without too much administrative complexity. Leases on demesne lands became longer from about the 1420s, and throughout the later fifteenth and early sixteenth centuries those of 20 years or more became very common. Where demesnes were split up among tenants leases were often converted to hereditary copyholds, though the rents which thereby became fixed were inevitably paid in cash rather than in labour or produce. In the Earls Colne court rolls enrolled leases became uncommon after 1443 because so much of the former demesne was now held by hereditary titles.[51] Elsewhere, as at Wivenhoe, demesnes were kept intact and remained as leasehold all through the late Middle Ages.[52] In both circumstances, however, the abandonment of direct demesne management, together with declining rural population, contributed to the formation of large sub-manorial tenures which were one of the more permanent effects of fifteenth-century agrarian development. Such tenures varied in status. At one end of the scale a spirit of aggrandisement in the countryside led to some large holdings gaining a reputation as manors even within the liberty of Colchester; Cooks in West Bergholt was called a manor in 1445; the accounts of Wivenhoe began to describe Battleswick as a manor by 1463; three St Botolph's properties, Canwick, Dilbridge and Shaws, were known as manors in the sixteenth century.[53] Early sixteenth-century accounts of the

---

[50] *Ibid.*, m. 3r,d. For a comparable case with some pertinent comments, see Butcher, 'Rent, Population and Economic Change', pp. 67–74.
[51] E.R.O., D/DPr 68, m. 25r and subsequently.
[52] E.R.O., T/B 122.
[53] *Essex Fines*, iv, p. 35; E.R.O., T/B 122; Morant, *Colchester*, ii, pp. 17, 39.

Duke of Norfolk's estates show Stoke by Nayland at the head of five petty manors all held by leasehold tenants.[54] Some smaller properties which did not qualify for manorial status nevertheless acquired an inflated esteem because they had tenures subordinate to them. Three tenements in Earls Colne occur as capital messuages in court proceedings of the 1450s and 1460s.[55]

Most accumulations were less tidy, claiming no particular unity other than the temporary accident of common ownership by a single person. The property of John Short of Feering, a relapsed Lollard whose lands were confiscated in 1466, comprised 10 copyhold tenements, each with its own attached lands, meadows and pastures.[56] Agglomerations like this, whether leasehold or hereditary, often broke up when leases fell in or when heritable lands were shared between female heirs. The frequent regrouping of tenures on Campsey Priory estates in Dedham or on those of the earls of Oxford at Earls Colne makes it difficult to follow through the century the entry fines paid on separate parcels of land.[57] However, underlying these kaleidoscopic variations, the forces making for accumulation were more powerful than those working in the opposite direction. Investment in land permitted richer villagers to live more comfortably than in the past and created opportunities for commercial farming among families who would not previously have enjoyed them. Such were the Audleys of Earls Colne, whose credit in the village was established by Ralph Audley in the 1450s and 1460s. By 1450, when he first occurs as a capital pledge in the manorial court rolls[58] he held at least two tenements as well as some parcels of demesne land.[59] In 1457 he was the Earl of Oxford's bailiff, a post he retained until about 1466.[60] He died about 1470–1, having allegedly drowned himself, leaving a son called John as his heir.[61] It was a younger son, Geoffrey, however, who accumulated tenements in Henry VII's reign[62] and who in turn was bailiff of Earls Colne in 1496 and 1497.[63] His death was reported at Whitsun 1504, when his two sons called Thomas came into their inheritance.[64] One of these became Colchester's famous town clerk.

Once embarked upon acquiring property, townsmen were likewise prepared to accumulate tenures of all sorts. They had no prejudice against

[54] B.L., Add. Roll 215, m. 1r.
[55] E.R.O., D/DPr 68, mm. 30r, 33r; D/DPr 69, m. 3d.
[56] P.R.O., S.C.2/171/81, m. 5r.
[57] E.R.O., D/DPr 66–71 (Earls Colne); P.R.O., D.L. 30/58/728–9; D.L.30/59/730–4 (Dedham).
[58] E.R.O., D/DPr 68, m. 25r.   [59] E.R.O., D/DPr 68, mm. 24d, 27(3)r.
[60] E.R.O., D/DPr 68, m. 31r; D/DPr 69, mm. 2r, 4d.
[61] E.R.O., D/DPr 70, m. 1d.
[62] For Geoffrey's paternity, see E.R.O., D/DPr 69, m. 3r. His acquisition of holdings is documented in D/DPr 70, mm. 1d, 2d, 4r,d.
[63] E.R.O., D/DPr 70, m. 4r,d.   [64] E.R.O., D/DPr 70, mm. 11r, 12r, 13r.

customary tenures. Thomas Bonham, esquire, the borough recorder,[65] performed fealty in West Bergholt in 1518 for 16 acres of land and 6 acres of meadow to be held by the rod at will.[66] The properties of John Clere the clothier contained scattered copyhold lands.[67] When leading burgesses showed no compunction in acquiring such properties it is only to be expected that lesser men should do likewise. John Craton the dyer, at the time of his death in 1490, held customary land, wood and meadows in West Bergholt called Great Hygyns.[68] A good example of a complex accumulation of properties in which customary tenures were prominent was that of William Bounde of Colchester who died in 1508. In Greenstead he had a customary tenement called Pykardys and a freehold of 30 acres, held by charter, called Cokkys. In Wivenhoe he held two customary tenements called Cristofers and Burrys, containing 38 acres, and a half-acre piece of customary land next to the church. He also held there a newly built brick house with a limekiln belonging to it.[69]

Townsmen did not acquire property in neighbouring villages to cultivate it themselves. They inserted themselves as intermediaries between manorial lords and the ultimate lessees, and drew rents from their acquisitions. It is impossible otherwise to account for the scattered and fragmented character of their acquisitions. Tenements which had once been the hereditary possessions of village families were acquired by these absentees as a form of investment. Thomas Jopson owed fealty in West Bergholt in 1488 for various parcels of freehold land called Collettes,[70] and in 1508 William Hunt performed fealty for lands and tenements called Sayers in Wivenhoe and Greenstead.[71] An awareness of this process underlies the complaint against Thomas Christmas II that he had converted to pasture 6 tenements in Fingringhoe whereby 50 or 60 people had lost their livelihood.[72] There was little difference in attitude between the townsman who accumulated property with his savings and the country gentleman who leased his properties in the country in order to earn an additional income in the town.

These developments reveal a frankly commercial attitude to land by men whose interests and culture were primarily urban. The relaxing of manorial organisation had been an important prelude to this commercialisation, since customary lands could not otherwise have become so readily

[65] CR 89/1r; CR 90/1r.
[66] E.R.O., D/DMa M3, m. 18d.
[67] Bindoff, *The House of Commons* i, p. 651.   [68] E.R.O. D/DMa M2, m. 6r.
[69] E.R.O., T/B 122, court held Monday after the Exaltation of the Holy Cross, 24 Henry VII.
[70] E.R.O., D/DMa M2, m. 5r.   [71] E.R.O., T/B 122.
[72] *The Domesday of Enclosures, 1517–1518*, ed. I. S. Leadam, Royal Historical Society (2 vols., London, 1897), i, p. 220.

assimilated to other types of land as income-earning assets. But these changes had not come about through the rapid growth of commercial opportunity. On the contrary, urban and rural sources alike show that the background was one of economic stagnation. Land was abundant and cheap, and capital was starved of exciting opportunities for investment. The period when an urban interest in land is most apparent was one when outlets for investment in trade and industry were even less inviting than those in agriculture.

SURVEY, 1415–1525

Variations in Colchester's fortunes during the fifteenth century were more dependent than in the past upon merchants from other ports. The town's own adventurers maintained direct contacts with Gascony and the Baltic until the middle of the century, but with faltering expectations and with no opportunity to expand their operations. The characteristic quality of Colchester cloth was raised to meet the challenge of new markets, with some temporary success. The good years for Colchester trade during the 1440s, when cloth output reached its medieval peak, were chiefly owing to the interest of Cologne merchants in Colchester's newer styles. But after 1450 exports decreased at the hands of both English and German merchants and the cloth industry contracted. The organisation of industry became more rigidly structured on capitalist lines as wealth accumulated in individual families and as smaller enterprises withdrew, but the number of men engaged in overseas trade fell. There was probably a decline in the number of merchants in the borough. The situation in the late fifteenth and earlier sixteenth centuries, when cloth exports for England as a whole were growing, is obscure in evidence from Colchester, but on balance it is unlikely that the cloth industry there revived and there is some reason to suppose that it was decaying. Industrial capitalism cannot be closely linked, therefore, with industrial growth in this period.

Colchester's population did not maintain the level it had attained by 1414. By implication, therefore, the cloth industry was more important for employment in the town in the 1440s than in the early years of the century. Recurrent losses of population through epidemics were no longer counterbalanced by immigration to the extent they had been in the later fourteenth century, and particularly after 1450 the number of residents fell; by 1525 there were only about 5,300. The cessation of growth and the onset of economic contraction were accompanied by falling levels of internal trade and an even more severe reduction of credit. Colchester's adverse fortune in this period has many parallels elsewhere, as at Coventry, York and Norwich,[1] all of which had experienced industrial growth comparable to Colchester's between 1350 and 1414. Other smaller cloth towns in eastern England also suffered some contraction, as at Clare and Sudbury, but it is possible that Lavenham was more fortunate than Colchester in the late fifteenth and early sixteenth centuries.

The borough constitution changed little during the years before 1519, but distinctions of rank between aldermen, councillors and commoners became more accentuated. This development, which started as no more than a weakness amongst wealthier townsmen for pomp and circumstance, acquired a new justification in the later fifteenth century as the community's income fell and the burgesses became more beholden to the wealthier among them for public spirit and forbearance in the matter of public debts. The growth of oligarchy was not the consequence of any particular interest group in the borough having become more powerful, since the social composition of the ruling families became more diverse rather than less. In the later fifteenth century there were more bailiffs whose income derived chiefly from land than at any time since the Black Death. Amongst leading townsmen, as amongst the ordinary tradesmen of the borough, there was a greater willingness after 1414 than before to implement statute law and to introduce by-laws in order to regulate trade and industry. Colchester acquired rudimentary gild organisations (though the borough's record in this respect lacks distinctive colour), partly to protect urban craftsmen against the consequences of a harsher commercial environment but partly for separate cultural and administrative purposes. As a result of the multiplication of borough officers and craft officers a larger proportion of the population became attached to the community through elective office. But economic misfortunes exacerbated tensions within the borough, and the threat of family feuds and public disorder was more acute in the early sixteenth century than ever before. It was in these circumstances that between 1519 and 1525 the burgesses undertook the first major overhaul of the borough constitution since 1372. The elected council was enlarged to broaden the basis of support among Colchester's wealthier families for the decisions of the borough officials. Simultaneously the rights of electing juries to change those officials were tightly circumscribed.

The advantages of Colchester's early fifteenth-century prosperity for local agriculture were not as great as might be supposed, partly because of the town's small size, partly because it had learned how to acquire large consignments of produce cheaply from other coastal regions of eastern England. As the town's requirements of food and raw materials shrank, opportunities available to local farmers became even poorer than before,

[1] Phythian-Adams, 'Urban Decay', pp. 168–9.

though as in the fourteenth century agriculture was not governed primarily by changes in urban demand. There is no evidence of agrarian recovery in the Colchester region in the late fifteenth and early sixteenth centuries. However, partly because of the cheapness of land but also because of the scarcity of attractive investment opportunities in commerce, Colchester men were apparently more willing to invest in land in the early Tudor period than they were in the days of Colchester's greatest prosperity.

SOME FURTHER REFLECTIONS

This study has not been designed to generate broad generalisations about medieval urban economies, but a few further comments on the exceptional nature of Colchester's economic history in the fourteenth and fifteenth centuries may now conveniently be drawn together. They concern the relevance of Colchester's experience for the general interpretation of English economic performance in this period. In 1334, having failed to benefit much from commercial developments of the twelfth and thirteenth centuries, Colchester's standing as an English town had been a humble one. By 1524 the position was considerably improved. In taxable wealth the borough ranked as England's twelfth largest town, after London, Norwich, Bristol, Coventry, Exeter, Salisbury, Southwark, Ipswich, King's Lynn, Canterbury and Reading.[1] Judged by its number of taxpayers it stood even higher, above Coventry, Reading, King's Lynn and Ipswich.[2] Colchester had overtaken some of England's foremost ports (notably Hull, Boston, Great Yarmouth and Southampton) as well as some major inland cities (Lincoln, Oxford, Gloucester, Winchester, Cambridge). This outstanding success, when set against the record of Colchester's economic performance, suggests a number of observations about the nature of urban prosperity in the late Middle Ages.

Colchester's medieval records confirm that personal wealth in the borough increased between 1334 and 1524 and that this was partly the result of industrial and commercial development. The merchant class increased rapidly in numbers and wealth during the later fourteenth century and remained in 1524 more prominent in the affairs of the borough than it had been two centuries before. The differences between Colchester's taxable wealth as registered at either end of this period are nevertheless

---

[1] A. R. H. Baker, 'Changes in the Later Middle Ages', in H. C. Darby, ed., *A New Historical Geography of England* (Cambridge, 1973), p. 243; Gottfried, *Bury St. Edmunds*, p. 125.

[2] Phythian-Adams, *Desolation of a City*, p. 12.

incapable of yielding any quantitative statement about the course of economic change. They were the net outcome of the townsmen's accumulations and sales of assets over 190 years, and do not testify to any continuous growth of wealth. Nor is there any way of converting statements about taxable wealth, as differently defined at two points in time, into statements about levels of income. The contrast between these taxations will give a very misleading impression of what happened in Colchester if it is interpreted as direct evidence of a high rate of economic growth. Comparison between different towns across this period is a satisfactory way of identifying which of them were most fortunate in the accumulation of wealth, but to understand good fortune in terms of economic development requires the course of change to be charted.[3] In a period when most towns went through long phases of contraction[4] good fortune did not imply a high rate of growth. In the final analysis, the most interesting feature of Colchester's case is how little sustained growth it required to achieve so great an advance relative to other towns.

In charting the course of Colchester's development, it appears that the town did not grow in any sustained fashion between 1334 and 1524. Even in the later fourteenth century the history of brewing activity suggests an unstable course of increase, with the years 1351–6, 1375–80 and 1398–1412 as the main phases of upsurge. After about 1414 there were over 20 years without indications of economic growth, and population may have fallen slightly. Industrial revival between 1437 and 1449 raised cloth output to new heights, but it is doubtful whether the urban population recovered its earlier peak. And after 1449 it is impossible to speak of economic growth on the available evidence, which favours more the proposition that the economy of the town decayed. In all, then, of the 190 years between 1334 and 1524 it is improbable that more than a quarter were years of growth to higher levels of output.

An account of these years of growth which explains them solely by reference to clothmaking is bound to be incomplete. It is unfortunate that other areas of industrial investment do not lend themselves to parallel analysis. On the other hand, the history of enterprise in the making and marketing of cloth must provide the main clue to Colchester's good fortune relative to other towns. This, at least, may be deduced from taxation records in conjunction with evidence of industrial location. The strength of the argument in a local context was discussed in Chapter 14. The link between clothmaking and wealth supplies by far the best explanation of the improved ranking of Colchester, Lavenham and Hadleigh amongst the

---

[3] This is the main respect in which my approach differs from that of Dr Bridbury, which is most recently represented by Bridbury, 'English Provincial Towns', pp. 1–24.

[4] Dobson, 'Urban Decline', pp. 1–22; Phythian-Adams, 'Urban Decay', pp. 164–70.

towns of eastern England.[5] Explanations of industrial growth are of particular interest for the general interpretation of the late Middle Ages, and here again Colchester's case has something to offer. The town's increasing output cannot be explained primarily by growth in the home market. An ability to compete in Gascony, Prussia, Italy and Central Europe was the main determinant of growth, and the industrial history of the borough is unintelligible except with reference to successful competition in new markets. It is true that improvements in the real income of some sectors of society may explain the increasing sale of Colchester's particular type of russets in the later fourteenth century and the switch into cloths of better quality in the earlier fifteenth. In both periods, however, there was more to the picture than a deepening of demand in existing markets. Industrial growth cannot be understood chiefly as a manifestation of more broadly based growth of expenditure.

Nor was growth in towns of Colchester's size capable of generating significant development in the agricultural sector. Examination of trends even in villages close to the borough shows a distinct independence from urban trends. On reflection this is not surprising, given the small proportion of the population which was urban and the small size of increases in industrial employment between 1350 and 1414 in comparison with the contemporary contraction of rural employment. It is fanciful to suppose that Colchester's industrial growth compensated for declining rural population as a source of demand for agricultural produce. The example of Colchester suggests that industrial development in settlements of only a few thousand inhabitants created little perceptible stimulus to economic development in other sectors of the economy.

Colchester was a larger and in aggregate a wealthier town in 1525 than it had been before the Black Death, even if by Italian standards it was still not a town at all.[6] To that extent an account of its development will be meat and drink to historians looking on the bright side of economic change in the late Middle Ages. It is good that local variations of experience should be understood and that excessively generalised pessimistic accounts of the years between 1300 and 1525 should be redrawn. Sound judgement on this issue is important both for the interpretation of economic change and for broader interpretations of developing urban culture. But Colchester's economic record also shows the limits to which optimism may be stretched. Evidence of urban prosperity, even when it can be supposed to indicate that urban wealth was greater than before the Black Death, is not enough to establish that urban income was characteristically increasing in the late Middle Ages. Colchester enjoyed some

---

[5] Bridbury, *Economic Growth*, pp. 112–13.
[6] Dobson, 'Urban Decline', pp. 3–4.

periods of rapid growth during the fourteenth and fifteenth centuries without this being its normal experience. And if Colchester did not grow through most of the period 1300–1525, it is very unlikely that any English town did so.

APPENDIX
SOME COLCHESTER STATISTICS

Table 1 *Brewers amerced in Colchester for brewing against the assize*

Year	Michaelmas no.	Hilary no.	Hocktide no.
1310/11	0	0	–
1311/12	112	21	31
1329/30	68	89	–
1333/4	100	–	79
1336/7	103	106	109
1340/1	100	97	–
1345/6	94	92	93
1351/2	70	73	75
1353/4	94	92	108
1356/7	115	113	105
1359/60	100	104	86
1360/1	–	101	–
1364/5	119	118	107
1366/7	126	114	119
1372/3	121	124	126
1374/5	129	125[a]	–
1376/7	–	132	–
1378/9	157	161	160
1379/80	–	161	175
1381/2	139	166	167
1382/3	164	174	175
1383/4	–	–	176
1384/5	167	178	183
1385/6	178	188	189
1387/8	186	109	190
1391/2	–	158	167
1392/3	172	166	166
1395/6	175	180	180
1398/9	164	186	186
1399/1400	192	186	195
1400/1	204	189	191

269

Table 1 (*cont.*)

Year	Michaelmas no.	Hilary no.	Hocktide no.
1403/4	–	239	233
1404/5	226	250	241
1405/6	235	224	241
1406/7	243	250	254
1409/10	–	213	–
1411/12	239	246	235
1413/14	252	251	–
1416/17	231	–	229
1418/19	212	–	234
1419/20	241	229	245
1422/3	206	234	236
1423/4	–	247	238
1424/5	–	238	232
1425/6	212	235	240
1426/7	–	–	219
1427/8	–	216	230
1428/9	–	218	222
1429/30	221	228	234
1432/3	216	226	223
1434/5	193	184	200
1435/6	211	210	219
1436/7	–	206	217
1437/8	203	205	211
1438/9	209	189	189
1439/40	161	164	173
1442/3	186	192	200
1443/4	187	202	202
1444/5	–	192	213
1446/7	–	190	203
1447/8	192	188	191
1448/9	172	191	194
1451/2	181	191	220
1452/3	206	201	201
1455/6	188	189	202
1456/7	203	204	206
1457/8	–	188	195
1458/9	193	191	195
1459/60	194	196	191
1460/1	185	185	177
1463/4	124[b]	0	0
1466/7	164	175	177
1470/1	160	164	161
1473/4	159	159	157
1476/7	166	159	169
1477/8	169	175	175

Table 1 (*cont.*)

Year	Michaelmas no.	Hilary no.	Hocktide no.
1480/1	150	153	149
1481/2	148	155	156
1483/4	–	168[a]	148[a]
1484/5	–	160	178
1509/10	–	94	–
1510/11	104	–	100
1511/12	92	–	–
1512/13	–	116	114
1514/15	112	96	114
1515/16	103	102	110
1516/17	105	103	–
1522/3	98	–	–

Notes:
[a] Close approximation
[b] Inquest *ex officio*, 8.xi.1463.
Source: CR1–96.

Table 2 *Vintners amerced in Colchester for selling wine against the assize*

Year	Michaelmas no.	Hilary no.	Hocktide no.
1311/12	5	3	6
1329/30	5	2	1
1336/7	0	0	0
1340/1	2	1	–
1345/6	3	1	0
1351/2	6	4	5
1353/4	12	8	–
1356/7	8	7	9
1359/60	12	4	7
1360/1	–	4	–
1364/5	15	12	–
1366/7	11	10	11
1372/3	4	3	4
1374/5	5	–	–
1376/7	–	7	–
1378/9	12	13	10
1379/80	–	9	7
1381/2	9	9	13
1382/3	12	6	8
1383/4	–	–	16
1384/5	12	13	14
1385/6	15	12	14
1387/8	14	21	13
1391/2	–	17	13
1392/3	22	9	8
1395/6	16	8	10
1398/9	18	12	16
1399/1400	12	15	17
1400/1	17	20	17
1403/4	–	9	6
1404/5	15	10	–
1405/6	3	1	6
1406/7	6	5	4
1409/10	13	–	–
1411/12	7	8	7
1413/14	5	5	7
1416/17	–	–	13
1418/19	6	–	8
1419/20	8	8	12
1422/3	6	6	19
1423/4	–	9	13
1424/5	–	7	9
1425/6	14	9	10
1426/7	–	–	5
1427/8	–	–	4

Table 2 (*cont.*)

Year	Michaelmas no.	Hilary no.	Hocktide no.
1428/9	–	6	7
1429/30	8	8	8
1432/3	4	4	7
1434/5	7	7	7
1435/6	9	6	6
1436/7	6	6	9
1437/8	6	3	2
1438/9	5	3	3
1439/40	3	3	8
1442/3	7	13	13
1443/4	11	9	9
1444/5	11	9	11
1446/7	–	8	7
1447/8	10	10	17
1448/9	10	11	11
1451/2	9	9	9
1452/3	10	10	10
1455/6	17	9	7
1456/7	6	5	5
1457/8	–	4	4
1458/9	2	2	2
1459/60	2	2	3
1460/1	9	11	12
1463/4	5	5	6
1466/7	6	8	6
1470/1	7	5	–
1473/4	2	8	2
1476/7	9	6	9
1477/8	8	8	8
1480/1	4	4	3
1481/2	4	4	4
1483/4	–	–	8
1484/5	–	11	11
1509/10	–	6	–
1510/11	3	–	6
1511/12	3	3	–
1512/13	–	3	3
1514/15	6	6	8
1515/16	7	0	6
1516/17	6	6	–
1522/3	6	–	–

Source: CR 1–96.

Table 3 *Bakers amerced in Colchester for baking bread for sale against the assize*

Year	Number of inquests known	Largest number amerced at a single inquest	Total number amerced during the year
1311/12	2	14	16
1333/4	1	10	10
1336/7	3	10	14
1340/1	3	17	18
1345/6	2	7	9
1351/2	3	7	7
1353/4	4	6	9
1356/7	2	6	8
1359/60	2	9	11
1364/5	1	11	11
1366/7	3	13	17
1372/3	3	12	13
1374/5	4	8	9
1376/7	2	9	11
1378/9	3	12	16
1379/80	3	9	10
1381/2	3	9	12
1382/3	2	9	10
1383/4	1	7	7
1384/5	2	10	10
1385/6	3	9	11
1387/8	1	10	10
1391/2	1	9	9
1392/3	1	10	10
1395/6	2	14	14
1398/9	2	12	14
1400/1	2	11	13
1403/4	3	15	16
1404/5	1	10	10
1405/6	5	13	20
1406/7	3	4	8
1411/12	2	5	9
1413/14	1	4	4
1418/19	2	9	13
1419/20	2	10	10
1422/3	2	8	12
1423/4	3	5	11
1424/5	1	6	6
1426/7	3	11	14
1427/8	2	12	15
1428/9	2	10	11
1434/5	3	12	15
1435/6	2	11	11

Table 3 (*cont.*)

Year	Number of inquests known	Largest number amerced at a single inquest	Total number amerced during the year
1436/7	2	11	14
1437/8	1	13	13
1438/9	4	14	20
1443/4	2	10	12
1447/8	1	11	11
1451/2	5	10	11
1452/3	1	10	10
1455/6	7	7	12
1456/7	4	8	10
1457/8	5	8	11
1458/9	4	8	10
1459/60	6	11	14
1460/1	4	6	9
1463/4	4	10	14
1466/7	6	11	11
1470/1	3	10	10
1473/4	5	11	13
1476/7	4	7	9
1477/8	5	6	7
1480/1	5	9	9
1481/2	6	7	11
1483/4	6	8	15
1484/5	7	9	17
1509/10	2	6	8
1510/11	2	7	10
1511/12	1	9	9
1512/13	9	11	18
1514/15	4	14	21
1515/16	3	9	18
1517/18	3	17	23
1518/19	3	17	23
1522/3	4	24	32

Source: CR 1–96.

Appendix

Table 4. *Common forestallers amerced in Colchester*

Year	Michaelmas no.	Hilary no.	Hocktide no.
1310/11	21	13	–
1311/12	25[a]	0	15
1329/30	5	7	–
1333/4	9	0	10
1336/7	10	10	10
1340/1	13	15	–
1345/6	13	13	12
1351/2	12	14	13
1353/4	9	8	–
1356/7	10	11	10
1359/60	7	7	17
1360/1	–	17	–
1364/5	10	–	–
1366/7	16	10	10
1372/3	12	12	12
1374/5	6	9	11
1378/9	14	15	13
1379/80	–	11	11
1381/2	14	12	12
1382/3	12	13	13
1383/4	–	–	12
1384/5	10	10	10
1387/8	7	7	7
1391/2	–	8	6
1392/3	4	3	9
1395/6	4	7	7
1398/9	4	4	8
1399/1400	10	13	11
1400/1	14	14	17
1403/4	–	16	15
1404/5	10	13	11
1405/6	9	9	9
1406/7	9	8	8
1411/12	2	1	1

Note:
[a] 12 other names cancelled.
Source: CR 1–38.

Table 5 *Enrolled borough leases*

Year	Hythe leases £	Water tolls £	Land tolls £	Moothall cellar £
1310/11	0	35		0
1311/12	0	35		0
1345/6	0	35		0
1351/2	0	35		0
1353/4	0	35		0
1356/7	0	$35\frac{1}{3}$		0
1359/60	0	35		0
1364/5	0	35		0
1372/3	0	35		0
1373/4	$2\frac{1}{2}$[a]	40[a]		4[a]
1374/5	$3\frac{1}{3}$	$41\frac{2}{3}$		$3\frac{1}{2}$[b]
1385/6	4	–		–
1387/8	14[c]	35		–
1392/3	–[d]	17	18	–
1395/6	–[d]	20	18	–
1398/9	36[e]	40		$5\frac{1}{3}$
1399/1400	36	40		$5\frac{1}{3}$
1400/1	39	40		$6\frac{2}{3}$
1404/5	–[f]	–		$7\frac{1}{3}$
1405/6	30[f]	40		$6\frac{2}{3}$
1406/7	35[f]	40		$7\frac{1}{3}$
1411/12	28[g,h]	20[g]	15	$9\frac{1}{3}$
1413/14	28	20	16	$9\frac{1}{3}$
1418/19	28	20	16	9
1419/20	20	20	16	9
1422/3	20	20	16	8
1425/6	22	22	16	8
1428/9	$22\frac{1}{2}$	$22\frac{1}{2}$	16	8
1429/30	23	23	14	6
1432/3	25	25	18	–
1434/5	26	26	12	–
1435/6	26	26	12	6
1436/7	26	26	$12\frac{1}{2}$	$6\frac{1}{2}$
1437/8	26	26	13	7
1438/9	28	28	13	7
1439/40	44		12	6
1442/3	52		12	8
1443/4	52		10	12
1447/8	52		–	–
1448/9	48		10	8
1455/6	42		17	
1456/7	44		17	
1458/9	43		18	
1459/60	–		18	

Table 5 (*cont.*)

Year	Hythe leases £	Water tolls £	Land tolls £	Moothall cellar £
1460/1	29		19	
1463/4	33½		19	
1466/7	–		18	
1470/1	35		18	
1473/4	32		18	
1476/7	35		–	
1480/1	35		–	
1481/2	35		–	
1484/5	35		16	
1504/5	24[i]		–	
1516/17	24		–	
1517/18	24		–	
1520/1	24		–	
1521/2	28[j]		–	

Notes:

[a] Supplied from RPB, fols. 6v, 7r. The income from Hythe was for measurage there.

[b] Supplied from RPB, fo. 9v.

[c] Receipt for measurage, poundage and a new crane.

[d] The tenant was to render an account of his receipts and expenses.

[e] Receipt for two cranes and some new buildings at Hythe, together with measurage, poundage, wharfage and quayage.

[f] Including £1 from a separate lease of porterage, which was subsequently combined with the other Hythe rents.

[g] Hythe rents and water tolls were leased together for £48. The division shown in the table follows that for 1413/14 and 1418/19.

[h] Excluding, from 1411/12 onwards the rent of William Mayhew's tenement and the great hall annexed to it.

[i] Supplied from RPB, fo. 78v. The profits of Hythe were leased to Ambrose Lowth for 10 years at £24 a year.

[j] The rent was still £28 in 1541/2: Colchester Borough Archives, indenture of 22 October 1541.

Source: CR 1–96, except where otherwise stated in the notes.

Table 6 *Numbers of new burgesses by election enrolled in Colchester*

Year	No.	Year	No.	Year	No.
1327/8	7	1373/4	44	1419/20	16
1328/9	12	1374/5	16	1420/1	9
1329/30	15	1375/6	12	1421/2	33
1330/1	11	1376/7	11	1422/3	21
1331/2	13	1377/8	19	1423/4	13
1332/3	14	1378/9	18	1424/5	21
1333/4	13	1379/80	18	1425/6	26
1334/5	20	1380/1	18	1426/7	8
1335/6	4	1381/2	23	1427/8	8
1336/7	8	1382/3	15	1428/9	16
1337/8	4	1383/4	28	1429/30	17
1338/9	9	1384/5	22	1430/1	34
1339/40	10	1385/6	18	1431/2	11
1340/1	22	1386/7	23	1432/3	10
1341/2	9	1387/8	16	1433/4	9
1342/3	20	1388/9	12	1434/5	15
1343/4	9	1389/90	14	1435/6	7
1344/5	16	1390/1	9	1436/7	5
1345/6	23	1391/2	10	1437/8	12
1346/7	?	1392/3	15	1438/9	16
1347/8	10	1393/4	23	1439/40	7
1348/9	18	1394/5	18	1440/1	12
1349/50	37	1395/6	20	1441/2	19
1350/1	17	1396/7	9	1442/3	14
1351/2	11	1397/8	8	1443/4	9
1352/3	20	1398/9	6	1444/5	18
1353/4	53	1399/1400	11	1445/6	12
1354/5	30	1400/1	12	1446/7	19
1355/6	23	1401/2	12	1447/8	7
1356/7	14	1402/3	31	1448/9	9
1357/8	12	1403/4	11	1449/50	7
1358/9	7	1404/5	18	1450/1	1
1359/60	22	1405/6	22	1451/2	16
1360/1	36	1406/7	71	1452/3	19
1361/2	21	1407/8	10	1453/4	6
1362/3	13	1408/9	7	1454/5	21
1363/4	27	1409/10	10	1455/6	8
1364/5	12	1410/11	7	1456/7	4
1365/6	29	1411/12	12	1457/8	15
1366/7	14	1412/13	18	1458/9	10
1367/8	9	1413/14	20	1459/60	10
1368/9	30	1414/15	23	1460/1	5
1369/70	26	1415/16	12	1461/2	0
1370/1	9	1416/17	8	1462/3	7
1371/2	24	1417/18	5	1463/4	9
1372/3	25	1418/19	25	1464/5	6

Table 6 (*cont.*)

Year	No.	Year	No.	Year	No.
1465/6	7	1485/6	11	1505/6	3
1466/7	7	1486/7	13	1506/7	9
1467/8	11	1487/8	5	1507/8	9
1468/9	6	1488/9	13	1508/9	9
1469/70	6	1489/90	9	1509/10	6
1470/1	3	1490/1	5	1510/11	0
1471/2	4	1491/2	2	1511/12	1
1472/3	6	1492/3	8	1512/13	10
1473/4	1	1493/4	1	1513/14	18
1474/5	3	1494/5	0	1514/15	12
1475/6	6	1495/6	5	1515/16	9
1476/7	12	1496/7	4	1516/17	4
1477/8	1	1497/8	2	1517/18	8
1478/9	15	1498/9	5	1518/19	2
1479/80	6	1499/1500	7	1519/20	10
1480/1	5	1500/1	1	1520/1	3
1481/2	5	1501/2	4	1521/2	6
1482/3	5	1502/3	7	1522/3	13
1483/4	2	1503/4	11	1523/4	4
1484/5	3	1504/5	11	1524/5	4

Note: when compiling the Oath Book index, clerks sometimes accidentally omitted entries which they overlooked. Because of the very imperfect state of preservation of the court rolls, I have not attempted to correct the Oath Book figures. Inaccuracies are slight, however, and do not affect any conclusions which I have drawn from this table.
Source: OB, fos. 29v–123r.

Table 7 *Number of pleas of debt in Colchester borough courts*

Year	No.	Year	No.
1311/12	22	1442/3	261
1336/7	26	1443/4	344
1351/2	12	1444/5	275
1353/4	32	1446/7	297[a]
1356/7	61	1447/8	379
1359/60	125	1448/9	328
1366/7	243	1451/2	216[a]
1372/3	173	1455/6	281[a]
1378/9	395	1456/7	276
1381/2	467	1457/8	326
1382/3	402	1458/9	243
1384/5	481	1459/60	219
1387/8	654	1460/1	233
1398/9	435	1463/4	321[a]
1399/1400	349	1466/7	418[a]
1400/1	357	1476/7	285[a]
1405/6	392	1477/8	294
1406/7	401	1481/2	263[a]
1411/12	396	1490/1	185
1419/20	348	1493/4	155
1422/3	346	1510/11	145
1423/4	269	1512/13	110
1424/5	292	1514/15	126
1425/6	291	1517/18	123
1427/8	348	1518/19	120
1429/30	343	1519/20	120
1432/3	288	1521/2	165
1434/5	212	1522/3	178
1435/6	315	1524/5	156
1437/8	332		

Note:
[a] These figures include some unavoidable double counting and are on average about one seventh too high.
Source: CR 1–96; Monday Courts, VI–XVII Henry VII; Thursday Courts, VI–XVI Henry VII.

LIST OF PRINTED WORKS CITED

PRIMARY SOURCES

The Black Book of the Admiralty, ed. T. Twiss, Rolls ser. (4 vols., London, 1871–6)
A Book of London English, 1384–1425, ed. R. W. Chambers and M. Daunt (Oxford, 1931)
British Borough Charters, 1216–1307, ed. A. Ballard and J. Tait (Cambridge, 1923)
Bronnen tot de Geschiedenis van den Handel met Engeland, Schotland en Ierland, 1150–1485, ed. H. J. Smit, Rijks Geschiedkundige Publikatiën, lxv, lxvi (2 vols., The Hague, 1928)
Building Accounts of King Henry III, ed. H. M. Colvin (Oxford, 1971)
Calendar of the Charter Rolls preserved in the Public Record Office, H.M.S.O. (6 vols., London, 1903–27)
Calendar of the Close Rolls preserved in the Public Record Office, Edward I–Henry VII, H.M.S.O. (47 vols., London, 1892–1963)
Calendar of the Fine Rolls preserved in the Public Record Office, H.M.S.O. (22 vols., London, 1911–62)
Calendar of Inquisitions Post Mortem and other Analogous Documents preserved in the Public Record Office, H.M.S.O. (19 vols., London, 1904–74)
Calendar of Letters from the Mayor and Corporation of the City of London, circa 1350–1370, ed. R. R. Sharpe (London, 1885)
Calendar of Patent Rolls preserved in the Public Record Office, Edward I–Henry VII, H.M.S.O. (48 vols., London, 1894–1916)
Calendar of Plea and Memoranda Rolls of the City of London, A.D. 1413–1437, ed. A. H. Thomas (Cambridge, 1943)
Calendar of Plea and Memoranda Rolls of the City of London, A.D. 1437–1457, ed. P. E. Jones (Cambridge, 1954)
Cartularium Monasterii Sancti Johannis Baptiste de Colecestria, ed. S. A. Moore, Roxburghe Club (2 vols., London, 1897)
The Charters and Letters Patent granted to the Borough, ed. W. G. Benham (Colchester, 1904)
Court Rolls of the Borough of Colchester, ed. I. H. Jeayes (4 vols., Colchester, 1921–41, n.d.)
The Coventry Leet Book or Mayor's Register, ed. M. D. Harris, Early English Text Society, cxxxiv, cxxxv, cxxxviii, cxlvi (4 parts, London, 1907–13)
A Descriptive Catalogue of Ancient Deeds in the Public Record Office, H.M.S.O. (6 vols., London, 1890–1915)

The Diplomatic Correspondence of Richard II, ed. E. Perroy, Camden 3rd ser., xlviii (London, 1933)

Documenti per la storia economica dei secoli xiii–xvi, ed. F. Melis, Istituto Internazionale di Storia Economica 'F. Datini' (Florence, 1972)

Documents illustrating the Crisis of 1297–98 in England, ed. M. C. Prestwich, Camden 4th ser., xxiv (London, 1980)

The Domesday of Enclosures, 1517–1518, ed. I. S. Leadam, Royal Historical Society (2 vols., London, 1897)

English Historical Documents, 1189–1327, ed. H. Rothwell (London, 1975)

Essex Sessions of the Peace, 1351, 1377–1379, ed. E. C. Furber, Essex Archaeological Society Occasional Publications, iii (Colchester, 1953)

Feet of Fines for Essex, ed. R. E. G. Kirk and others, Essex Archaeological Society (4 vols., Colchester, 1899–1964)

The Grey of Ruthin Valor, ed. R. I. Jack (Sydney, 1965)

Die Handelsbücher des hansischen Kaufmannes Veckinchusen, ed. M. P. Lesnikov, Forschungen zur mittelalterlichen Geschichte, xix (Berlin, 1973)

Handelsrechnungen des Deutschen Ordens, ed. C. Sattler, Verein für die Geschichte von Ost- und Westpreussen, v (Leipzig, 1887)

Hanseakten aus England, 1275 bis 1412, ed. K. Kunze (Halle, 1891)

Hanserecesse von 1431–76, ed. G. von der Ropp (8 vols., Leipzig, 1876–92)

Hansisches Urkundenbuch, ed. K. Höhlbaum and others (11 vols., Halle, 1876–1916)

Henry of Huntingdon, *Historia Anglorum, 55 B.C.–A.D. 1154*, ed. T. Arnold, Rolls ser. (London, 1879)

Inquisitions and Assessments relating to Feudal Aids; with other Analogous Documents preserved in the Public Record Office, A.D. 1284–1431, H.M.S.O. (6 vols., London, 1899–1920)

Jack Upland, Friar Daw's Reply and Upland's Rejoinder, ed. P. L. Heyworth (Oxford, 1968)

The Lay Subsidy of 1334, ed. R. E. Glasscock, The British Academy: Records of Social and Economic History, new ser., ii (London, 1975)

Letters and Papers, Foreign and Domestic, of the Reign of Henry VIII, preserved in the Public Record Office, the British Museum and elsewhere in England, H.M.S.O., 2nd edn (23 vols. in 38, London, 1862–1932)

The Map of Great Britain c. *A.D. 1360*, issued by the Bodleian Library (Oxford, 1958)

The Medieval Essex Community: The Lay Subsidy of 1327, ed. J. C. Ward, Essex Record Office Publications, lxxxviii (Chelmsford, 1983)

The Medieval Records of a London City Church (*St. Mary at Hill*), *A.D. 1420–1559*, ed. H. Littlehales, Early English Text Society, cxxviii (London, 1905)

The Oath Book or Red Parchment Book of Colchester, ed. W. G. Benham (Colchester, 1907)

The Parlement of the Thre Ages, ed. I. Gollancz (London, 1915)

Paston Letters and Papers of the Fifteenth Century, ed. N. Davis (2 vols. out of 3, Oxford, 1971, 1976)

The Peasants' Revolt of 1381, ed. R. B. Dobson (London, 1970)

Quellen zur Geschichte des Kölner Handels und Verkehrs im Mittelalter, ed. B. Kuske, Publikationen der Gesellschaft für Rheinische Geschichtskunde, xxxiii (4 vols., Bonn, 1917–34)

Records of the Borough of Leicester, 1103–1327, ed. M. Bateson (London, 1899)

Records of the Borough of Northampton, ed. C. A. Markham and J. C. Cox (2 vols., Northampton, 1898)
Recueil de documents relatifs à l'histoire de l'industrie drapière en Flandre, ed. H.-E. Sagher and others, part ii (3 vols., Brussels, 1951–66)
The Red Paper Book of Colchester, ed. W. G. Benham (Colchester, 1902)
Die Rezesse und andere Akten der Hansetage von 1256–1430, ed. K. Koppmann (8 vols., Leipzig, 1870–97)
Rotuli Hundredorum temporibus Henrici III et Edwardi I in Turri Londinensi et in Curia Receptae Scaccarii Westmonasterii Asservati, ed. W. Illingworth, Record Commission (2 vols., London, 1812–18)
Rotuli Parliamentorum; ut et Petitiones et Placita in Parliamento, Record Commission (6 vols., London, 1783)
Select Cases concerning the Law Merchant, ed. C. Gross and H. Hall, Selden Society, xxiii, xlvi, xlix (3 vols., London, 1908–32)
Skelton, John, *The Complete English Poems*, ed. J. Scattergood (Harmondsworth, 1983)
The Statutes of the Realm, from Original Records and Authentic Manuscripts, ed. A. Luders and others, Record Commission (11 vols. in 12, London 1810–28)
Suffolk in 1327, being a Subsidy Return (a Twentieth), ed. S. H. A. Hervey, Suffolk Green Books, ix, vol. ii (Woodbridge, 1906)
Suffolk in 1524, being the Return for a Subsidy Granted in 1523, ed. S. H. A. Hervey, Suffolk Green Books, x (Woodbridge, 1910)
Tudor Economic Documents, ed. R. H. Tawney and E. Power (3 vols., London, 1924)
The Vision of William concerning Piers the Plowman, ed. W. W. Skeat (2 vols., Oxford, 1886)
Thomas of Walsingham, *Historia Anglicana*, ed. H. T. Riley, Rolls ser. (2 vols., London, 1863–4)
York City Chamberlains' Account Rolls, 1396–1500, ed. R. B. Dobson, Surtees Society, cxcii (Durham, 1980)

SECONDARY SOURCES

Ammann, H., 'Deutschland und die Tuchindustrie Nordwesteuropas im Mittelalter', *Hansische Geschichtsblätter*, lxxii (1954)
Die Diesbach-Watt-Gesellschaft: ein Beitrag zur Handelsgeschichte des 15 Jahrhunderts (St Gallen, 1928)
Ashley, W. J., *The Bread of our Forefathers: An Inquiry in Economic History* (Oxford, 1928)
An Introduction to English Economic History and Theory, 4th edn (2 vols., London, 1906, 1909)
Ashtor, E., 'L'Exportation de textiles occidentaux dans le Proche-Orient musulman au bas Moyen Âge (1370–1517)', in *Studi in memoria di Federigo Melis* (5 vols., Naples, 1978), ii
Studies in the Levantine Trade in the Middle Ages (London, 1978)
Baker, A. R. H., 'Changes in the Later Middle Ages', in H. C. Darby, ed., *A New Historical Geography of England* (Cambridge, 1973)
Baratier, E., 'De 1291 à 1423', in G. Rambert, ed., *Histoire du commerce de Marseille* (7 vols., Paris, 1949–66), ii

Bartlett, J. N., 'The Expansion and Decline of York in the Later Middle Ages', *Ec.H.R.*, 2nd ser., xii (1959)

Bautier, R. H., 'La Place de la draperie brabançonne et plus particulièrement bruxelloise dans l'industrie textile du Moyen Âge', *Annales de la Société Royale d'Archéologie de Bruxelles*, li (1966)

Bennett, H. S., *Life on the English Manor: A Study of Peasant Conditions, 1150–1400* (Cambridge, 1937)

Beresford, M. W. and Hurst, J. G., *Deserted Medieval Villages: Studies* (London, 1971)

Bindoff, S. T., *The House of Commons, 1509–1558*, The History of Parliament (3 vols., London, 1982)

Bird, B., 'The Rising of the Commons, 1381', *Colchester Historical Studies*, Colchester Local History Research Group, i (Colchester, c. 1980)

Bird, B. and Stephenson, D., 'Who was John Ball?', *Essex Archaeology and History*, viii (1976)

Bolton, J. L., *The Medieval English Economy, 1150–1500* (London, 1980)

Boutruche, A., *La Crise d'une société: Seigneurs et paysans du Bordelais pendant la Guerre de Cent Ans* (Paris, 1963)

Bridbury, A. R., *Economic Growth: England in the Later Middle Ages* (London, 1962)

'English Provincial Towns in the Later Middle Ages', *Ec.H.R.*, 2nd ser., xxxiv (1981)

Medieval English Clothmaking: An Economic Survey (London, 1982)

Britnell, R. H., 'Agricultural Techniques in Eastern England', in E. Miller, ed., *The Agrarian History of England and Wales*, iii (Cambridge, forthcoming)

'Agricultural Technology and the Margin of Cultivation in the Fourteenth Century', *Ec.H.R.*, 2nd ser., xxx (1977)

'Agriculture in a Region of Ancient Enclosure, 1185–1500', *Nottingham Medieval Studies*, xxvii (1983)

'Burghal Characteristics of Market Towns in Medieval England', *Durham University Journal*, new ser., xlii (1981)

'Colchester Courts and Court Records, 1310–1525' *Essex Archaeology and History*, xvii (forthcoming, 1986)

'Essex Markets before 1350', *Essex Archaeology and History*, xiii (1981)

'Minor Landlords in England and Medieval Agrarian Capitalism', *Past and Present*, lxxxix (1980)

'The Oath Book of Colchester and the Borough Constitution, 1372–1404', *Essex Archaeology and History*, xiv (1982)

'The Pastons and their Norfolk' (forthcoming)

'Production for the Market on a Small Fourteenth-Century Estate', *Ec.H.R.*, 2nd ser., xix (1966)

'Utilization of the Land in Eastern England, 1350–1500', in E. Miller, ed., *The Agrarian History of England and Wales*, iii (Cambridge, forthcoming)

Brown, E. H. Phelps and Hopkins, S. V., *A Perspective of Wages and Prices* (London, 1981)

Bruns, F., 'Die Lübeckischen Pfundzollbücher von 1492–1496', *Hansische Geschichtsblätter*, xiii (1907)

Butcher, A. F., 'The Origins of Romney Freemen, 1433–1523', *Ec.H.R.*, 2nd ser., xxvii (1974)

'Rent, Population and Economic Change in Late-Medieval Newcastle', *Northern History*, xiv (1978)

Cam, H. M., *The Hundred and the Hundred Rolls* (London, 1930)

Liberties and Communities in Medieval England (Cambridge, 1933)

Carrère, C., *Barcelone, centre économique à l'époque des difficultés, 1380–1462* (2 vols., Paris, 1967)

Carsten, F. L., *The Origins of Prussia* (Oxford, 1954)

Carus-Wilson, E. M., 'Evidences of Industrial Growth on some Fifteenth-Century Manors', in *idem*, ed., *Essays in Economic History* (3 vols., London, 1954, 1962)

Medieval Merchant Venturers: Collected Studies, 2nd edn (London, 1967)

'The Medieval Trade of the Ports of the Wash', *Medieval Archaeology*, vi, vii (1962–3)

'The Oversea Trade of Late Medieval Coventry', in *Économies et sociétés au Moyen Age: Mélanges offerts à Edouard Perroy* (Paris, 1973)

'The Woollen Industry', in M. M. Postan and E. E. Rich, eds., *The Cambridge Economic History of Europe*, ii: *Trade and Industry in the Middle Ages* (Cambridge, 1952)

Carus-Wilson, E. M. and Coleman, O., *England's Export Trade, 1275–1547* (Oxford, 1963)

Chapman, J. and André, P., *A Map of the County of Essex* (London, 1777, reprinted Chelmsford, 1950)

Clark, A., 'Serfdom on an Essex Manor', *E.H.R.*, xx (1905)

Clark, E., 'Debt Litigation in a Late Medieval English Vill', in J. A. Raftis, ed., *Pathways to Medieval Peasants* (Toronto, 1981)

Coleman, O., 'Trade and Prosperity in the Fifteenth Century: Some Aspects of the Trade of Southampton', *Ec.H.R.*, 2nd ser., xvi (1963)

Coornaert, E., 'Draperies rurales, draperies urbaines. L'évolution de l'industrie flamande au Moyen Âge et au xvie siècle', *Revue belge de philologie et d'histoire*, xxviii (1950)

Cotgrave, R., *A Dictionarie of the French and English Tongues* (London, 1611)

Crummy, P., *Aspects of Anglo-Saxon and Norman Colchester*, Colchester Archaeological Report, i; Council for British Archaeology Report xxxix (London, 1981)

Colchester: Recent Excavations and Research (Colchester, 1974)

Cunningham, W., *The Growth of English Industry and Commerce during the Early and Middle Ages*, 5th edn (3 vols., Cambridge, 1910)

Cutts, E. L., *Colchester* (London, 1897)

Day, J., 'The Great Bullion Famine of the Fifteenth Century', *Past and Present*, lxxix (1978)

Delisle, L., *Études sur la condition de la classe agricole et l'état de l'agriculture en Normandie au Moyen Âge* (Évreux, 1851)

Dewindt, E. B., *Land and People in Holywell-cum-Needingworth* (Toronto, 1971)

Dobson, R. B., 'Admissions to the Freedom of the City of York in the Later Middle Ages', *Ec.H.R.*, 2nd ser., xxvi (1973)

'Urban Decline in Late Medieval England', *Transactions of the Royal Historical Society*, 5th ser., xxvii (1977)

Dollinger, P., *The German Hansa*, trans. D. S. Ault and S. H. Steinberg (London, 1970)

Doolittle, I. G., 'Population Growth and Movement in Colchester and the Tendring Hundred, 1500–1800', *Essex Journal*, vii (1972)

Duby, G., *L'Économie rurale et la vie des campagnes dans l'Occident médiéval* (2 vols., Paris, 1962)

Dyer, C., 'English Diet in the Later Middle Ages', in T. H. Aston, P. R. Coss, C. Dyer and J. Thirsk, eds., *Social Relations and Ideas: Essays in Honour of R. H. Hilton*, Past and Present Publications (Cambridge, 1983)

Lords and Peasants in a Changing Society: The Estates of the Bishopric of Worcester, 680–1540, Past and Present Publications (Cambridge, 1980)

Dymond, D. and Betterton, A., *Lavenham: 700 Years of Textile Making* (Woodbridge, 1982)

Elton, G. R., *Policy and Police: The Enforcement of the Reformation in the Age of Thomas Cromwell* (Cambridge, 1972)

Espinas, G., *La Draperie dans la Flandre française au Moyen Âge* (2 vols., Paris, 1923)

Everitt, A., 'The Marketing of Agricultural Produce', in J. Thirsk, ed., *The Agrarian History of England and Wales, iv: 1500–1640* (Cambridge, 1967)

Feiling, K. G., 'An Essex Manor in the Fourteenth Century', *E.H.R.*, xxvi (1911)

Florio, J., *A Worlde of Wordes* (London, 1598)

Genicot, L., 'Les Grandes Villes de l'Occident en 1300', in *Économies et sociétés au Moyen Âge: Mélanges offerts à Edouard Perroy* (Paris, 1973)

Glasscock, R. E., 'England circa 1334', in H. C. Darby, ed., *A New Historical Geography of England* (Cambridge, 1973)

Goetz, L. K., *Deutsch-Russische Handelsgeschichte des Mittelalters*, Hansische Geschichtsquellen, new ser., v (Lübeck, 1922)

Gottfried, R. S., *Bury St. Edmunds and the Urban Crisis: 1290–1539* (Princeton, 1982)

Epidemic Disease in Fifteenth-Century England: The Medical Response and the Demographic Consequences (Leicester, 1978)

Gray, H. L., 'The Production and Exportation of English Woollens in the Fourteenth Century', *E.H.R.*, xxxix (1924)

Green, A. S., *Town Life in the Fifteenth Century* (2 vols., London, 1894)

Gross, C., *The Gild Merchant* (2 vols., Oxford, 1890)

Hadwin, J. F., 'Evidence on the Possession of "Treasure" from the Lay Subsidy Rolls', in N. J. Mayhew, ed., *Edwardian Monetary Affairs (1279–1344)*, *B.A.R.*, 36 (Oxford, 1977)

'The Medieval Lay Subsidies and Economic History', *Ec.H.R.*, 2nd ser., xxxvi (1983)

Harvey, B., *Westminster Abbey and its Estates in the Middle Ages* (Oxford, 1977)

Hatcher, J., *Plague, Population and the English Economy, 1348–1530* (London, 1977)

Hauschild, U., *Studien zu Löhnen und Preisen in Rostock im Spätmittelalter*, Quellen und Darstellungen zur Hansischen Geschichte, new ser., xix (Cologne, 1973)

Heers, J., *Gênes au xve siècle: Activité économique et problèmes sociaux* (Paris, 1961)

'La Mode et les marchés des draps de laine: Gênes et la montagne à la fin du Moyen Âge', *Annales E.S.C.*, xxvi (1971)

Herlihy, D. and Klapisch-Zuber, C., *Les Toscans et leurs familles* (Paris, 1978)

Hibbert, A. B., 'The Economic Policies of Towns', in M. M. Postan, E. E. Rich and E. Miller, eds., *The Cambridge Economic History of Europe, iii: Economic Organization and Policies in the Middle Ages* (Cambridge, 1963)

Hill, F., *Medieval Lincoln* (Cambridge, 1948)

Hilton, R. H., *The Economic Development of some Leicestershire Estates in the Fourteenth and Fifteenth Centuries* (Oxford, 1947)

The English Peasantry in the Later Middle Ages (Oxford, 1975)

'Lords, Burgesses and Hucksters', *Past and Present*, xcvii (1982)

A Medieval Society: The West Midlands at the End of the Thirteenth Century (London, 1966)

'Women Traders in Medieval England', *Women's Studies*, ii (1984)

Hirsch, T., *Danzigs Handels- und Gewerbsgeschichte unter der Herrschaft des Deutschen Ordens*, Preisschriften hrsg. von der fürstlich jablonowski'schen Gesellschaft zu Leipzig (Leipzig, 1858)

Holmes, G. A., *The Estates of the Higher Nobility in Fourteenth-Century England* (Cambridge, 1957)

House of Commons, *Every Member of the Lower House of the Parliaments of England, Scotland and Ireland, i: Parliaments of England, 1213–1702* (London, 1878)

Houtte, J. A. van, *An Economic History of the Low Countries, 800–1800* (London, 1977)

Irsigler, F., 'Kölner Wirtschaft im Spätmittelalter', in H. Kellenbenz, ed., *Zwei Jahrtausende Kölner Wirtschaft* (2 vols., Cologne, 1975)

James, M. K., *Studies in the Medieval Wine Trade*, ed. E. M. Veale (Oxford, 1971)

Jones, C. A., *A History of Dedham* (Colchester, 1907)

Jones, G. F., 'Sartorial Symbols in Medieval Literature', *Medium Aevum*, xxv (1956)

Kermode, J. I., 'Urban Decline? The Flight from Office in Late Medieval York', *Ec.H.R.*, 2nd ser., xxxv (1982)

Ketner, F., *Handel en Scheepvaart van Amsterdam in de Vijftiende Eeuw* (Brill, 1946)

Kowaleski, M., 'The Commercial Dominance of a Medieval Provincial Oligarchy: Exeter in the Later Fourteenth Century', *Medieval Studies*, xlvi (1984)

Kurath, H. and Kuhn, S. M., eds., *Middle English Dictionary* (Michigan, 1956–in progress)

Laurent, H., *Un Grand Commerce d'exportation au Moyen Âge: La draperie des Pays-Bas en France et dans les pays méditerranéens (xiie–xve siècles)* (Paris, 1935)

Liagre-de Sturler, L., *Les Relations commerciales entre Gênes, la Belgique et l'Outremont, d'après les archives notariales génoises (1320–1400)* (2 vols., Brussels and Rome, 1969)

Lipson, E., *The Economic History of England*, i, 12th edn (London, 1959)

Lloyd, T. H., *Alien Merchants in England in the High Middle Ages* (Brighton, 1982)

The English Wool Trade in the Middle Ages (Cambridge, 1977)

The Movement of Wool Prices in Medieval England, *Ec.H.R.* Supplement vi (Cambridge, 1973)

'Overseas Trade and the English Money Supply in the Fourteenth Century', in N. J. Mayhew, ed., *Edwardian Monetary Affairs (1279–1344)*, B.A.R., 36 (Oxford, 1977)

Luzzatto, G., *An Economic History of Italy from the Fall of the Roman Empire to the Beginning of the Sixteenth Century*, trans. P. Jones (London, 1961)

McClenaghan, B., *The Springs of Lavenham* (Ipswich, 1924)

McFarlane, K. B., *England in the Fifteenth Century: Collected Essays* (London, 1981)

   Lancastrian Kings and Lollard Knights (Oxford, 1972)

McKisack, M., *The Fourteenth Century, 1307–1399* (Oxford, 1959)

Macpherson, D., *Annals of Commerce, Manufactures, Fisheries and Navigation* (4 vols., London, 1805)

Maitland, F. W., *Township and Borough* (Cambridge, 1898)

Martin, G. H., *The Early Court Rolls of the Borough of Ipswich*, Department of English Local History Occasional Papers, v (Leicester, 1954)

Mate, M., 'Agrarian Economy after the Black Death: The Manors of Canterbury Cathedral Priory, 1348–91', *Ec.H.R.*, 2nd ser., xxxvii (1984)

Mazzaoui, M. F., *The Italian Cotton Industry in the Later Middle Ages, 1100–1600* (Cambridge, 1981)

Melis, F., *Aspetti della vita economica medievale*, i (Siena, 1962)

   'La diffusione nel Mediterraneo occidentale dei panni di Wervicq e delle altre città della Lys attorno al 1400', in *Studi in onore di Amintore Fanfani* (6 vols., Milan, 1962), iii

   Mercaderes italianos en España (Siglos xiv–xvi) (Seville, 1976)

   'Uno sguardo al mercato dei panni di lana a Pisa nella seconda metà del trecento', *Economia e storia*, vi (1959)

Miller, E., 'The Fortunes of the English Textile Industry during the Thirteenth Century', *Ec.H.R.*, 2nd ser., xviii (1965)

   'Medieval York', in P. M. Tillott, ed., *A History of Yorkshire: The City of York*, The Victoria History of the Counties of England (Oxford, 1961)

Miskimin, H. A., *The Economy of Early Renaissance Europe, 1300–1460* (Eaglewood Cliffs, 1969)

Mollat, M., *Études sur l'économie et la société de l'Occident médiéval, xiie–xve siècles* (London, 1977)

Moorman, J., *A History of the Franciscan Order from its Origins to the Year 1517* (Oxford, 1968)

Morant, P., *The History and Antiquities of the most Ancient Town and Borough of Colchester* (London, 1748)

   The History and Antiquities of the County of Essex (2 vols., London, 1768)

Morris, W. A., *The Frankpledge System* (Cambridge, Mass., 1910)

Munro, J. H., 'Monetary Contraction and Industrial Change in the Late-Medieval Low Countries, 1335–1500', in N. J. Mayhew, ed., *Coinage in the Low Countries (880–1500)*, *B.A.R.*, International Series, 54 (Oxford, 1979)

   Wool, Cloth, and Gold: The Struggle for Bullion in Anglo-Burgundian Trade, 1340–1478 (Toronto, 1972)

Newton, K. C., *The Manor of Writtle* (Chichester, 1970)

   Thaxted in the Fourteenth Century (Chelmsford, 1960)

Nicholas, D. M., 'The English Trade at Bruges in the Last Years of Edward III', *Journal of Medieval History*, v (1979)

   Town and Countryside: Social, Economic and Political Tensions in Fourteenth-Century Flanders (Bruges, 1971)

Nie, W. L. J. de, *De Ontwikkeling der Noord-Nederlandsche Textielververij van de Veertiende tot de Achttiende Eeuw* (Leiden, 1937)

Origo, I., *The Merchant of Prato*, 2nd edn (Harmondsworth, 1963)

Page, F. M., *The Estates of Crowland Abbey* (Cambridge, 1934)

Phythian-Adams, C., *Desolation of a City: Coventry and the Urban Crisis of the Late Middle Ages*, Past and Present Publications (Cambridge, 1979)

'Urban Decay in Late Medieval England', in P. Abrams and E. A. Wrigley, eds., *Towns in Societies: Essays in Economic History and Historical Sociology*, Past and Present Publications (Cambridge, 1978)

Platt, C., *Medieval Southampton: The Port and Trading Community, A.D. 1000–1600* (London, 1973)

Plucknett, T. F. T., *Legislation of Edward I* (Oxford, 1949)

Poerck, G. de, *La Draperie médiévale en Flandre et en Artois: Technique et terminologie*. Rijksuniversiteit te Gent, Werken uitgeven door de Faculteit van de Wijsbegeerte en Letteren, cx, cxi, cxii (3 vols., Bruges, 1951)

Poos, L. R., 'The Social Context of Statute of Labourers Enforcement', *Law and History Review*, i (1983)

Postan, M. M., *Essays on Medieval Agriculture and General Problems of the Medieval Economy* (Cambridge, 1973)

'Medieval Agrarian Society in its Prime: England', in *idem*, ed., *The Cambridge Economic History of Europe, i: The Agrarian Life of the Middle Ages*, 2nd edn (Cambridge, 1966)

Medieval Trade and Finance (Cambridge, 1973)

Powell, E., *The Rising in East Anglia in 1381* (Cambridge, 1896)

Power, E., *The Paycockes of Coggeshall* (London, 1920)

Power, E. and Postan, M. M., eds., *Studies in English Trade in the Fifteenth Century* (London, 1933)

Prescott, A., 'London in the Peasants' Revolt: A Portrait Gallery', *The London Journal*, vii (1981)

Putnam, B. H., *The Enforcement of the Statute of Labourers during the First Decade after the Black Death, 1349–59* (New York, 1908)

Raftis, J. A., *The Estates of Ramsey Abbey*, Pontifical Institute of Medieval Studies, Studies and Texts, iii (Toronto, 1957)

Tenure and Mobility: Studies in the Social History of the Medieval English Village, Pontifical Institute of Medieval Studies, Studies and texts, viii (Toronto, 1964)

Razi, Z., *Life, Marriage and Death in a Medieval Parish: Economy, Society and Demography in Halesowen, 1270–1400*, Past and Present Publications (Cambridge, 1980)

Renken, F., *Der Handel der Königsberger Grossschäfferei des Deutschen Ordens mit Flandern um 1400*, Abhandlungen zur Handels- und Seegeschichte, v (Weimar, 1937)

Renouard, Y., ed., *Bordeaux sous les rois d'Angleterre*, Histoire de Bordeaux, iii (Bordeaux, 1965)

Réville, A., *Le Soulèvement des travailleurs d'Angleterre en 1381* (Paris, 1898)

Reynolds, S., *An Introduction to the History of English Medieval Towns* (Oxford, 1977)

Rickword, G., 'Taxations of Colchester, A.D. 1296 and 1301', *T.E.A.S.*, new ser., ix (1906)

Ritchie, N. (née Kenyon), 'Labour Conditions in Essex in the Reign of Richard II', in E. M. Carus-Wilson, ed., *Essays in Economic History* (3 vols., London, 1954, 1962)

Round, J. H., 'The Arms of Colchester', *T.E.A.S.*, new ser., v (1895)

'Berryfield, Colchester', *T.E.A.S.*, new ser., xvii (1926)

Russell, J. C., *British Medieval Population* (Albuquerque, 1948)

Medieval Regions and their Cities (Newton Abbot, 1972)

Salzman, L. F., *English Trade in the Middle Ages* (Oxford, 1931)

Schofield, R. S., 'The Geographical Distribution of Wealth in England, 1334–1649', *Ec.H.R.*, 2nd ser., xviii (1965)

Schulz, F., *Die Hanse und England von Eduards III bis auf Heinrichs VIII Zeit*, Abhandlungen zur Verkehrs- und Seegeschichte im Auftrag des Hansischen Geschichtsvereins, v (Berlin, 1911)

Sherborne, J. W., 'The Battle of La Rochelle and the War at Sea, 1372–5', *Bulletin of the Institute of Historical Research*, xlii (1969)

Shrewsbury, J. F. D., *A History of Bubonic Plague in the British Isles* (Cambridge, 1971)

Smith, R. A. L., *Canterbury Cathedral Priory* (Cambridge, 1943)

Sprandel, R., *Das mittelalterliche Zahlungssystem nach hansisch-nordischen Quellen des 13.–15. Jahrhunderts*, Monographien zur Geschichte des Mittelalters, x (Stuttgart, 1975)

Stenton, F. M., *Preparatory to Anglo-Saxon England*, ed. D. M. Stenton (Oxford, 1970)

Tait, J., *The Medieval English Borough* (Manchester, 1936)

Thornton, G. A., *A History of Clare, Suffolk* (Cambridge, 1928)

Thrupp, S., *The Merchant Class of Medieval London* (Chicago, 1948)

Titow, J. Z., *English Rural Society, 1200–1350* (London, 1969)

Tuck, A., *Richard II and the English Nobility* (London, 1973)

Unwin, G., *Studies in Economic History*, ed. R. H. Tawney (London, 1927)

Uytven, R. van, 'Cloth in Medieval Literature of Western Europe', in N. B. Harte and K. Ponting, eds., *Cloth and Clothing in Medieval Europe: Essays in Memory of Professor E. M. Carus-Wilson* (London, 1983)

Verlinden, C., 'Draps des Pays-Bas et du Nord-Ouest de l'Europe au Portugal du xve siècle', *Anuario de estudios medievales*, iii (1966)

Way, A., 'Illustrations of Medieval Manners, Chivalry and Costume, from Original Documents', *The Archaeological Journal*, v (1848)

Wee, H. van der, *The Growth of the Antwerp Market and the European Economy (Fourteenth–Sixteenth Centuries)* (3 vols., The Hague, 1963)

Wilkinson, B., *The Later Middle Ages in England, 1216–1485* (London, 1969)

Willard, J. F., *Parliamentary Taxes on Personal Property, 1290 to 1334: A Study in Medieval English Financial Administration* (Cambridge, Mass., 1934)

Williams, G. A., *Medieval London: From Commune to Capital*, 2nd edn (London, 1970)

Wolff, P., *Commerces et marchands de Toulouse (vers 1350–vers 1450)* (Paris, 1954)

Wolffe, B. P., *The Royal Demesne in English History: The Crown Estate in the Governance of the Realm from the Conquest to 1509* (London, 1971)

Woodcock, B. L., *Medieval Ecclesiastical Courts in the Diocese of Canterbury* (Oxford, 1952)

Young, A., *General View of the Agriculture of the County of Essex* (2 vols., London, 1807)

Young, C. R., *The Royal Forests of Medieval England* (Leicester, 1979)

INDEX

Printed in the United Kingdom
by Lightning Source UK Ltd.
130831UK00002B/130-132/P